KS3 Maths

Complete Revision and Practice

Contents

Section One — Numbers

Multiples and Factors 1
Factors and Prime Numbers 2
Special Number Sequences 4
Practice Questions 6
Equivalent Fractions 8
Fractions, Decimals and Percentages 9
Rounding Off 10
Accuracy 12
Estimating 13
Practice Questions 14
Conversion Factors 16
Metric and Imperial Units 17
Fractions without a Calculator 18
Fractions with a Calculator 20
Practice Questions 21
Percentages 23
Ratios 25
Practice Questions 28
Standard Index Form 30
Powers or Indices 32
Square Roots and Cube Roots 33
Practice Questions 34
Calculator Buttons 36
Revision Summary 40

Section Two — Algebra

Turning Words into Algebra 41
Basic Algebra 42
Expanding Double Brackets – Two Methods 45
Practice Questions 46
Number Patterns 48
Finding the nth Term 49
Negative Numbers 51
Letters 52
Practice Questions 53
Substituting Values into Formulae 55
Solving Equations the Easy Way 57
Trial and Improvement 59
The Balance Method for Equations 60
Solving Equations 61
Rearranging Formulae 62
Practice Questions 63
Formula Triangles 65
Density and Speed 66
Two Hints When Using Formulae 67
Practice Questions 69
x- and y-Coordinates 71
x-, y- and z-Coordinates 72
Easy Graphs You Should Know 73
Finding the Gradient of a Line 75
What the Gradient Means 76
Practice Questions 77
Four Graphs You Should Recognise 79
Practice Questions 83
Plotting Straight Line Graphs 85
Typical Graph Questions 88
Practice Questions 92
Simultaneous Equations 94
Inequalities 96
Graphical Inequalities 97
Practice Questions 98
Revision Summary 101

Contents

Section Three — Shapes

Regular Polygons ... 102
Symmetry ... 104
The Shapes You Need to Know ... 107
Practice Questions ... 108
Areas ... 110
Circle Questions ... 112
Perimeters and Areas ... 114
Volume and Capacity ... 116
Solids and Nets ... 117
Practice Questions ... 118
Geometry ... 121
Circle Geometry ... 124
Three-letter Angle Notation ... 125
Practice Questions ... 126
Length, Area and Volume ... 129
Similarity and Enlargement ... 130
Enlargements — The Four Key Features ... 131
The Four Transformations ... 132
Practice Questions ... 134
Pythagoras' Theorem ... 136
Bearings ... 137
Trigonometry — SIN, COS, TAN ... 138
Loci and Constructions ... 140
Practice Questions ... 142
Revision Summary ... 144

Section Four — Statistics & Probability

Probability ... 145
Theoretical Probability ... 146
Estimated Probability ... 147
Combined Probability ... 148
Practice Questions ... 150
Graphs and Charts ... 152
Practice Questions ... 155
Mean, Median, Mode and Range ... 157
Frequency Tables ... 158
Grouped Frequency Tables ... 160
Cumulative Frequency Tables ... 161
The Cumulative Frequency Curve ... 162
Practice Questions ... 163
Revision Summary ... 165

Practice Exam — Paper 1 ... 166
Practice Exam — Paper 2 ... 177
Practice Exam — Mental Maths Test ... 188
Answers ... 190
Index ... 202

Published by Coordination Group Publications Ltd.

Editors:
Simon Little, Kate Redmond, Kate Manson.

Contributors:
Martin Chester, Janet Dickinson, Angela Duffy, Garry Rowlands, Karen M Rowlands, Emma Singleton.

With thanks to Peter Caunter and Joanna Lyall for the proofreading.

ISBN 1 84146 383 3
Website: www.cgpbooks.co.uk
Printed by Elanders Hindson, Newcastle upon Tyne.
Clipart source: CorelDRAW

Multiples and Factors

Multiple and factors are a nice topic to start the book.
It's quite easy to confuse them, so learn the definitions below.

Multiples

The multiples of a number are simply its times table.

E.g. the multiples of 15 are: 15 30 45 60 75 90 105 120 ...

Factors

The factors of a number are all the numbers that divide into it.

There's a special way to find them:

Example 1

"Find all the factors of 20."

Start off with 1 × the number itself, then try 2 ×, then 3 ×, and so on, listing the pairs in rows like this. Try each one in turn and put a dash if it doesn't divide exactly. Eventually, when you get a number repeated (number 4 in this example), you stop.

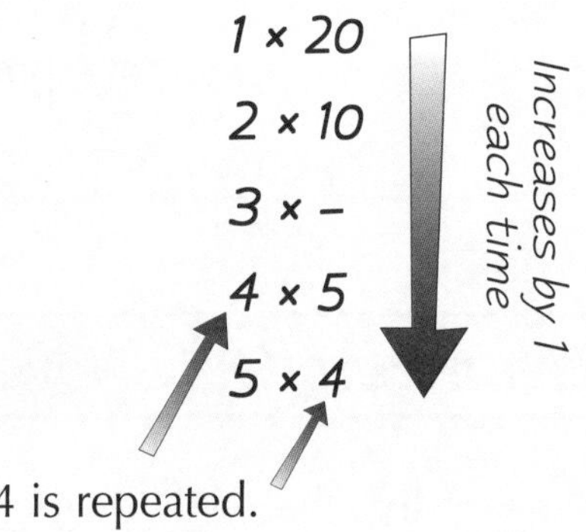

So the factors of 20 are 1, 2, 4, 5, 10, 20

This method guarantees you find them all — but don't forget 1 and 20!

Example 2

"Find the factors of 36."

1 × 36
2 × 18
3 × 12
4 × 9
5 × –
6 × 6

Check each number in turn to see if it divides or not. Use your calculator if you're not totally confident.

Careful not to include this one when it comes to writing out your answer.

The 6 has repeated so stop here.

So the factors of 36 are 1, 2, 3, 4, 6, 9, 12, 18, 36

Factors and Prime Numbers

Finding **Prime Factors** — The **Factor Tree**

Any number can be broken down into a string of prime numbers (see below) all multiplied together — this is called "expressing it as a product of prime factors", and to be honest it's pretty tedious — but it's in the exam, and it's not difficult so long as you know what it is.

The mildly entertaining "Factor Tree" method is best, where you start at the top and split your number off into factors as shown. Each time you get a prime, you ring it and you finally end up with all the prime factors, which you can then arrange in order.

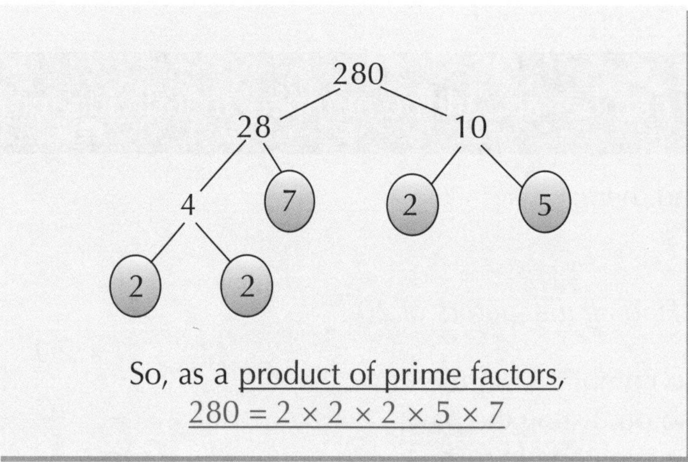

So, as a product of prime factors,
$280 = 2 \times 2 \times 2 \times 5 \times 7$

Prime Numbers Only Have Two Factors ...

... which means that they only divide by 1 and themselves — and that's the best way to think of them.

So prime numbers are all the numbers that DON'T come up in times tables:

2 3 5 7 11 13 17 19 23 29 31 37 ...

As you can see, they're an awkward-looking bunch (that's because they don't divide by anything sensible).

Example

The only numbers that multiply to give 5 are 1×5

The only numbers that multiply to give 23 are 1×23

In fact the only way to get any prime number is $1 \times$ ITSELF.

Factors and Prime Numbers

Prime Numbers **All End** in **1**, **3**, **7** or **9** — with **Two Exceptions**

Only the circled numbers are primes.

1) 1 is NOT a prime number (it doesn't even have two factors).
2) The first four prime numbers are 2, 3, 5 and 7.
3) 2 and 5 are the exceptions because all the rest end in 1, 3, 7 or 9.
4) But not all numbers ending in 1, 3, 7 or 9 are primes, as shown on the left.

How to **Find** Prime Numbers — A Very Simple Method

1) Since all primes (above 5) end in 1, 3, 7, or 9, then to find a prime number between say, 50 and 60, the only possibilities are: 51, 53, 57 and 59.
2) Now, to find which of them actually are primes you only need to divide each one by 3 and 7. If it doesn't divide exactly by either 3 or 7 then it's a prime. (This simple rule using just 3 and 7 is true for checking primes up to 120.)

Example *"Find the primes between 50 and 60."*

Just try dividing 51, 53, 57 and 59 by 3 and 7:

$51 \div 3 = 17$	17 is a whole number, so 51 is not a prime number because it will divide by 3 ($3 \times 17 = 51$).
$53 \div 3 = 17.666$ $53 \div 7 = 7.571$	So 53 is a prime number because it ends in 1, 3, 7 or 9 and it doesn't divide by 3 or 7.
$57 \div 3 = 19$	19 is a whole number, so 57 is not a prime number because it will divide by 3 ($3 \times 19 = 57$).
$59 \div 3 = 19.666$ $59 \div 7 = 8.429$	So 59 is a prime number.

Remember — prime numbers only divide by 1 and themselves

If this stuff is new to you, you might have to read through it a few times before it goes in. Trying to scribble it down from memory is a good way to see if you really know it or not.

Special Number Sequences

There are FIVE special sequences of numbers that you should know:

1 Even Numbers

*...all **divide by 2***

2 4 6 8 10 12 14 16 18 20 ...

All EVEN numbers end in 0, 2, 4, 6 or 8.
e.g. 64, 192, 1000, 518

2 Odd Numbers

*...**don't** divide by 2*

1 3 5 7 9 11 13 15 17 19 21 ...

All ODD numbers end in 1, 3, 5, 7 or 9.
e.g. 121, 89, 403, 627

3 Square Numbers

The first 12 are shown below:

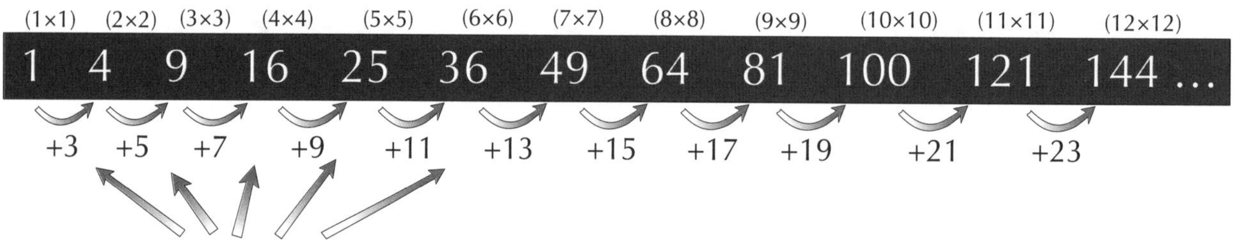

Note that the differences between the square numbers are all the odd numbers.

They're called square numbers because they're like the areas of this pattern of squares:

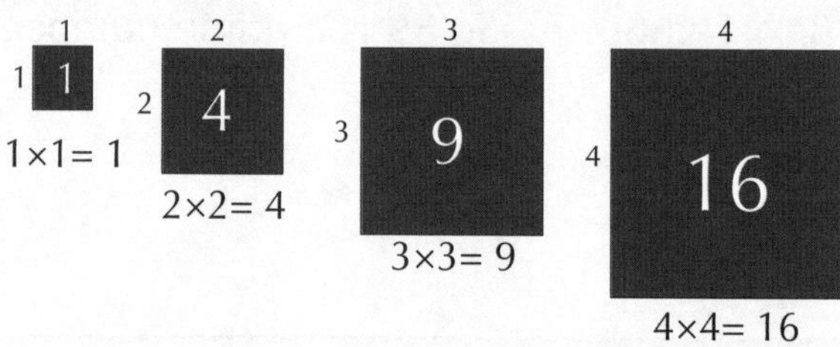

Special Number Sequences

4 Cube Numbers

Below are the first 10:

(1×1×1)	(2×2×2)	(3×3×3)	(4×4×4)	(5×5×5)	(6×6×6)	(7×7×7)	(8×8×8)	(9×9×9)	(10×10×10)...
1	**8**	**27**	**64**	**125**	**216**	**343**	**512**	**729**	**1000...**

They're called cube numbers because they're like the volumes of this pattern of cubes:

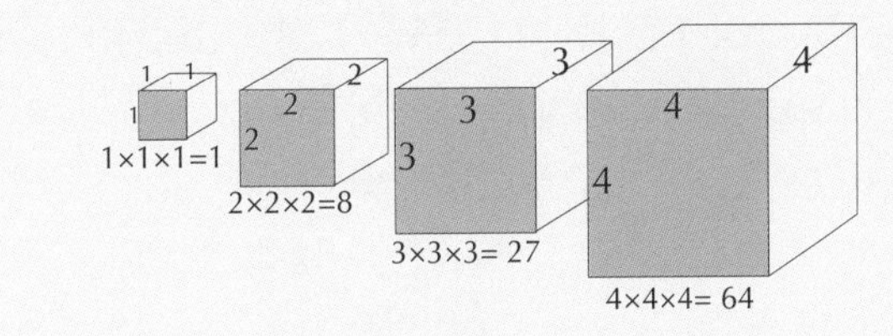

5 Triangle Numbers

To remember the triangle numbers you have to picture in your mind this increasing pattern of triangles, where each new row has one more blob than the previous row.

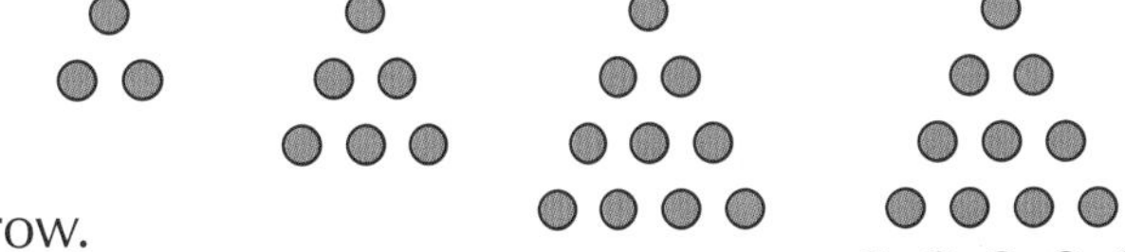

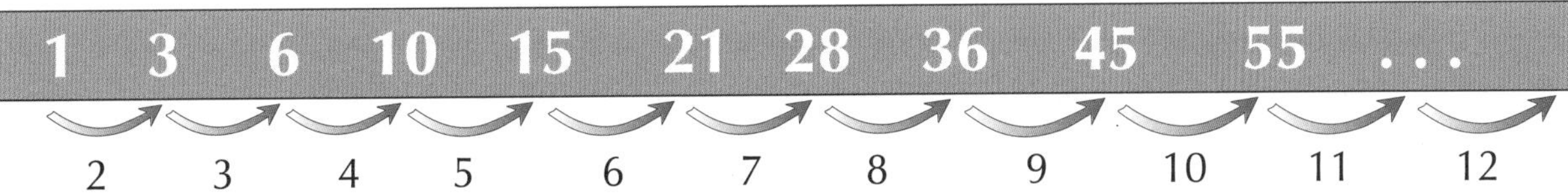

Pattern of Difference

It's definitely worth learning this simple pattern of differences, as well as the formula for the nth term (see page 50) which is:

$$nth\ term = \tfrac{1}{2} n (n + 1)$$

You should be able to spot any of these number sequences

The first two types are very easy, so breeze through them first, then spend a bit longer on the harder ones. Don't just learn the numbers, you need to understand how each pattern works.

Warm-up and Worked Exam Questions

These warm-up questions will test whether you've learnt the facts properly. Go back over any bits you don't know, then there'll be no nasty surprises when it comes to the exam-type questions.

Warm-up Questions

1) Choose from the numbers 10, 11, 12, 13, 14, 15, 16, 17, 18, 19, 20 to answer the following.
   Which numbers are (a) multiples of 3? (b) multiples of 5? (c) prime numbers?
2) Find the next two numbers in each of these sequences:
   (a) 7, 9, 11, 13, ... (b) 1, 3, 6, 10, ... (c) 9, 16, 25, 36, ...
3) Find all the prime numbers between 30 and 50. (There are five of them.)
4) Find the missing number in each sequence:
   (a) 42, ? , 46, 48, 50, ... (b) 8, 27, 64, ? , 216, ... (c) 42, 35, ? , 21, 14, ...
5) Find all the factors of: (a) 56 (b) 36
6) Choose from the numbers 3, 8, 12, 16, 21, 25, 27, 30, 36, 43 to answer the following.
   Which numbers are (a) square? (b) cube? (c) triangle? (d) even? (e) odd?
7) Find the prime factors of (a) 150 (b) 168
8) How do you know that 273 is not a prime number?
9) Draw a pattern of dots to show that 21 is a triangle number.

Once you've managed the warm-ups, you can dive into the trickier exam questions. Here's a worked example to start you off, and then you're on your own for some serious exam practice.

Worked Exam Question

Calculator Not Allowed

1 Peter has to draw a rectangle with an area of 48 cm^2. The sides must be whole numbers of centimetres. He makes his rectangle 4 cm wide and 12 cm long.

There are four other possible correct answers. Write them down below.

This is really a factors question in disguise. The area of a rectangle is length times width (see page 110), so if you use the method for finding factors from page 1, you should get all the possible pairs of lengths that would give a rectangle with an area of 48 cm^2.

1 x 48

2 x 24

3 x 16

4 x 12 — *This was Peter's answer.*

5 x —

6 x 8

7 x —

8 x 6 — *Here you get 8 and 6 repeated, so you know you've now found all the factors.*

The four other possible answers were: 1 cm by 48 cm, 2 cm by 24 cm, 3 cm by 16 cm, and 6 cm by 8 cm.

(2 marks)

Exam Questions

Exam Questions

Calculator Not Allowed

2 (a) The number chain below is part of an odd number chain.
Fill in the two missing numbers.

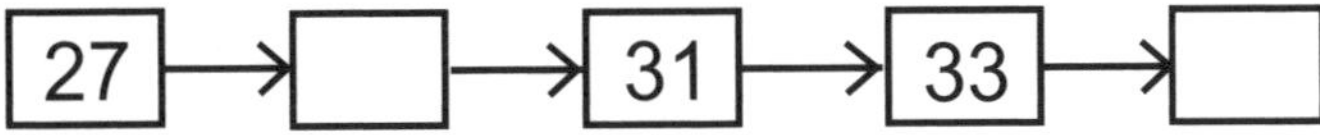

(2 marks)

(b) The number chain below is part of an even number chain.
Fill in the two missing numbers.

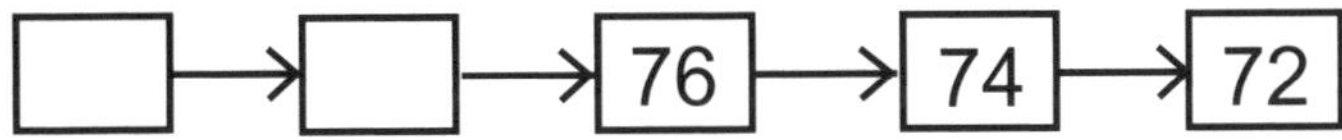

(2 marks)

3 A teacher has five number cards. He says: "Each card shows a different positive number between 10 and 20. None of the cards show an even number."
What numbers are on the cards?

(2 marks)

4 Write down the numbers from the list below which are factors of 16.

1 2 3 4 5 6 7 8 9 10 11 12 13 14 15 16

(2 marks)

5 There is a number between 30 and 40 which is a square number and also a triangle number. Write down this number and draw two patterns of dots to show how this number is a square number and also a triangle number.

(3 marks)

Calculator Allowed

6 (a) Write the number 210 as the product of its prime factors.

(2 marks)

(b) Write the number 165 as the product of its prime factors.

(2 marks)

(c) Emma has to find the highest number which will divide exactly into 210 **and** into 165. Use your answers to (a) and (b) to find this number, which is the highest factor that these two numbers have in common.

(1 mark)

Equivalent Fractions

Equivalent fractions are fractions that are equal in value, even though they look different.

Multiply ***Top*** *and* ***Bottom*** *by the* ***Same*** *Number*

Starting with any fraction you like, you can make up a list of equivalent fractions by simply multiplying top and bottom by the same number each time:

$$\frac{1}{2} = \frac{2}{4} = \frac{6}{12} = \frac{30}{60} \qquad (\times 2,\ \times 3,\ \times 5)$$

$$\frac{1}{5} = \frac{2}{10} = \frac{6}{30} = \frac{30}{150} \qquad (\times 2,\ \times 3,\ \times 5)$$

Cancelling *Down*

Going the other way, you will sometimes need to simplify a fraction by "cancelling down" — which just means dividing top and bottom by the same number:

$$\frac{3}{15} = \frac{1}{5} \qquad (\div 3)$$

$$\frac{22}{33} = \frac{2}{3} \qquad (\div 11)$$

Changing ***Fractions*** *to* ***Percentages*** *and Back*

If you can spot equivalent fractions then you can jump from fractions to percentages and back nice and easily, like this:

Examples

$$\frac{1}{2} = \frac{5}{10} = \frac{50}{100} = 50\%$$

$$20\% = \frac{20}{100} = \frac{2}{10} = \frac{1}{5}$$

Fractions, Decimals and Percentages

Fractions, decimals and percentages are just three different ways of expressing a proportion of something — and it's important you see them as closely related and completely interchangeable with each other. This table shows the really common conversions which you should know without having to work them out:

Fraction	Decimal	Percentage
1/2	0.5	50%
1/4	0.25	25%
3/4	0.75	75%
1/3	0.333333	33% (rounded)
2/3	0.666667	67% (rounded)
1/10	0.1	10%
2/10	0.2	20%
x/10	0.x	x0%
1/5	0.2	20%
2/5	0.4	40%

The more of those conversions you learn, the better — but for those that you don't know, you must also learn how to convert between the three types. These are the methods:

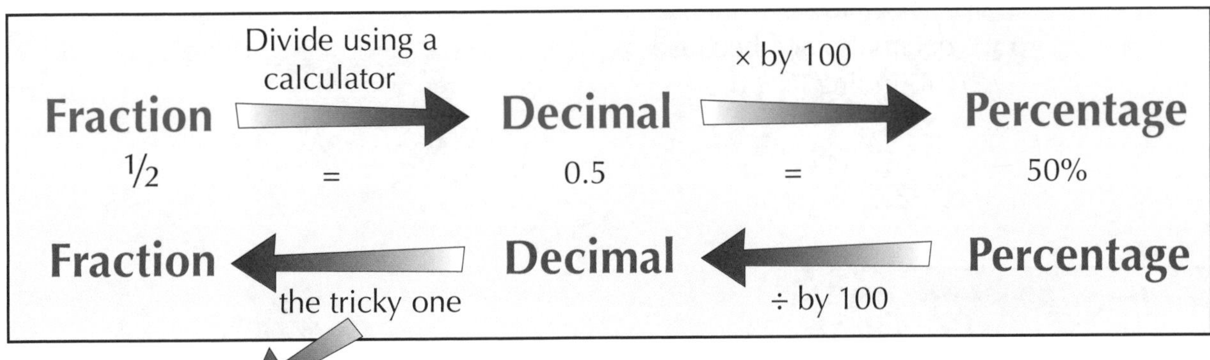

Converting decimals to fractions is only possible for exact decimals that haven't been rounded off.

It's simple enough, but it's best illustrated by examples so look now at page 18 and work out what the simple rule is. You should then be able to fill in the rest of this table:

Fraction	Decimal	Percentage
3/4		
	0.2	
		70%
	0.55	
13/20		
	0.28	

Fractions, decimals and percentages are all about proportion

Make sure you're totally happy converting between fractions, percentages and decimals. And learn that pink table — those conversions will help with all kinds of maths questions.

Rounding Off

The two most common ways of specifying where a number should be rounded off are decimal places and significant figures.

Doing decimal places is easier, but whichever way is used, the basic method is always the same and is shown below:

*The **Basic Method** has **Three Steps***

1) Identify the position of the last digit.
2) Then look at the next digit to the RIGHT — called the DECIDER.
3) If the DECIDER is 5 or more, then round up the last digit.
   If the DECIDER is 4 or less, then leave the last digit as it is.

Example *"What is 8.35692 to 3 decimal places?"*

8.35692 = **8.357**

LAST DIGIT to be written (3rd decimal place because we're rounding to 3 d.p.)

DECIDER

The last digit rounds UP because the decider is "5 or more".

Decimal Places (d.p.)

This is pretty easy:

1) To round off to, say, 4 decimal places, the last digit will be the 4th one after the decimal point.
2) There must be no more digits after the last digit (not even zeros).

Decimal Places Examples

Original number: 65.228371

Rounded to 5 decimal places (5 d.p.)	65.22837	(DECIDER was 1, so don't round up)
Rounded to 4 decimal places (4 d.p.)	65.2284	(DECIDER was 7, so do round up)
Rounded to 3 decimal places (3 d.p.)	65.228	(DECIDER was 3, so don't round up)
Rounded to 2 decimal places (2 d.p.)	65.23	(DECIDER was 8, so do round up)

Rounding Off

Significant Figures (s.f.)

The method for s.f. is identical to that for d.p., except that finding the position of the last digit is more difficult — it wouldn't be so bad, but for the ZEROS...

1) The 1st significant figure of any number is simply the first digit which isn't a zero.
2) The 2nd, 3rd, 4th, etc. significant figures follow on immediately after the 1st, regardless of being zeros or not zeros.

Examples

0.003409 — Significant Figures: **1st** (3), **2nd** (4), **3rd** (0), **4th** (9)

3.04070 — **1st** (3), **2nd** (0), **3rd** (4), **4th** (0)

(If we're rounding to, say, 3 s.f. then the LAST DIGIT is simply the 3rd s.f.)

3) After rounding off the last digit, end zeros must be filled in up to, but not beyond, the decimal point. No extra zeros must ever be put in after the decimal point.

Examples

	to 4 s.f.	**to 3 s.f.**	**to 2 s.f.**	**to 1 s.f.**
1) 34.875 1	34.88	34.9	35	30
2) 16.005 7	16.01	16.0	16	20
3) 0.002 390 4	0.002 390	0.002 39	0.002 4	0.002
4) 10 795.2	10 800	10 800	11 000	10 000

*Possible **Error** of **Half a Unit** when **Rounding***

Whenever a measurement is rounded off to a given UNIT the actual measurement can be anything up to half a unit bigger or smaller.

Examples

1) A wall is given as being "6 m high to the nearest metre" — its actual height could be anything between 5.5 m and 6.5 m — i.e. half a metre either side of 6 m.
2) If it was given as "6.4 m to the nearest 0.2 m", then it could be anything from 6.3 m to 6.5 m — i.e. 0.1 m either side of 6.4 m.
3) "A school has 2800 pupils to 2 s.f." (i.e. to the nearest 100) — the actual figure could be anything from 2750 to 2849. — (Why isn't it 2850?)

The first significant figure is never a zero

Rounding off to a certain number of decimal places is pretty straightforward. Significant figures are a bit trickier, but if you remember the rules about zeros, you'll soon get the hang of it.

Accuracy

Appropriate Accuracy

In your exam you may well get a question asking for "an appropriate degree of accuracy" for a certain measurement.

So how do you decide what the appropriate degree of accuracy is? The key to this is how many significant figures (see page 11) you round it to, and these are the three rules:

1) For fairly casual measurements, 2 significant figures is most appropriate.

Examples

Cooking — 250 g (2 s.f.) of sugar, (not 253 g (3 s.f.), or 300 g (1 s.f.))

Distance of a journey — 320 miles or 15 miles or 2400 miles.

Area of a garden or floor — 480 m^2 or 18 m^2.

2) For more important or technical things, 3 significant figures is essential.

Examples

A length that will be cut to fit, e.g. you'd measure a shelf as 75.6 cm long (not 76 cm or 75.63 cm).

A technical figure, e.g. 35.1 miles per gallon (not 35 m.p.g.).

Any accurate measurement with a ruler, e.g. 44.5 cm (not 40 cm or 44.54 cm).

If you can't decide, choose 3 s.f.

3) Only for really scientific work would you have more than 3 s.f.

Examples

Only someone really keen would want to know the length of a piece of pipe to the nearest tenth of a mm — like 34.46 cm, for example.

Estimating

Estimating Calculations

As long as you realise what's expected, this is very easy. People get confused because they over-complicate it. To estimate something this is all you do:

1) Round everything off to nice easy convenient numbers.
2) Then work out the answer using those nice easy numbers — and that's it.

Don't worry about the answer being "wrong", because we're only trying to get a rough idea of the proper answer, e.g. is it about 50 or about 500? Don't forget though, in the exam you'll need to show all the steps you've done, to prove you didn't just use a calculator.
Look at the example below:

Example

Question: *"Estimate the value of $\frac{48.6 \times 5.2}{117.4 + 375.9}$ showing all your working".*

Answer: $\frac{48.6 \times 5.2}{117.4 + 375.9} \approx \frac{50 \times 5}{120 + 380} = \frac{250}{500} = \frac{1}{2}$

"≈" means "roughly equal to"

Estimating Areas and Volumes

This isn't bad either — so long as you learn the two steps of the method:

1) Draw or imagine a RECTANGLE OR CUBOID of similar size to the object.
2) Round off all lengths to the NEAREST WHOLE NUMBER, and work it out — easy.

Example 1

"Estimate the area of Australia":

Area of Australia is approximately equal to area of dashed rectangle:

i.e. 1892km × 4025km = 7 615 300 km^2
(or, without a calculator:
2000 × 4000 = 8 000 000 km^2)

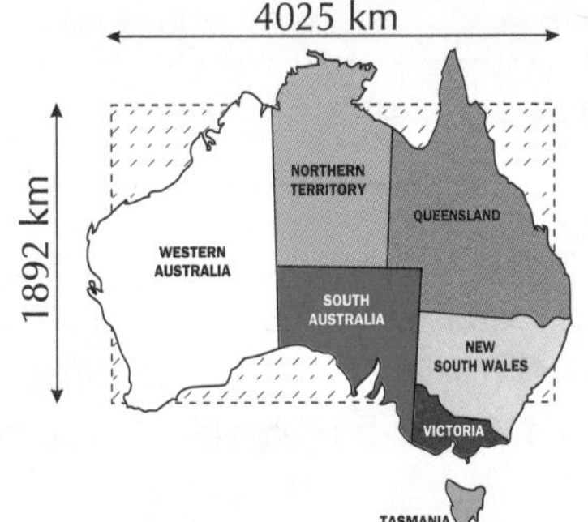

Example 2

"Estimate the volume of the vase":
Volume of vase is approximately equal to volume of dashed cuboid
= 5 × 5 × 13
= 325 cm^3

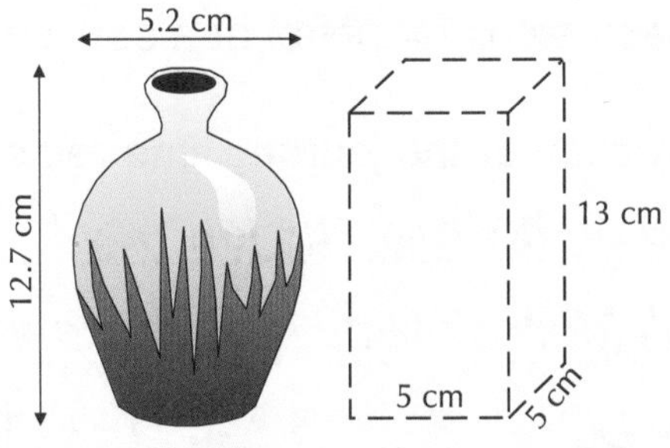

Estimating is just rounding everything off to easy numbers

Simple enough, but you still have to make sure you do it properly and show your working.
Don't forget to learn the method for estimating areas and volumes — it's easy marks in the exam.

Warm-up and Worked Exam Questions

There's nothing too scary in this section, but you've still got to check whether or not you've remembered it all. Have a go at these warm-up questions to find out.

Warm-up Questions

1) Simplify the following fractions:
   (a) $\frac{9}{27}$ (b) $\frac{15}{60}$ (c) $\frac{13}{104}$
2) Convert these fractions to percentages:
   (a) $\frac{7}{10}$ (b) $\frac{2}{5}$ (c) $\frac{3}{20}$
3) Convert these percentages to fractions:
   (a) 84% (b) 60% (c) 30%
4) Round the number 7.8953 to the following number of decimal places:
   (a) 1 decimal place (b) 2 decimal places (c) 3 decimal places
5) Round the number 72.567 to the following number of significant figures (s.f.):
   (a) 1 s.f (b) 2 s.f. (c) 3 s.f.
6) Round these numbers to 3 significant figures.
   (a) 12 765 (b) 3.785 (c) 0.000 559 7

Oooh, some exam questions — with the answers helpfully written in. Must be your birthday.

Worked Exam Questions

1 Estimate the answer to: $\frac{495 \times 0.52}{4.87}$ (Give your answer to 1 significant figure.)

Remember, estimating is easy — it just means rounding everything off to nice convenient numbers.

$$\frac{495 \times 0.52}{4.87} \approx \frac{500 \times 0.5}{5} = \frac{250}{5} = 50$$

This symbol (≈) means "roughly equal to". It's pretty useful when you're doing estimations.

The question asks you to give your answer to 1 significant figure. That means you should put 50, not 49 or 55 or anything like that.

(2 marks)

2 The journey time for a school coach trip is planned at 2 hours 20 minutes.
The coach stops for petrol at a service station after 1 hour 20 minutes.

What fraction of the journey time remains?

There's an hour of the journey left.

The full journey time is 2 hours and 20 minutes.

This is $\frac{60}{140} = \frac{6}{14} = \frac{3}{7}$

Here you just need to cancel down by dividing the top and bottom values by the same number. First you can divide by 10, and then by 2, to give the fraction in its simplest form.

These are just the journey times expressed in minutes instead of hours — much easier to work with.

(3 marks)

Exam Questions

Exam Questions

Calculator Not Allowed

3 (a) Which of the following is the best estimate of the answer to 48.24 ÷ 5.92?

6 7 8 9 10 11

(1 mark)

(b) Which of the following is the best estimate of the answer to 123.6 × 0.49?

6 6.5 60 65 600 650

(1 mark)

(c) Estimate the answer to: $\dfrac{38.4 \times 28.2}{6.67 \times 4.02}$

(2 marks)

4 In a basketball tournament the Bingham Bears won 17 out of 20 games, while the Hockley Hares won 21 out of 25 games.
For each team calculate the percentage of games won, and hence state which team has performed better in the tournament.

(3 marks)

Calculator Allowed

5 A groundsman marks out a tennis court.

(a) He makes the court 23 metres long, to the nearest metre.
What is the shortest possible length of the court?

(1 mark)

(b) He makes the court 10 metres wide, to the nearest metre.
What is the shortest possible width of the court?

(1 mark)

(c) Jordan wants to know how many times she should run round the outside of this court to be sure of running at least 1 km. Use your answer to parts (a) and (b) to find how many times she should run around the court.
Show your working, and give your answer to 2 significant figures.

(3 marks)

Conversion Factors

Conversion factors are a really handy tool for dealing with a wide variety of questions, and the method is dead easy.

Method

1) Find the conversion factor (always easy).
2) Multiply by it AND divide by it (to get 2 answers).
3) Choose which is the common sense answer.

Three Important Examples

Example 1

"Convert 4.45 hours into minutes."
(This is NOT 4hrs 45mins.)

1) Conversion factor = 60 (simply because 1 hour = 60 mins).
2) 4.45 hrs × 60 = 267 mins (makes sense)
   4.45 hrs ÷ 60 = 0.0742 mins (ridiculous answer!)
3) So plainly the answer is that 4.45hrs = 267 mins (= 4 hrs 27 mins)

Example 2

"If £1 = 2.75 Australian dollars, how much is 15.43 Australian dollars in £?"

1) Obviously, conversion factor = 2.75 (the "exchange rate").
2) 15.43 × 2.75 = £42.43
   15.43 ÷ 2.75 = £5.61
3) Not quite so obvious this time, but if roughly 3 Australian dollars = £1, then 15 Australian dollars can't be much — certainly not £42 — so the answer must be £5.61

Example 3

"A map has a scale of 1:50 000. How big in real life is a distance of 6 cm on the map?"

1) Conversion factor = 50 000
2) 6 cm × 50 000 = 300 000 cm (looks OK)
   6 cm ÷ 50 000 = 0.00012 cm (not good)
3) So 300 000 cm is the answer.
   How do we convert to metres?

To Convert 300 000 cm to m:

1) C.f. = 100 (cm ⟷ m)
2) 300 000 × 100 = 30 000 000 m (hmm)
   300 000 ÷ 100 = 3000 m (more like it)
3) So answer = 3000 m (or 3 km).

Metric and Imperial Units

This topic is easy marks — make sure you get them.

Metric *Units*

1) Length — mm, cm, m, km
2) Area — mm^2, cm^2, m^2, km^2,
3) Volume — mm^3, cm^3, m^3, ml, litres
4) Weight — g, kg, tonnes
5) Speed — m/s, km/h

MEMORISE THESE KEY FACTS:

1cm = 10 mm	1 tonne = 1000 kg
1m = 100 cm	1 litre = 1000 ml
1km = 1000 m	1 litre = 1000 cm^3
1kg = 1000 g	1 cm^3 = 1 ml

Imperial *Units*

1) Length — Inches, feet, yards, miles
2) Area — Square inches, square feet, square yards, square miles
3) Volume — Cubic inches, cubic feet, pints, gallons
4) Weight — Ounces, pounds, stones, tons
5) Speed — mph

LEARN THESE TOO!

1 foot = 12 inches
1 yard = 3 feet
1 gallon = 8 pints
1 pound = 16 ounces (oz)
1 stone = 14 pounds (lbs)

Metric-Imperial *Conversion*

You need to learn these — because they don't promise to tell you them in the exam, so if they're feeling mean (as they often are), they won't.

Approximate Conversions

1 kg ≈ 2¼ lbs	1 inch ≈ 2.5 cm
1 metric tonne ≈ 1 imperial ton	1 foot ≈ 30 cm
1 litre ≈ 1¾ pints	1 m ≈ 1 yard (+ 10%)
1 gallon ≈ 4.5 litres	1 mile ≈ 1.6 km or 5 miles ≈ 8 km

Using ***Metric-Imperial*** *Conversion Factors*

1) *Convert 36 mm into cm.*
   ANSWER: C.F. = 10, so × or ÷ by 10, which gives 360 cm or 3.6 cm. (Sensible)
2) *Convert 45 inches into cm.*
   ANSWER: C.F. = 2.5, so × or ÷ by 2.5, which gives 18 cm or 112.5 cm.
3) *Convert 2.77 litres into pints.*
   ANSWER: C.F. = 1¾, so × or ÷ by 1.75, which gives 1.58 or 4.85 pints.

Conversion factors sound complicated, but they're not

There is a lot to learn on this page. But all these conversions are the kind of thing that it's really handy to know anyway, not just for passing maths exams... so get learning.

Fractions without a Calculator

Terrifyingly, they may force you (under exam conditions!) to demonstrate your prowess at doing fractions by hand... better learn this little lot first then, hmm?

1) Converting **Fractions to Decimals** – Just Divide

Just remember that "/ " means " ÷ ", as shown below:

A/B – What does it mean?

This is confusing unless you know it's just a way of writing a fraction on a single line, and you should know that a fraction actually means one thing divided by another.

So A/B, $\frac{A}{B}$, $^{A}/_{B}$ and A ÷ B all mean the same thing.

For example, 5/11, $\frac{5}{11}$, $^{5}/_{11}$ and 5 ÷ 11 (= 0.4545....) are all the same thing.

2) Converting **Decimals to Fractions**

It's a simple rule, so work it out yourself...

$0.2 = {}^{2}/_{10}$, $0.9 = {}^{9}/_{10}$, $0.6 = {}^{6}/_{10}$, etc.

$0.15 = {}^{15}/_{100}$, $0.32 = {}^{32}/_{100}$, $0.06 = {}^{6}/_{100}$, $0.68 = {}^{68}/_{100}$, etc.

$0.234 = {}^{234}/_{1000}$, $0.085 = {}^{85}/_{1000}$, $0.505 = {}^{505}/_{1000}$, etc.

These can then be cancelled down — see below.

3) **Cancelling down** — easy

Divide top and bottom by the same number, till they won't go any further:

$$\frac{16}{48} \overset{\div 8}{=} \frac{2}{6} \overset{\div 2}{=} \frac{1}{3}$$

Fractions without a Calculator

4) Doing **Fraction Arithmetic** by Hand

Multiplying – easy

Multiply top and bottom separately:

$$\frac{2}{3} \times \frac{5}{7} = \frac{2 \times 5}{3 \times 7} = \frac{10}{21}$$

Dividing – quite easy

Turn the 2nd fraction upside down and then multiply:

$$\frac{1}{2} \div \frac{6}{7} = \frac{1 \times 7}{2 \times 6} = \frac{7}{12}$$

Adding and Subtracting — Match the Denominators First

Before you add or subtract fractions, you need to check that the bottom numbers (the denominators) are the same.

WHEN THE DENOMINATORS ARE THE SAME:

Just add or subtract the top numbers only and leave the bottom number alone.

E.g. $\frac{3}{5} + \frac{1}{5} = \frac{4}{5}$ $\quad \frac{7}{8} - \frac{3}{8} = \frac{4}{8}$ Easy.

WHEN THE DENOMINATORS ARE DIFFERENT:

It gets tricky now. You need to match the bottom numbers (find a "common denominator") by multiplying them. Then you have to multiply the tops by the same as the bottoms to avoid changing the value of the fractions. Remember, the idea is to make the bottom numbers match.

E.g. $\frac{3}{4} + \frac{1}{3} = \frac{9}{12} + \frac{4}{12}$

Multiply the top of each fraction by the same number as the bottom (So it's 3 × 3 = 9 and 1 × 4 = 4 in this case).

Multiply by 3... *...multiply by 4...* *...to make both denominators 12.*

Once the denominators are the same, just add or subtract the top numbers as normal...

So: $\frac{3}{4} + \frac{1}{3} = \frac{9}{12} + \frac{4}{12} = \frac{13}{12}$

Raise your hands and step away from the calculator...

Your calculator is such a faithful friend in this scary world of maths, and that can make it hard to let go. But you really do have to learn how to handle fractions all by yourself. Be brave.

Fractions with a Calculator

In your calculator paper, it's best to use your calculator for all fractions.

The Fraction Button

Use this as much as possible in the exam. It's very easy, so make sure you know how to use it — you'll lose a lot of marks if you don't.

1) To Enter a **Normal** Fraction like **1/5**

Just press:   

2) To Enter a **Mixed** Fraction like **1 3/4**

Just press:     

3) To do a **Regular Calculation** like **2/5 × 1/4**

Just press:        

4) To **Reduce a Fraction** to its Lowest Terms

Just enter it and then press: 

e.g 12/24     

i.e. 1/2

5) To **Convert** between **Mixed and Top Heavy Fractions**

Just press:  

E.g. to give 3 5/7 as a top heavy fraction:      ,  

which gives an answer of 26/7.

Warm-up and Worked Exam Questions

Bit of a warm-up first as usual, just to get your brain ready. If you can handle these boring old conversions you'll be ready to go on to the exciting exam questions. Whoopee.

Warm-up Questions

1) Convert the following lengths to the units given in brackets:
   (a) 10 000 cm (m) (b) 78 956 cm (km) (c) 0.000 56 km (cm)
2) Convert the following volumes to the units given in brackets:
   (a) 600 000 ml (litres) (b) 1067 cm^3 (ml) (c) 0.0065 litres (cm^3)
3) Convert the following weights to the units given in brackets:
   (a) 0.000 08 kg (g) (b) 72 kg (tonnes) (c) 2 100 000 g (tonnes)
4) Convert the following fractions to decimals:
   (a) 2/5 (b) 1/8 (c) 3/7
5) Convert the following decimals to fractions:
   (a) 0.26 (b) 0.08 (c) 0.625
6) Calculate the following:
   (a) $1\frac{3}{5}+\frac{4}{5}$ (b) $\frac{6}{16}-\frac{15}{16}$ (c) $\frac{2}{3}\times\frac{6}{7}$ (d) $\frac{3}{5}\div\frac{2}{5}$

I've gone through these and written in the answers for you so you can get an idea of what to do. But don't get upset — there are still plenty left for you over the page.

Worked Exam Questions

1 A pet shop has a 30 kilogram sack of bird food. The food needs to be repacked into bags, each containing three quarters of a kilogram. How many bags of food can be made? (Calculators must not be used.)

You need to divide 30 kilograms by 3/4 of a kilogram. Easy with a calculator, but as you're not allowed one you're best using the method from page 19.

$$\frac{30}{1}\div\frac{3}{4} = \frac{30}{1}\times\frac{4}{3} = \frac{120}{3} = 40$$

30/1 is just the same as 30. *To divide fractions without a calculator, turn the 2nd fraction upside down and multiply.*

(2 marks)

2 Approximately 70 000 people attended the last FA Cup Final. Five eighths of these were male. How many females were in the crowd?

This question just requires you to find 3/8ths of 70 000. One method you could use is shown below.

If 5/8 are male then 1 – 5/8 = 3/8 are female.

1/8 of 70 000 = 70 000 ÷ 8 = 8750

So 3/8 of 70 000 = 3 x 8750 = 26 250 females.

(2 marks)

Exam Questions

Exam Questions

Calculator Not Allowed

3 (a) Place the following numbers in order of size, starting with the smallest.

0.45 3/5 1/3 0.3 0.2 4/10

(2 marks)

(b) Place the following volumes in order of size, starting with the smallest.

2 pints 500 cm^3 0.5 gallons 1 litre

(2 marks)

4 Helen has 21 marbles. 2/7 of them are blue, 1/3 are red and the rest are green. How many green marbles does Helen have?

(3 marks)

Calculator Allowed

5 The Bennett family are on holiday in Europe.

(a) Whilst driving Mr Bennett sees a sign saying 24 kilometres to the next town. How many miles are there in 24 kilometres?

(2 marks)

(b) The Bennetts stop in the town to draw out some money from a local cash point and fill their car up with petrol. The exchange rate for pounds to Euros on that day is £1 : 1.445 Euros.

(i) Mrs Bennett draws out 100 Euros. How much is this in pounds?

(2 marks)

(ii) Mr Bennett fills up the car with 135 litres of petrol. The total cost is 20.25 Euros. How much is this in pence per gallon? (Use 1 gallon = 4.5 litres.)

(3 marks)

(c) The Bennetts are going on a scenic walk along a coastal path. The map they are following has a scale of 1 : 50 000. The path they decide to take measures 5.5 cm on the map. What is the actual distance of the path in kilometres?

(2 marks)

Percentages

Contrary to popular belief there are three distinct types of percentage question. Obviously then, it's going to be pretty essential that you can:

1) Distinguish between the three types.
2) Remember the method for each of them.

Type 1

These are identified by the "%" symbol in the question. This is the easiest type — they're always of the form:

FIND "some" % OF "something else"

For example: *"Find 35% of £200"*

Method

1) Write: 35% of £200

2) Translate: $\frac{35}{100} \times 200 = £70$

3) Check that it's a sensible answer.

Remember:

1) "OF" means "×"

2) "Per cent" means "out of 100", so 35% means "35 out of 100", i.e. $\frac{35}{100}$

Type 2

These are identified by the word "percentage" in the question. They're always of the form:

EXPRESS "one thing" AS A PERCENTAGE OF "another"

For example: *"Express £12 as a percentage of £80."*

Method – FDP

F.D.P. : Fraction → Decimal → Percentage

(See page 9)

$\frac{12}{80}$ —(12 ÷ 80)→ **0.15** —(× 100)→ **15%**

Make a fraction using the two numbers — always with the smallest on top.

Divide them to get a decimal.

Then multiply by 100 to get a percentage.

Percentages

Percentage Change

(An important example of type 2.)

It's quite common to give a change in value as a percentage.
This is the formula for doing so — learn it, and use it:

$$\text{Percentage “Change”} = \frac{\text{“Change”}}{\text{Original}} \times 100$$

By "change", we could mean all sorts of things such as "profit", "loss", "appreciation", "depreciation", "increase", "decrease", "error", "discount", etc.

For example, **Percentage "profit"** $= \dfrac{\textbf{"profit"}}{\textbf{original}} \times \mathbf{100}$

Don't forget the huge importance of using the original value in this formula.

Type 3

These are identified by them not giving you the "original value".

These are the type most people get wrong — but only because they don't recognise them as a type 3 and don't apply this simple method:

Example: ***"A house increases in value by 25% to £90 000. Find its value before the rise."***

Method

÷ 125	**£90 000**	**=**	**125%**
	£720	**=**	**1%**
× 100	**£72 000**	**=**	**100%**

So the original price was £72 000

An increase of 25% means that £90 000 represents 125% of the original value.

If it was a drop of 25%, then we would put "£90 000 = 75%" instead, and then divide by 75 on the left hand side, instead of 125.

Always set them out exactly like this example. The trickiest bit is deciding the top % figure on the right hand side. The 2nd and 3rd rows are always 1% and 100%.

Be able to tell the difference between the three types

Percentages can be tricky, but just learn the three different types and the method for each and you won't go far wrong. Don't forget about percentage change either, which is a special kind of type 2.

Ratios

The whole grisly subject of ratios gets a whole lot easier when you do this:

Treat RATIOS like FRACTIONS

So for the ratio 3 : 4 you'd treat it as the fraction 3/4, which is 0.75 as a decimal.

*What the **Fraction** form of the Ratio **Actually Means***

Suppose in a class the girls and boys are in the ratio 3 : 4.
This means there's 3/4 as many girls as boys.
So if there were 20 boys, there would be 3/4 × 20 = 15 girls.

You've got to be careful — it doesn't mean
3/4 of the people in the class are girls.

*Reducing **Ratios** to their **Simplest Form***

You reduce ratios just like you'd reduce fractions to their simplest form.

Example

For the ratio 15 : 18 both numbers have a factor of 3,
so divide them by 3 — that gives 5 : 6.
We can't reduce this any further. So the simplest form of 15 : 18 is 5 : 6.

*Treat them just like **Fractions** — use your **Calculator** if you can*

Now this is really sneaky. If you stick in a fraction using the $a\frac{b}{c}$ button, your calculator automatically cancels it down when you press =.

So for the ratio 8 : 12, just press 8 $a\frac{b}{c}$ 12 =, and you'll get the reduced fraction 2/3. Now you just change it back to ratio form, i.e. 2 : 3. Ace.

Ratios

*The More **Awkward Cases***

*1 The a b/c Button will **only** accept **Whole Numbers***

So if the ratio is awkward (like "2.4 : 3.6" or "$1\frac{1}{4} : 2\frac{3}{4}$") then you must multiply both sides by the same number until they are both whole numbers.

Then you can use the a b/c button as before to simplify them down.

e.g. With "$1\frac{1}{4} : 2\frac{3}{4}$", multiplying both sides by 4 gives "5 : 11."
(Try a b/c, but it won't cancel further.)

*2 The Ratio is **Mixed Units***

You must convert both sides into the same units — usually the smaller unit is best. Use the relevant conversion factor (see page 17), and then carry on as normal.

E.g. "36 mm : 5.4 cm" — first multiply 5.4 cm by 10 to give the figure in mm
⇒ 36 mm : 54 mm
= 2:3 (using a b/c)

*3 To **Reduce a Ratio** to the form **1 : n***

(n can be any number at all.)

Simply divide both sides by the smallest side.

e.g. "5 : 27" — the smaller number is 5, so divide both sides by 5.
to give: 1 : 5.4
(i.e. 1 : n)

The 1 : n form is often the most useful because it shows the ratio very clearly.

Ratios

Using the Formula Triangle in Ratio Questions

EXAMPLE: *"Mortar is made from sand and cement in the ratio 9 : 2.*
If 7 buckets of sand are used, how much cement is needed?"

This is a fairly common type of exam question and it's pretty tricky for most people — but once you start using the formula triangle method, it's all a bit of a breeze really.

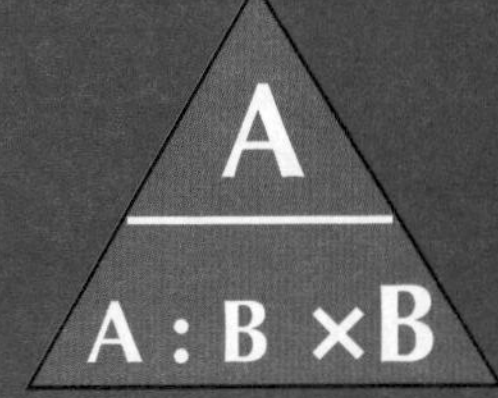

This is the basic formula triangle for ratios, but note:

1) The ratio must be the right way round, with the first number in the ratio relating to the item on top in the triangle.
2) You'll always need to convert the ratio into its equivalent fraction or decimal to work out the answer.

The formula triangle for the mortar question is shown below, and the trick is to replace the ratio 9 : 2 by its equivalent fraction: 9/2, or 4.5 as a decimal (i.e. 9 ÷ 2).
So, covering up cement in the triangle gives us:
"cement = sand / (9 : 2)"
= 7 ÷ 4.5
= 1.56 or about 1½ buckets of cement.

Proportional Division

In a proportional division question, a total amount is to be split in a certain ratio.

EXAMPLE: *"£1800 is to be split in the ratio 2 : 3 : 1. Find the 3 amounts."*

The key word when you're doing these is PARTS.
Concentrate on "parts" and it all becomes quite painless:

Method

1) Add up the parts:
The ratio 2 : 3 : 1 means there will be a total of 6 parts, i.e. 2 + 3 + 1 = 6.
2) Find the amount for one part:
Just divide the total amount by the number of parts:
£1800 ÷ 6 = £300 (= 1 part).
3) Hence find the three amounts:
2 parts = 2 × 300 = £600, 3 parts = 3 × 300 = £900, 1 part = £300.

Complicated terms, simple methods

Things like "proportional division" and "the 1 : n form" sound hard, but the methods used are surprisingly easy. Better than having simple-sounding words with really hard methods, I'd say.

Warm-up and Worked Exam Questions

Some more of your good friends the warm-up questions below, all about percentages and ratios. This is the time to go back over any stuff that you're not sure of, before it's too late...

Warm-up Questions

1) Calculate the following: (a) 20% of £200 (b) 45% of £560 (c) 30% of £12.50
2) The following marks were obtained by a student in practice exams. Express these marks as a percentage value.
   (a) 26/40 (b) 18/30 (c) 64/80
3) A video game console is priced £64 after a 30% discount. What was its original price?
4) The attendance at Rovers United was 25 000 last week. This week it was 30 000. Calculate the percentage increase in attendance.
5) £6200 needs to be shared amongst Dan, Chris and Angela in the ratio 2 : 3 : 5. How much does each person receive?
6) A computer is priced at £850, which includes VAT at 17.5%. What was its price before VAT was added?

You know the routine by now — work through the example and make sure you understand what's going on. That'll help when you come to do the real exam questions on the next page.

Worked Exam Question

1 (a) A parrot in a pet shop was priced at £35. Nobody bought it, so its price was reduced by 40%. How much did the parrot cost after the reduction?

40% of £35 = 40/100 of £35

This is a type 1 percentage question, so translate it into a fraction first.

(40 ÷ 100) × 35 = £14

£35 − £14 = £21

Don't forget, £14 is not your answer in this case — you still need to take that away from the original price.

(2 marks)

(b) One day the takings from the shop were £490. £55 of this was from hamster sales. What percentage of the takings came from selling hamsters?

This is asking you to express £55 as a percentage of £490. Use the FDP (fraction – decimal – percentage) method from page 23.

55 ÷ 490 = 0.112 (to 3 s.f.)

Your calculator will give you a whole line of numbers for this answer, but remember that 3 significant figures is usually the most appropriate degree of accuracy to use.

0.112 × 100 = 11.2%

(2 marks)

Exam Questions

Exam Questions

Calculator Not Allowed

2 The table on the right shows some percentages of amounts of money.

	£15	**£60**	**£85**
5%	75p	£3	£4.25
10%	£1.50	£6	£8.50

Use the table to help you work out the missing values below.

(a) 15% of £60 = £ ....

(b) £12.75 = 15% of £ ....

(c) 5% of £170 = £ ....

(d) £1.50 = 5% of £ ....

(4 marks)

Calculator Allowed

3 A DVD rental shop recorded the most popular rentals in a week:

Film	No. of rentals	Takings
X-men	20	£70.00
The Lord of the Rings	38	£133.00
Tomb Raider	19	£66.50
Buffy	5	£15.00
Charlie's Angels	3	£7.50
Totals:	85	£292.00

(a) What percentage of the total number of DVDs rented were "The Lord of the Rings"?

(1 mark)

(b) What percentage of the total takings were due to "The Lord of the Rings"?

(1 mark)

(c) A DVD player is on sale in the shop. It is now priced at £69.99 after a reduction of 28%. What was its original price?

(2 marks)

(d) (i) Express as a ratio in its simplest terms the number of rentals for "Buffy" to the number of rentals for "X-men".

(1 mark)

(ii) The week after the above results were recorded there were 36 rentals of "X-men". If the ratio of Buffy rentals to "X-men" rentals remained the same as above, how many copies of "Buffy" were rented in the second week?

(2 marks)

Standard Index Form

Standard Form and Standard Index Form are the same thing.
So remember both names as well as what it actually is:

Ordinary Number: 5 200 000 In Standard Form: 5.2×10^6

Standard form is only really useful for writing very big or very small numbers in a more convenient way.

E.g. 37 000 000 000 would be 3.7×10^{10} in standard form.
0.000 000 004 16 would be 4.16×10^{-9} in standard form.

What it Actually is

A number written in standard form must always be in exactly this form:

This number must always be between 1 and 10.

This number is just the number of places the decimal point moves.

The fancy way of writing this is "$1 \le a < 10$" — they sometimes write it like that in exam questions — don't let it put you off, just remember what it means.

Learn the Three Rules:

1) The front number must always be between 1 and 10.
2) The power of 10, n, is just how far the decimal point moves.
3) n is positive for big numbers and negative for small numbers.
(This is easier to remember than rules based on which way the point moves.)

Example 1

"Express 79 800 in standard form."

METHOD:

1) Move the decimal point until 79 800 becomes 7.98 ($1 \le a < 10$):

7.9800.

2) The point has moved 4 places so n = 4, giving 10^4.
3) 79 800 is a big number, so n is +4, not –4.

ANSWER:

$79\ 800 = 7.98 \times 10^4$

Example 2

"Express 3.51×10^{-3} as an ordinary number."

METHOD:

1) 10^{-3} tells us that the decimal point must move 3 places:

. 3.51

2) The "–" sign tells us to move the point to make the number small (i.e. 0.003 51 rather than 3510).

ANSWER:

$3.51 \times 10^{-3} = 0.003\ 51$

Standard Index Form

Standard Form and the *Calculator*

People usually manage all that stuff about moving the decimal point well enough (apart from always forgetting that for a big number it's "ten to the power +ve something" and for a small number it's "ten to the power –ve something"), but when it comes to doing standard form on a calculator it's often a sorry saga of confusion and ineptitude. But it's not so bad really — you just have to learn it, that's all...

1) *Entering* Standard Form Numbers EXP

The button you must use to put standard form numbers into the calculator is the EXP (or EE) button — but don't go pressing X 10 as well, like a lot of people do, because that makes it wrong.

EXAMPLE:

"Enter 5.74 x 10^9 into the calculator."

Just press: 5.74 EXP 9 and the display will be 5.74 ^{09}

Note that you only press the EXP (or EE) button — you don't press X or 10 at all.

2) *Reading* Standard Form Numbers

The big thing you have to remember when you write any standard form number from the calculator display is to put the "×10" in yourself. Don't just write down what it says on the display.

EXAMPLE:

"Write down the number 3.265 ^{06} *as a finished answer."*

As a finished answer this must be written as 3.265×10^6.

It is not 3.265^6 so don't write it down like that — you have to put the $\times 10^n$ in yourself, even though it isn't shown in the display at all. That's the bit people forget.

Standard form and standard index form are the same thing

Standard form is just a quick way of writing very big or small numbers. Your calculator makes it easy to use numbers in standard form, so make sure you know how to use it.

Powers or Indices

Powers are a very useful shorthand:

$6\times6 = 6^2$ ("six squared")
$2\times2\times2\times2 = 2^4$ ("two to the power four")
$9\times9\times9\times9\times9 = 9^5$ ("nine to the power five")
$4\text{x}4\text{x}4 = 4^3$ ("four cubed")

That bit is easy to remember. Unfortunately, there are seven special rules for powers that are not quite so easy, but you do need to know them for the exam:

*The Seven **Rules***

1) When multiplying, you ADD the powers.

e.g. $2^3 \times 2^4 = 2^{3+4} = 2^7$ $5^2 \times 5^7 = 5^{2+7} = 5^9$

2) When dividing, you SUBTRACT the powers.

e.g. $4^6 \div 4^3 = 4^{6-3} = 4^3$ $10^8/10^3 = 10^{8-3} = 10^5$

3) When raising one power to another, you MULTIPLY the powers.

e.g. $(2^2)^4 = 2^{2\text{x}4} = 2^8$ $(5^3)^6 = 5^{18}$

4) Anything to the power 1 is just itself — $x^1 = x$.

e.g. $3^1 = 3$, $2 \times 2^6 = 2^7$, $5^1 = 5$, $8^3 \div 8^2 = 8^{3-2} = 8^1 = 8$

5) Anything to the power 0 is just 1 — $x^0 = 1$.

e.g. $4^0 = 1$ $28^0 = 1$ $2^3 \div 2^3 = 2^{3-3} = 2^0 = 1$

6) 1 to any power is still just 1 — $1^x = 1$.

e.g. $1^{19} = 1$ $1^{63} = 1$ $1^3 = 1$ $1^{202} = 1$

7) Fractional powers mean one thing: roots

The power ½ means square root,

e.g. $25^{\frac{1}{2}} = \sqrt{25} = 5$

The power $\frac{1}{3}$ means cube root,

e.g. $27^{\frac{1}{3}} = \sqrt[3]{27} = 3$

Square Roots and Cube Roots

Square Roots

"Squared" means "times by itself": $P^2 = P \times P$ — square root is the reverse process.

The best way to think of it is this:

"Square root" means "what number times by itself gives..."

Example

"Find the square root of 49." (i.e. " Find $\sqrt{49}$ " or "Find $49^{1/2}$")

To do this you should say it as: "What number times by itself gives 49?"

Now, if you'd learnt the number sequences on page 4,

then of course you'd know instantly that the answer is 7.

However, it has to be said the best way to find any square root is simply to use the square root button on your calculator: Press [√] [49] [=] 7

Cube Roots

"Cubed" means "times by itself twice": $T^3 = T \times T \times T$ — cube root is the reverse process.

"Cube root" means "what number times by itself twice gives..."

Example

"Find the cube root of 64." (i.e. "find $\sqrt[3]{64}$ " or " find $64^{\frac{1}{3}}$ ")

You should say "what number times by itself TWICE gives 64?"

From your in-depth revision of page 5, you will of course know the answer is 4.

However, for others that you may not know, there's no better method than to use the cube root button: Press [∛] [27] [=] 3

And Don't Forget

"Something to the power ½" is just a different way of asking for a square root,

e.g. $81^{\frac{1}{2}}$ is the same as $\sqrt{81}$ which is just 9.

"Something to the power 1/3" is just a different way of asking for a cube root,

e.g. $27^{\frac{1}{3}}$ is the same as $\sqrt[3]{27}$ which is just 3.

Learn all seven rules about powers

Seven rules sounds like a lot, but they're actually very quick to learn, so don't panic.
Then there's just roots to contend with, and your calculator can help you there.

Warm-up and Worked Exam Questions

There's really no point just rushing straight on to the next section — practice is the best thing you can do to improve your performance in exams, so don't neglect it.

Warm-up Questions

1) Write the following numbers in standard form:
   (a) 5 600 000 (b) 72 853 462 (c) 10 089
2) Write the following numbers in standard form:
   (a) 0.000 076 (b) 0.003 788 (c) 0.000 506 7
3) Work out the following:
   (a) $6^2 \times 6^3$ (b) $7^8 \div 7^2$ (c) $5^0 \times 5$
   (d) $49^{1/2}$ (e) $\sqrt[3]{64}$
4) Use your calculator to find the following. Give your answers to 3 significant figures.
   (a) $\sqrt{108}$ (b) $\sqrt[3]{72}$ (c) 6^8 (d) $48^{1/3}$ (e) $92^{1/2}$

It's no good learning all the facts if you then go to pieces in the exam and start writing complete nonsense. These worked examples show you how to turn those facts into good answers.

Worked Exam Questions

Calculator Allowed

1 In a large department store 2.4×10^4 purchases are made in one day. The total amount spent on the day was £1.5 million.

Calculate the average amount spent on each purchase.

Easy — you just divide the amount spent by the number of purchases. The only thing that makes it at all complicated is the big numbers involved.

$1.5 \times 10^6 \div 2.4 \times 10^4 = 62.5 = £62.50$

(2 marks)

If you really wanted to, you could turn the standard form numbers into ordinary numbers before working out the answer, i.e. 1 500 000 ÷ 24 000. But it's much simpler just to use the standard form button on your calculator. That's why it's so important to know which button it is.

Calculator Not Allowed

2 Work out $\dfrac{4 \times 10^9}{8 \times 10^5}$

Give your answer in standard form.

You're not allowed to use a calculator here, so you need to use rule 2 from page 32 — when dividing, you subtract the powers. It's easier to do sums like this in two parts — first divide 4 by 8, and then sort out the tens.

$4 \div 8 = 0.5$

$10^9 \div 10^5 = 10^4$

So the answer is 0.5×10^4 which is 5×10^3 in standard form.

(3 marks)

Exam Questions

Exam Questions

Calculator Allowed

3 A government spends £2.7×10^7 on education in total.
It spends £8.9×10^6 on secondary education.

What percentage of its total education budget is spent on secondary education?

(2 marks)

4 In 2003 the population of Madville was 6 278 000.

(a) Give this population in standard form.

(1 mark)

(b) In 2003, there was an average in Madville of one doctor for every 82.2 people.
How many doctors were there in Madville?
Give your answer to an appropriate degree of accuracy.

(2 marks)

Calculator Not Allowed

5 (a) Work out $4 \times 10^7 \times 3 \times 10^4$.
Give your answer in standard form.

(2 marks)

(b) Work out 0.003×0.002.
Give your answer in standard form.

(2 marks)

6 Look at the table on the right.
It shows some of the powers of 8.

Power	Answer
8^0	1
8^1	8
8^2	64
8^3	512
8^4	4096
8^5	32 768
8^6	262 144
8^7	2 097 152
8^8	16 777 216

(a) Explain how the table shows that
$64 \times 4096 = 262\ 144$.

(2 marks)

(b) Use the table to help you work out
the value of $16\ 777\ 216 \div 32\ 768$.

(2 marks)

(c) Use the table to work out the value of $(8^2)^3$.

(2 marks)

Calculator Buttons

The next few pages are full of lovely calculator tricks to save you a lot of button-bashing. Most people now have two line display calculators, but some still have the old style ones. I've included the buttons you'll need to know for both types, just in case.

The **Old Style** Calculators

These ones only display numbers. They do the calculation each time you press an operation key.

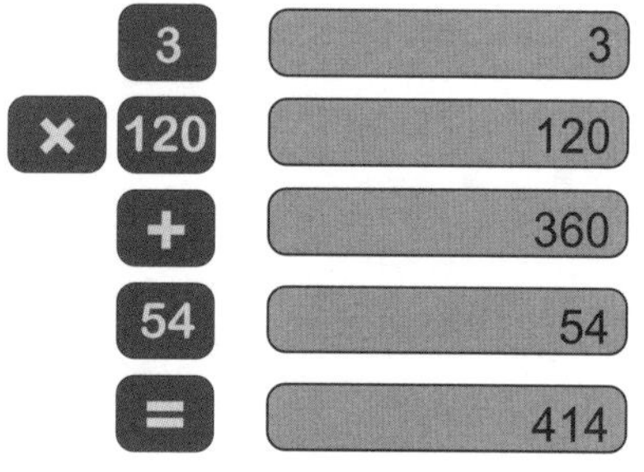

C Semi-Cancel and AC All Cancel

The C button only cancels the number you're entering. AC clears the whole calculation. Using C instead of AC when you hit the wrong key will save you loads of time.

2-Line Display Calculators

These are the most common now. They're easy to use because you just type most calculations exactly as they're written. Like this:

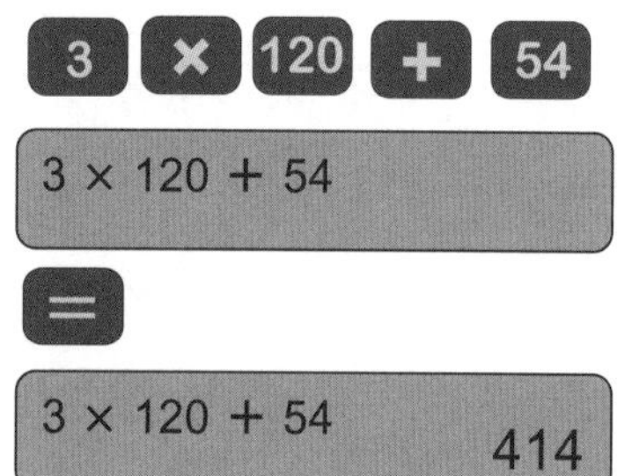

DEL The Delete Button

Pressing the DEL button deletes what you've typed, one key at a time (just like on a computer), so it's much quicker than pressing AC and re-typing the whole lot.

Cursor Buttons ◄ ►

The cursor buttons ◄ and ► are pretty useful for editing what you've typed in. (You'll probably find you overwrite what was there before, but you can change this with the INS key to insert, rather than overwrite.)

1 Entering **Negative** Numbers

On some calculators, there's a +/– button. To enter a minus number, you need to press this after you've entered the number. Most calculators just have a minus button (–), which you press before entering the number. Why can't they all just be the same...

So to work out – 5 × – 6 you'd either press...

or...

The examples in this book will use the (–) button, but if yours is different make sure you know how to use it.

Calculator Buttons

2 Square, Square Root and Cube Root

The square, square root and cube root buttons are [x^2], [√] and [∛].

1) The [x^2] button squares the number you typed, i.e. it multiplies it by itself.
It's ideal for finding the area of a circle, using the formula $A = \pi r^2$.
E.g. if r = 5 then press [3.14] [×] [5] [x^2] [=] which gives you 78.5.

For a more accurate answer use the π button, which is usually the second function of the EXP key.

2) [√] is the reverse process of [x^2] —
it calculates the square root of the number you enter.
Pressing [√] [25] [=] gives [5]
then [x^2] [=] takes you back to [25].

3) [∛] gives the cube root (see page 33) which is the reverse of cubing a number.
E.g. [∛] [27] [=] gives [3]
then pressing [x^3] [=] takes you back to [27].

3 Older Calculators do Stuff Backwards

On some calculators, especially older ones, you need to enter a lot of calculations backwards.
E.g. if you're working out the square root of a number,
you'd enter the number first and then press the square root: [25] [√] [5]

Or if you were typing a trigonometry function like sin 45°: [45] [SIN] [0.707106781]

You don't need to press equals when you do functions on one of these calculators.
It'll work it out automatically. Bless it.

4 The Memory Buttons ([STO] Store, [RCL] Recall)

On some calculators the memory buttons are called [Min] (memory in) and [MR] (memory recall) instead.

Contrary to popular belief, the memory is not intended for storing your favourite phone number. In fact it's a really useful feature for keeping a number you've just calculated, so you can use it again shortly afterwards.

For something like $\frac{16}{15 + 12 \sin 40}$ you could just work out

the bottom line first and stick it in the memory:

Press [15] [+] [12] [SIN] [40] [=] and then [STO] (Or [STO] [M] or [STO] [1] or [Min])
to keep the result of the bottom line in the memory.
Then you simply press [16] [÷] [RCL] [=], and the answer is 0.7044.
(Instead of [RCL], you might need to type [RCL] [M] or [RCL] [1] or [MR], depending on your calculator.)
Once you've practised with the memory buttons a bit, you'll soon find them very useful.
They can speed things up no end.

Calculator Buttons

5 BODMAS and the Brackets Buttons

The brackets buttons are (and).

One of the biggest problems people have with calculators is not realising that they always work things out in a certain order, which is summarised by the word BODMAS. BODMAS stands for:

Brackets, Other, Division, Multiplication, Addition, Subtraction

This becomes really important when you want to work out even a simple thing like $\frac{23+45}{64\times 3}$ — it's no good just pressing 23 + 45 ÷ 64 × 3 =

— it will be completely wrong. The calculator will think you mean $23+\frac{45}{64}\times 3$ because it will do the division and multiplication before it does the addition.

The secret is to override the automatic BODMAS order of operations using the brackets buttons. Brackets are the ultimate priority in BODMAS, which means anything in brackets is worked out before anything else happens to it. So all you have to do is:

1) Write a couple of pairs of brackets into the expression: $\frac{(23+45)}{(64\times 3)}$

2) Then just type it as it's written:

(23 + 45) ÷ (64 × 3) =

You might think it's difficult to know where to put the brackets in. It's not that difficult, you just put them in pairs around each group of numbers. It's OK to have brackets within other brackets too, e.g. (4 + (5 ÷ 2)). As a rule, you can't cause trouble by putting too many brackets in, so long as they always go in pairs.

6 The Fraction Button

— It's absolutely essential that you learn how to use this button for doing fractions. Full details are given on page 20.

7 The Power Button

On some calculators, the power button is ^

It's used for working out powers of numbers quickly. For example, to find 3^4, instead of pressing 3 × 3 × 3 × 3, you should just press 3 x^y 4 =

Calculator Buttons

8 The Standard Form Button

The standard form button is EXP or EE.

All you ever use this for is entering numbers written in standard form into the calculator.

It would be a lot more helpful if the calculator manufacturers labelled it as $\times 10^n$ because that's what you should call it as you press it: "Times ten to the power..."

For example, to enter 5×10^3, you must only press: 5 EXP 3

and NOT, as a lot of people do: 5 × 10 EXP 3 .

Some calculators then display this number as:

5^3

REMEMBER — it doesn't mean 5^3, but 5×10^3.

Pressing × 10 as well as EXP is horribly wrong because the EXP already contains the "× 10" in it. That's why you should always say to yourself "times ten to the power..." every time you press the EXP button, to prevent this very common mistake.

9 Modes

This is tricky and you wouldn't really need to know about it except that you'll sometimes accidentally get into the wrong mode, and it can make life pretty difficult if you don't know how to get back to normality.

There are 3 separate modes that your calculator has to make a choice about:

Calculation Modes You want COMP mode. This is the mode for doing normal calculations. On CASIOs, this is on the first menu you get from pressing MODE .
Angles Modes You want degrees mode (there'll be a small DEG or D on the display when you're in this mode). On CASIOs, you'd press MODE twice to get the right menu.
Display Modes You want NORM mode most of the time. The other display modes are for showing a certain number of decimal places (FIX) or significant figures (SCI).

*Make sure you can do all of this on **your** calculator*

All calculators are different — it's up to you to make sure you can do all this stuff on yours. Spend a bit of time now finding out which are the right buttons to use for each of these tasks.

Revision Summary for Section One

The questions below will test how much you've learnt from this first section. They follow the sequence of pages in the section, so it's easy to look up anything you don't know. They're pretty hard-going, but they really are the best way to find out what you know and what you don't know.

Keep learning these basic facts until you know them

1) What are the multiples of a number? What are the factors of a number?
2) What is the best method for finding all the factors of a number?
3) What are the prime factors of a number? How do you find them?
4) State the two rules for finding prime numbers (below 120).
5) List the first ten terms in each of these sequences:
   (a) odd numbers (b) even numbers (c) prime numbers
   (d) square numbers (e) cube numbers (f) triangle numbers
6) List the first six equivalent fractions for one fifth.
7) Outline the four methods used for converting between fractions, decimals and percentages.
8) What are the three steps for rounding off?
9) What are the 3 extra details concerning s.f. rounding?
10) State three rules for deciding on appropriate accuracy.
11) State two rules for estimating the answer to a calculation.
12) State two rules for estimating an area or volume.
13) State the 3 steps of the method for applying conversion factors.
14) Give 8 different conversions from one metric unit to another.
15) Give 5 different conversions from one imperial unit to another.
16) Give 8 conversions between metric and imperial units.
17) What does a/b mean?
18) How do you cancel down fractions by hand?
19) Describe in words how you multiply, divide, add and subtract fractions by hand.
20) Which is the fraction button? What must you press to enter $5\frac{1}{4}$?
21) How would you convert it to a top heavy fraction?
22) Describe the 3 types of percentage question and how to identify them.
23) Give details of the method for each of the 3 types.
24) Give the formula for percentage change, and give 3 examples of it.
25) How can a calculator help to simplify ratios?
26) What is the formula triangle for ratios?
27) What are the three rules for expressing a number in standard form?
28) What are the seven rules for powers?
29) Explain what a square root is. Explain what a cube root is.
30) Explain the difference between the 2 cancel buttons on your calculator.
31) Which are the memory buttons on your calculator? What are they used for?
32) What does BODMAS mean and what has it got to do with your calculator?
33) When would you use the brackets buttons?
34) Which is the power button? What must you press to find 7^{12}?
35) Which is the standard form button? What must you press to enter 2×10^{-6}?
36) What would the number 8×10^4 look like on the calculator display?

Turning Words into Algebra

This is all about taking a maths problem which is written as a sentence and turning it into an equation or formula.

Example 1 *"A number is doubled, then three is added to the total, and the result is fifteen. What was the original number?"*

Somehow you need to be able to turn that sentence into this equation:

"Solve $2x + 3 = 15$"

You have to be the translator:

From long-winded **English**		To ink-saving **algebra**
A number	——	x
double it	——	$2x$
then add three	——	$2x + 3$
the result is 15	——	$2x + 3 = 15$

And there you have it. You just have to think about each bit of the sentence and convert it into a bit of maths. Keep doing it bit by bit and before you know it you have an equation which you can solve. The answer to the above is clearly 6. ($2 \times 6 + 3 = 15$)

Example 2 *"A gang of four workers were paid £15 per hour plus a tip of £6. They shared this money equally between the four of them and each got £9. How many hours did they work?"*

$$\frac{15x + 6}{4} = 9$$

£15 per hour → $15x$; plus a £6 tip → $+6$; shared between 4 workers → 4; each got £9 → 9

x represents the number of hours worked. So all you have to do now is solve the equation to find x. The answer comes out as $x = 2$ hours.

Just watch out when translating "LESS": "Three less than a number" means "a number, less three" → i.e. $x - 3$, not $3 - x$

Remember — x is the unknown

Turning words into algebra might sound a bit baffling at first, but stick with it. It'll really help you understand what equations actually mean — which will make them easier to deal with.

Basic Algebra

The next four pages cover some of the real meat of algebra.
They're hugely important, so take your time and make sure you take it all in.

1) Terms

Before you can do anything else, you MUST understand what a TERM is:

1) **A TERM is a collection of numbers, letters and brackets, all multiplied / divided together.**

2) Terms are separated by + and – signs. E.g. $5x^2 - 2dy - 3x + 6$

3) Terms always have a + or – attached to the front of them.

4) E.g.

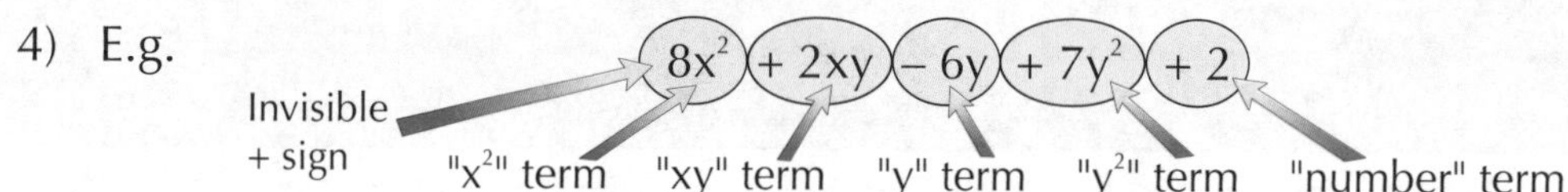

2) Simplifying — "Collecting Like Terms"

EXAMPLE: *"Simplify* $2x^2 - 5x + 7x^2 + 6x - 3$*"*

$2x^2$ $-5x$ $+7x^2$ $+6x$ -3 = $+2x^2$ $+7x^2$ $-5x$ $+6x$ -3

x^2-terms, x-terms, number term = $9x^2$ $+x$ -3 = $9x^2 + x - 3$

1) Put bubbles round each term — be sure you capture the +/– sign in front of each.

2) Then you can move the bubbles into the best order so that like terms are together.

3) "Like terms" have exactly the same combination of letters, e.g. "x-terms" or "xy-terms".

4) Combine like terms using the number line (see page 51).

Basic Algebra

3) Expanding (Multiplying out) Brackets

SINGLE BRACKETS

1) The thing outside the brackets multiplies each separate term inside the brackets.
2) When letters are multiplied together, they are just written next to each other, e.g. $p \times q = pq$.
3) Remember, $R \times R = R^2$, and TY^2 means $T \times Y \times Y$, whilst $(TY)^2$ means $T \times T \times Y \times Y$.
4) Remember, a minus outside the bracket reverses all the signs when you multiply.

EXAMPLES:

1) $2(4x + 6) = \underline{8x + 12}$

2) $3q(5r - 4q) = \underline{15qr - 12q^2}$

3) $-5(2a - 3b) = \underline{-10a + 15b}$ *(note that the a- and b-term signs have been reversed — Rule 4)*

DOUBLE BRACKETS

You get 4 terms after multiplying them out and usually 2 of them combine to leave 3 terms, like this:

For more detail on expanding brackets, see page 45.

$$\begin{aligned}(2A - 5)(3A + 1) &= (2A \times 3A) + (2A \times 1) + (-5 \times 3A) + (-5 \times 1) \\ &= 6A^2 + 2A - 15A - 5 \\ &= 6A^2 - 13A - 5\end{aligned}$$

these 2 combine together

Basic Algebra

SQUARED BRACKETS

ALWAYS write these out as two brackets and work them out CAREFULLY like this:

$$(5t + 3)^2 = (5t + 3)(5t + 3)$$
$$= 25t^2 + 15t + 15t + 9$$
$$= 25t^2 + 30t + 9$$

You should always get four terms from squared brackets, and two of these will combine together to leave three terms in the end.

(The usual WRONG ANSWER, by the way, is $(5t + 3)^2 = 25t^2 + 9$ — eeek!)

4) Factorising — Putting Brackets In

This is the exact reverse of multiplying out brackets. Here's the method to follow:

1) Take out the biggest NUMBER that goes into all the terms.
2) Take each letter in turn and take out the highest power (e.g. x, x^2 etc.) that will go into EVERY term.
3) Open the brackets and fill in all the bits needed to reproduce each term.

EXAMPLE: *"Factorise $6x^4y + 8x^2y^3z - 12x^3yz^2$"*

$$2x^2y(3x^2 + 4y^2z - 6xz^2)$$

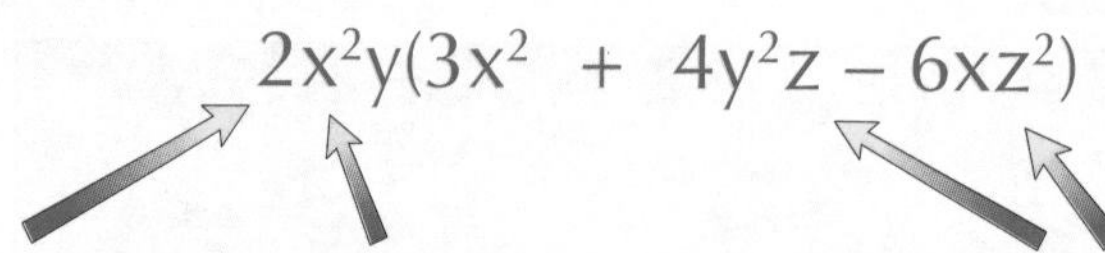

Biggest number that'll divide into 6, 8 and 12

Highest powers of x and y that will go into all three terms

z wasn't in all terms so it can't come out as a common factor

Remember:
1) The bits taken out and put at the front are the common factors.
2) The bits inside the brackets are what's needed to get back to the original terms if you were to multiply the brackets out again.

Expanding Double Brackets — Two Methods

This can get quite tricky and it's all too easy to get it wrong.
Learn these two very handy methods and always use one or the other:

*The Jolly Old "**Area**" Method*

You can imagine the result of multiplying two brackets is a bit like an area.
This is done by looking at something like (x + 3)(x + 2), and thinking of it as a rectangle which is "(x + 3) long" by "(x + 2) wide".

	x	+ 3
x	This bit is x long by x wide: AREA x^2	This bit is 3 long by x wide: AREA 3x
+ 2	This bit is x long by 2 wide: AREA 2x	This bit is 3 long by 2 wide: AREA 6

Multiply to get each of the 4 bits, then add the 4 bits together

... and you get the "area" of the entire (x + 3)(x + 2) rectangle:

$$x^2 + 3x + 2x + 6 = x^2 + 5x + 6$$

*The Fiendish **FOIL method***

The other method, which is a more "grown up" method, is just to multiply each of the four bits straight off without using the area idea or drawing any boxes.
For reasons which should be obvious we call this the FOIL method:

Firsts: (x + 3) (x + 2) — times

Outsides: (x + 3) (x + 2) — times

Insides: (x + 3) (x + 2) — times

Lasts: (x + 3) (x + 2) — times

So we end up with:

F + O + I + L =

$x^2 + 2x + 3x + 6 =$

$x^2 + 5x + 6$ (again)

This is the better method to use.

These topics are pure algebra...

The processes on these pages are so fundamental to algebra you need to make an extra special effort to learn them. Then go on to the next page to get some good practice using them.

Warm-up and Worked Exam Questions

Algebra can seem pretty weird if you're not used to it, but that's why you need to learn the basics really well. Even if you find it easy, it's practice that really fixes things in your brain.

Warm-up Questions

1) Janice thinks of a number. She doubles it and adds 5. She calls the number x. Which of these expressions is correct?
   (a) $2x + 5$ (b) $5x + 2$ (c) $5 + x + 2$ (d) $2(x + 5)$
2) Bob has x apples in a bag. Charlotte has 3 times as many apples as Bob. Write an expression involving x to show how many apples she has.
3) Simplify: (a) $3x + 2x + 4$ (b) $2y - y + x - 1$ (c) $3x^2 + 2x - x^2 - 3$
4) Multiply out the brackets:
   (a) $2(a + 3)$ (b) $3(2u - 5)$ (c) $x(3x + 2)$ (d) $2b(2b - 3)$
5) Expand and simplify:
   (a) $(y + 2)(y + 1)$ (b) $(w - 3)^2$ (c) $(2p + 1)(3p - 1)$ (d) $(q + 1)(q - 1)$
6) Factorise:
   (a) $2y + 4$ (b) $4xy - 6x$ (c) $3x^2 + 9x$ (d) $4a^2 - 8a$ (e) $3u^2 - 7u$

Now that you've had some good practice of these basic algebra techniques, it's time to see how you fare with some exam-style questions.

Worked Exam Questions

Questions covering this topic can occur on both calculator and non-calculator papers — but the numbers are usually so easy that you won't need your calculator anyway.

1 Peter the plumber charges £10 to come out and do some work, plus £15 for every hour he works.

(a) How much money would he get if he worked for 6 hours on a single visit?

He charges 6 x 15 for the hours worked, plus his £10 for coming out.

So he would get (6 x 15) + 10 = £100

(1 mark)

(b) Write an expression to show how much he earns for working for h hours on a single visit.

He earns 15 x h for the hours he works, plus the £10 call out charge,

so he charges 15h + 10.

(1 mark)

2 Expand and simplify

(a) $3(2w + 4)$

$3(2w + 4) = (3 \times 2w) + (3 \times 4) = 6w + 12$

(1 mark)

(b) $(p + 2)(3p + 1)$

$(p + 2)(3p + 1) = (p \times 3p) + (p \times 1) + (2 \times 3p) + (2 \times 1)$

$= 3p^2 + p + 6p + 2 \quad = 3p^2 + 7p + 2$

(2 marks)

Exam Questions

Exam Questions

Calculator Not Allowed

3 Freda has 6 bags of chocolate coins and 5 extra chocolate coins.
The number of coins in each bag is the same.
Call the number of coins in each bag "N". Which two expressions below correctly represent the number of coins that Freda has?

5N + 6   **5 × 6 × N**   **6 + 5N**   **6N + 5**   **6 + 5 + N**   **5 + 6N**

(2 marks)

4 Alice, Bill and Clive all collect comics.
Bill has five times as many comics as Alice and Clive has 4 more comics than Alice.
Let the number of comics that Alice has be **y**. Write expressions involving y to show the number of comics that Bill and Clive have.

(2 marks)

5 Simplify:

(a) $2x + 3y + 4x - y + 7$

(1 mark)

(b) $x + 2 + x + 2$

(1 mark)

6 (a) Expand the brackets: $(u - v)(u + v)$

(2 marks)

(b) Expand and simplify: $-2x(-3x + y - 2) - x^2$

(2 marks)

7 Show that $(a + 2)^2$ is not the same as $a^2 + 4$

(2 marks)

8 Several possible factorisations of $36b + 12$ are shown below.

12(3b + 1)   **6(6b + 2)**   **2(18b + 6)**   **36(b + 1)**   **4(9b + 3)**

(a) One of the expressions is incorrect. Which is it?

(1 mark)

(b) Which expression is completely factorised?

(1 mark)

Number Patterns

This is an easy topic, but make sure you know all six types of sequence, not just the first few. The main secret is to write the differences in the gaps between each pair of numbers. That way you can usually see what's happening whichever type it is.

1 "Common Difference" Type — Dead Easy

E.g. 4 7 10 13 16 ... 532 527 522 517 512 ...

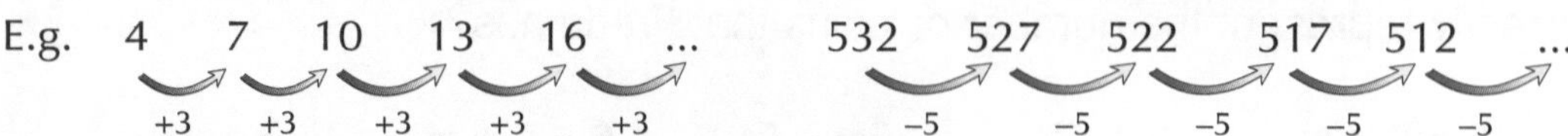

+3 +3 +3 +3 +3 –5 –5 –5 –5 –5

2 "Increasing Difference" Type

Here the differences increase by the same amount each time:

E.g. 3 5 8 12 17 23 ...

+2 +3 +4 +5 +6 +7

3 "Decreasing Difference" Type

Here the differences decrease by the same amount each time:

E.g. 76 66 57 49 42 36 ...

-10 -9 -8 -7 -6 -5

4 "Multiplying Factor" Type

This type has a common MULTIPLIER linking each pair of numbers:

E.g. 3 6 12 24 48 ...

× 2 × 2 × 2 × 2 × 2

5 "Dividing Factor" Type

This type has a common DIVIDER linking each pair of numbers:

E.g. 625 125 25 5 ...

÷ 5 ÷ 5 ÷ 5 ÷ 5

6 "Adding Previous Terms" Type

Add the first two terms to get the 3rd, then add the 2nd and 3rd to get the 4th, etc.

E.g. 1 1 2 3 5 8 13 21 ....

1 + 1 1 + 2 2 + 3 3 + 5 5 + 8 8 + 13 13 + 21

This example is a special sequence called the Fibonacci sequence.

Number patterns should be easy marks in the exam

Learn the six patterns on this page, and look back at the special sequences on pages 4 and 5. Spotting the pattern and finding the next term (which is what questions usually ask for) is easy.

Finding the nth Term

"The nth term" is a formula with "n" in it which gives you every term in a sequence when you put different values for n in.

There are two different types of sequence (for "n^{th} term" questions) which have to be done in different ways:

Common Difference Type

For any sequence such as 3, 7, 11, 15, where there's a common difference
(differences: 4, 4, 4)

you can always find "the nth term" using this formula:

$$n^{th} \text{ term} = dn + (a-d)$$

Don't forget:

1) "a" is simply the value of the first term in the sequence.
2) "d" is simply the value of the common difference between the terms.
3) To get the nth term, you just find the values of "a" and "d" from the sequence and stick them in the formula.
4) You don't replace n though — that wants to stay as n.

Of course you have to learn the formula, but life is like that...

Example *"Find the nth term of this sequence: 5, 7, 9, 11, ..."*

ANSWER:

1) The formula is $dn + (a - d)$
2) The first term is 5, so $a = 5$
3) The common difference is 2 so $d = 2$

Putting these in the formula gives:

n^{th} term $= 2n + (5 - 2)$

so n^{th} term $= 2n + 3$

Finding the nth Term

Changing Difference Type

$$n^{th} \text{ term} = a + (n-1)d + \tfrac{1}{2}(n-1)(n-2)C$$

If the number sequence is one where the difference between the terms is increasing or decreasing then it gets a whole lot more complicated (as you'll have spotted from the above formula — which you'll have to learn)!

This time there are three letters you have to fill in:

"a" is the first term,

"d" is the first difference (between the first two numbers),

"C" is the change between one difference and the next.

Example *"Find the nth term of this sequence: 2, 4, 7, 11, ..."*

(differences: 2, 3, 4)

ANSWER:

1) The formula is "$a + (n-1)d + \tfrac{1}{2}(n-1)(n-2)C$"

2) The first term is 2, so $a = 2$

3) The first difference is 2 so $d = 2$

4) The differences increase by 1 each time so $C = +1$

Putting these in the formula gives:

"$2 + (n-1)2 + \tfrac{1}{2}(n-1)(n-2)\times 1$"

Which becomes:

$2 + 2n - 2 + \tfrac{1}{2}n^2 - 1\tfrac{1}{2}n + 1$

Which simplifies to:

$\tfrac{1}{2}n^2 + \tfrac{1}{2}n + 1$

so the nth term $= \tfrac{1}{2}n^2 + \tfrac{1}{2}n + 1$

n^{th} term formula — you stick in values for n to find different terms

These last two pages aren't too bad — you just need to do some learning. Make sure you've got both formulae in your head, and that you know how and when to use them.

Negative Numbers

Dealing with Minus Signs

Everyone knows rule 1, but sometimes rule 2 applies instead, so make sure you know both rules and when to use them.

RULE 1

+	+	makes	+
+	–	makes	–
–	+	makes	–
–	–	makes	+

Only use Rule 1 when...

1) Multiplying or dividing

E.g. $-1 \times 6 = \underline{-6}$ $\quad -6 \div -3 = \underline{+2}$ $\quad -2y \times -2 = \underline{+4y}$

Careful when you're multiplying a negative number by itself. "-2^2" is a bit ambiguous — you should really write it as "$-(2^2)$" (= $\underline{-4}$). Otherwise someone could think you meant "$(-2)^2$" (= $\underline{+4}$).

2) Two signs appear next to each other

E.g. $8 - -7 = 8 + 7 = \underline{15}$ $\qquad 3 + -4 - -6 = 3 - 4 + 6 = \underline{5}$

RULE 2

USE THE NUMBER LINE

EXAMPLE: *"Simplify 7x – 11x – 2x + 4x"*

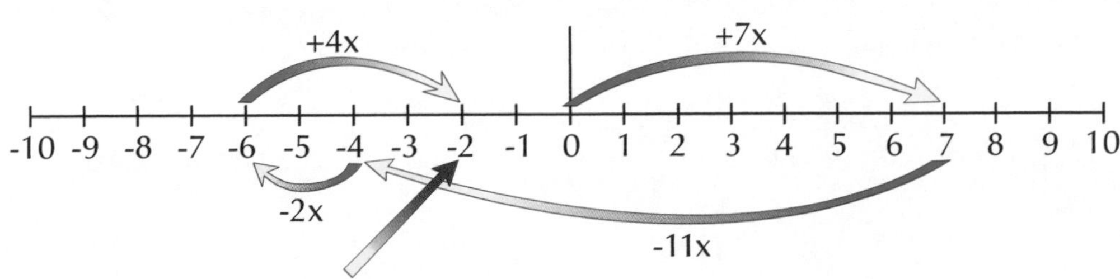

So $7x - 11x - 2x + 4x = \underline{-2x}$

Use Rule 2 when Adding or Subtracting

Letters

Multiplying and *Dividing* Letters

This is the super-slick notation they like to use in algebra which just ends up making life difficult for folks like you. You've got to remember these five rules:

1) **"abc" means "$a \times b \times c$"**

The ×'s are often left out to make it clearer.

2) **"pq^2" means "$p \times q \times q$"**

Note that only the q is squared, not the p as well.

3) **"$(pq)^2$" means "$p \times p \times q \times q$"**

The brackets mean that both letters are squared.

4) **"$p(q-r)^3$" means "$p \times (q-r) \times (q-r) \times (q-r)$"**

Only the brackets get cubed.

5) **"$p \div q$" means "$\frac{p}{q}$"**

You might hear "p divided by q" or "p over q" — but they mean the same thing.

When letters are together it means they're multiplied

These two pages on negative numbers and letters are both hugely important algebra basics. They crop up everywhere in algebra, so try to get your head round it all now.

Warm-up and Worked Exam Questions

Stuff like "find the nth term" will sound like complete gibberish if you haven't worked through this section carefully. So try these warm-up questions and check they make sense to you.

Warm-up Questions

1) Find the next two terms in each of the following sequences. In each case say how you found the next terms.
   (a) 2, 5, 8, ... , ... (b) 10, 11, 14, 19, ... , ... (c) 4, 12, 36, ... , ...
   (d) 128, 32, 8, ... , ... (e) 0, 2, 2, 4, 6, 10, ... , ...
2) Find the nth term of the following sequences: (a) 8, 6, 4, ... (b) 3, 6, 11, 18, ...
3) Work out:
   (a) 3×-2 (b) -3×-2 (c) $3 + -4$ (d) $3 - -4$
   (e) $(-3)^2$ (f) -3^2 (g) $(2 \times -3) + (4 \times -2)$ (h) $(2 \times -3) - (4 \times -2)$
4) Which of the following are correct?
   $(2p)^2 = 4p^2$ $(2p)^2 = 2^2 \times p^2$ $(2p)^2 = 4 + p^2$
   $(2p)^2 = 2p \times 2p$ $(2p)^2 = 2 \times 2p$ $(2p)^2 = 2 \times p^2$
5) Work out:
   (a) $(xy)^2$ (b) $(2x)^3$

It's easy just to scan these worked examples with your brain on auto-pilot. In fact, it can be hard not to. But make the effort to really concentrate on what's going on — it'll be worth it.

Worked Exam Questions

1 (a) Find the next term in this sequence: 1, 3, 8, 16 ...

This is an increasing difference type of sequence.

Look at the differences between each number in the sequence: +2 +5 +8

The difference increases by 3 each time, so the next difference must be 8 + 3 = 11. So the next term is 16 + 11 = 27.

(2 marks)

(b) Find the 8th term. *Use the formula from page 50.*

$a + (n - 1)d + ½(n - 1)(n - 2)C$. For the 8th term, n = 8.

a is the 1st term = 1. d is the 1st difference = 2.

C is the change between one difference and the next = 3.

Putting these in the formula gives: $1 + (8 - 1)2 + ½(8 - 1)(8 - 2)3$.

$= 1 + 14 + (½ \times 7 \times 6 \times 3) = 78$.

(3 marks)

2 Simplify: $3k - (-2k)$

$3k - -2k = 3k + 2k$ *Just remember, two minuses make a plus.*

$= 5k$

(1 mark)

Exam Questions

Exam Questions

Calculator Allowed

3 (a) Two whole numbers multiply to give -20 and add to give 1.
What are the numbers?

(2 marks)

(b) Two whole numbers multiply to give -12.
What is the largest number they can add up to?

(2 marks)

4 The first three terms in a sequence are **2**, **6** and **18**.

(a) What is the next term in this sequence?

(1 mark)

(b) What is the fifth term?

(1 mark)

Calculator Not Allowed

5 Find the missing terms in these sequences:

(a) 6, ... , 0, ... , -6, ...

(2 marks)

(b) 27, ... , ... , 1, 1/3, ...

(2 marks)

(c) 5, 10, 15, 25, ... , 65 , ...

(2 marks)

6 The nth term of a sequence is $n^2 + 1$.
The first term is 2. What are the next two terms?

(2 marks)

7 What does $a^2(b - c)^3$ mean? Choose from the options below.

a + (b – c) + (b – c)

a × a × (b – c) × (b – c) × (b – c)

a × (b – c) + a × (b – c) + a × (b – c)

a × (b – c) × a × (b – c) × a × (b – c)

(1 mark)

Substituting Values into Formulae

*This Topic is a lot **Easier** than **You Think***

Generally speaking, algebra is a pretty grim subject, but you should realise that some bits of it are very easy. This is definitely the easiest bit of all, so whatever you do, don't lose out on these easy exam marks.

Example

"The formula shown below is used to convert temperatures in degrees Fahrenheit (F) to degrees Celsius (C). Use the formula to find 80 degrees Fahrenheit in Celsius."

$$C = \frac{5}{9}(F - 32)$$

Method

If you don't follow this STRICT METHOD you'll just keep getting them wrong — it's as simple as that.

1) Write out the formula.

e.g. $C = \frac{5}{9}(F - 32)$

2) Write it again, directly underneath, but substituting numbers for letters on the RHS (Right Hand Side).

$$C = \frac{5}{9}(80 - 32)$$

3) Work it out in stages. Use BODMAS to work things out in the right order. Write down values for each bit as you go along.

(See next page)

$$C = \frac{5}{9}(48)$$

$$C = 5 \div 9 \times 48$$

$$C = 26.7^{\circ} \text{ (3 s.f.)}$$

You'll make fewer mistakes if you do it step by step, as shown. If you do it in one go, use the brackets buttons on your calculator to help and be extra careful about checking your answer.

Substituting Values into Formulae

BODMAS

Brackets, Other, Division, Multiplication, Addition, Subtraction

BODMAS tells you the ORDER in which these operations should be done:

Work out brackets first, then other things like squaring, then multiply or divide groups of numbers before adding or subtracting them.

This set of rules works really well for simple cases, so remember the word: BODMAS. (See page 38.)

Example *"A mysterious quantity, Q, is given by the formula*

$$Q = (R - 5)^2 + \frac{7T}{W}$$

Find the value of Q when R = 8, T = 3 and W = -7"

ANSWER:

1) Write down the formula: $Q = (R - 5)^2 + 7T/W$

2) Put the numbers in: $Q = (8 - 5)^2 + 7\times3/-7$

3) Then work it out in stages: $= (3)^2 + 7\times3/-7$

$= 9 + 21/-7$

$= 9 + -3$

$= 9 - 3 = \underline{6}$

Note BODMAS in operation:

Brackets worked out first, then squared. Multiplications and divisions done before finally adding and subtracting.

BODMAS tells you why 3 × 2 + 1 and 3 × (2 + 1) aren't the same

BODMAS might seem like a stupid word (fair comment) and a completely pointless invention. But it's not, it's actually immensely important. If you don't get it sussed now, you'll go on making the most basic of mistakes and needlessly losing marks in all the algebra you do...

Solving Equations the Easy Way

The "proper" way to solve equations is shown on page 61. In practice the "proper way" can be pretty difficult, so there's a lot to be said for the much easier methods shown on the next two pages.

The drawback with these is that you can't always use them on very complicated equations.

In most exam questions though, they do just fine.

1 The **Common Sense** Approach

The trick here is to realise that the unknown quantity "x" is after all just a number and the "equation" is just a cryptic clue to help you find it.

Example *"Solve the equation $2x + 3 = 27$"*

(i.e. find what number x is)

ANSWER:

This is what you should say to yourself:

"Something + 3 = 27"

Hmm, so that "something" must be 24.

So that means $2x = 24$ ...

... which means "2 times something = 24".

So it must be $24 \div 2$, which is 12.

So the answer is $x = 12$.

In other words don't think of it as algebra, but as "find the mystery number".

Solving Equations the Easy Way

2 The *Trial and Error* Method

This is a perfectly good method, and although it won't work every time it usually does, especially if the answer is a whole number.

The big secret of trial and error methods is to find two opposite cases and keep taking values in between them.

In other words, find a number that makes the RHS bigger, and then one that makes the LHS bigger, and then try values in between them. (See next page.)

Example *"Solve this equation: $4x + 2 = 20 - 5x$"* (i.e. find the number x)

ANSWER:

Try x = 1: $4 + 2 = 20 - 5$,

$6 = 15$ — no good, RHS too big

Try x = 3: $12 + 2 = 20 - 15$,

$14 = 5$ — no good, now LHS too big

So try in between...

Try x = 2: $8 + 2 = 20 - 10$,

$10 = 10$ — YES, so $x = 2$.

Remember — these methods won't work every time

These two methods work best when the answer is a whole number. If the answer is 4.53645, it could take you a very long time to get there. But the good news is you can usually tell from the question if the answer's going to be a whole number.

Trial and Improvement

In principle, this is an easy way to find approximate answers to quite complicated equations, especially "cubics" (ones with x^3 in). BUT... you have to make an effort to learn the finer details of this method, otherwise you'll never get the hang of it.

Method

1) Substitute TWO initial values into the equation that give opposite cases. Opposite cases means one result too big, one too small, or one +ve, one –ve, for example. These values are usually suggested in the question — if not, you'll have to keep trying different values until you find two that give opposite results.
2) Now choose your next value in between the previous two and substitute it into the equation. Continue this process, always choosing a new value between the two closest opposite cases (and preferably nearer to the one closest to the answer you want).
3) After only 3 or 4 steps you should have 2 numbers which are to the right degree of accuracy but differ by 1 in the last digit. E.g. if you had to get your answer to 2 d.p. then you'd eventually end up with say 5.43 and 5.44, with these giving opposite results.
4) At this point you might be able to tell which is the answer — it'll be the one that gives the closest result — but it's best to check using the exact middle value. So for 5.43 and 5.44, you'd try 5.435 to see if the real answer was between 5.43 and 5.435 or between 5.435 and 5.44 (see below).

Example

"The equation $x^3 + x = 16$ has a solution between 2 and 2.5. Find this solution to 1 d.p."

Try $x = 2$: $2^3 + 2 = 10$ (Too small)
Try $x = 2.5$: $2.5^3 + 2.5 = 18.125$ (Too big)

16 is closer to 18.125 than it is to 10 so we'll choose our next value for x closer to 2.5 than 2.

You can work out that 2 is too small and 2.5 is too big from the question, without substituting ... so you could try an in-between value straight off. BUT it's easy to get muddled — if in doubt, use the method shown.

Try $x = 2.3$: $2.3^3 + 2.3 = 14.467$ (Too small)

This means the solution is between 2.3 and 2.5, so try 2.4 next.

Try $x = 2.4$: $2.4^3 + 2.4 = 16.224$ (Too big)

So the solution must be between 2.3 and 2.4. Since we're only asked for the solution to 1 d.p., and since 2.4 gives the result closest to 16, the answer must be 2.4.
To check — which is always a good idea — we can try the exact middle value:

Try $x = 2.35$: $2.35^3 + 2.35 = 15.328$ (Too small)

This tells us with certainty that the solution must be between 2.35 (too small) and 2.4 (too big). So to 1 d.p. it must round up to 2.4.

If at first you don't succeed... try a little higher... or lower...

This method's basically the same as the one on the previous page — it just gets a bit more complicated here. In questions like this, you know you can't find x exactly, so you've just got to get as close to it as the question asks you to — e.g. 1 decimal place in the example above.

The Balance Method for Equations

Or, "How to peel off the wrapping from your x"...

*You Must Take the " = " Sign **Seriously***

When you see an "=" sign you must realise what it actually means:

What's on one side is exactly equal to what's on the other — no matter how different they may look.

That means you're allowed to do anything you like to one side — so long as you do exactly the same thing to the other. That's really important, so don't forget it.

***Anything** Divided by Itself = 1*

You ought to know what's really going on when, for example, you change an equation from $Ax = B$ to $x = \frac{B}{A}$. The big trick here is to remember that anything divided by itself = 1.

EXAMPLE: *"Solve the equation 5x = 18."*

ANSWER: First you should divide by 5 on both sides like this: $\frac{5x}{5} = \frac{18}{5}$

(This is what you would always do: divide both sides by what the x had been multiplied by — in this case, 5.)

The really important bit to get into your head is this: $\frac{5x}{5} = \left(\frac{5}{5}\right)x = 1x = x$

So that means we end up with $x = \frac{18}{5} = 3.6$

***Peeling off** the + and – terms*

Compare these "before" and "after" shots and you'll see the reason why the rule "change the sign when crossing from one side of the = to the other" actually works.

Before: $2x - y = 7$

$2x \underbrace{- y + y}_{\text{zero}} = 7 + y$

After: $2x = 7 + y$

Before: $2x + y = 7$

$2x \underbrace{+ y - y}_{\text{zero}} = 7 - y$

After: $2x = 7 - y$

The big mystery of crossing the equals sign finally revealed...

If you've understood this page, you can see why moving across the equals sign means numbers move from the top of a fraction to the bottom, or change sign from + to –.

Solving Equations

Solving equations means finding the value of x from something like: $6x + 7 = 1 - 4x$.
Now, not a lot of people know this, but exactly the same method applies to solving equations and to rearranging formulae, as illustrated on the next page.

1) EXACTLY THE SAME METHOD APPLIES TO BOTH FORMULAE AND EQUATIONS.
2) THE SAME SEQUENCE OF STEPS APPLIES EVERY TIME.

To illustrate the sequence of steps we'll use this equation: $\sqrt{3-\frac{2x+2}{x+4}} = 2$

*The **Six Steps** Applied to **Equations**:*

1) Get rid of any square root signs by squaring both sides:

$$3-\frac{2x+2}{x+4} = 4$$

2) Get everything off the bottom by cross-multiplying up to EVERY OTHER TERM:

$$3-\frac{2x+2}{x+4} = 4 \quad \Rightarrow \quad 3(x+4)-(2x+2) = 4(x+4)$$

3) Multiply out any brackets:

$$3x + 12 - 2x - 2 = 4x + 16$$

4) Collect all subject terms (those with an x in) on one side of the "=" and all non-subject terms on the other side, remembering to reverse the +/– sign of any term that crosses the "=" :

+3x moves across the "=" and becomes -3x
-2x moves across the "=" and becomes +2x
+16 moves across the "=" and becomes -16

$$12 - 2 - 16 = 4x - 3x + 2x$$

5) Combine like terms on each side of the equation, and reduce it to the form "Ax = B", where A and B are just numbers (or bunches of letters in the case of formulae):

$3x = -6$
("Ax = B": A = 3, B = -6, x is the subject.)

6) Finally slide the A underneath the B to give "$x = \frac{B}{A}$", divide, and that's your answer:

$x = \frac{-6}{3} = -2$ So x = -2

Learn the 6 steps for solving equations — they always work

The example on this page is a nasty one because it's a "worst case scenario". But once you can follow this method through you'll be able to tackle anything they throw at you.

Rearranging Formulae

Rearranging formulae means making one letter the subject,
e.g. getting "y = " from something like $3x + z = 5(y + 4w)$.
Generally speaking "solving equations" is easier, but don't forget:

1) EXACTLY THE SAME METHOD APPLIES TO BOTH FORMULAE AND EQUATIONS.
2) THE SAME SEQUENCE OF STEPS APPLIES EVERY TIME.

We'll illustrate this by making "y" the subject of this formula: $x = \sqrt{b - \dfrac{a}{2y + 1}}$

*The **Six Steps** Applied to **Formulae***

1) Get rid of any square root signs by squaring both sides:

$$x^2 = b - \frac{a}{2y + 1}$$

2) Get everything off the bottom by cross-multiplying up to EVERY OTHER TERM:

$$x^2 = b - \frac{a}{2y + 1} \Rightarrow x^2(2y + 1) = b(2y + 1) - a$$

3) Multiply out any brackets:

$$2yx^2 + x^2 = 2yb + b - a$$

4) Collect all subject terms on one side of the "=" and all non-subject terms on the other side, remembering to reverse the +/– sign of any term that crosses the "=" :

+2yb moves across the "=" and becomes -2yb
$+x^2$ moves across the "=" and becomes $-x^2$

$$2yx^2 - 2yb = -x^2 + b - a$$

5) Combine like terms on each side of the equation, and reduce it to the form "Ax = B", where A and B are just bunches of letters which don't include the subject (y). Note that the LHS has to be factorised.

$$(2x^2 - 2b)y = b - x^2 - a$$

("Ax = B" i.e. $A = (2x^2 - 2b)$, $B = b - x^2 - a$, y is the subject.)

6) Finally slide the A underneath the B to give "$x = \dfrac{B}{A}$", cancel if possible and that's your answer:

$$\text{So } y = \frac{b - x^2 - a}{2x^2 - 2b}$$

Learn the six steps for... deja vu...

You won't usually need to do all 6 steps — usually the equations will be simpler than this. So if there's no square root, you can skip step 1, and so on...

Warm-up and Worked Exam Questions

I like algebra, because you can feel clever without actually doing anything that complicated. Don't worry if you're still finding it all a bit of a mystery — it'll come with practice.

Warm-up Questions

1) Solve the equations: (a) $3x + 4 = 13$ (b) $17 - 2x = 5$ (c) $2(x + 3) = 8$ (d) $4x - 5 = 10$ (e) $5x + 13 = 8$
2) p is the subject of $p = q + 3w$. Rearrange the equation to make (a) q the subject (b) w the subject.
3) The equation $x^2 + 3x - 1 = 0$ has a positive solution. Use trial and improvement to find two numbers between which this solution lies, correct to 1 decimal place.
4) If $a = 3$, $b = 2$, $c = 5$ and $d = -2$, find the values of
   (a) ad (b) d^2 (c) $-(d^2)$ (d) $a + b + c + d$
   (e) $a - b + c - d$ (f) $ab + bc + cd$ (g) $(a + b) \div d$ (h) $a + b \div d$

Now you can go on to these exam questions. What a treat. They're not all that different to the warm-up questions, so if you coped alright with those you should do fine.

Worked Exam Questions

1 Make d the subject of $a = \frac{(2b - d)}{3}$

multiply both sides by 3 $3a = 2b - d$

add d to both sides $d + 3a = 2b$

take 3a from both sides $d = 2b - 3a$

(2 marks)

2 The volume of a cube of side length L is L^3.
What is the volume of a cube of length 2.7 cm?

Volume $= 2.7^3 = 2.7 \times 2.7 \times 2.7 = 19.7\ \text{cm}^3$ (3 s.f.)

(2 marks)

3 The cost, £C, of calling out a technician to repair a computer is $C = 25 + 18h + p$, where h is the number of hours worked, and p is the cost of any parts.

(a) Find the cost when the technician needs £30 of parts and works for 2.5 hours.

$p = 30$, $h = 2.5$, so $C = 25 + (18 \times 2.5) + 30 = 25 + 45 + 30 = £100$

(2 marks)

(b) If the technician didn't need any parts and charged £79, how long did he work for?

$p = 0$ and $C = 79$, so $79 = 25 + 18h$ *take 25 from both sides*

$18h = 79 - 25 = 54$

$h = 54 \div 18 = 3$. So he worked for 3 hours.

(2 marks)

Exam Questions

Exam Questions

Calculator Not Allowed

4 Draw lines to connect pairs of expressions that are **equal** when $u = 4$, $v = 5$, and $w = 2$.

$\mathbf{vw \div u}$	$\mathbf{2u + v - w}$
$\mathbf{u + v + w}$	$\mathbf{2v}$
$\mathbf{uv \div w}$	$\mathbf{v \div w}$

(3 marks)

5 Solve:

(a) $7k - 3 = 11$

(1 mark)

(b) $3t + 5 = t + 12$

(2 marks)

6 s is the subject of the equation $s = 3(t - v)$.
Rearrange it to make t the subject.

(1 mark)

Calculator Allowed

7 Use the equations $\mathbf{2a + 4b = 16}$ and $\mathbf{3b - d = 7}$ to help you answer the following questions.

(a) Find the value of the expressions below. The first one has been done for you.

(i) $6b - 2d$ **= 14** (ii) $a + 2b$

(iii) $2d - 6b$ (iv) $2a + 7b - d$

(3 marks)

(b) Use the equations to write an expression equal to 30.

(2 marks)

8 The formula for the volume, V, of a square-based pyramid with base length l and perpendicular height h is $V = \frac{1}{3} l^2 h$.

(a) A square-based pyramid has base length 3 cm and perpendicular height 7 cm. Find its volume.

(2 marks)

(b) The volume of a square-based pyramid is 48 cm^3 and its height is 9 cm. What is the length of the square base?

(2 marks)

Formula Triangles

You may have already come across these in physics, but whether you have or you haven't, the fact remains that they're extremely potent tools for quite a number of tricky maths problems — so make sure you know how to use them. They're very easy to use and very easy to remember.

If 3 things are related by a formula that looks either

like this: $A = B \times C$ or like this: $B = \frac{A}{C}$

then you can put them into a FORMULA TRIANGLE like this:

1 First **Decide** Where the Letters Go

1) If there are two letters multiplied together in the formula then they must go on the bottom of the formula triangle (and so the other one must go on the top).

   For example the formula "F = ma" fits into a formula triangle like this.

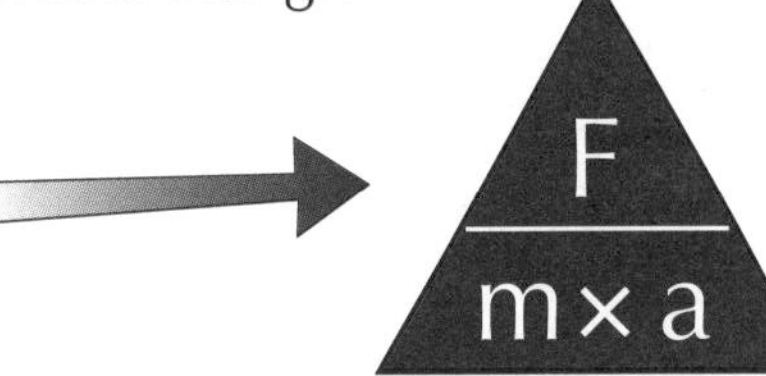

2) If there's one thing divided by another in the formula then the one on top of the division goes on top in the formula triangle (and so the other two must go on the bottom — it doesn't matter which way round).

   For example the formula "SIN θ = Opp / Hyp" fits into a formula triangle like this.
   (See page 138 for more trigonometry formula triangles.)

2 Using the **Formula Triangle**

Once you've got the formula triangle sorted out, the rest is easy:

1) Cover up the thing you want to find and just write down what's left showing.
2) Put in the values for the other two things and just work it out.

EXAMPLE:

"Using " F = ma" , find the value of "a" when F = 15 and m = 50."

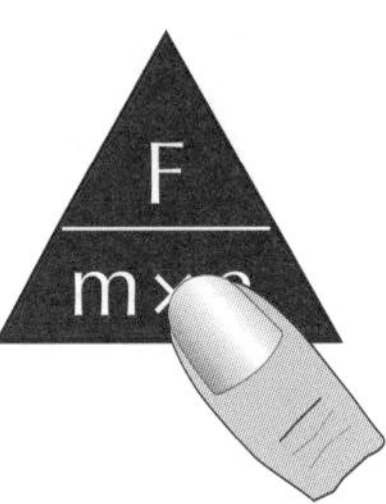

ANSWER:

Using the formula triangle, we want to find "a" so we cover it up, and that leaves "F/m" showing (i.e. F ÷ m). So "a = F/m", and putting the numbers in we get: a = 15 / 50 = 0.3.

Formula triangles are incredibly useful

With this method you don't need to worry about changing the subjects of formulas and horrible things like that. So make sure you understand formula triangles and use them whenever you can.

Density and Speed

Now let's see the formula triangles in action with two formulas you need to know.

Density = Mass ÷ Volume

You might think this is physics, but density is in the maths syllabus, and it's quite likely to come up in your exam. The formula for density is Density = Mass / Volume which you can put it in a formula triangle like this:

Example *"Find the volume of an object which has a mass of 60 g and a density of 2.4 g/cm³."*

ANSWER: To find volume, cover up V in the formula triangle.
This leaves M/D showing, so V = M ÷ D
= 60 ÷ 2.4
= 25 cm³

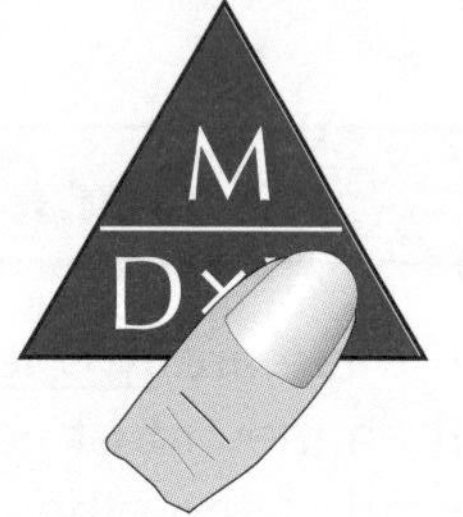

Speed = Distance ÷ Time

This is very common. In fact it probably comes up every single year — and they never give you the formula! Either learn it beforehand or wave goodbye to lots of easy marks.

Life isn't all bad though — there's an easy formula triangle:

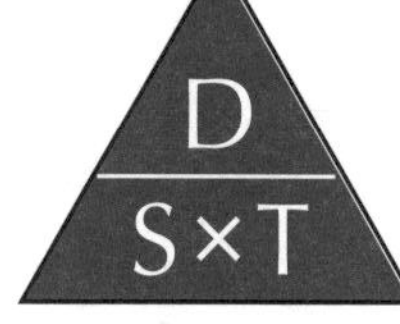

Example *"A car travels 140 miles at 40 miles per hour. How long does it take?"*

ANSWER: We want to find the time, so cover up T in the triangle which leaves D/S,

so T = D / S = distance ÷ speed = 140 ÷ 40 = 3.5 hours

Learn the formula triangle, and you'll find questions on speed, distance and time very easy.

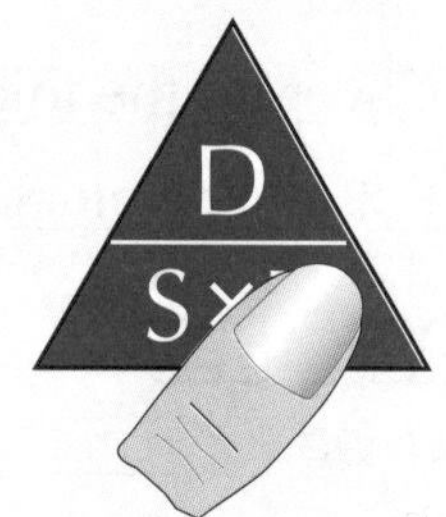

Density and Speed — learn those formulae...

One way or another you must remember the formulae for density and speed.
The best way is to come up with a name or phrase to help you remember the order of letters in the triangle. For density, I use DiMoV (the Russian Agent).
For speed, how about SoDarnTired, which I bet is how you're feeling right now...

Two Hints When Using Formulae

These are just the kind of little details that you really do need to know but somehow never quite get to learn — well learn them now.

1 Units — Getting them Right

By units we mean things like cm, m, m/s, km^2 etc., and as a rule you don't have to worry too much about them. However, when you're using a formula triangle, there's one special thing you need to know. It's simple enough but you must know it:

The UNITS you get OUT of a formula DEPEND ENTIRELY upon the units you put INTO IT

So if you put a distance in cm and a time in seconds into the formula triangle to work out speed, the answer must come out in cm per second (cm/s).

Or, if the time is in hours and the speed in miles per hour (mph) then the distance you'd calculate would come out as miles.

It's pretty simple when you think about it.
Where you really have to watch out is when you get this sort of question:

Example

"A boy walks 600m in 15 minutes. Find his speed in km/h."

If you just do "600 m ÷ 15 minutes" your answer will be a speed, sure, but in metres per minute (m/min) which is no good at all.

Instead you must convert into km and hours first:

600 m = 0.6 km   15 mins = 0.25 hours (mins ÷ 60).

Then you can work it out in the right units:

Speed = Distance ÷ Time
= 0.6 km ÷ 0.25
= 2.4 km/h   which is much more like it.

Two Hints When Using Formulae

2 Converting **Time** to Hours, Minutes and Seconds with °’”

Here's a tricky detail that comes up when you're doing speed, distance and time:

Converting an answer like 1.45 HOURS into HOURS AND MINUTES.

What it definitely isn't is 1 hour and 45 mins — remember, your calculator does not work in hours and minutes unless you tell it to, as shown below.

You'll need to practise with this button, but you'll be glad you did.

1) Entering a time in hours, minutes and seconds:

E.g. to enter 5 hours 34 minutes and 23 seconds,
press 5 °’” 34 °’” 23 °’” = to get 5°34°23 .

2) Converting hours, minutes and seconds to a decimal time:

Enter the number in hours, minutes and seconds as above.

Then just press °’” and it should convert it to a decimal like this 5.573055556 .

So 5 hours 34 minutes and 23 seconds is equal to 5.57 hours (3 s.f.).

(Some older calculators will automatically convert it to decimal when you enter a time in hours, minutes and secs.)

3) Converting a decimal time into hours, minutes, and seconds:

E.g. To convert 2.35 hours into hours, minutes and seconds.
Simply press 2.35 = to enter the decimal, then press SHIFT °’” .

The display should become 2°21°0 ,

which means 2 hours 21 minutes (and 0 seconds).

Learn how to do it on your calculator

It's easy to make mistakes with times if you're not thinking carefully about it. Never ever enter 5 h 25 min as 5.25. That'd be a disaster. 5.25 is $5\frac{1}{4}$, so would actually be 5 h 15 mins.

Warm-up and Worked Exam Questions

Now, as a bit of a change, you're going to do some... warm-up questions!
Try to contain your excitement, or you'll do yourself an injury.

Warm-up Questions

1) Write formula triangles for:
   (a) force = mass × acceleration (F = m × a)
   (b) SIN = opposite ÷ hypotenuse (S = O ÷ H)
   (c) COS = adjacent ÷ hypotenuse (C = A ÷ H)
   (d) TAN = opposite ÷ adjacent (T = O ÷ A)
2) An enlargement is described by a scale factor with the formula:
   new length = scale factor × old length.
   A 5 × 3 cm rectangle is enlarged to give an 8 × w cm rectangle.
   Find the scale factor of the enlargement and the width of the new rectangle.
3) The mass, volume and density of various pieces of metal are recorded in the table on the right. However some of the values are missing. Fill in the gaps to complete the table.

Mass	Volume	Density
10 kg	100 cm^3	
	1 cm^3	0.02 kg/cm^3
500 g		125 g/cm^3
	15 cm^3	1.2 kg/cm^3

4) How many minutes in 1 hour 15 minutes? How many minutes in 1.15 hours?

Time for another worked example, then you're on your own again on the next page.

Worked Exam Question

1 Fred walks 5400 m in 72 minutes.

(a) What is his average speed in km/h? *First convert the values into the units you need.*

5400 m = 5.4 km, 72 minutes = 1.2 hours.

Then use the formula triangle: 

Average speed = distance ÷ time = 5.4 ÷ 1.2 = 4.5 km/h

(2 marks)

(b) How far will he travel in 48 minutes at this speed?

48 minutes = 48 ÷ 60 = 0.8 hours

Distance = speed x time = 4.5 x 0.8 = 3.6 km

(2 marks)

(c) If he kept at the same speed and had travelled 14 km and 400 m by the end of the day, how long had he been walking, in hours and minutes?

14 km 400 m = 14.4 km

Time = distance ÷ speed = 14.4 ÷ 4.5 = 3.2 hours

0.2 hrs = 0.2 x 60 min = 12 min, so time taken = 3 hrs 12 minutes.

(3 marks)

Exam Questions

Exam Questions

Calculator Allowed

2 (a) A car travels 45 miles at 60 mph. How long will it take?

(1 mark)

(b) A plane travels 1800 km in 2 hours 30 minutes.
What is its average speed?

(2 marks)

(c) A train travels for 285 minutes at an average speed of 45 km/h.
How far will it travel?

(2 marks)

3 How long in hours, minutes and seconds will it take to travel 750 m at 1.2 km/h?

(2 marks)

4 (a) A lioness walks 0.8 km in 10 minutes. Find her speed in km/h.

(2 marks)

(b) The lioness spots an antelope and chases it.
She runs 150 m in 15 seconds. What is her speed in km/h now?

(3 marks)

5 (a) A block of butter, 5 cm by 4 cm by 4 cm, has a mass of 300 g.
What is its density?

(2 marks)

(b) Some of the block of butter is used for cooking.
It is now 3 cm by 4 cm by 4 cm. Its density remains the same.
What is mass of butter is left?

(2 marks)

6 Force, mass and acceleration are related by the formula:

force = mass × acceleration

(a) A force acts on an object of mass 7 kg and makes it accelerate at 3 m/s^2. What is the size of the force (in $kg.m/s^2$)?

(1 mark)

(b) The same force acts on another object and makes it accelerate at 5 m/s^2.
What is the mass of this object?

(2 marks)

x- and y-Coordinates

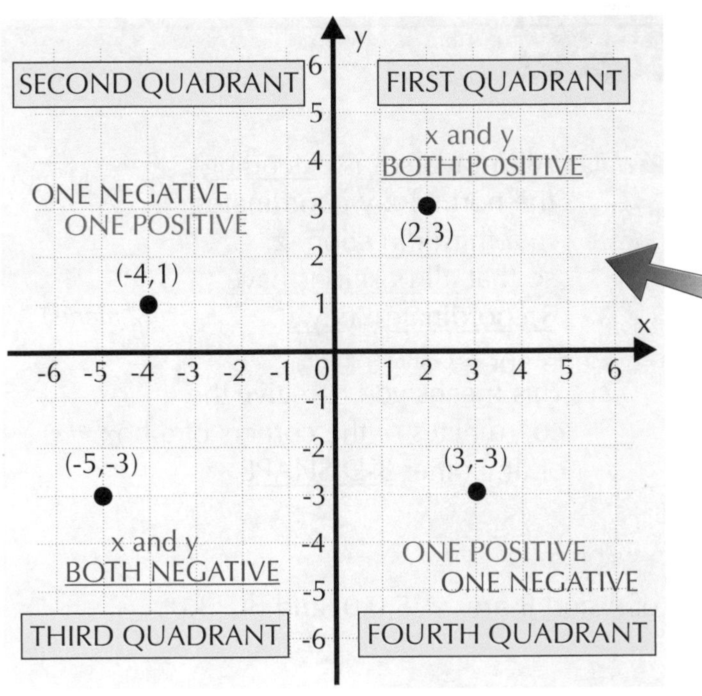

A graph has four regions — called quadrants — where the x- and y- coordinates are either positive or negative.

This is the easiest quadrant by far because here all the coordinates are positive.

You have to be very careful in the other quadrant though, because the x- and y- coordinates could be negative, and that always makes life difficult.

*Getting **x-** and **y-Coordinates** in the **Right Order***

You must always give coordinates in brackets like this: **(x, y)**

E.g. (2, 3), (13, -4), (-3, -5)

And you always have to be really careful to get them the right way round — x first, then y.

Here are three points to help you remember:

1) The two coordinates are always in alphabetical order — x then y.

2) x is always the flat axis going across the page.
In other words "x is a..cross". *Get it — x is a "x". (Hilarious, isn't it.)*

3) Remember it's always in the house (→) and then up the stairs (↑), so it's along first and then up.
x-coordinate first, and then y-coordinate.

x-, y- and z-Coordinates

3-D Coordinates — A Very Easy Topic

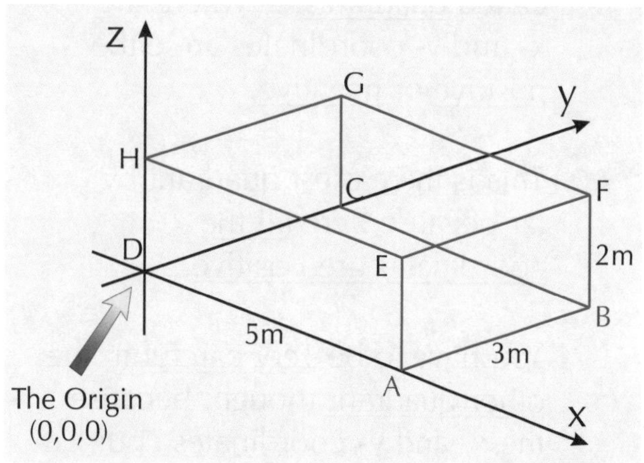

1) All it involves is <u>extending</u> the normal x-y coordinates in a <u>third direction</u>, z, so that <u>all positions have 3 coordinates</u>: (<u>x,y,z</u>).

2) This means you can give the coordinates of the <u>corners of a box</u> or any other <u>3-D SHAPE</u>.

For example, in this drawing the coordinates of A and B are: A(5,0,0) and B(5,3,0).

Example *"The diagram below shows a shape with square base ABCD. The top point E is 7 units vertically above the centre of square ABCD. Find the coordinates of points C, D and E."*

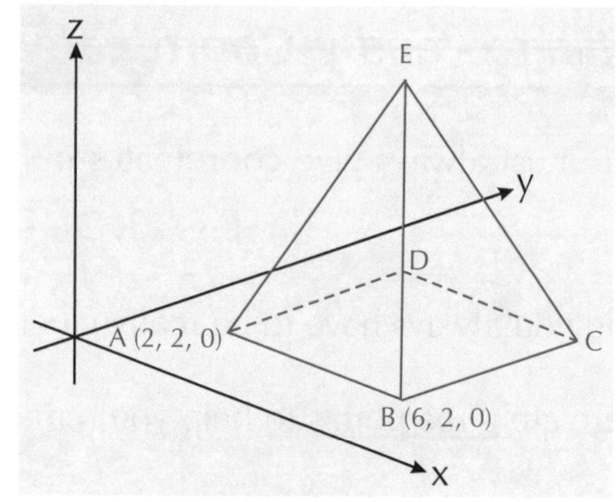

1) <u>First find the length of the square's sides</u>:

   The x-coordinates of A and B are 2 and 6, so they're 4 units apart.
   So square ABCD has <u>sides of length 4</u>.

2) <u>Now it's easy to find D and C</u>:

   C has the same x- and z- coordinates as <u>B</u>, but it's <u>4 units</u> further along the <u>y-axis</u>.

   <u>So C is (6, 6, 0)</u>

   D has the same x- and z- coordinates as <u>A</u>, but it's <u>4 units</u> further along the <u>y-axis</u>.

   <u>So D is (2, 6, 0)</u>

3) <u>To find E, work out the coordinates one by one</u>:

   As E is above the centre point of ABCD...

   ...its <u>x-coordinate</u> is halfway between 2 and 6, i.e. <u>4</u>...

   ...and its <u>y-coordinate</u> is also halfway between 2 and 6, i.e. <u>4</u>.

   The question tells you the vertical height is 7, which means the <u>z-coordinate is 7</u>.

   <u>So E is (4, 4, 7)</u>

Don't be scared by 3-D coordinates...

3-D coordinates aren't nearly as scary as you might think. Questions won't ask you to do much more than identify points on a diagram, like the examples on this page. You just need to be careful to give the coordinates in the <u>right order</u>.

Easy Graphs You Should Know

If you want to make life easy for yourself, then you definitely need to know a few simple graphs straight off without even having to blink. These are they:

1 "x = a" — VERTICAL LINES

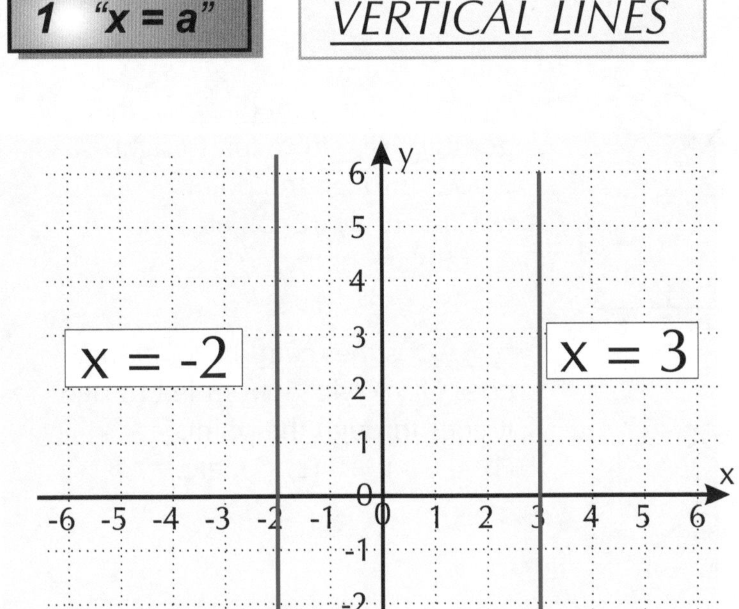

"x = a number" is a line that goes straight up through that number on the x-axis, e.g. x = 3 goes straight up through 3 on the x-axis as shown.

Don't forget: the y-axis is also the line "x = 0"

2 "y = a" — HORIZONTAL LINES

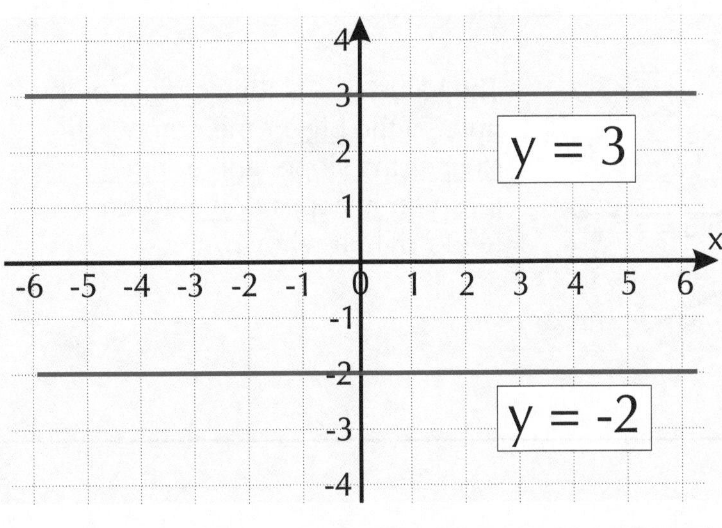

"y = a number" is a line that goes straight across through that number on the y-axis, e.g. y = -2 goes straight across through -2 on the y-axis as shown.

Don't forget: the x-axis is also the line "y = 0"

Easy Graphs You Should Know

3 "y = x" and "y = -x"

THE MAIN DIAGONALS

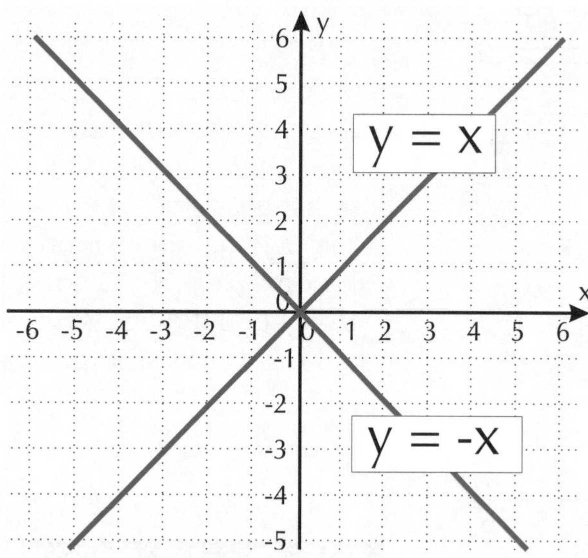

"$y = x$" is the main diagonal that goes UPHILL from left to right. It goes through the points (1, 1), (-1, -1), (2, 2), etc.

"$y = -x$" is the main diagonal that goes DOWNHILL from left to right. It goes through the points (1, -1), (-1, 1), (2, -2), etc.

4 "y = ax" and "y = -ax"

OTHER SLOPING LINES

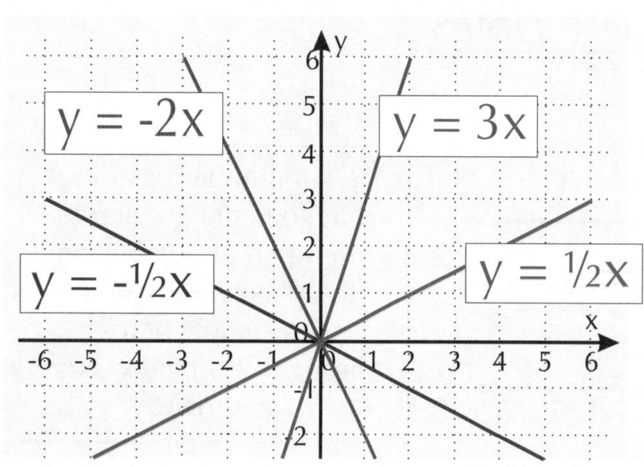

$y = ax$ and $y = -ax$ are the general equations for a sloping line through the origin.

The value of a is the gradient of the line, so the bigger the number the steeper the slope, and a minus sign tells you it slopes downhill from left to right as shown.

Look back at these when you've read about y = mx + c lines

You need to be able to tell what a line will look like from its equation (and vice versa). On page 79, we'll cover the general equation for straight lines ($y = mx + c$). But the ones on this page are a good place to start, so get learning them.

Finding the Gradient of a Line

Working out the gradient of a straight line is a slightly involved business, and there are quite a few things that can go wrong.

Once again though, if you learn and follow the steps below and treat it as a strict method, you'll have a lot more success than if you try and fudge your way through it.

Strict Method for **Finding Gradient**

1) Find two accurate points reasonably far apart

Both in the first quadrant if possible, to keep all the numbers positive and reduce the chance of making a mistake.

2) *Complete the triangle* as shown

3) Find the change in y and the change in x

Make sure you do this using the scales on the y- and x- axes, not by counting cm! So in the example shown, the change in y is not 4 cm but 50 – 10 = 40 units, and the change in x is 8 – 1 = 7 units.

4) Learn this formula, and use it:

$$\text{GRADIENT} = \frac{\text{VERTICAL}}{\text{HORIZONTAL}}$$

Make sure you get it the right way up, too! Remember it's VERy HOt — VERtical over HOrizontal.

5) Finally, is the gradient positive or negative?

If it slopes UPHILL left → right (↗) then it's +ve.
If it slopes DOWNHILL left → right (↘) then it's –ve (so put a minus(–) in front of it).

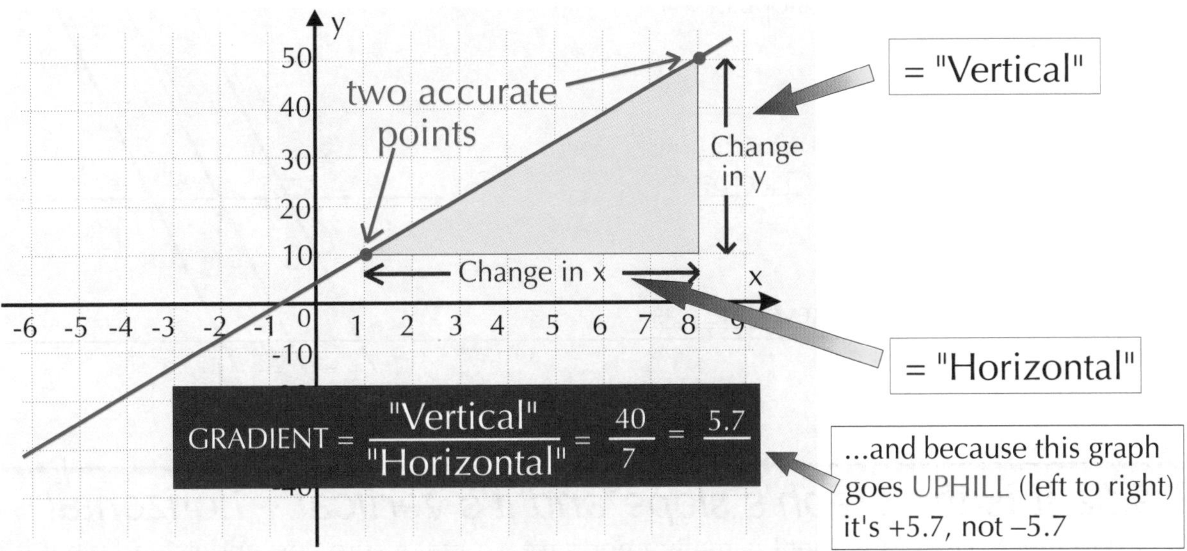

What the Gradient Means

1 In Real Life

No matter what the graph, the meaning of the gradient is always simply:

(y-axis units) PER (x-axis units)

Examples

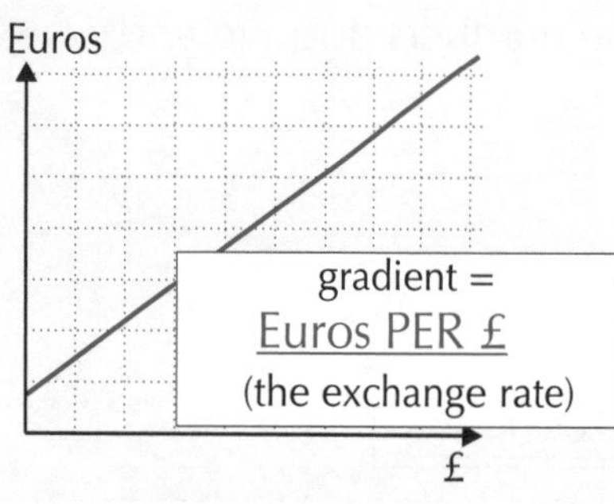

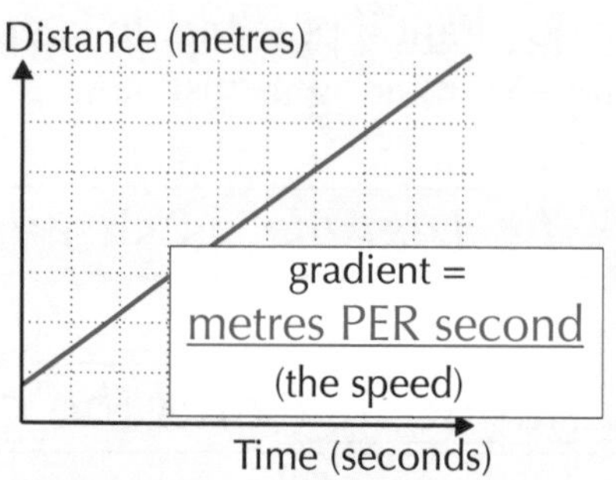

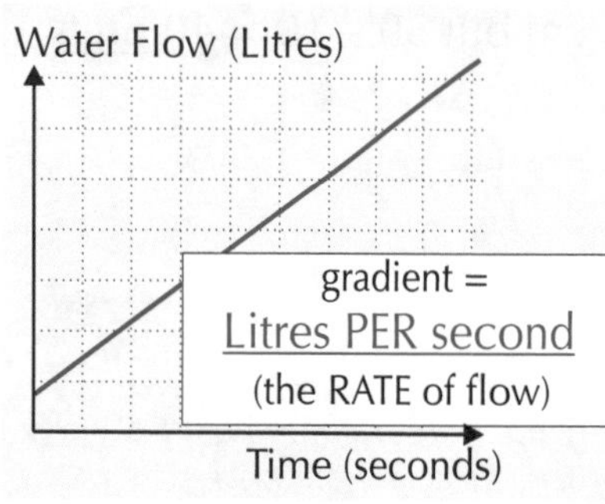

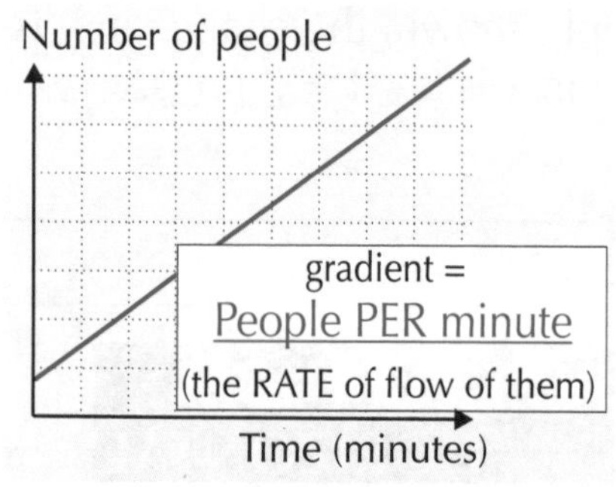

Some gradients have special names like exchange rate or speed, but once you've written down "something PER something" using the y-axis and x-axis units, it's then pretty easy to work out what the gradient represents.

2 In the Equation of the Line

(See page 79)

Here you see the 2x family of slopes.

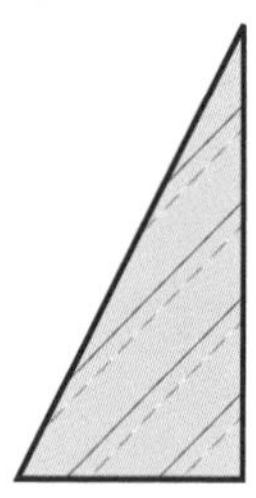

Each section of them goes up 2 for every 1 across.

The slope, or gradient, is whatever the x is multiplied by, in this case 2.

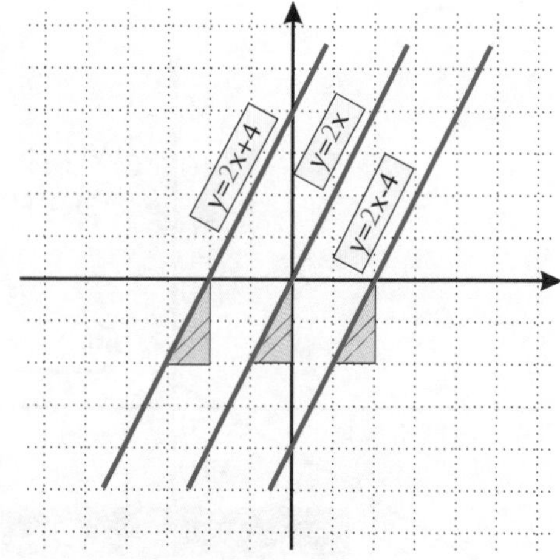

Gradient is the graph's slope and it's vertical ÷ horizontal

Don't skip these pages. Gradient is really important, so make sure you understand what it is, how to measure it and how to use the graph's units to work out what the gradient represents.

Warm-up and Worked Exam Questions

Graphs, gradients and coordinates — far more fun than watching paint dry. Try them and see.

Warm-up Questions

1) The coordinates of three corners of a rectangle are (0, 0), (5, 0) and (0, 10). Find the fourth corner, and write down the gradients of the two diagonals.

2) A square is shown on the right.

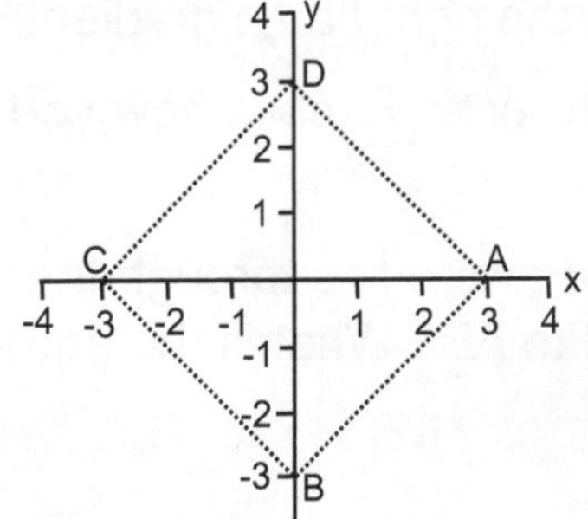

(a) Find the gradients of the sides AB and AD.

(b) Write down the equation of line joining:
(i) B to D (ii) A to C

3) Find the gradient of the lines through the points
(a) (0, 0) and (5, 5) (b) (1, 2) and (4, 5) (c) (5, 5) and (10, 15) (d) (2, 4) and (6, 2)

4) What is given by the gradient of each graph below, and what is the unit of measurement?

(a)

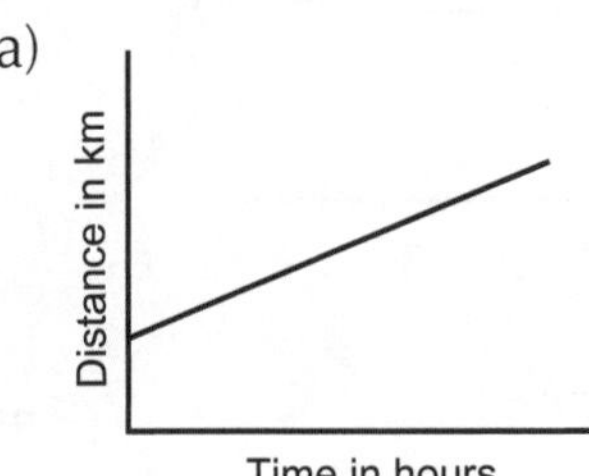

(b)

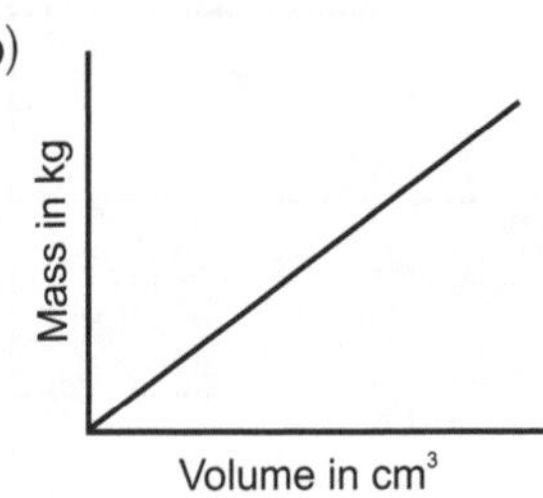

(c)

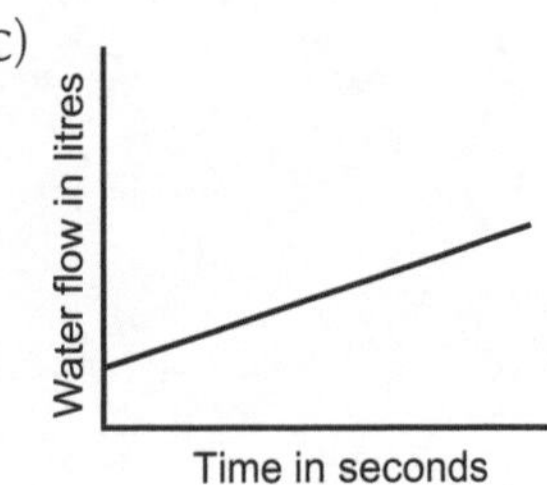

Alright, possibly not **far** more fun...

Worked Exam Question

Calculator Allowed

1 OABC is a parallelogram.

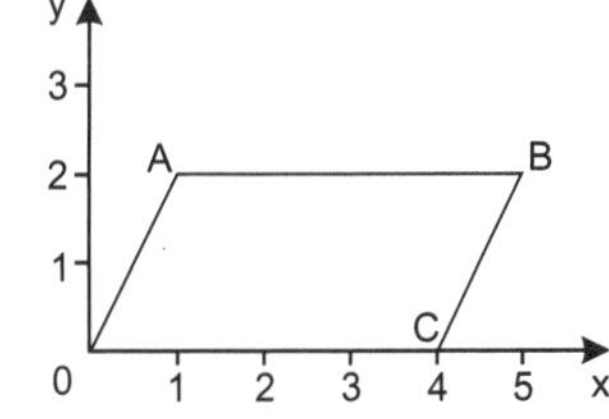

(a) Match each equation with the line it describes.

(2 marks)

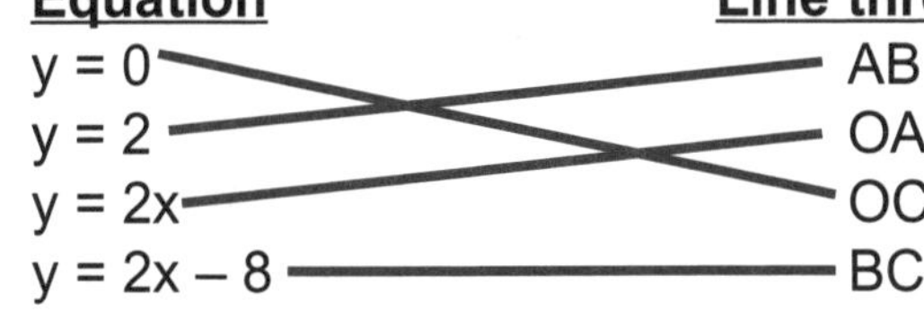

You should identify y = 0, y = 2 and y = 2x as standard lines to learn. Check the final line by substituting the coordinates of B and C into y = 2x – 8. So B is (5, 2): 2 = 2 × 5 – 8 (correct). C is (4, 0): 0 = 2 × 4 – 8 (also correct).

(b) Find the equation of OB.

y = (gradient of OB) × x — *You know that a line through the origin has an equation in the form y = ax, where a is the gradient of the line.*

Gradient of OB is 2 ÷ 5 = 0.4, so equation is y = 0.4x

(1 mark)

(c) Circle the correct equation of the straight line through A and C.

(y = 8/3 – 2/3x) (circled) — *You can make sure you've picked the right one by substituting the coordinates of point C (4, 0) into each equation and checking if it works.* — **y = 2/3 – 8/3x**

(1 mark)

Exam Questions

Exam Questions

Calculator Not Allowed

2 John says the line through A and B in the diagram on the right has a gradient of 2/3.

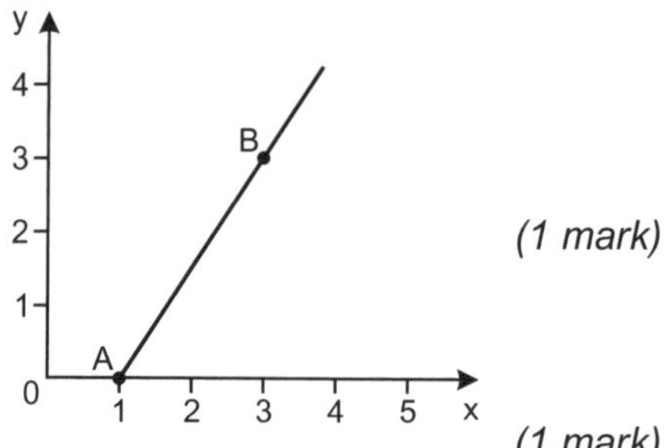

(a) Is he correct? Explain how you know. *(1 mark)*

(b) Lorna draws a line through the origin (0,0) parallel to AB. What is the equation of this line? *(1 mark)*

3 Look at the rectangle in the diagram. Give the equations of the lines joining:

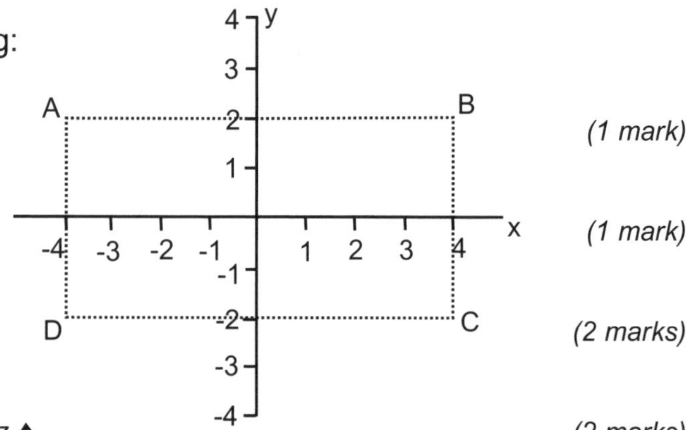

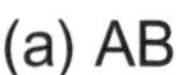
(a) AB *(1 mark)*

(b) BC *(1 mark)*

(c) AC *(2 marks)*

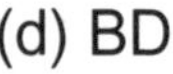
(d) BD *(2 marks)*

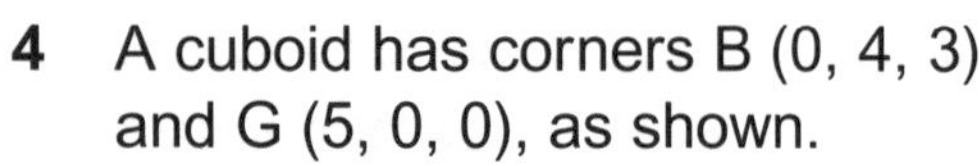
4 A cuboid has corners B (0, 4, 3) and G (5, 0, 0), as shown.

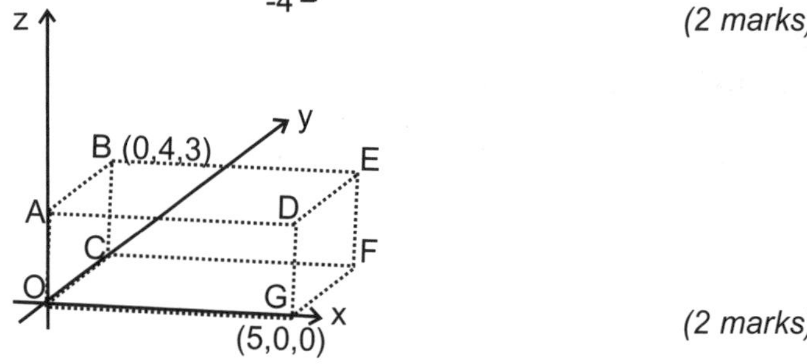

Find the coordinates of

(a) Point A (b) Point E *(2 marks)*

Calculator Allowed

5 Selina is doing a sponsored walk. At 10:00 am she's 2 km from her start point. By 12:30 she's 12 km from her start point. She walks at a steady speed the whole way.

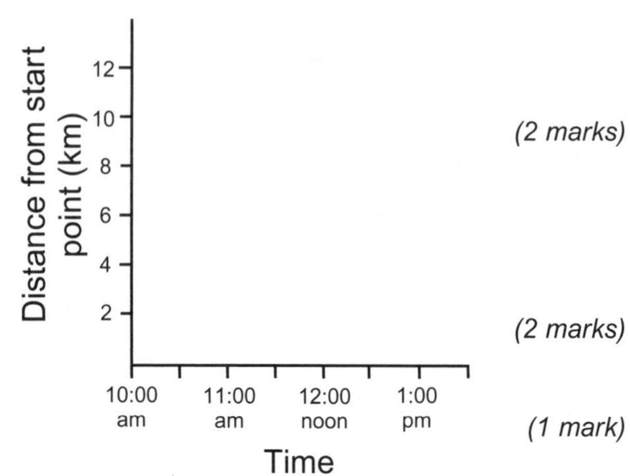

(a) Complete the graph on the right to show this. *(2 marks)*

(b) Work out the gradient of the line. *(2 marks)*

(c) Write down Selina's speed. *(1 mark)*

Four Graphs You Should Recognise

There are four types of graph that you should know the basic shape of just from looking at their equations — it really isn't as difficult as it sounds.

1 **Straight Line** Graphs: "y = mx + c"

— which means y = gradient times x + place where it crosses the y-axis (usually called the y-intercept).

So m = gradient and c = y-intercept.

Straight line equations are easy to spot — they have an x-term, a y-term and usually a number and that's it. There's no x^2, x^3 or 1/x terms, or any other fancy things.

Straight lines		Rearranged into "y = mx +c"	
y = 4 + 2x	→	y = 2x + 4	(m = 2, c = 4)
x – 3y = 0	→	y = 1/3x + 0	(m = 1/3, c = 0)
2y + 2x = 8	→	y = -x + 4	(m = -1, c = 4)

Always make sure your rearranged equations begin with "y" on its own, not "2y" or "0.5y" or whatever.

These are not straight lines:

$x^3 = 2 - y$ $\quad$ $y = x^2 + 2$ $\quad$ $1/y + 2/x = 5$

Examples

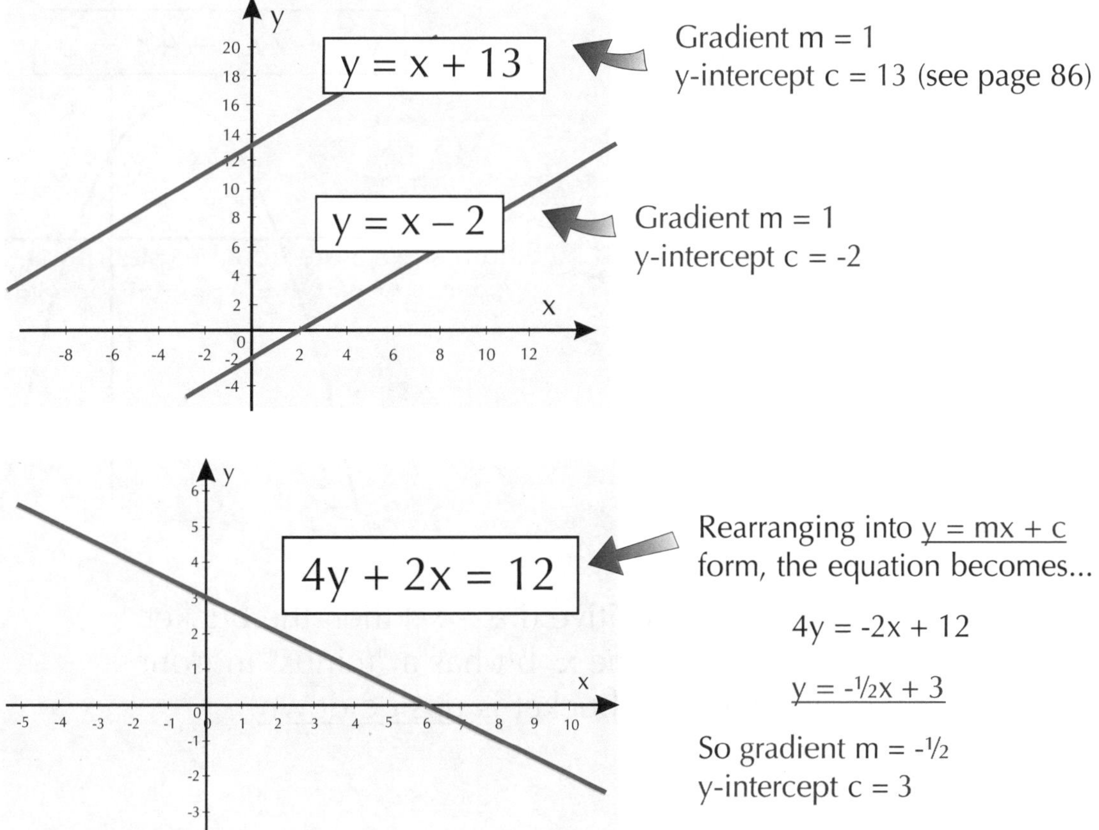

Four Graphs You Should Recognise

2 x^2 Bucket Shapes

y = anything with x^2 in it, but not x^3

All x^2 graphs have the same <u>SYMMETRICAL bucket shape</u>.

Examples

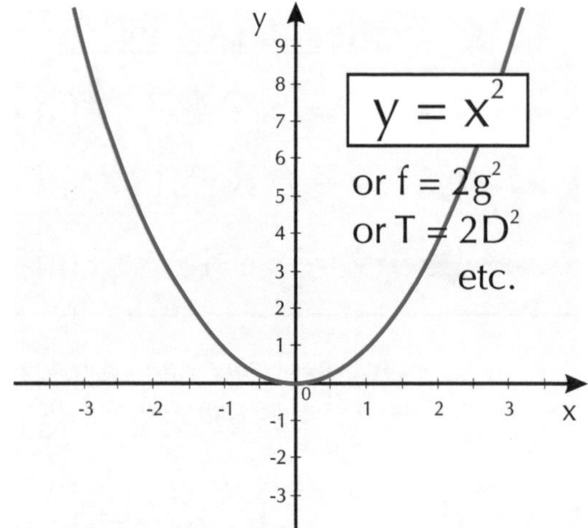

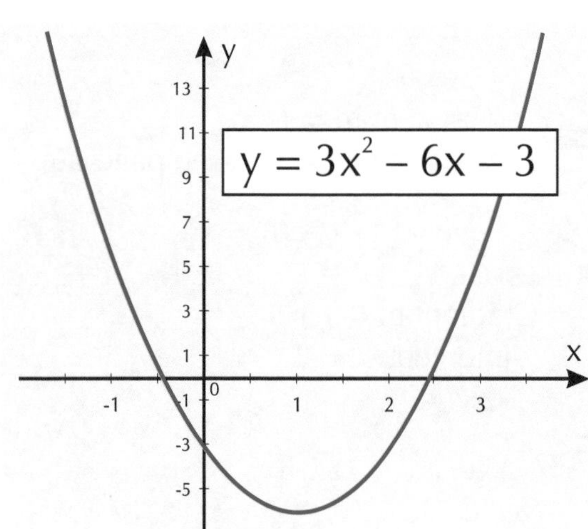

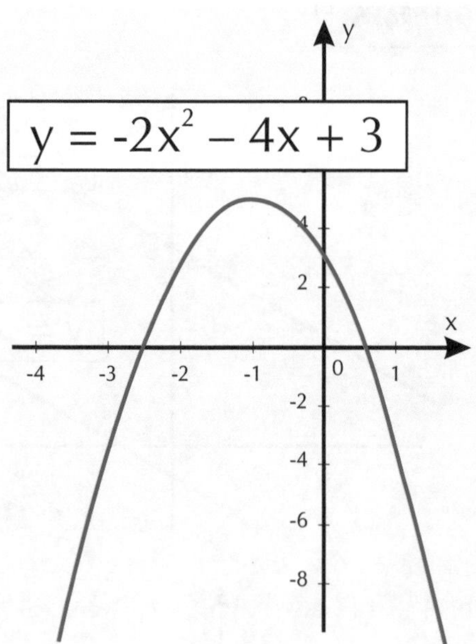

Notice that if the x^2 bit is positive (i.e. $+x^2$) then the bucket is the normal way up, but if the x^2 bit has a "minus" in front of it (i.e. $-x^2$) then the bucket is <u>upside down</u>.

Four Graphs You Should Recognise

3 x^3 Graphs

y = "something with x^3 in it"

All x^3 graphs have the same basic wiggle in the middle, but it can be a flat wiggle or a more pronounced wiggle.

Examples

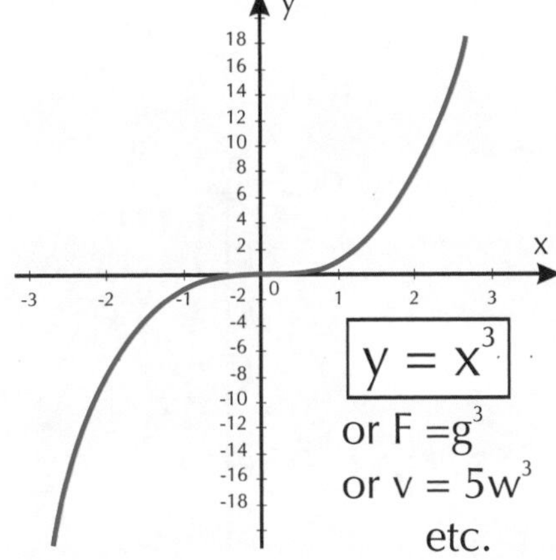

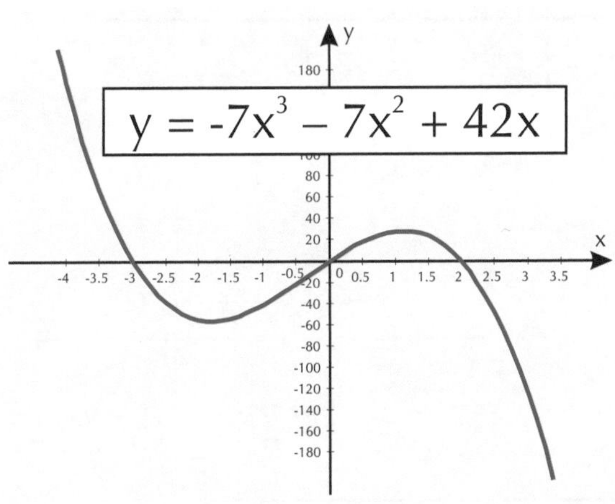

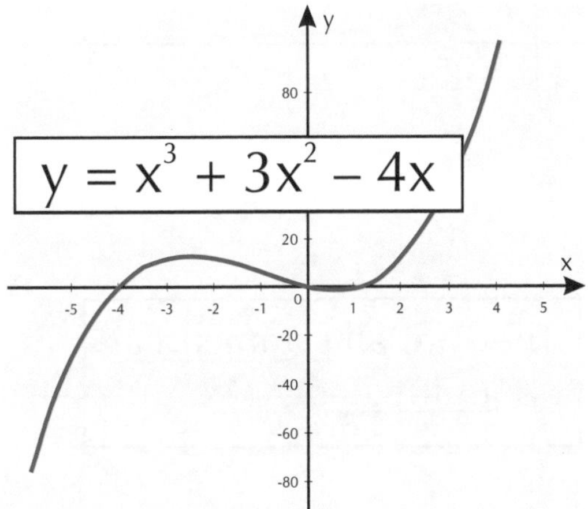

Notice that "$-x^3$ graphs" always come down from top left whereas the $+x^3$ ones go up from bottom left.

Four Graphs You Should Recognise

4 1/x Graphs

$$y = \frac{a}{x}, \text{ where a is some number}$$

These graphs are all EXACTLY the same shape, the only difference being how close they get to the corner.

Examples

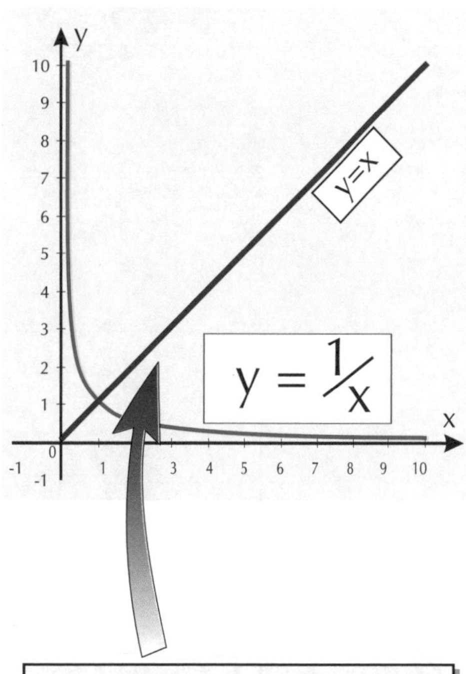

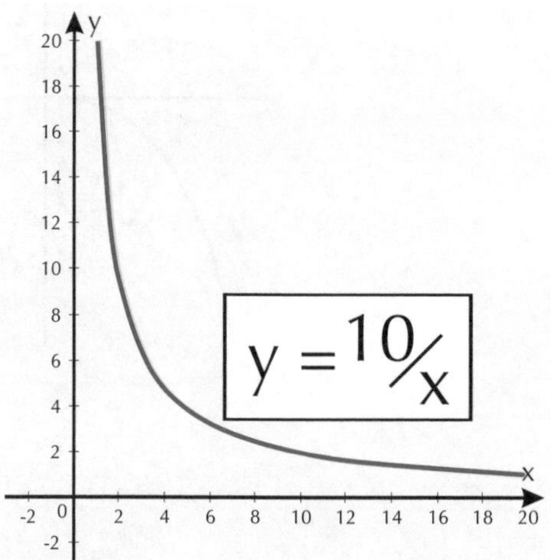

They are all symmetrical about the line y = x.

This is also the graph you get when x and y are in inverse proportion.

"Inverse proportion" means that if y doubles, x halves, and so on.

Four very different graphs — you need to learn all the details...

Learn all the details about the four types of graph, their equations and their shapes. Then turn over and sketch three examples of each of the four types of graph. Remember, if you don't learn it, then it's a waste of time even reading it. This is true for all revision.

Warm-up and Worked Exam Questions

Some people find these easy — they only need to glance at an equation to know what sort of graph it'd give. If you're one of them, you're a lucky swine. If not, don't worry, you'll get there.

Warm-up Questions

1) Below are four different equations:

   A: $y = x^2 + 4$ B: $y = 2x + 4$ C: $y = 3/x + 2$ D: $y = 3x - 7$

   Think about the graphs of these equations. Which of them would be straight lines?

2) Look at the three graphs below. Each has four equations under it.
   In each case, choose which equation will give the graph shown.

(a)

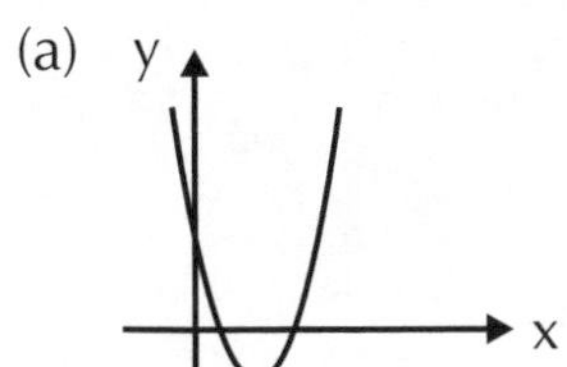

(i) $y = x^2$
(ii) $y = x^3 + x^2 + 1$
(iii) $y = x^2 - 5x + 4$
(iv) $y = -x^2 + 3x - 4$

(b)

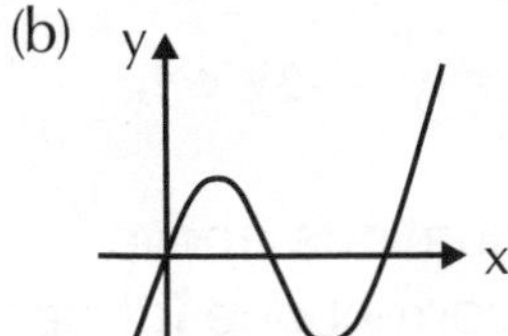

(i) $y = 4x + x^2 - 2x^3$
(ii) $y = x^3 - 3x^2 + 2x$
(iii) $y = 5 - x^3$
(iv) $y = 2x^3 + 4$

(c)

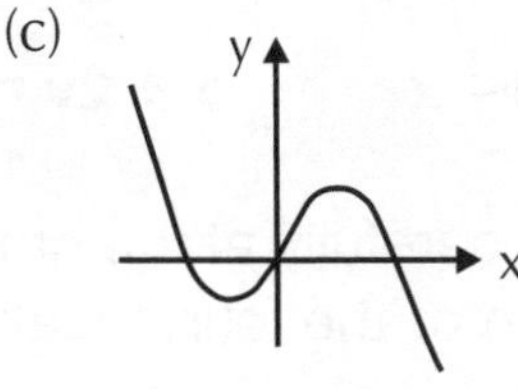

(i) $y = x^3 - 4x^2$
(ii) $y = x^3 + 3x^2 - 5x$
(iii) $y = 6 - 2x^3$
(iv) $y = 12x + x^2 - x^3$

If it turns out that you do find these hard, one thing that'll make them easier is lots of practice. And by a lucky coincidence, here are four exam questions just waiting for you. Amazing.

Worked Exam Question

Calculator Not Allowed

1 For each of these graphs you are given two possible equations.
In each case tick the correct equation.

(a)

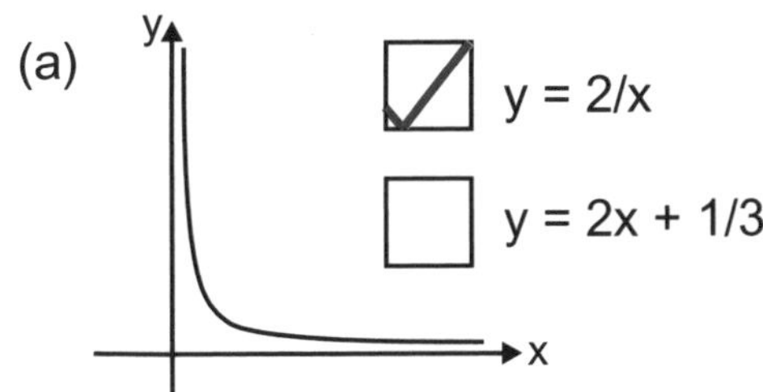

This is the shape you get when y is something over x *(see page 82)**.*

(b)

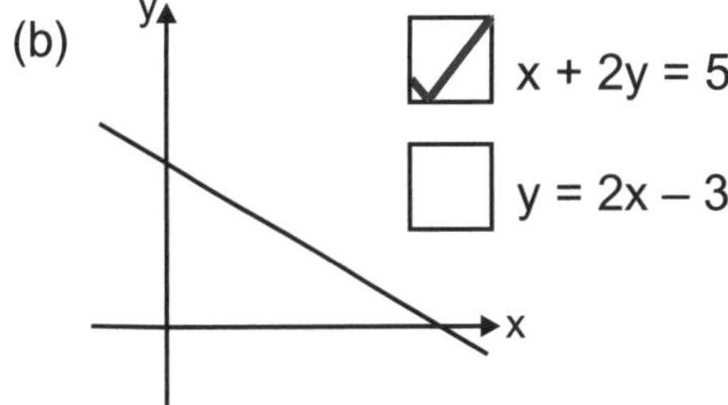

It's clearer if you rearrange the 1st equation by moving the x to the other side, giving $2y = -x + 5$. Now you can tell it's the 1st equation, because the graph has a negative gradient (slopes down) and crosses the y-axis at a positive value.

(c)

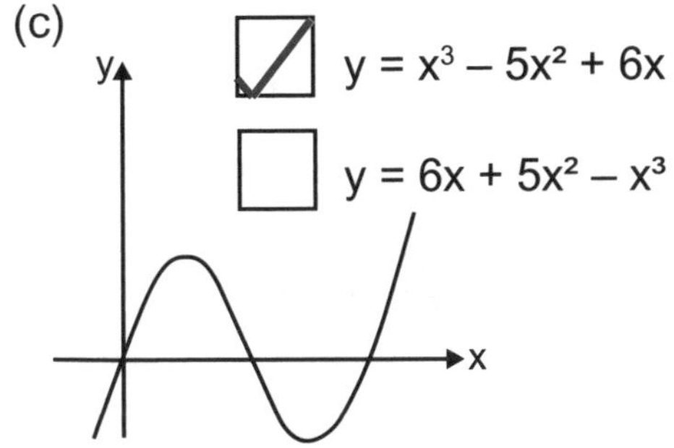

This graph goes up from bottom left, so the x^3 bit must be positive.

(d)

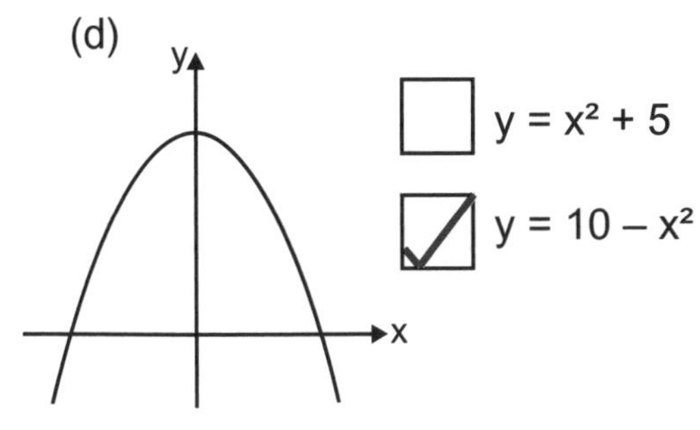

This is an upside down bucket shape, so the x^2 bit must be negative.

(4 marks)

Exam Questions

Exam Questions

Calculator Not Allowed

2

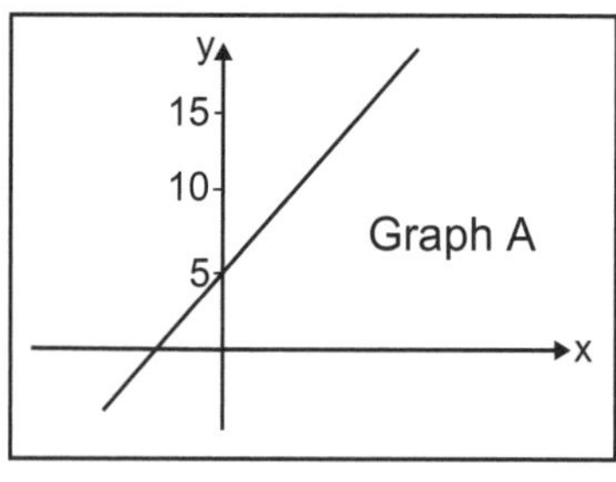

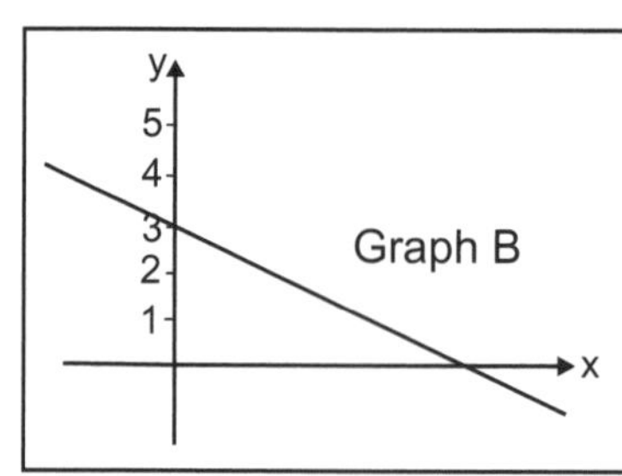

$y = 5 - x$ **$x + 2y = 6$** **$y = -3x + 5$** **$y = 2x + 5$**

Look carefully at the graphs and equations above.
Which of the four equations is the correct one for each graph?

(2 marks)

3 Here are six different equations labelled A to F.

A: $y = x^2$ **B: $y = 2x + 3$** **C: $y = -3$**

D: $x + y = 8$ **E: $y = 4 - x^2$** **F: $x = 5$**

Think about the graphs of these equations.

(a) Which graph is a straight line with a gradient of 2?

(1 mark)

(b) Which graph is parallel to the x-axis?

(1 mark)

(c) Which **two** graphs go through (5, 3)?

(2 marks)

(d) Which graph goes through (0, 0)?

(1 mark)

4 (a)

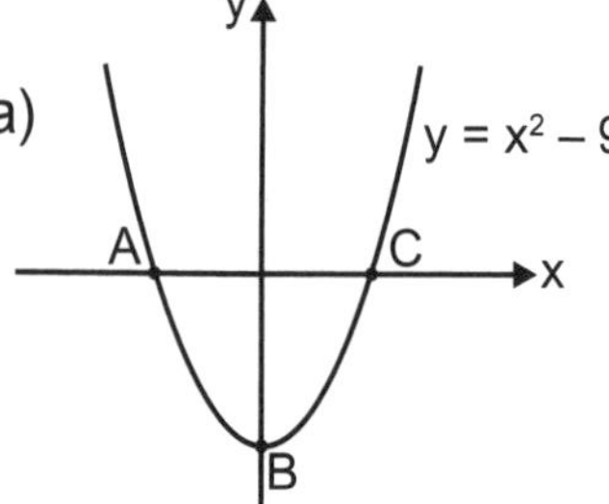

This is the graph of $y = x^2 - 9$.
What are the coordinates of A, B, and C?

(3 marks)

(b) The graph of $y = x^2 - 9$ is reflected in the line $y = 2$. What are the coordinates of D, the reflection of B?

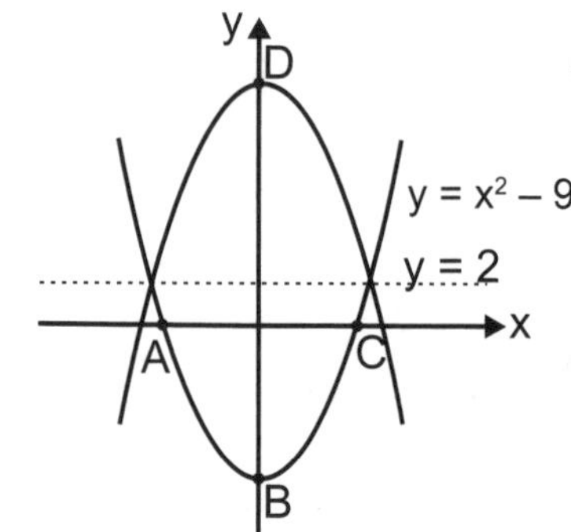

(1 mark)

Plotting Straight Line Graphs

The next page will show you how to plot straight line graphs using "y = mx + c". But first, here's an easy way to do it...

The "Table of 3 Values" Method

You can draw ANY STRAIGHT LINE from its equation using this EASY method.

Method

1) Choose 3 values of x and draw up a table.
2) Work out the value of y for each value of x.
3) Plot the coordinates and draw the line.

If it's a straight line equation, the three points will be in a straight line with each other. If they aren't, first check that you've correctly plotted the values in your table, then make sure it's definitely a straight line equation, and that your values for y are right.

Example

"Draw the graph of $y = 2x - 4$."

1) DRAW UP A TABLE with some suitable values of x. Choosing x = 0, 2, 4 usually works, i.e.

x	0	2	4
y			

2) FIND THE y-VALUES by putting each x-value into the equation:

x	0	2	4
y	-4	0	4

e.g. When x = 4...

$$y = 2x - 4 = (2 \times 4) - 4 = 8 - 4 = 4$$

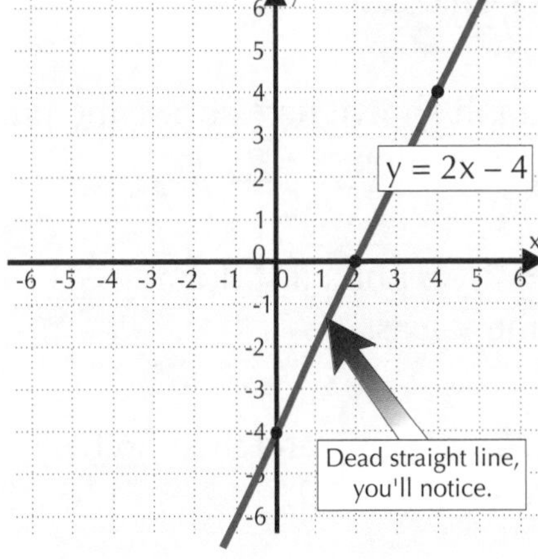

3) PLOT THE POINTS and DRAW THE LINE right across the graph (as shown). (The points should always lie in a perfect straight line. If they don't, check your calculations.)

Plotting Straight Line Graphs

This page shows you how to plot a straight line from the equation in "y = mx + c" form. You need to remember:

> Any straight line can be written in the form y = mx + c.
>
> "m" is equal to the gradient of the graph.
> "c" is the value where it crosses the y-axis and is called the y-intercept.

Remember, it's always just "y" — meaning "1 × y" — when the equation is in this form.

Drawing a **Straight Line** using "y = mx + c"

The main thing is being able to identify "m" and "c" and knowing what to do with them.

But watch out — people often mix up "m" and "c", especially with say, "y = 5 + 2x".
So remember: "m" is the number in front of x and "c" is the number on its own.

Method

1) Get the equation into the form "y = mx + c".
2) Identify "m" and "c" carefully.
3) Put a dot on the y-axis at the value of c.
4) Then go along one unit and up or down by the value of m and make another dot.
5) Repeat the same "step" in the other direction as shown below.
6) Finally check that the gradient looks right.

Example

The graph shown here shows the process for the equation "y = 2x + 3":

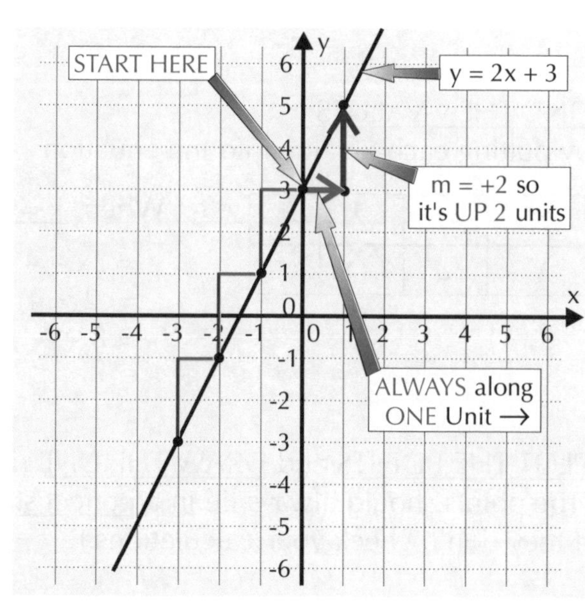

1) "c" = 3, so put a first dot at y = 3 on the y-axis.

2) Go along 1 unit and then up by 2 because "m" = +2.

3) Repeat the same step in the other direction (i.e. 1 ← 2 ↓ the other way).

4) CHECK:
A gradient of +2 should be quite steep and uphill left to right — which it is.

Plotting Straight Line Graphs

Finding the Equation of a Straight Line graph

This is basically the opposite process. You have to decode a graph to put together the equation. And it's not nearly as hard as you might think...

Method

1) Find where the graph crosses the y-axis. This is the value of "c".
2) Find the value of the gradient. This is the value of "m".
3) Now just put these values for "m" and "c" into "$y = mx + c$" and there you have it!

The only bit which can be slightly tricky is finding the gradient. Remember — gradient is change in y / change in x.

(The method for finding the gradient was covered on page 75.)

Example

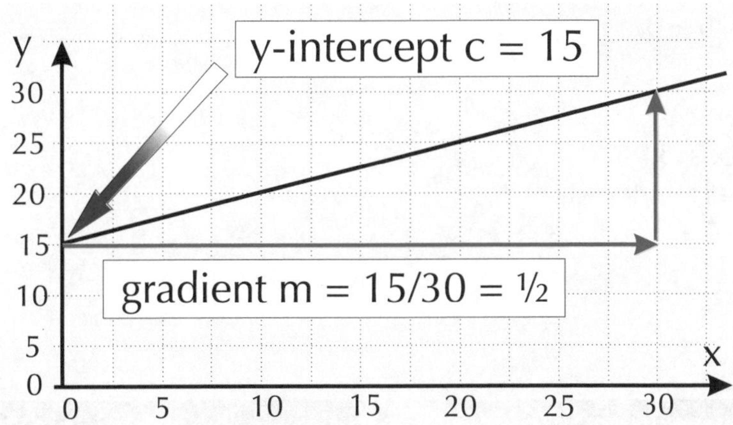

For the graph shown here, $m = \frac{1}{2}$ and $c = 15$ so "$y = mx + c$" becomes:

$$y = \tfrac{1}{2}x + 15$$

These 3 pages tell you all you need to know about straight lines

Make sure you learn the three methods fully and practise using each one. The "plotting points from a table" method on page 85 is easy and will work for any graph — see the next page...

Typical Graph Questions

Over the next four pages, we'll cover some of the most common graph questions that you get in exams.

There's often a lot of fiddly detail involved in graph questions: getting the right values in the table, plotting the right points and getting the final answers from your graph. If you want to get all these easy marks, then you've got to learn all these little tricks:

1 Filling in The **Table of Values**

A Typical Question

"Complete the table of values for the equation $y = x^2 - 4x + 3$."

x	-2	-1	0	1	2	3	4	5	6
y				0			3		15

What you don't do is try to punch it all into the calculator in one go. Not good. The rest of the question hinges on this table of values and one silly mistake here could cost you a lot of marks. This might look like a long-winded method but it takes far less time than you think and is the only really safe method.

1) For EVERY value in the table you should WRITE THIS OUT:

For $x = 4$:
$$\begin{aligned} y &= x^2 - 4x + 3 \\ &= 4^2 - (4 \times 4) + 3 \\ &= 16 - 16 + 3 \\ &= \underline{3} \end{aligned}$$

For $x = -1$:
$$\begin{aligned} y &= x^2 - 4x + 3 \\ &= (-1 \times -1) - (4 \times -1) + 3 \\ &= 1 \; - \; -4 + 3 = 1 + 4 + 3 \\ &= \underline{8} \end{aligned}$$

2) Make sure you can reproduce the y-values they've already given you...

(i.e. 0, 3 and 15 in the table above)

... before you fill in the spaces in the table. This is really important to make sure you're doing it right, before you start cheerfully working out a pile of wrong values!

I wouldn't tell you all this without good reason, so ignore it at your peril.

Typical Graph Questions

2 *Plotting* **the Points** *and Drawing* **the Curve**

Here again there are easy marks to be won and lost — this all matters:

1) GET THE AXES THE RIGHT WAY ROUND
   The values from the first row are always plotted on the x-axis.
2) PLOT THE POINTS CAREFULLY...
   ...and don't mix up the x and y values.
3) Join the points with a line or a curve. The points should ALWAYS form a PERFECT STRAIGHT LINE or a COMPLETELY SMOOTH CURVE. If they don't, they're wrong.

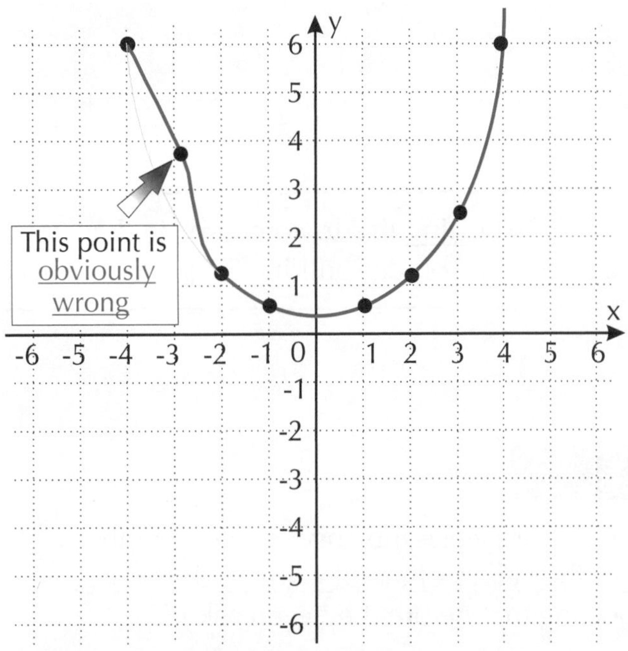

Never ever let one point drag your line off in some ridiculous direction — if one point seems out of place, check the value in the table and then check the position where you've plotted it. When a graph is generated from an equation, you never get spikes or lumps.

Algebra equations always give straight lines or smooth curves

Remember — a graph from an ALGEBRA EQUATION must always be drawn as a smooth curve or a dead straight line. You only use lots of short straight line sections to join points in "Data Handling" when it's called a "frequency polygon". (See page 152.)

Typical Graph Questions

3 Getting Answers *from your Graph*

There are two types of "reading the answer from your graph" questions you can get.

1) FOR A SINGLE CURVE OR LINE

— you always get the answer by drawing a straight line to the graph from one axis, and then down or across to the other axis.

Example *"Find the value of y when x is equal to 3 in the graph shown."*

All you do is this...

1) Start at 3 on the x-axis
2) Go straight up to the graph
3) Then straight over to the y-axis
4) And read off the value — which in this case is $y = 3.3$ (as shown opposite)

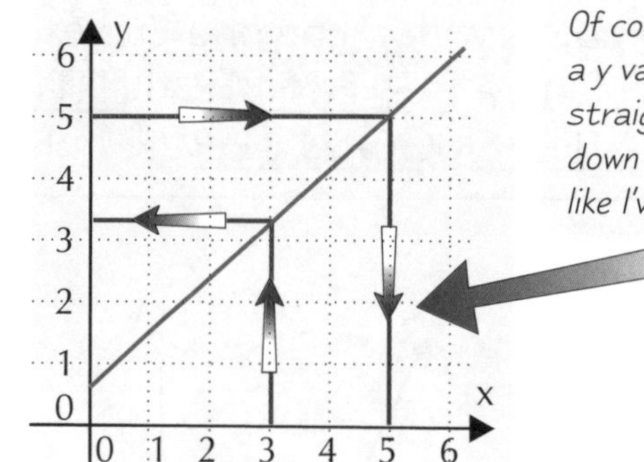

Of course they could also give you a y value, and you'd have to read straight across and then straight down to find the value of x — like I've shown here.

You should be fully expecting this to come up, so that even if you don't understand the question, you can still have a pretty good stab at it.

2) IF TWO LINES CROSS

— you can bet your very last fruitcake the answer to one of the questions will simply be: the values of x and y where they cross and you should be expecting that before they even ask it! (See page 95.)

When a question asks you to find the point that satisfies two equations, this is what it means.

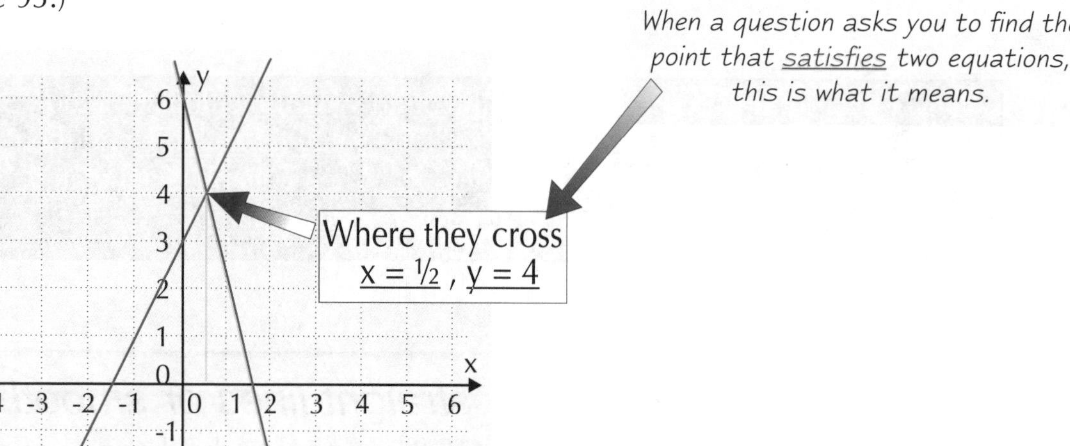

Typical Graph Questions

4 Travel Graphs

Travel graphs are very different from "algebra" graphs. There are no equations, no ys or xs. Instead, the graph just tells a story (kind of). Here are the main things to know about them:

The Four Key Points

1) A TRAVEL GRAPH is always DISTANCE (↑) against TIME (→).
2) For any section, SLOPE (gradient) = SPEED, but watch out for the UNITS.
3) FLAT SECTIONS are where it's STOPPED.
4) The STEEPER the graph the FASTER it's going.

A Typical Tricky Question

"What's the speed of the return section on the graph shown?"

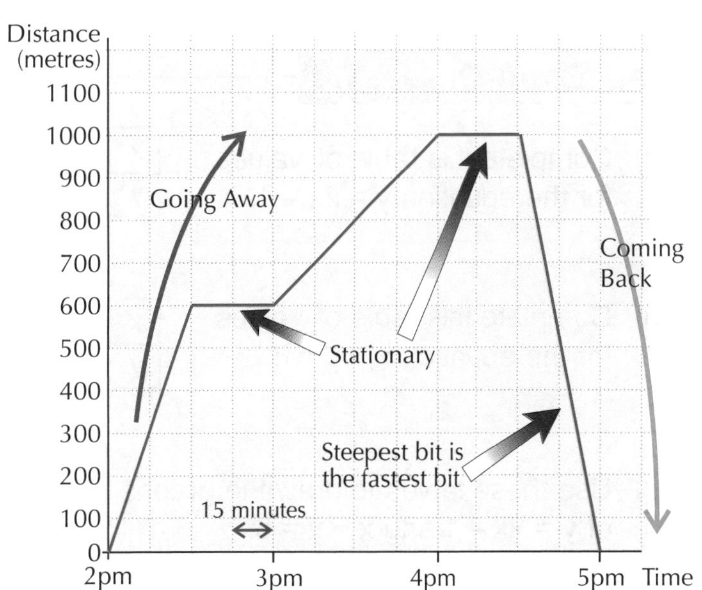

ANSWER:

Speed = gradient

= 1000 m ÷ 30 min = 33.33 m/min (metres per minute)
or 1 km ÷ ½ hr = 2 km/h (kilometres per hour)
or 1000 m ÷ 1800 s = 0.56 m/s (metres per second)

Note that the answer (and its units) depends very much on the units you use to work it out.

Travel graphs are easy once you know how to read them...

Make sure you understand what is happening in each section of the travel graph above. Exam questions often ask you to describe this — it should be easy marks.

Warm-up and Worked Exam Questions

Questions on this type of graph stuff tend to be pretty much all the same. That's good in a way, because you won't get any surprises in the exam. It's a bit boring though.

Warm-up Questions

1) Complete the table of values for the equation $y = 3x - 2$.

x	-2	0	2	4
y	-8			

2) Complete the table of values for the equation $y = 2x^2 + 3x - 1$.

x	-4	-3	-2	-1	0	1	2	3
y	19		1					26

3) Give the general equation for a straight line graph.
4) A straight line graph has the equation $y = 7 - 5x$. What is the gradient of this graph?
5) A straight line graph has a gradient of 3 and a y-intercept of -4. What is the equation of this straight line graph?
6) What does the gradient of a travel graph tell you?
7) What is always plotted up the vertical axis of a travel graph?

Blah blah worked examples... blah blah exam questions...
See, you're not the only one getting bored.

Worked Exam Question

Calculator Allowed

1 (a) Complete this table of values for the equation $y = 2x - 1$.

x	0	2	4
y	-1	3	7

Just stick each value of x from the table into the equation, e.g. for the first x value of 0, y = (2 × 0) − 1 = 0 − 1 = -1.

(2 marks)

(b) Complete this table of values for the equation $x + y = 8$.

x	0	2	4
y	8	6	4

(2 marks)

(c) Use these tables to draw the graphs of $y = 2x - 1$ and $x + y = 8$.

(4 marks)

When a question asks you to draw 2 graphs like this, that doesn't mean use 2 sets of axes. The graph is just the line that you draw, and usually you'll need to draw them both on the same set of axes.

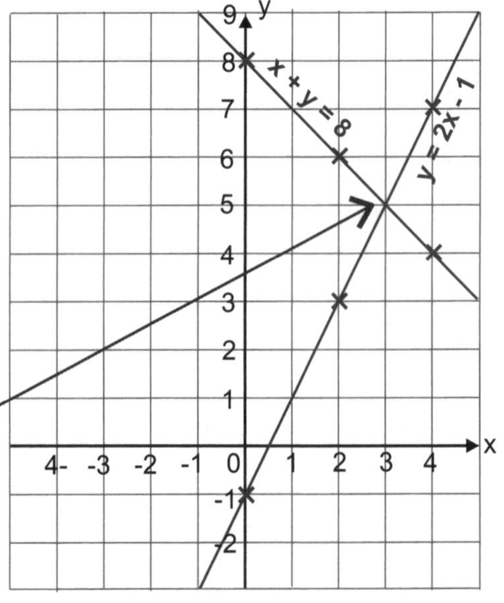

(d) Write down the coordinates of the point where the graphs intersect.

(3, 5)

(1 mark)

The point where the graphs intersect is here. Read down to get the x-coordinate, which comes first — you can see that it's 3. Next read across to get the y-coordinate, which is 5.

Exam Questions

Exam Questions

Calculator Allowed

2 (a) Complete the table of values for the equation $y = 2x^2 + 1$.

x	-3	-2	-1	0	1	2	3
y	19		3			9	

(2 marks)

(b) Draw the graph with equation $y = 2x^2 + 1$. Use graph paper. *(2 marks)*

(c) Use your graph to find the value of y when x = 1.5. *(1 mark)*

(d) Use your graph to find the values of x when y = 13 (to 1 d.p.). *(2 marks)*

3 (a) Complete the table of values for the equation $y = x + 3$.

x	0	2	4
y			

(1 mark)

(b) Complete the table for the equation $2x + y = 12$.

x	0	2	4
y			

(1 mark)

(c) Draw the graphs of the equations $y = x + 3$ and $2x + y = 12$ on the same axes. Use graph paper. *(2 marks)*

(d) Write down the coordinates of the point where the graphs intersect. *(1 mark)*

4 Kara and Kerry did a sponsored walk. They set off at noon and jogged for the first quarter of an hour. Then they walked for the next hour. After a rest, they set off to walk back. Kerry's mother drove to meet them and, as it started to rain, gave them a lift back.

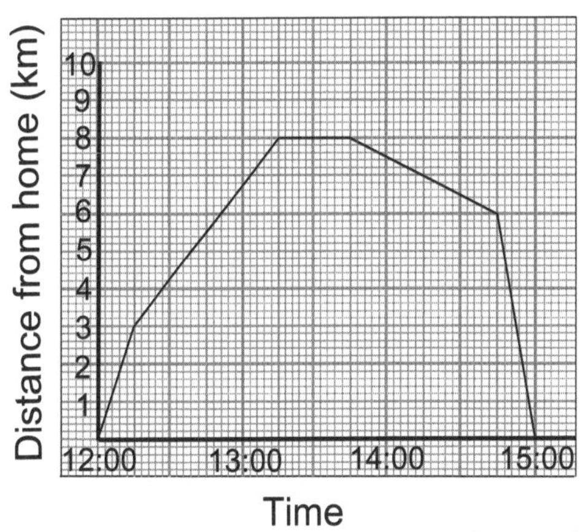

(a) For how many kilometres did they jog? *(1 mark)*

(b) How many minutes did they have for the break? *(1 mark)*

(c) What was their average speed from the start until they stopped for the break? *(1 mark)*

(d) At what time did Kerry's mother pick them up? *(1 mark)*

(e) What was their average speed in the car? *(1 mark)*

(f) How far did they jog and walk altogether? *(1 mark)*

Simultaneous Equations

These are OK as long as you learn these six steps in meticulous detail.

The Six Steps

We'll use these two equations for our example:

$$y + 6x = -1 \text{ and } 2y = 13 + 3x$$

1) REARRANGE BOTH EQUATIONS INTO THE FORM: $ax + by = c$
where a, b, c are numbers (which can be negative).

Also LABEL THE TWO EQUATIONS —① and —②

$$6x + y = -1 \quad —①$$
$$-3x + 2y = 13 \quad —②$$

2) You need to MATCH UP THE NUMBERS IN FRONT (the "coefficients") of either the x's or y's in BOTH EQUATIONS.

To do this you may need to MULTIPLY one or both equations by a suitable number.
You should RELABEL any that you change:

$$6x + y = -1 \quad —①$$
②×2 : $$-6x + 4y = 26 \quad —③$$

This gives us -6x in new equation ③ to match the +6x in equation ①.

3) ADD OR SUBTRACT THE TWO EQUATIONS ...
...to eliminate the terms with the same coefficient.
If the coefficients are the SAME (both +ve or both –ve) then SUBTRACT.
If the coefficients are OPPOSITE (one +ve and one –ve) then ADD.

SSS — if the Signs are the Same, then Subtract.

①+③ $$0x + 5y = 25$$

In this case we have +6x and -6x so we ADD.

4) SOLVE THE RESULTING EQUATION to find whichever letter is left in it.

$$5y = 25 \Rightarrow y = 5$$

5) SUBSTITUTE THIS BACK into equation ① and solve it to find the other quantity.

Sub in ①: $6x + 5 = -1 \Rightarrow 6x = -6 \Rightarrow x = -1$

6) Then SUBSTITUTE BOTH THESE VALUES INTO EQUATION ②, to make sure it works.
If it doesn't then you've done something wrong and you'll have to do it all again!

Sub x and y in ②: $-3 \times -1 + 2 \times 5 = 3 + 10 = 13$,

Which is right, so it's worked.

So the solutions are: $x = -1$, $y = 5$

Simultaneous Equations

On the previous page is the tricky algebra method for solving simultaneous equations.
On this page is the nice easy graph method for solving them.
You could be asked to do either method in the exam so make sure you learn them both.

Solving ***Simultaneous Equations*** *Using* ***Graphs***

This is a very easy way to find the x- and y-solutions to two simultaneous equations.
Here's the simple rule:

The solution of two simultaneous equations is simply the x- and y-values where their graphs cross.

Three Step Method

1) Do a "table of 3 values" for both equations.

2) Draw the two graphs.

3) Find the x- and y-values where they cross.

Example *"Draw the graphs for "y = 2x + 1" and "y = 4 – x" and then use your graphs to solve them."*

1) DO A TABLE OF 3 VALUES for both equations:

y = 2x + 1

x	0	1	2
y	1	3	5

y = 4 – x

x	0	2	4
y	4	2	0

2) DRAW THE GRAPHS

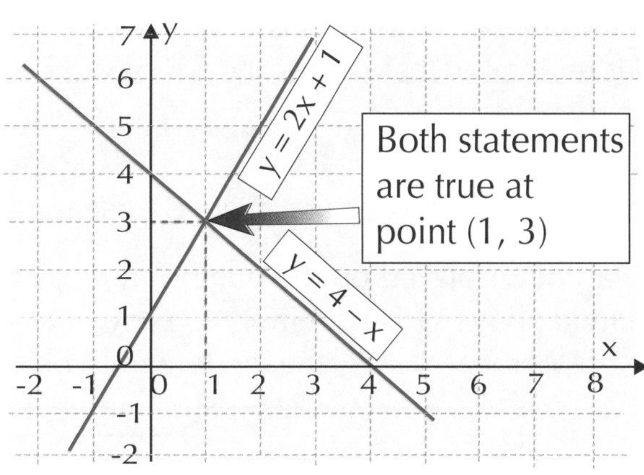

3) FIND WHERE THEY CROSS:
The graphs cross at x = 1 and y = 3.
So that's the answer.

Simultaneous equations means 2 equations and 2 unknowns

Simultaneous equations are a "classic" algebra topic if ever there was one — there's a big scary method to learn, which you'll find isn't half as bad as it first looks, and the questions are pretty much always the same. That's algebra for you...

Inequalities

This is quite difficult, but it's still worth learning the easy bits in case they ask a very easy question on it, as well they might. Here are the easy bits:

The 4 Inequality Symbols

$>$ means "is greater than" $\geqslant$ means "is greater than or equal to"

$<$ means "is less than" $\leqslant$ means "is less than or equal to"

REMEMBER, the one at the BIG end is BIGGER.

So "$x > 3$" and "$3 < x$" both say: "x is greater than 3"

Algebra with Inequalities — this is a bit more tricky.

The thing to remember here is that inequalities are just like regular equations:

$6x > x + 4$

$6x = x + 4$

in the sense that all the normal rules of algebra (see pages 42 to 45) apply...

with one big exception: **Whenever you multiply or divide by a negative number, you must flip the inequality sign.**

Example *"Solve $3x < 4x + 3$"*

ANSWER:

First take 4x from both sides:

$3x - 4x < 3$

Combining the x-terms gives:

$-x < 3$

To get rid of the "–" in front of x you need to divide both sides by -1
— but remember that means the "<" has to be flipped as well, which gives:

$x > -3$

The < has flipped around into a >, because we divided by a –ve number.

So the answer is "x is greater than -3", meaning that x has a value above -3, but is not -3.

This can be displayed on the number line, as shown below.
The circle above -3 is left empty to show that -3 is not included.
If the answer was $x \geq -3$, the circle would be coloured in.

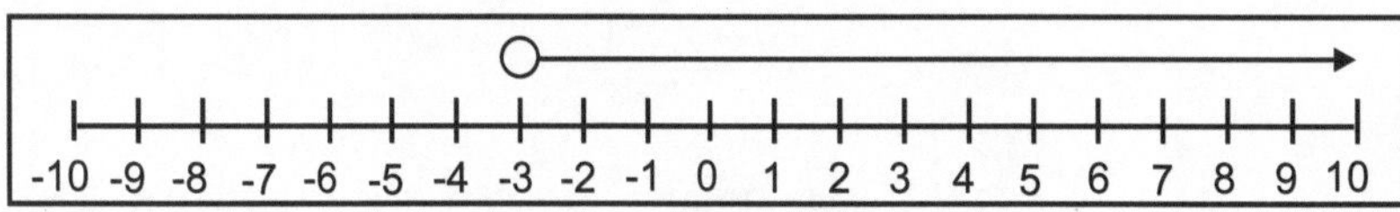

The main thing you should realise is that most of the time you just treat the "<" or ">" as though it was an "=" and do all the usual algebra that you would for a regular equation. The "big exception" is the only thing you really have to look out for.

Graphical Inequalities

This is easy so long as you remember the easy method for drawing graphs — i.e. a table of 3 values (see page 85). The questions always involve <u>shading a region</u> on a graph, which is represented by some horrid-looking algebra.

This could put you right off before you even start, but once you realise that the horrid-looking algebra means something really simple then the whole thing is mind-numbingly easy...

Method

1) <u>Convert each inequality to an equation</u>
   by simply putting an "=" in place of the "<".
2) <u>Do a table of 3 values for each equation</u> (see page 85)
   and then <u>draw the lines</u> on the graph.
3) <u>Shade the enclosed region</u>.
   The lines you've drawn will always enclose the region that you're after — and they nearly always ask you to <u>shade it</u>.

Example

"Shade the region represented by : $y > 2$, $y < x + 1$ and $x + y < 7$ "

See what I mean about the horrid-looking algebra...

<u>ANSWER</u>:

1) <u>CONVERT EACH INEQUALITY TO AN EQUATION</u>:
   $y > 2$ becomes $y = 2$
   $y < x + 1$ becomes $y = x + 1$
   $x + y < 7$ becomes $x + y = 7$
2) <u>DO A TABLE OF 3 VALUES</u> for each equation, and draw the lines on a graph.
   e.g. for $x + y = 7$:

x	0	3	6
y	7	4	1

3) <u>SHADE THE ENCLOSED REGION</u>, and Bob's your Uncle, it's done.

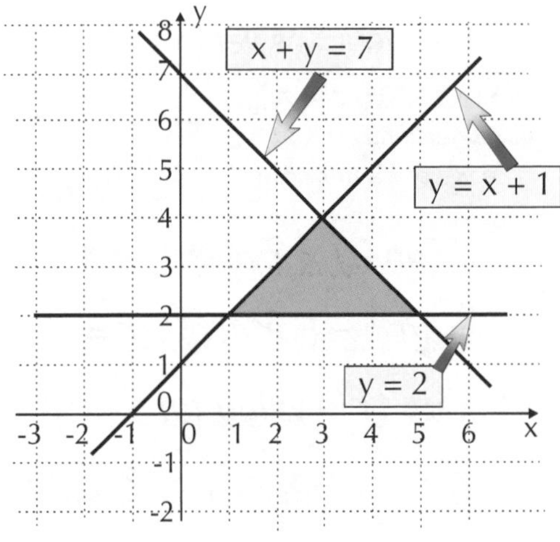

Inequalities are just like normal algebra — more or less...

Remember — the trick with inequalities is to treat them like normal algebra except you write < or > instead of =. Just remember to switch the sign if you ever times or divide by a negative number — it's really easy to forget this.

Warm-up and Worked Exam Questions

Last few questions, and then this monster section is over. The next one is about shapes, which should be a nice change after all these crazy equations. And it's a lot shorter too.

Warm-up Questions

1) Look at the equations below:

$$x + y = 10 \qquad 3x + 2y = 12$$

Outline briefly the method you would use to solve the equations

a) algebraically b) graphically

2) Show these inequalities on a number line diagram.
Use a scale from -10 to 10 on each of your number lines.
(a) $x > 2$ (b) $x < 5$ (c) $x \leq -2$ (d) $x \geq -4$

Algebra is really important for passing maths exams, but too much of it can be dangerous. All those equations can trigger a very strange response in certain oook oook eeky eeky ooooo...

Worked Exam Questions

1 Solve the inequality $6x + 5 > 29$.

Take 5 from both sides to give $6x > 24$

Divide both sides by 6 to give $x > 4$

(2 marks)

2 Claire buys 4 mangos and 5 kiwi fruit for £1.65. Later that day, she goes back to buy 2 more mangos 3 more kiwi fruit which costs her 95p.

a) If m and k represent the costs (in pence) of one kiwi and one mango respectively, write down two equations involving m and k.

$4m + 5k = 165$ *$2m + 3k = 95$*

4 mangos... plus.... 5 kiwi fruit... is 165p *2 mangos... plus.... 3 kiwi fruit... is 95p*

(2 marks)

b) Use your answer to part a) to find values for k and m.

First, multiply one of the equations so that the m's or k's match.

$4m + 5k = 165$ — Eqn 1

$2m + 3k = 95$ — Eqn 2

(Eqn 2) × 2 gives $4m + 6k = 190$ — Eqn 3

The m's in eqn 1 and eqn 3 match now, so you can eliminate them by subtracting one eqn from the other.

Eqn 3 – Eqn 1: $k = 25$

Put this value for k into Eqn 1:

$4m + (5 \times 25) = 165$, so $4m = 165 - 125 = 40$, so $m = 40 \div 4 = 10$

Answer: $k = 25$, $m = 10$

(3 marks)

Questions like this look horrible because there's so many steps, but if you take your time, you'll be able to follow the method through...

Exam Questions

Exam Questions

Calculator Allowed

3 Find the range of values of x which satisfy the inequality

5x – 2 < 2x + 13. Show your working.

(3 marks)

4 (a) Complete this table of values for the equation **y = x**.

x	0	2	4
y			

(1 mark)

(b) Draw the graph of y = x on the grid below.

(1 mark)

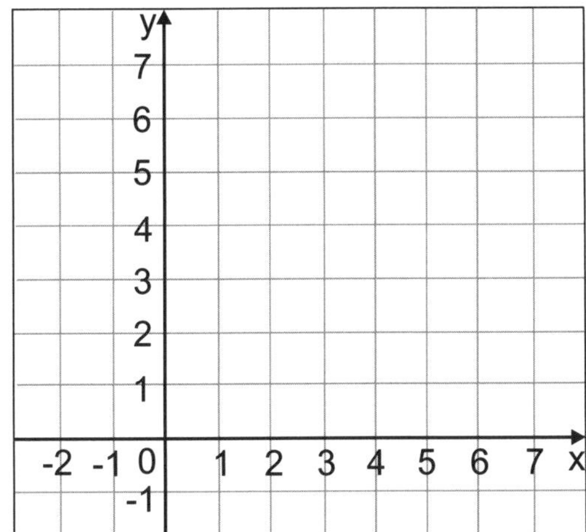

(c) Complete the same table of values for the equation **x + y = 6**.

(1 mark)

(d) Draw the graph of x + y = 6 on the grid above.

(1 mark)

(e) Draw the graph of y = 1 on the grid above.

(1 mark)

(f) Shade the region on your diagram represented by the inequalities

y < x, **x + y < 6** and **y > 1**.

(1 mark)

Exam Questions

Exam Questions

Calculator Allowed

5 Dave takes 33 minutes to iron 5 shirts and 2 pairs of jeans.
He takes 14 minutes to iron 2 shirts and 1 pair of jeans.

Let x be the number of minutes Dave takes to iron one shirt.
Let y be the number of minutes Dave takes to iron one pair of jeans.

Use algebra to find out how long it takes Dave to iron one shirt and how long it takes him to iron one pair of jeans.

(5 marks)

6 (a) On the grid below draw and label the graph of the equation $y = 2x + 1$.

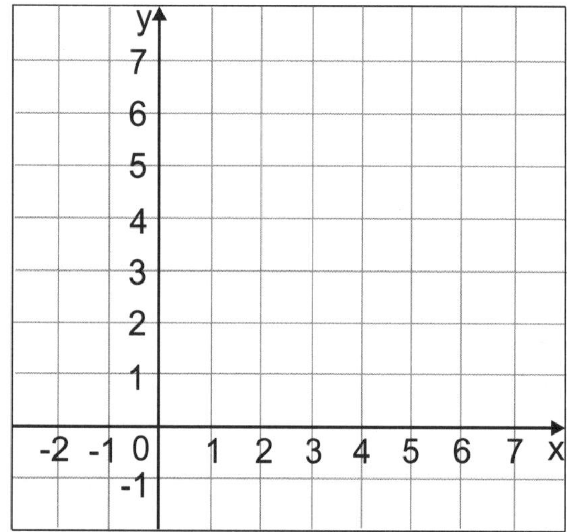

(1 mark)

(b) On the grid draw and label the graph of the equation $x + y = 7$.

(1 mark)

(c) Use the graphs you have drawn for (a) and (b) to find the values of x and y which satisfy the simultaneous equations

$y = 2x + 1$ and **$x + y = 7$**.

(1 mark)

7 Solve the inequality $7 + 3x < 2 + 5x$.
Show your answer by completing the number line diagram below.

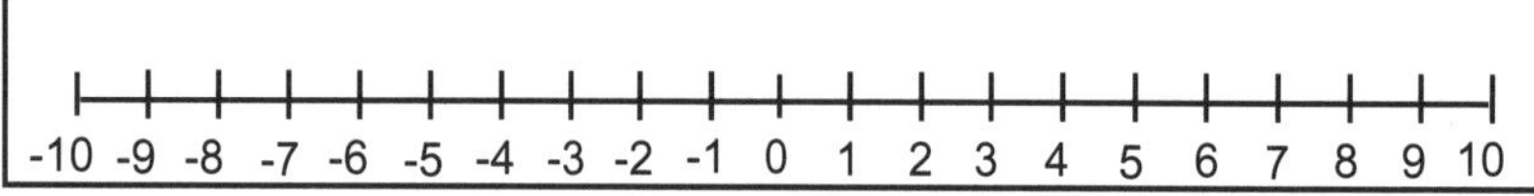

(3 marks)

Revision Summary for Section Two

These questions might seem like the last thing you want to do to celebrate reaching the end of the section. But they're important — they show you which bits of algebra you're weakest on. Then you can go back to those bits and spend some extra time on them. Otherwise you might waltz into the exam thinking you've done loads of revision, only to find that you don't know it at all.

Keep learning these basic facts until you know them

1) Write down three examples of translating a question from English into algebra.
2) In algebra, what is a term? What are the four steps for simplifying an expression?
3) Give the four most important details to do with multiplying out brackets.
4) What happens with double and squared brackets? Give the 3-step method for factorising.
5) Give all six different types of number pattern with an example of each.
6) What are the two formulae for finding the nth term of a number pattern?
7) What are the two rules for negative numbers? When are they used?
8) List 5 combinations of letters that cause confusion in algebra, e.g. ab^2.
9) What are the 3 steps of the method for substituting numbers into formulae?
10) What has BODMAS got to do with putting numbers into formulae?
11) What are the two easier alternative methods for tackling simple equations?
12) Demonstrate your prowess at these methods by doing an example of each.
13) Give the 4 steps for solving an equation by trial and improvement.
14) Explain what the "balance method" is for solving equations.
15) What do solving equations and rearranging formulae have in common?
16) List the 6 step method for doing equations and formulae. What is meant by $Ax = B$?
17) What are the two steps for using a formula triangle?
18) What is the formula triangle for: (a) density? (b) speed?
19) What do you know about the units that come out of a formula?
20) Explain what 3-D coordinates are. Give an example.
21) What type of line is: (a) $x = a$ (b) $y = b$ (c) $y = ax$.
22) Sketch the graphs $y = x$ and $y = -x$.
23) What is the formula for gradient? How do you remember it?
24) Write down the 5 step method for finding gradient.
25) What are the 4 different types of graph that you should know the basic shape of?
26) What does the equation of a straight line look like?
27) What makes them different from equations that aren't straight lines?
28) What sort of equation has a bucket-shaped graph? What about an upside-down bucket?
29) What sort of equation produces a graph with a wiggle in the middle?
30) Sketch one example of each of the above three types of graph, giving the equations.
31) What are the 2 rules for filling in a table of values?
32) What are the 4 rules for plotting the graph from a table of values?
33) Explain what "$y = mx + c$" means, including the significance of "m" and "c".
34) Detail the 3 steps for getting the equation of a straight line graph.
35) What are the two rules for getting answers from a graph or graphs?
36) What are the four main details concerning travel graphs?
37) What are "simultaneous equations"? Give an example.
38) Give the 6 step method for solving simultaneous equations.
39) Detail 3 steps of the method for solving simultaneous equations using graphs.
40) What are the 4 inequality symbols and what do they mean?
41) What are the rules of algebra for inequalities? What is the big exception?
42) What are the 3 steps for doing graphical inequalities?

Regular Polygons

A polygon is a many-sided shape.
A regular polygon is one where all the sides and angles are the same.
The regular polygons are a never-ending series of shapes with some fancy features.
They're very easy to learn. Here are the first few but they don't stop — you can have one with 16 sides or 30, etc.

EQUILATERAL TRIANGLE

(3)

3 equal sides
3 lines of symmetry
Rotational symmetry order 3

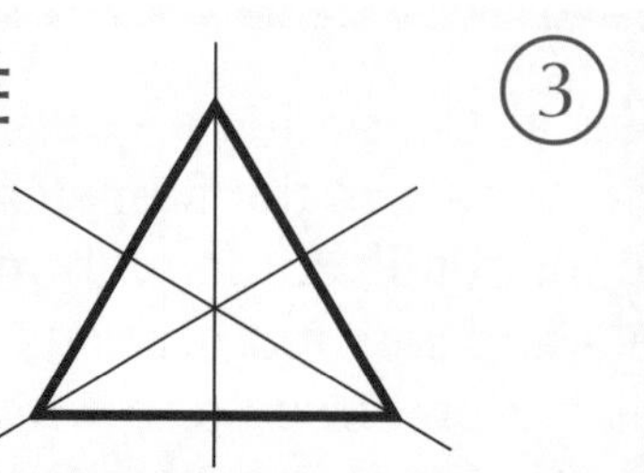

SQUARE

(4)

4 equal sides
4 lines of symmetry
Rotational symmetry order 4

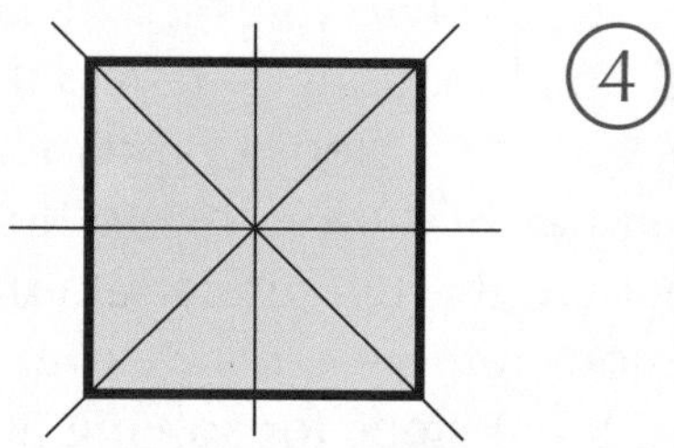

REGULAR PENTAGON

(5)

5 equal sides
5 lines of symmetry
Rotational symmetry order 5

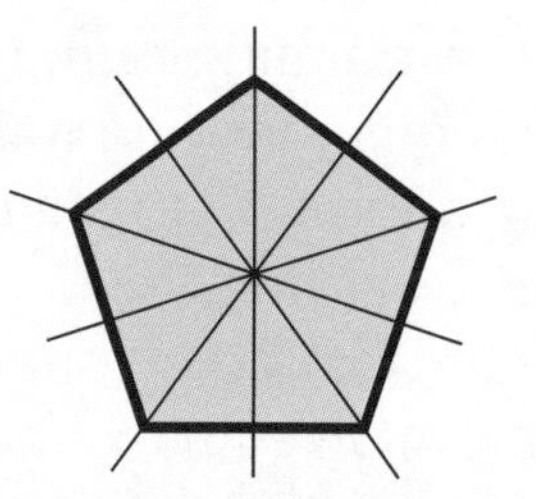

REGULAR HEXAGON

(6)

6 equal sides
6 lines of symmetry
Rotational symmetry order 6

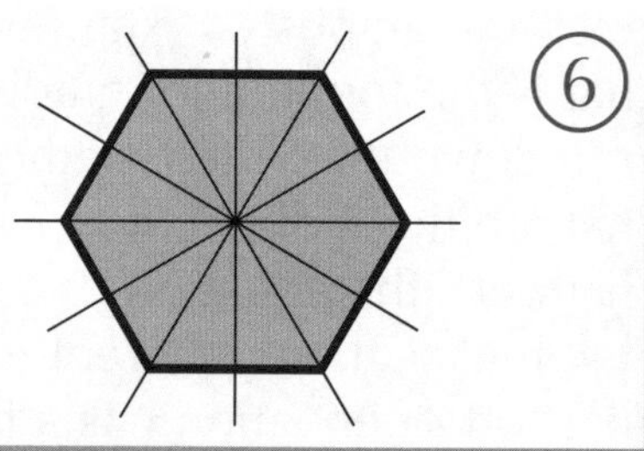

REGULAR HEPTAGON

(7)

7 equal sides
7 lines of symmetry
Rotational symmetry order 7

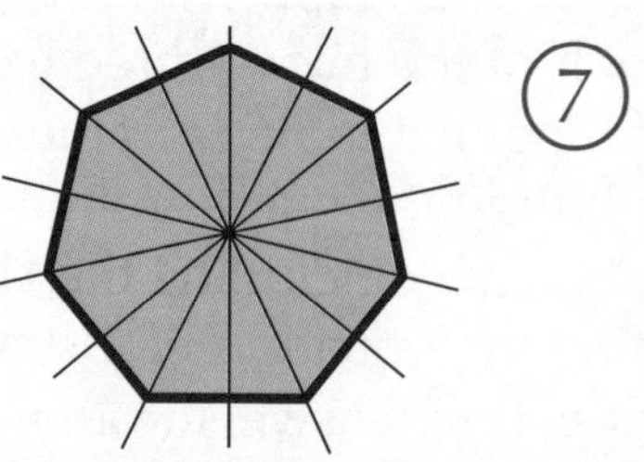

A 50p piece is a heptagon.

REGULAR OCTAGON

(8)

8 equal sides
8 lines of symmetry
Rotational symmetry order 8

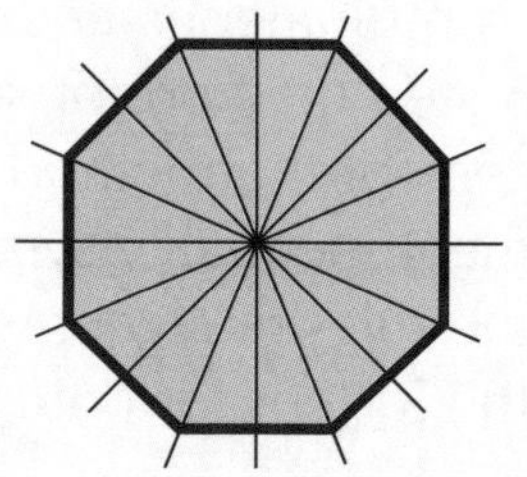

Regular Polygons

Interior and Exterior Angles

This is the main business with regular polygons.
Whenever you get one in an exam, it's a cosmic certainty they'll want you to work out the interior and exterior angles.
They are the key to it all, so if you can do that you won't have a problem.

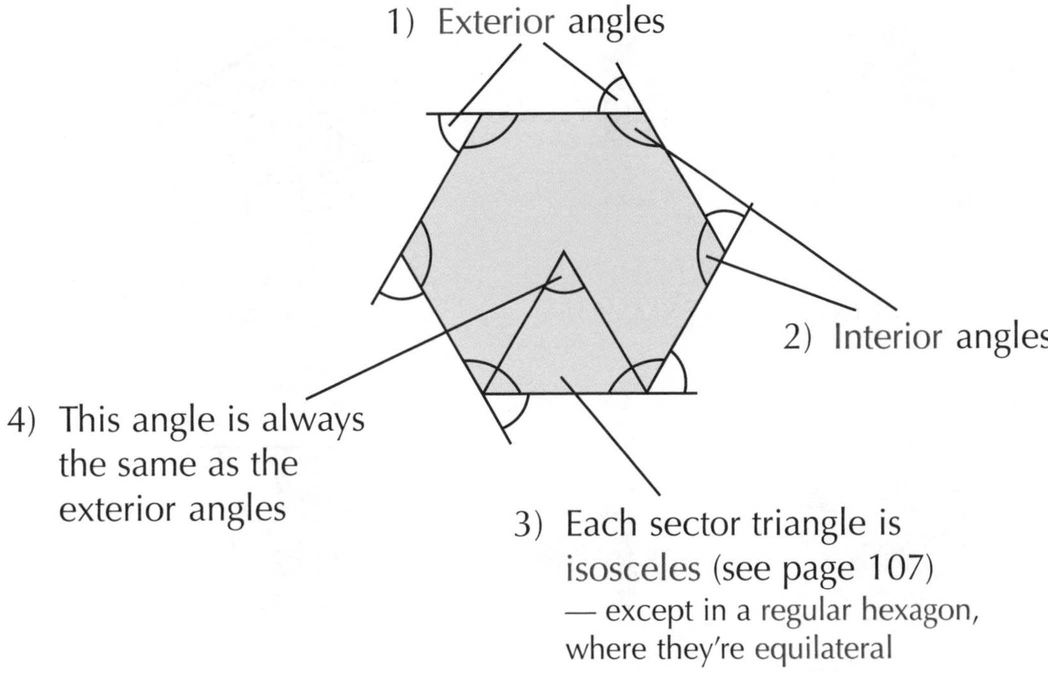

Here are all the formulae you'll need:

Sum of exterior angles = 360°

Exterior angle = $\dfrac{360°}{\text{No. of Sides}}$

Sum of interior angles = (n – 2) × 180°
(where n is the number of sides)

Interior angle = 180° – Exterior angle

These easy formulae could get you lots of easy marks

It'll only take you a minute to learn them and it's well worth it. No matter what funny-looking polygon question they try to spring on you in an exam, these formulae will give you the answer.

Symmetry

Symmetry is where a shape or picture looks exactly the same when put in different positions. There are three types of symmetry:

1 Line Symmetry

This is where you can draw a mirror line (or more than one) across a picture and both sides will fold exactly together.

How to Draw a Reflection

1) Reflect each point one by one.
2) Use a line which crosses the mirror line at 90^0 and goes exactly the same distance on the other side of the mirror line, as shown.

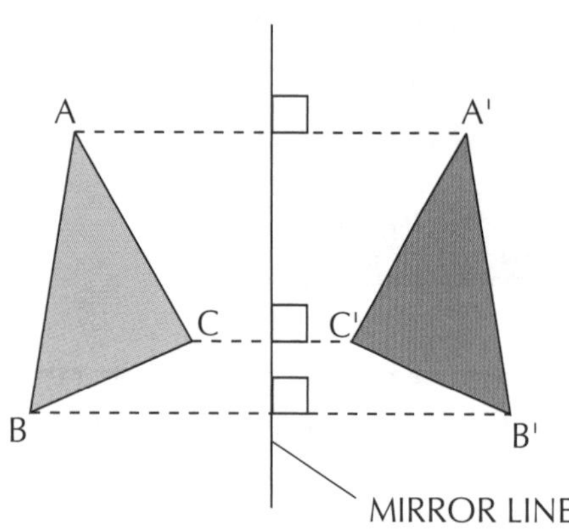

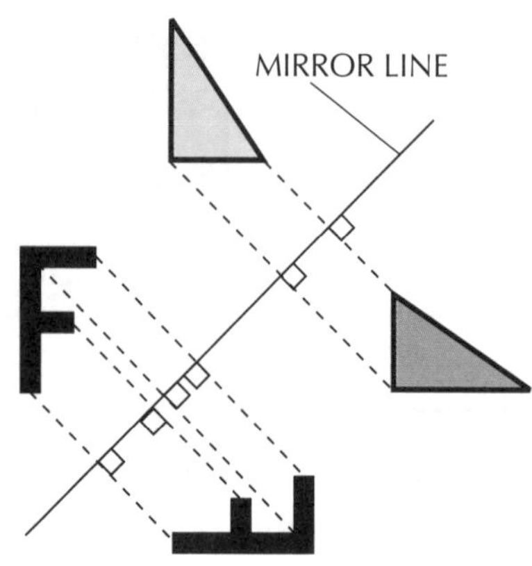

Symmetry

2 Plane Symmetry

Plane Symmetry is all to do with 3-D SOLIDS.
Whereas flat shapes can have a mirror line,
solid 3-D objects can have planes of symmetry.

A plane mirror surface can be drawn through many regular solids, but the shape must be exactly the same on both sides of the plane (i.e. mirror images), like these:

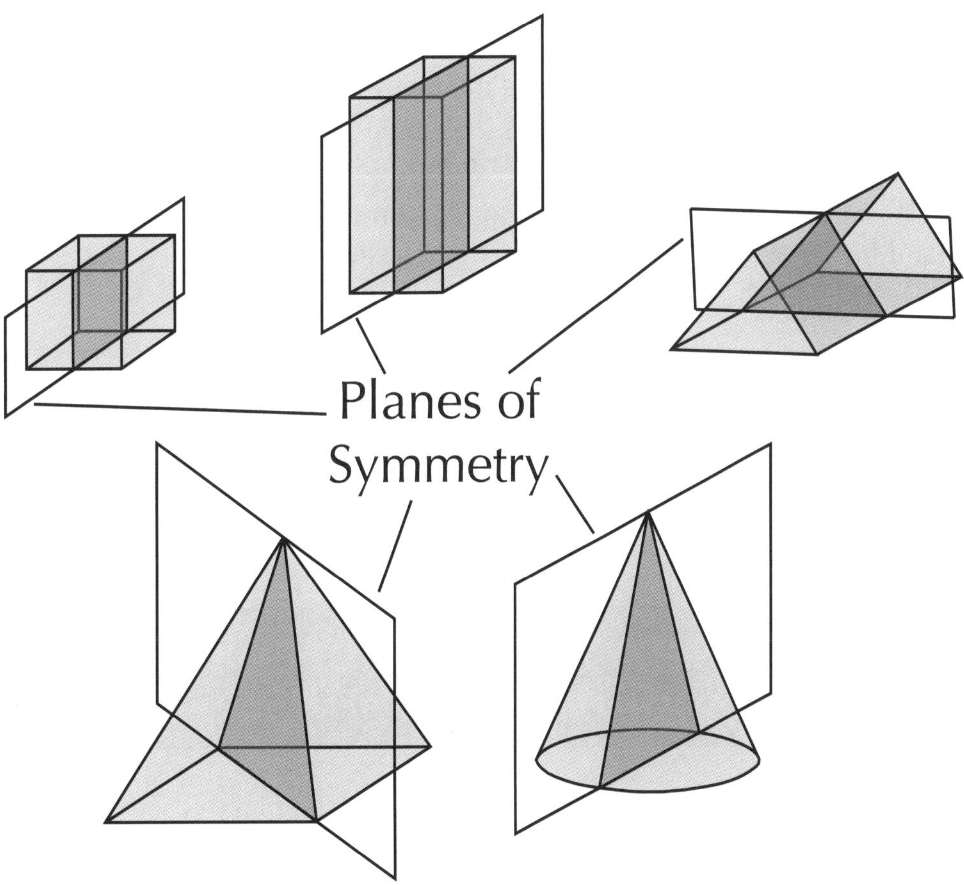

The shapes drawn here have more planes of symmetry but there's only one drawn in for each shape, because otherwise it would all get really messy and you wouldn't be able to see anything.
You could try finding some more though — it'd be good practice.

Symmetry

3 Rotational Symmetry

This is where the shape or drawing looks exactly the same when rotated into different positions.

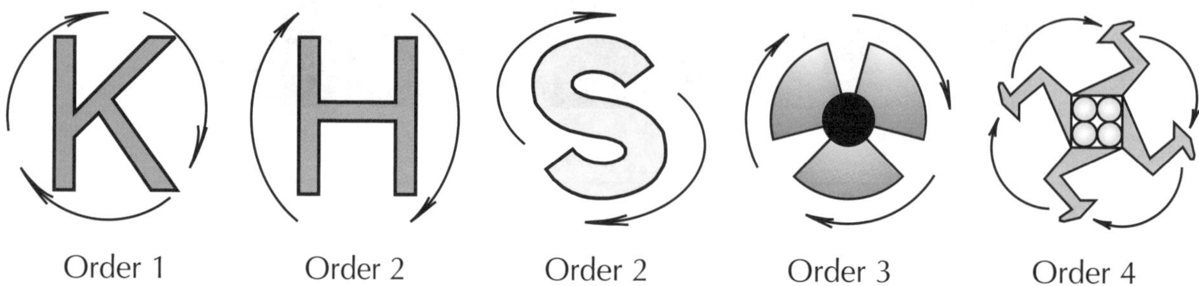

Two Key Points

1) The order of rotational symmetry is the fancy way of saying: "how many different positions look the same". e.g. you should say the S shape above has "rotational symmetry order 2".
2) BUT... when a shape has only 1 position you can either say that it has "rotational symmetry order 1" OR that it has "NO rotational symmetry".

Tracing Paper

SYMMETRY IS ALWAYS A LOT EASIER WITH TRACING PAPER

1) For reflections, trace one side of the drawing and the mirror line too. Then turn the paper over and line up the mirror line in its original position again. (If you put a blob on the mirror line it helps you get it back in position again.)
2) For rotations, just swizzle the tracing paper round. It's really good for finding the centre of rotation (by trial and error) as well as the order of rotational symmetry.
3) You can use tracing paper in the exam — so ask for it, or else take your own in with you.

You'll need to know about all three types of symmetry

You need to learn the details about line and plane symmetry, the 2 key points about rotational symmetry, and the 3 points about tracing paper. Make sure you learn some examples too.

The Shapes You Need to Know

These are easy marks in the exam — make sure you know them all.

1) SQUARE

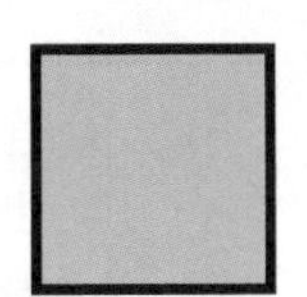
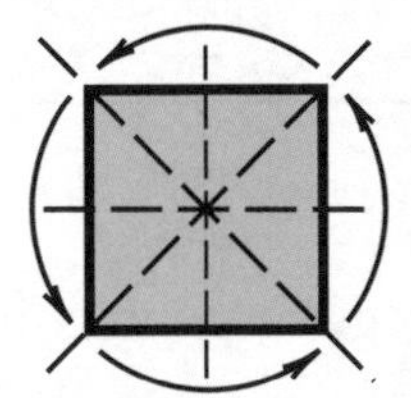

4 equal sides.
4 lines of symmetry.
Rotational symmetry order 4.

2) RECTANGLE

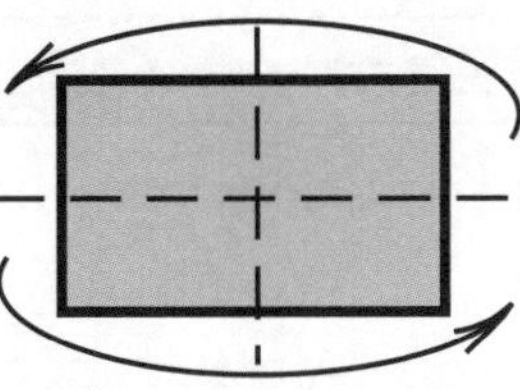

2 pairs of equal sides.
2 lines of symmetry.
Rotational symmetry order 2.

3) RHOMBUS

(A square pushed over — also a diamond)

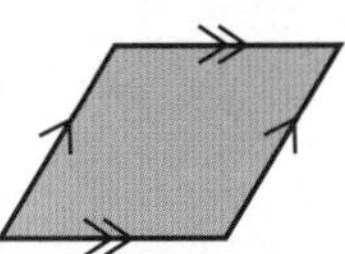
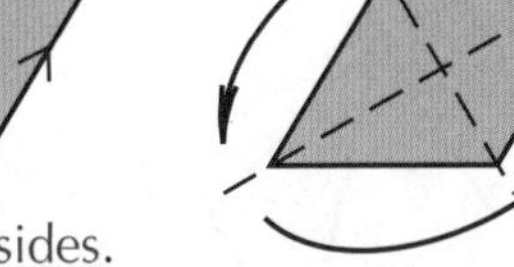
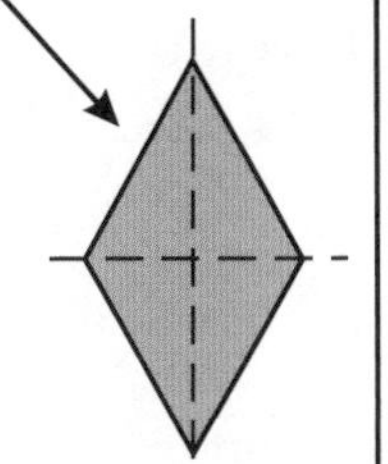

4 equal sides.
2 lines of symmetry.
Rotational symmetry order 2.

4) PARALLELOGRAM

(A rectangle pushed over — two pairs of parallel sides)

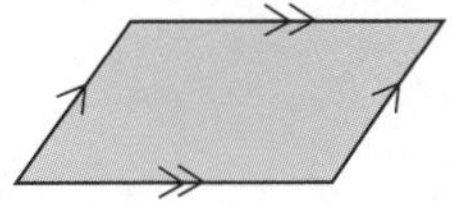
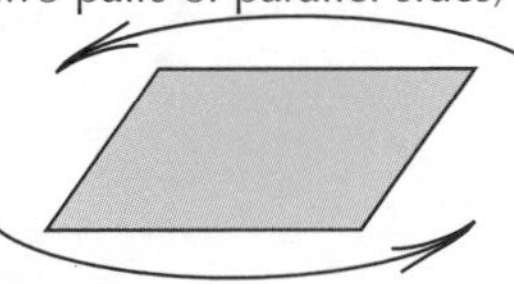

2 pairs of equal sides.
NO lines of symmetry.
Rotational symmetry order 2.

5) TRAPEZIUM

(One pair of parallel sides)

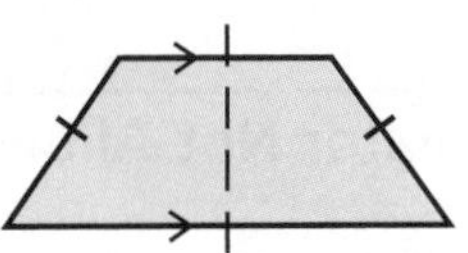
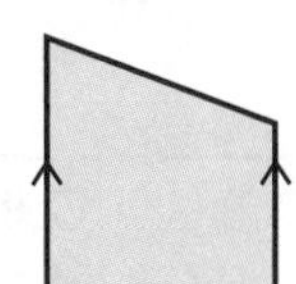
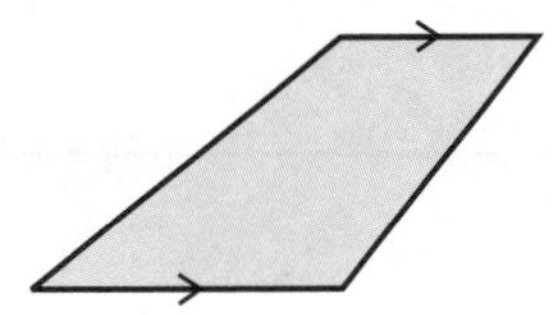

Only the isosceles trapezium has 2 equal sides and 1 line of symmetry.
None have rotational symmetry.

6) KITE

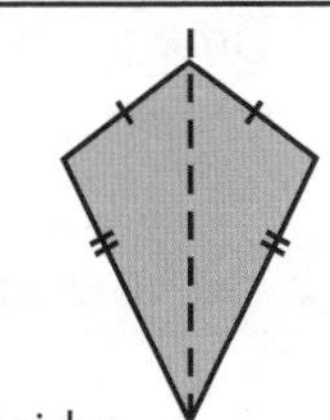

2 pairs of equal sides.
1 line of symmetry.
No rotational symmetry.

7) EQUILATERAL Triangle

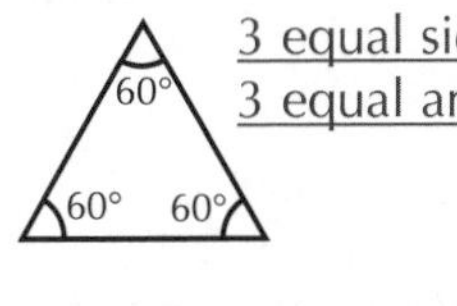

3 equal sides.
3 equal angles.

3 lines of symmetry.
Rotational symmetry order 3.

8) RIGHT-ANGLED Triangle

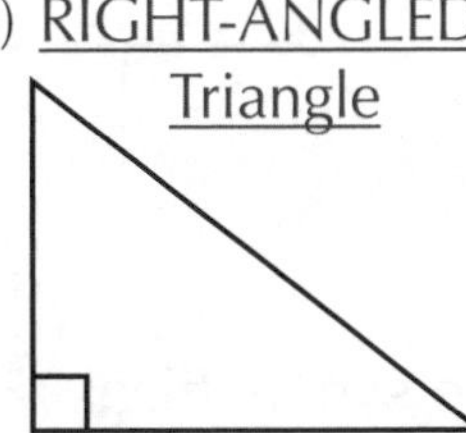

No symmetry unless angles are 45°.

9) ISOSCELES Triangle

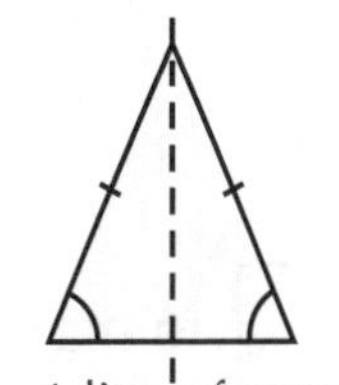
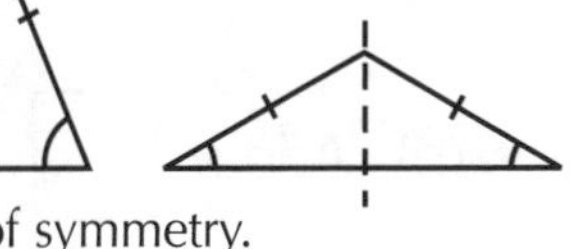

2 equal sides.
2 equal angles.

1 line of symmetry.
No rotational symmetry.

10) SOLIDS

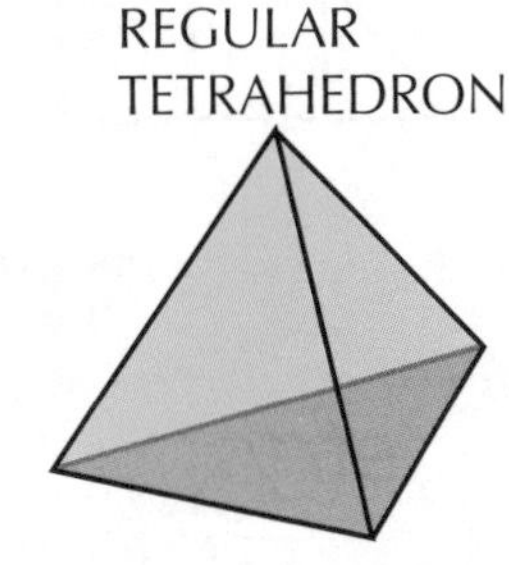

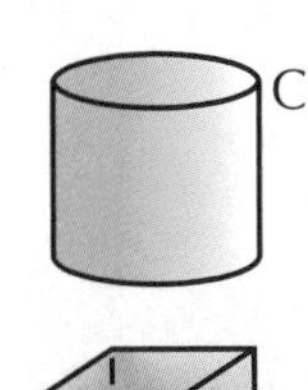

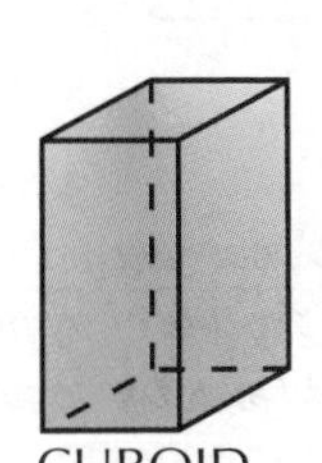

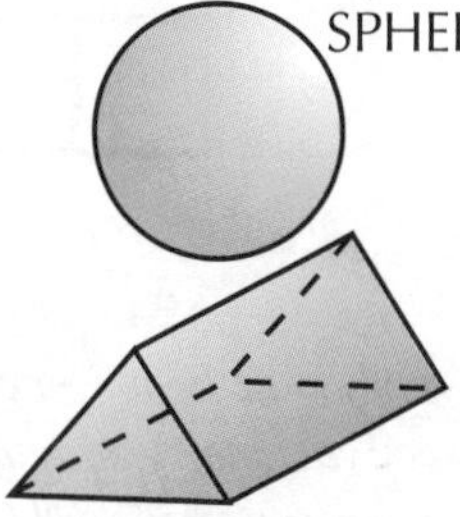

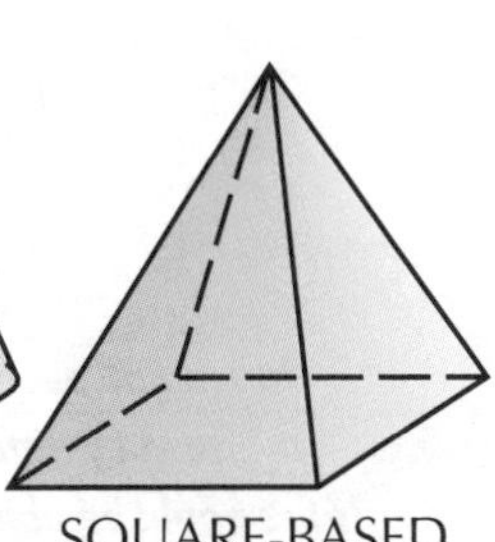

Warm-up and Worked Exam Questions

Same old, same old — race through these warm-up questions first to check you've learnt it all. There's no point struggling with the proper exam-type ones if there's stuff you don't know yet.

Warm-up Questions

1) How many lines of symmetry has a rectangle?
2) What is the order of rotational symmetry of a regular pentagon?
3) A regular polygon has interior angles of 140°. What is the size of each exterior angle?
4) Which quadrilateral has no lines of symmetry but has rotational symmetry of order 2?
5) (a) A regular polygon has exterior angles of 45°. How many sides has the polygon?
   (b) What size are the interior angles of this polygon?
6) (a) What name is given to the shape shown below?
   (b) How many lines of symmetry does it have?

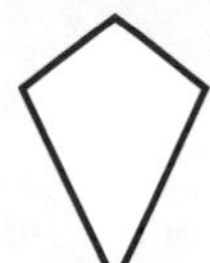

7) What name is given to this 3-D shape?

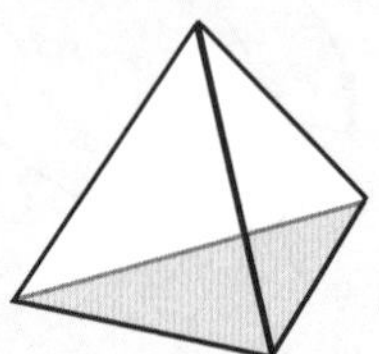

Time to see if all your hard work has paid off. If you haven't done any hard work you are very naughty and have to do them all twice as punishment.

Worked Exam Question

Calculator Not Allowed

1 (a) Draw the lines of symmetry on this square.

You should know from page 107 that a square has 4 lines of symmetry. That way you won't forget any.

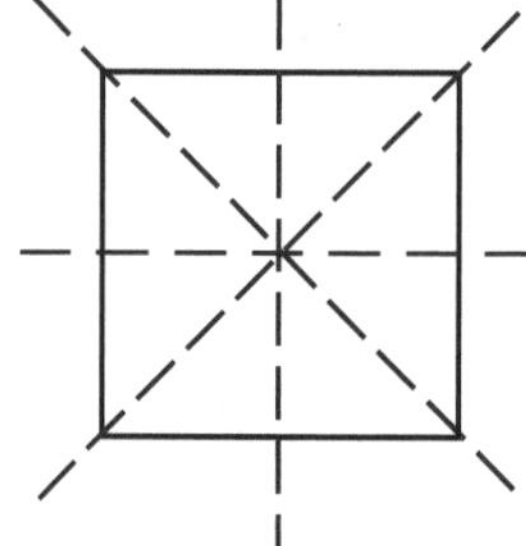

Remember, a line of symmetry is a line along which the two halves of a shape will fold exactly together.

(2 marks)

(b) Add a  to make this shape symmetrical. Find the 3 different ways to do it.

(i)

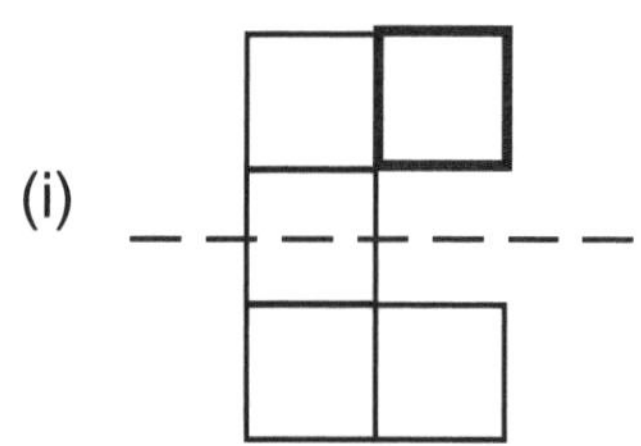

(ii)

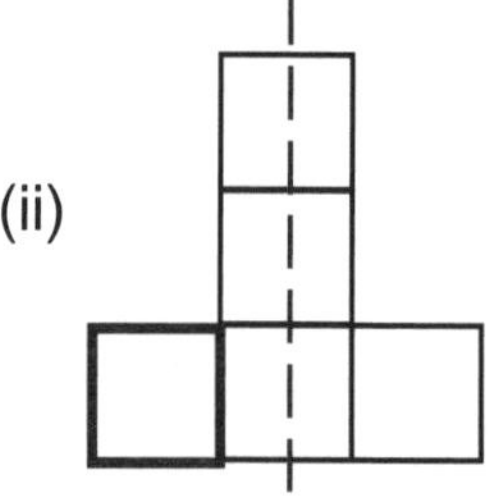

(iii)

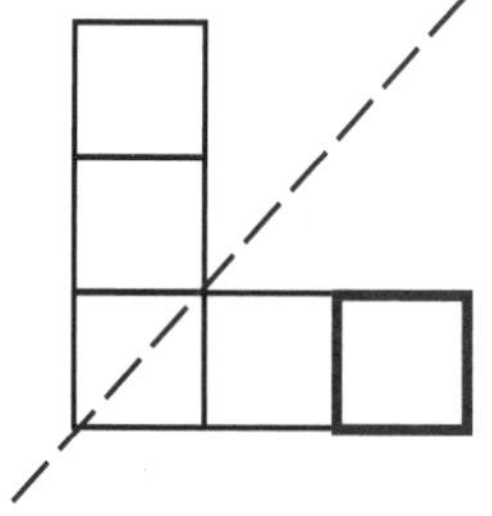

(3 marks)

This might seem harder than it really is at first — but once you get the idea it's pretty simple. Check what you've done by adding the line of symmetry. You should be able to see whether your new shape will fold exactly together along it.

Exam Questions

Exam Questions

Calculator Not Allowed

2 Draw in any lines of symmetry on this isosceles triangle.

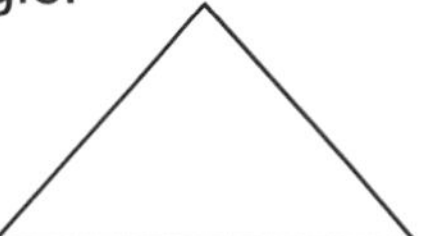

(1 mark)

3 Part of these squares have been shaded. Draw in their lines of symmetry.

(a)

(1 mark)

(b)

(2 marks)

4 (a) Reflect this shape in the mirror line.

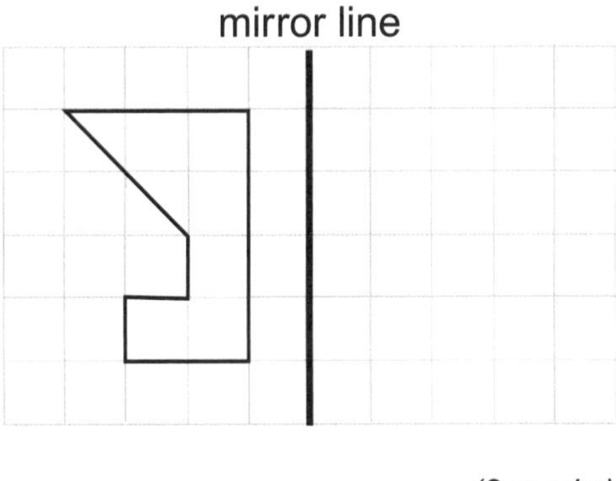

(2 marks)

(b) Reflect this triangle in the line y = x.

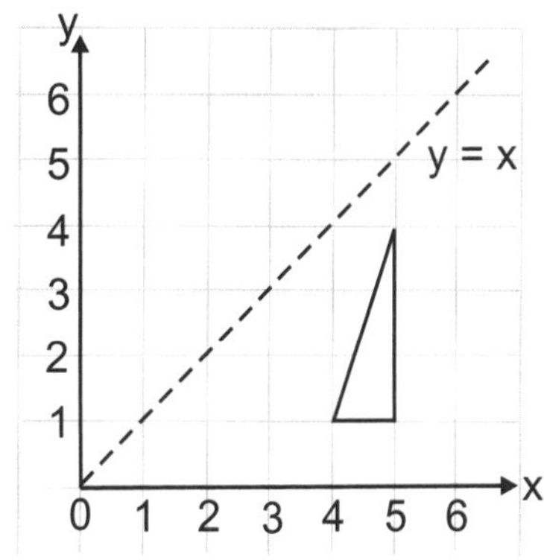

(2 marks)

5 (a) What is the order of rotational symmetry of a regular hexagon?

(1 mark)

(b) What is the order of rotational symmetry of the shaded hexagon on the right?

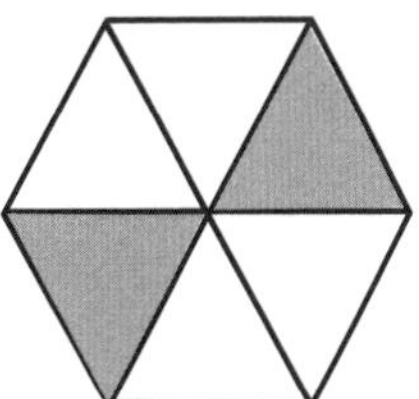

(1 mark)

(c) In this regular hexagon, find the sizes of the lettered angles. Do **not** use a protractor. (You may use a calculator for this question.)

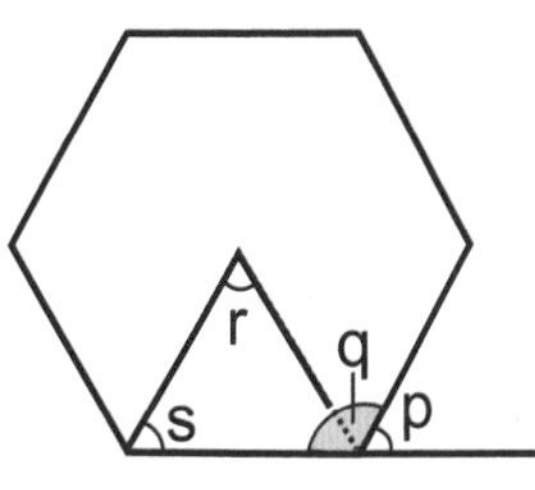

Diagram not drawn to scale

(4 marks)

Areas

You need to have all these area formulae firmly fixed in your brain. That includes the ones given to you inside the front cover of the exam paper — I guarantee that if you don't actually learn them, you'll be incapable of using them when it comes to the exam.

YOU MUST LEARN THESE FORMULAE:

1 Rectangle

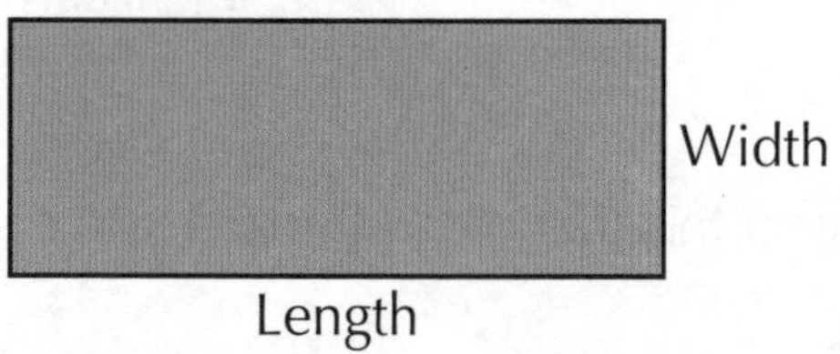

Area of RECTANGLE = length × width

$$A = l \times w$$

2 Triangle

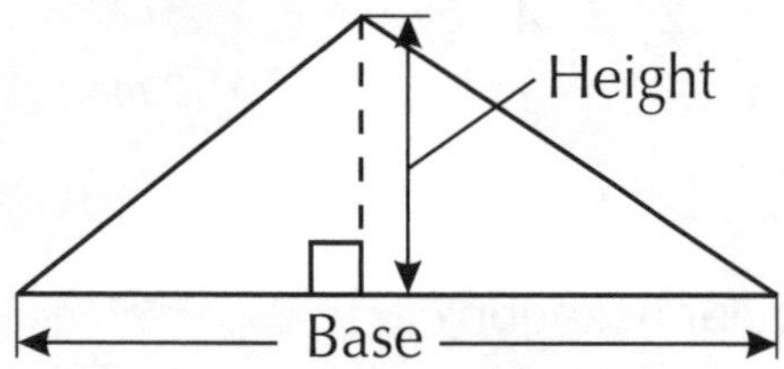

Area of TRIANGLE = ½ × base x vertical height

$$A = \frac{1}{2} \times b \times h_v$$

Note that the height must always be the vertical height, not the sloping height.

3 Parallelogram

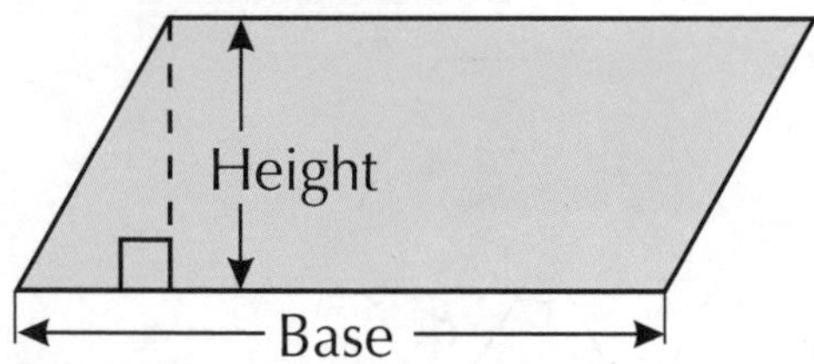

Area of PARALLELOGRAM = base × vertical height

$$A = b \times h_v$$

Areas

4 Trapezium

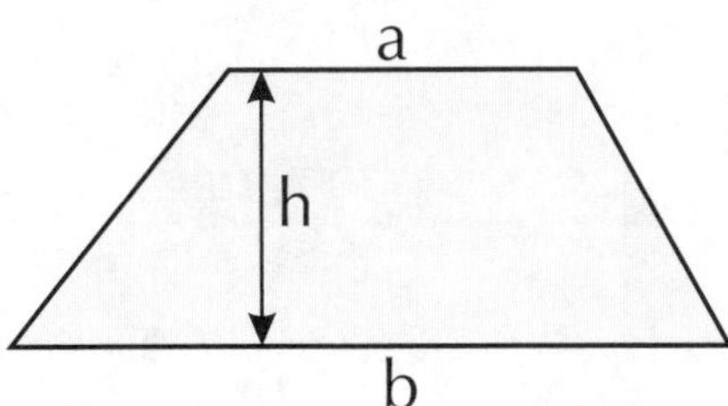

Area of <u>TRAPEZIUM</u> =
half the sum of the parallel sides × distance between them

$$A = \frac{1}{2} \times (a + b) \times h$$

5 Circle

π = 3.141592....
= <u>3.14</u> (approx)

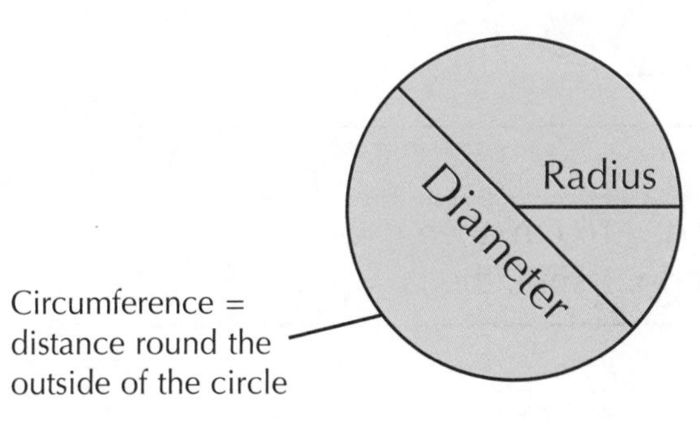

<u>Don't</u> muddle up these <u>two circle formulae</u>.

<u>AREA</u>
= π × (radius)^2

$$A = \pi \times r^2$$

For example, if the radius is 3cm, then
A = 3.14 × (3×3) = <u>28 cm^2</u> (to nearest whole number)

<u>CIRCUMFERENCE</u>
= π × diameter
(= 2πr because diameter = 2 × radius)

$$C = \pi \times d$$

If these circle formulae are worrying you, <u>don't panic</u>. Just have a look at the next page — that's got more on the strange bits, like π. Then <u>page 113</u> explains how you decide <u>which formula</u> to use. It's all much simpler than it looks at first glance.

Don't forget — you MUST learn these formulae

Once you've learnt these pages on <u>areas</u>, close the book and <u>write down</u> as much of it as you can from memory. Have a look to see how well you've done, then try it <u>again</u>.

Circle Questions

Here are a few circle-type words that you'll need to understand before you can answer any circle-type questions.

1 π "A Number a Bit Bigger than 3"

The big thing to remember is that π, called "pi" (pronounced like apple pie), is just an ordinary number. It's 3.14159... , which is often rounded off to either 3 or 3.14 or 3.142.

And that's all it is — a number a bit bigger than 3.

For calculations, get used to using the π button on your calculator instead of 3.14 or 3.142 — it's just as easy and way more accurate.

2 Diameter is Twice the Radius

The DIAMETER goes right across the centre of the circle.
The RADIUS only goes halfway across.

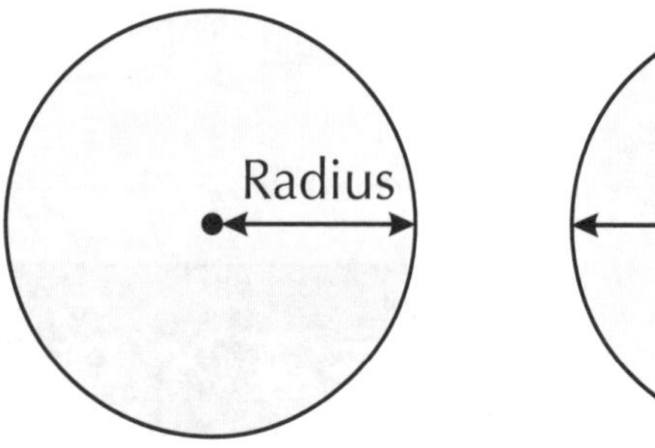

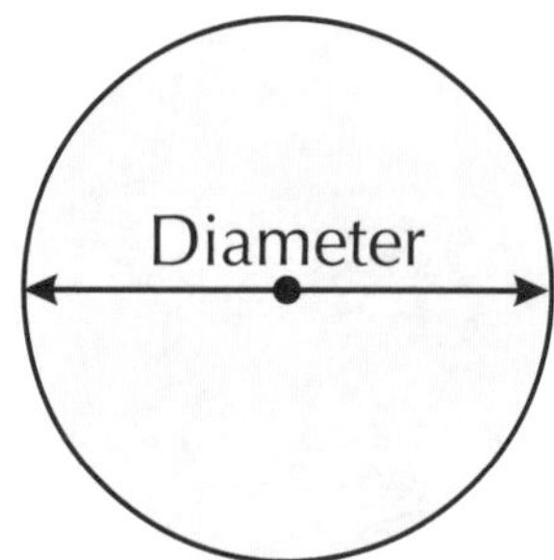

EXAMPLES:
If the radius is 4 cm, the diameter is 8 cm. If d = 16 cm, then r = 8 cm.
If the radius is 9 m, the diameter is 18 m. If d = 6 mm, then r = 3 mm.

3 Arc, Chord and Tangent

A TANGENT is a straight line that just touches the outside of the circle.

A CHORD is any line drawn across the inside of a circle. (It could even be a diameter.)

An ARC is just part of the circumference of the circle.

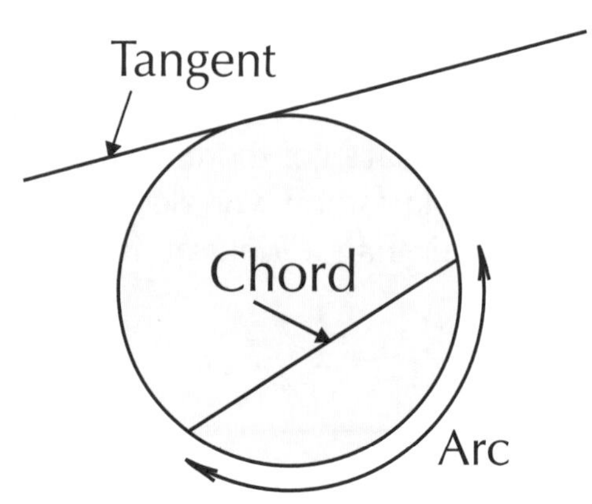

Circle Questions

4 The **Big** Decision:

"Which circle formula do I use?"

WORKING OUT AREA OR CIRCUMFERENCE — there is a difference you know!

1) If the question asks for "the area of the circle", you must use the formula for area:

$$A = \pi \times r^2$$

2) If the question asks for "circumference" (the distance around the circle) you must use the formula for circumference:

$$C = \pi \times d$$

And remember, it makes no difference at all whether the question gives you the radius or the diameter, because it's dead easy to work out one from the other.

EXAMPLE: *"Find the circumference and the area of the circle shown below."*

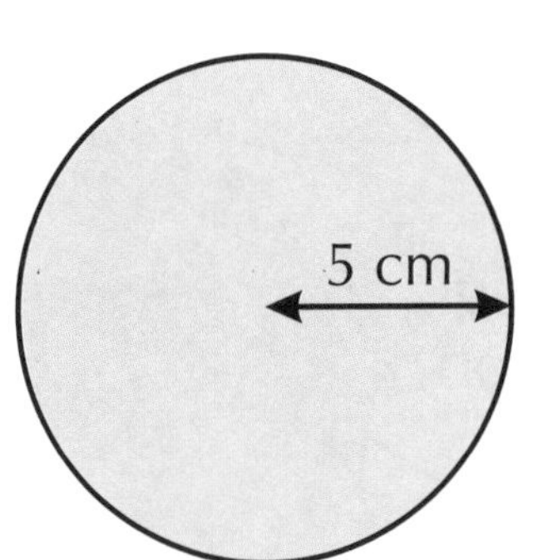

ANSWER: Radius = 5 cm, so diameter = 10 cm

Formula for circumference is:
$C = \pi \times d$, so
$C = \pi \times 10$
$= 31.4$ cm (3 s.f.)

Formula for area is:
$A = \pi \times r^2$, so
$A = \pi \times (5 \times 5)$
$= \pi \times 25 = 78.5\text{ cm}^2$ (3 s.f.)

When you're using the π button, just leave the π sign in your working, and show your rounding at the end.

π is just a number that's useful in circle questions

You've got to learn both the circle equations, but it's just as important that you know when to use each one. It's pretty simple once you've got that sorted out.

Perimeters and Areas

You can work out the perimeters and areas of all kinds of funny-looking shapes — it's easy when you know how.

1 Perimeters of Complicated Shapes

Make sure you know these nitty gritty details about perimeter:

1) Perimeter is the distance all the way around the outside of a 2D shape.
2) To find a perimeter, you add up the lengths of all the sides, but.... the only reliable way to make sure you get all the sides is this:

The Big Blob Method

1) Put a big blob at one corner and then go around the shape.
2) Write down the length of every side as you go — even sides that seem to have no length given — you must work them out.
3) Keep going until you get back to the big blob.

It's easy enough to work out the length of a side if none is given. For example, if the 6 cm side on the diagram below wasn't labelled, you'd just add up the 3 short vertical sides (2 cm + 2 cm + 2 cm) to get 6 cm. Easy.

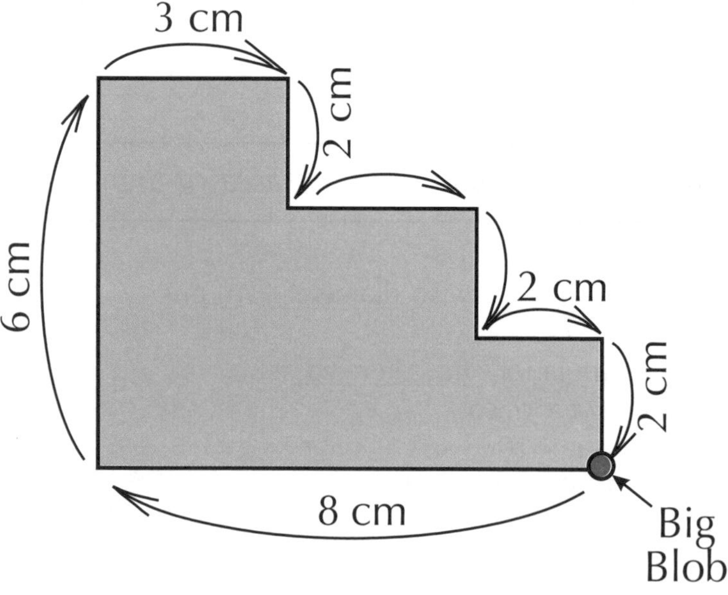

e.g. 8 + 6 + 3 + 2 + 3 + 2 + 2 + 2 = 28 cm

Yes, I know you think it's yet another fussy method, but believe me, it's so easy to miss a side. You must use good reliable methods for everything — or you'll be losing marks everywhere.

Perimeters and Areas

2 *Areas* of Complicated Shapes

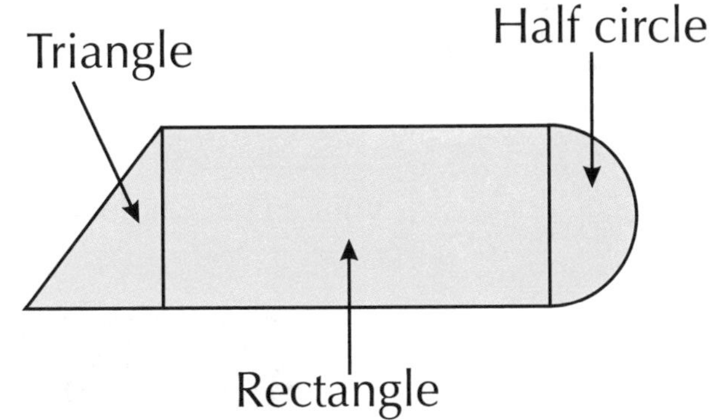

1) Split them up into the 3 basic shapes: rectangle, triangle, and circle.
2) Work out the area of each bit separately.
3) Then add them all together (or sometimes subtract them).

Example *"Work out the area of this shape."*

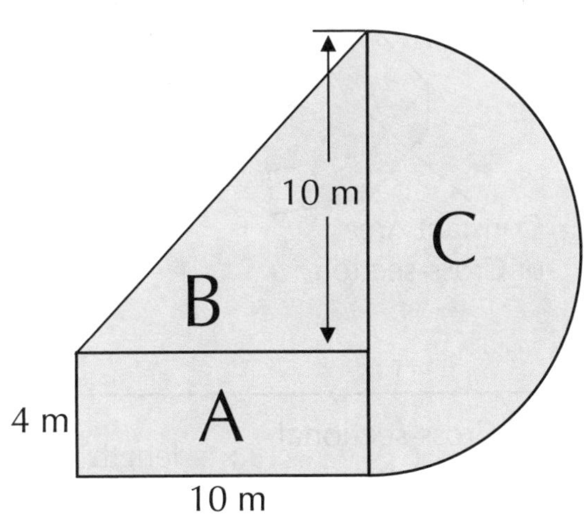

ANSWER:

Rectangle A:

Area $= l \times w$
$= 10 \times 4$
$= 40\ m^2$

Triangle B:

Area $= \frac{1}{2} \times b \times h$
$= \frac{1}{2} \times 10 \times 10$
$= 50\ m^2$

Semicircle C:

Area $= (\pi \times r^2) \div 2$
$= (\pi \times 7^2) \div 2$
$= 76.97\ m^2$ (3 s.f.)

TOTAL AREA = 40 + 50 + 76.97 = $166.97\ m^2$

The shapes may be complicated, but the method isn't

In fact it's really easy splitting up shapes into circles, triangles and squares. Just make sure you know how to work out the perimeters and areas of the simple shapes and you'll be fine.

Volume and Capacity

Volumes — You Must Learn These Too!

1 Cuboid *(rectangular block)*

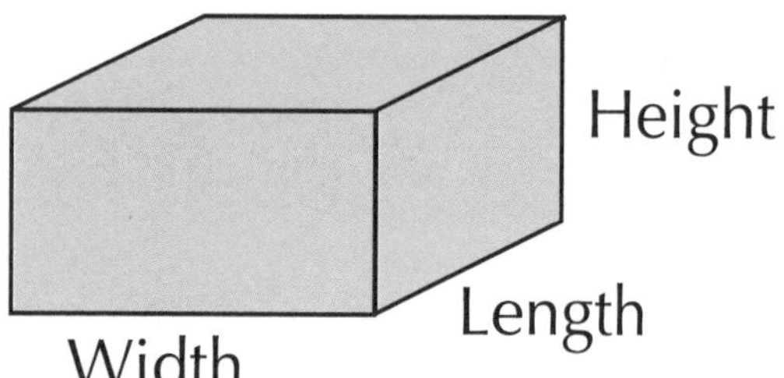

Volume of Cuboid = length × width × height

(The other word for volume is capacity.)

2 Prism

A prism is a solid (3-D) object which has a constant area of cross-section — i.e. it's the same shape all the way through.

Now, for some reason, not a lot of people know what a prism is, but they come up all the time in exams, so make sure you know.

Circular Prism
(or Cylinder)

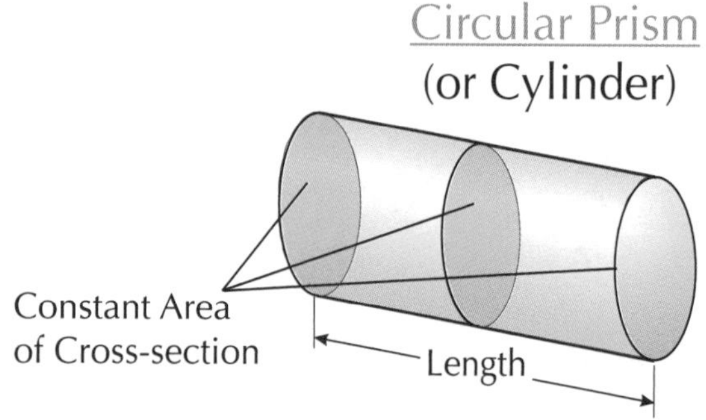

Hexagonal Prism
(a flat one, certainly, but still a prism)

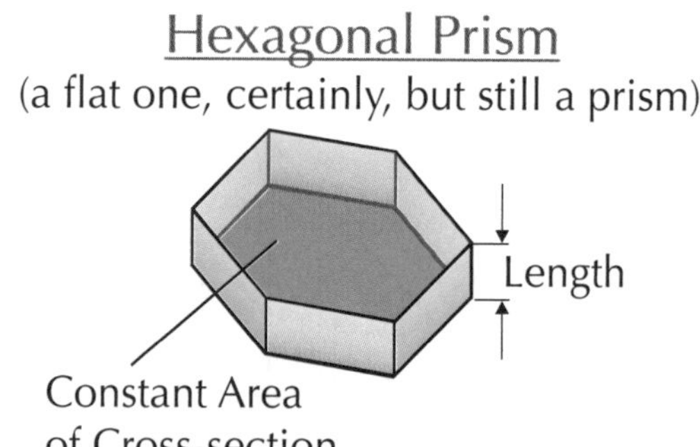

Triangular Prism

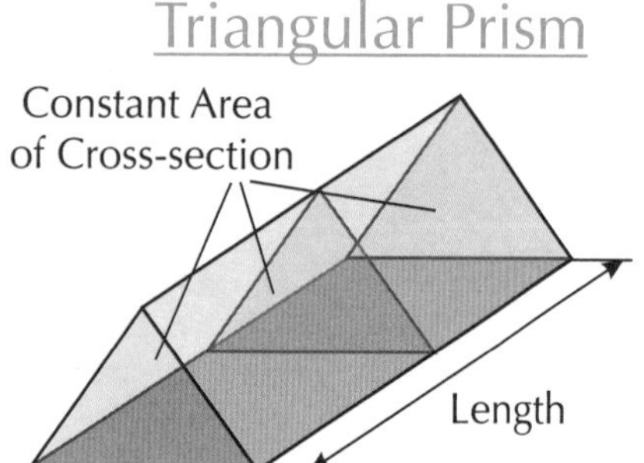

Volume of prism = Cross-sectional area × length

V = A × l

As you can see, the formula for the volume of a prism is very simple. The difficult part, usually, is finding the area of the cross-section.

Solids and Nets

You need to know what face, edge and vertex mean:

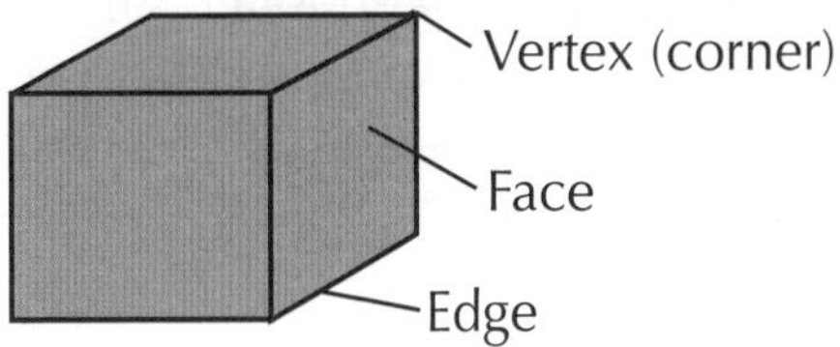

Surface Area and Nets

1) Surface area only applies to solid 3D objects, and it's simply the total area of all the outer surfaces added together. If you were painting it, it's all the bits you'd paint.
2) There is never a simple formula for surface area — you have to work out the area of each face in turn and then add them all together.
3) A net is just a solid shape folded out flat.
4) So obviously: surface area of solid = area of net.

There are 4 nets that you need to know really well for the exam, and they're shown below. They may well ask you to draw one of these nets and then work out its area.

1 Triangular Prism

4 cm
6 cm
15 cm

Net of Triangular Prism
5 cm
6 cm
4 cm
15 cm
5 cm

2 Cube

5 cm
Net of Cube
5 cm

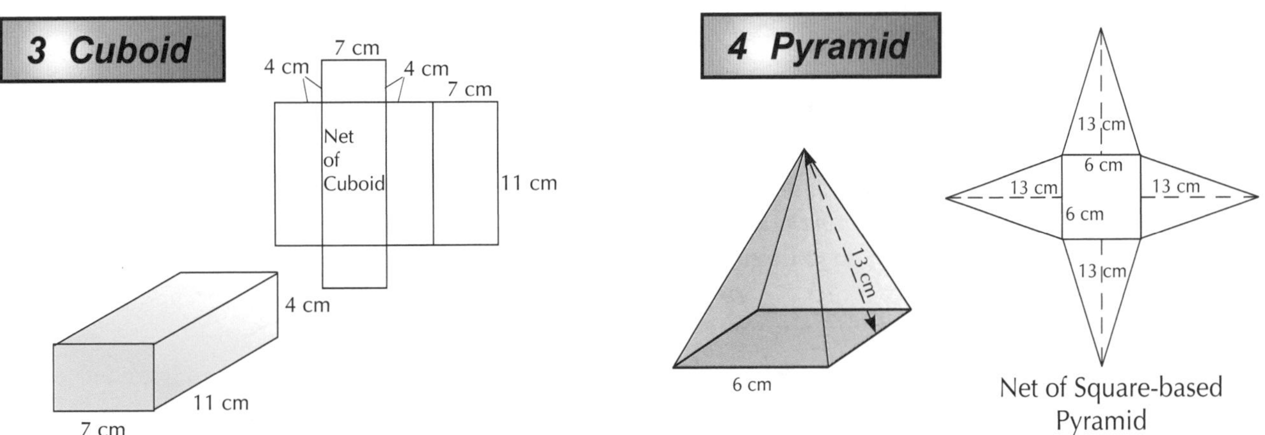

Make sure you can draw each of the four nets

Of course the lengths of the sides will be different — they'll be given to you in the exam. But the basic shape will be the same, and knowing it before the exam will save loads of time.

Warm-up and Worked Exam Questions

I'm not trying to pretend that doing warm-up questions is a fun way to pass the time — it isn't. It's just the best way to check that you've really been learning this stuff, not just kidding yourself.

Warm-up Questions

1) A triangle is 5 cm tall and the length of its base is 12 cm. Find its area.
2) How many edges does a cube have?
3) A rectangle has an area of 20 cm^2 and a length of 5 cm. Find its width.
4) If the diameter of a circle is 6 cm, what is its radius?
5) What is the mathematical name for the shape of a tin of beans?
6) How many vertices does a cuboid have?
7) A square has a perimeter of 24 cm. Find its area.
8) Find the area of a circle with radius 10 cm, to the nearest cm.
9) What name is given to the straight line which touches the circumference of a circle at one point?
10) Find the total surface area of a cube with edges of length 5 cm.

Don't just skim through these worked examples —
I've gone to the effort of showing all this working out, and I want it appreciated.

Worked Exam Question

1 Look at the shape below. Find:

(a) its area *(3 marks)*

(b) its perimeter *(2 marks)*

6 cm

10 cm – 6 cm = 4 cm

8 cm

5 cm

10 cm

The easiest way to find the area of this shape is to split it into 2 rectangles. I've split it vertically into a rectangle of 8 cm by 6 cm and a rectangle of 4 cm by 5 cm.

(a) Area of 1st rectangle = 8 × 6 = 48 cm².

Area of 2nd rectangle = 5 × (10 – 6) = 5 × 4 = 20 cm².

So total area of shape = 48 + 20 = 68 cm².

To find the perimeter of the shape, you need to add together the lengths of all its sides using the big blob method as shown in the diagram. However there are a couple of sides where lengths haven't been given, so you need to work those out first.

(b) Vertical missing side = 8 – 5 = 3 cm.

Horizontal missing side = 10 – 6 = 4 cm.

Perimeter = 6 + 3 + 4 + 5 + 10 + 8

= 36 cm.

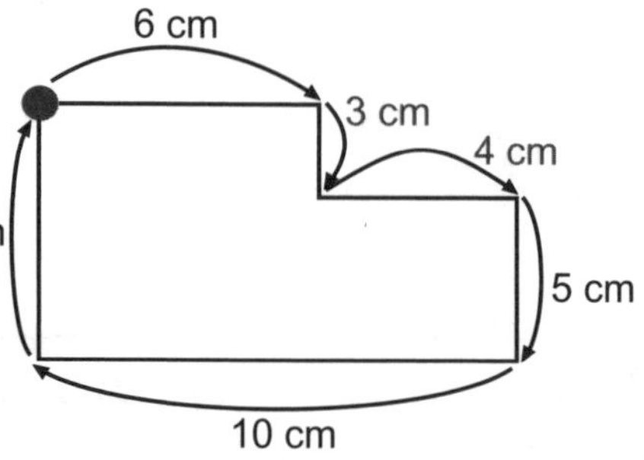

Exam Questions

Exam Questions

Calculator Allowed

2 This arrow-head is formed from two parallelograms of the same area.
Find the area of the shape. Include the units.

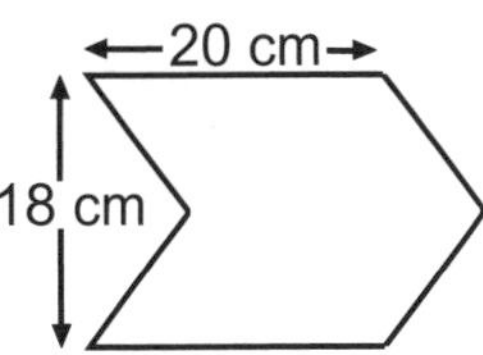

(3 marks)

3 A malt loaf has dimensions 20 cm by 10 cm by 10 cm.

(a) Work out its approximate volume.

(2 marks)

(b) The malt loaf is cut into 25 slices of the same thickness.
Find the thickness of each slice.

(2 marks)

4 These shapes each have an area of 12 cm^2. Find the missing lengths.

(a) p, 8 cm

(b)

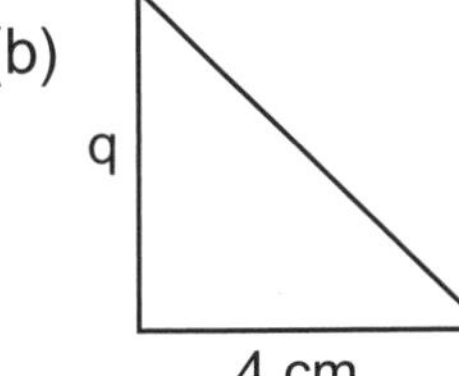

(c)

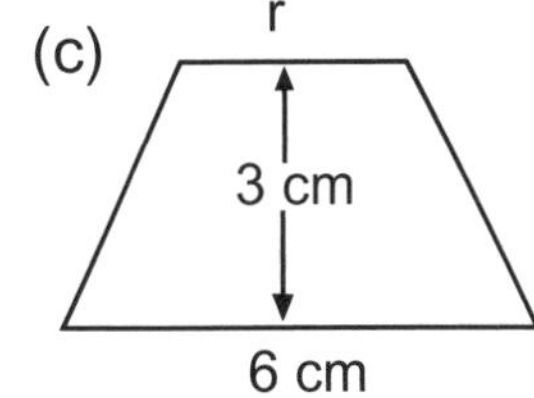

(6 marks)

5 A bicycle wheel has a diameter of 60 cm.

(a) Find the circumference of the wheel.

(2 marks)

(b) How many complete revolutions will the wheel make in covering a distance of 1 km?

(3 marks)

6 The perimeter of the rectangle shown below is 24 cm.

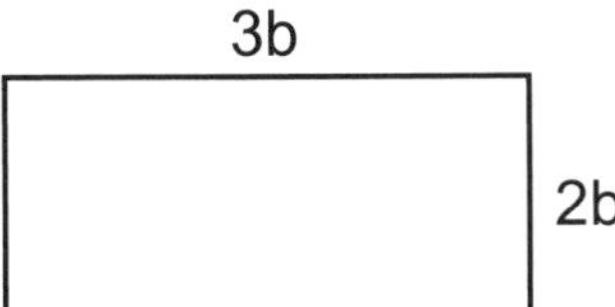

(a) Find b.

(2 marks)

(b) Find the area of the rectangle, to one decimal place.

(3 marks)

Exam Questions

Exam Questions

7 Find the shaded area:

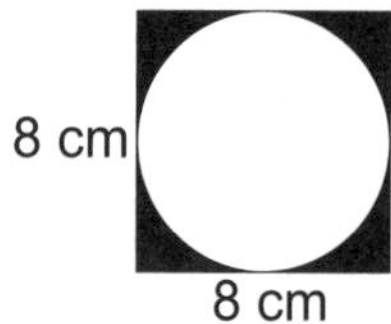

(4 marks)

8 Find the volume of this triangular prism.

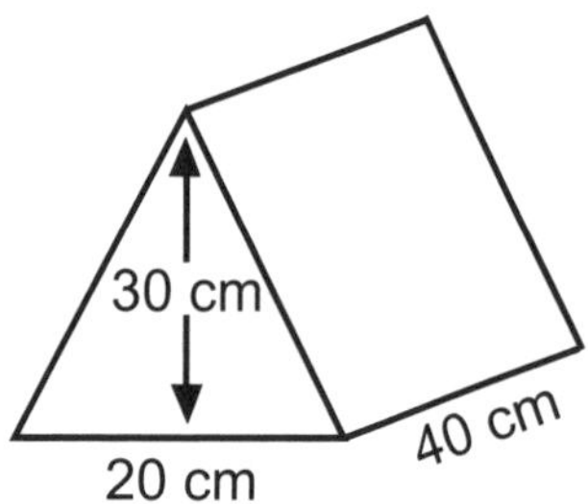

(3 marks)

9 Find (a) the area

(3 marks)

(b) the perimeter of this quarter-circle.

(3 marks)

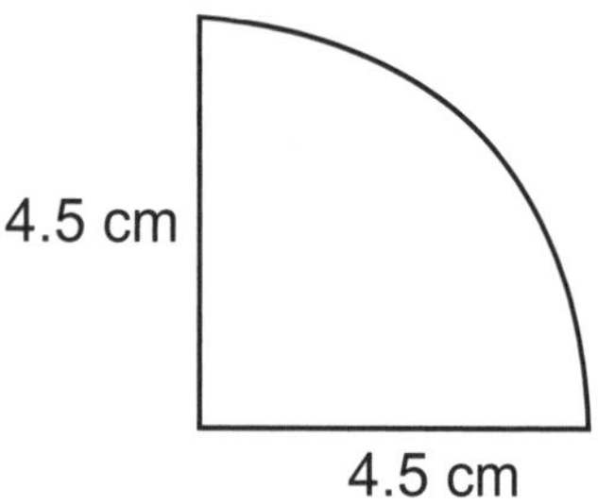

10 This cuboid and this triangular prism have the same volume.

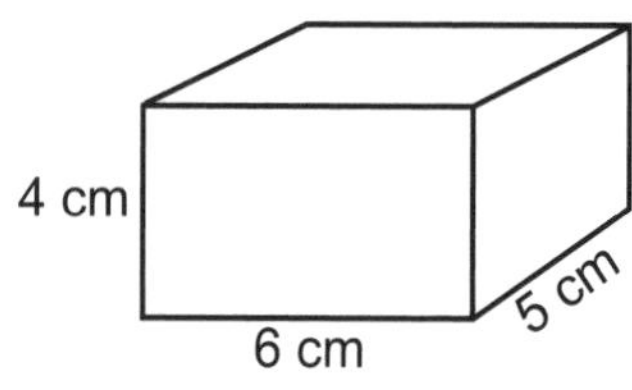

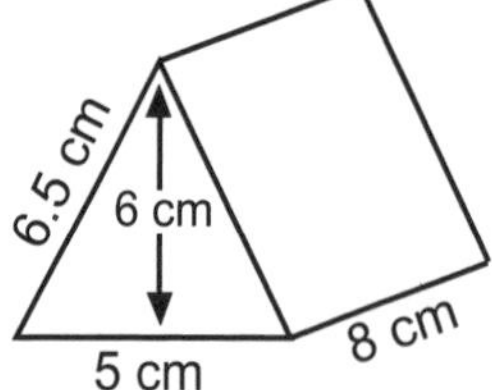

(a) Sketch a net for each of them. The nets need not be drawn accurately, but you must include labels to show their dimensions where necessary.

(6 marks)

(b) Do they have the same surface area? Show your working.

(5 marks)

Geometry

8 Simple Rules — that's all

If you know them all thoroughly, you at least have a fighting chance of working out problems with lines and angles. If you don't — you've no chance.

1 Angles in a Triangle

Add up to 180°.

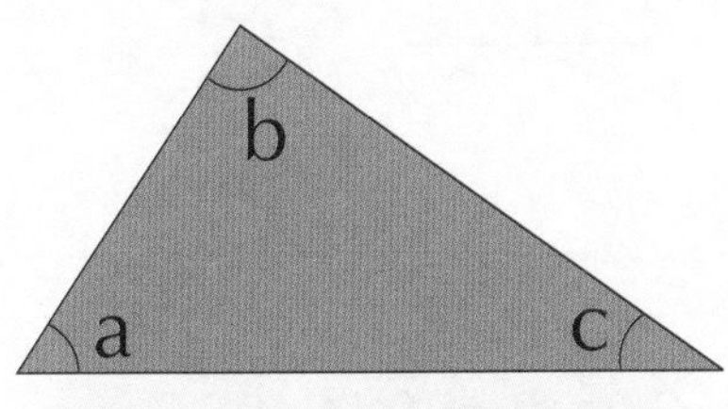

a + b + c = 180°

2 Angles on a Straight Line

Add up to 180°.

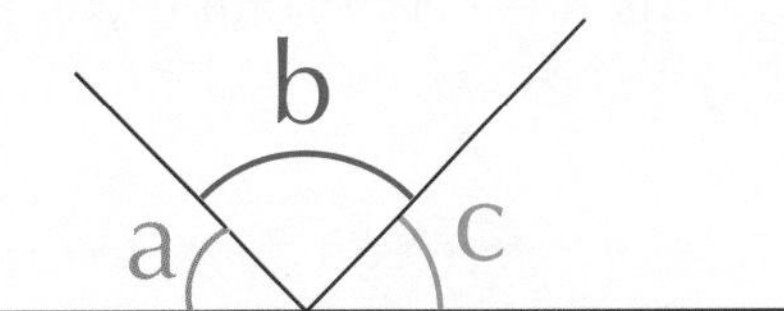

a + b + c = 180°

ACUTE angles are sharp pointy ones (between 0° and 90°).
OBTUSE angles are flatter (between 90° and 180°).

3 Angles in a 4-sided Shape

Add up to 360°.

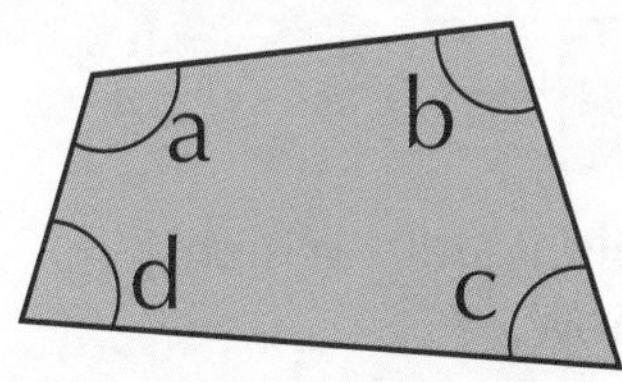

a + b + c + d = 360°

4 Angles Round a Point

Add up to 360°.

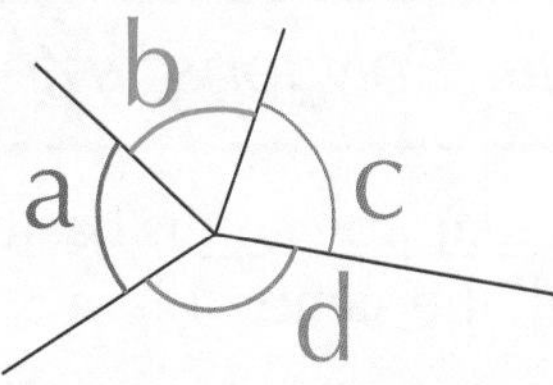

a + b + c + d = 360°

A QUADRILATERAL is just any four-sided shape. So squares, rectangles, parallelograms, etc. are all quadrilaterals. And so are lots of other more random ones.

5 Exterior Angle of Triangle

Exterior angle of triangle
= sum of opposite interior angles

a + b = d

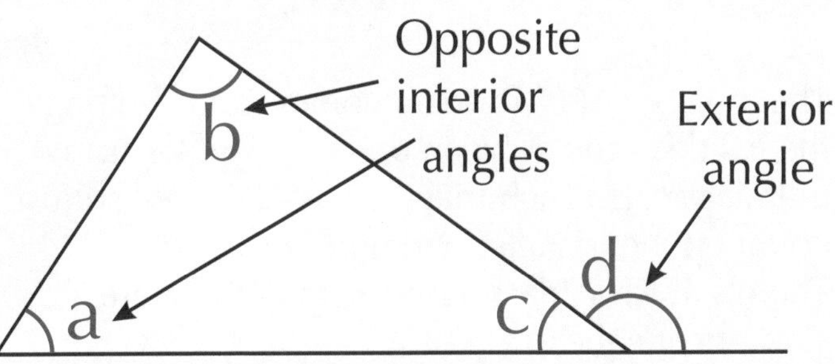

Geometry

6 Isosceles Triangles

2 sides the same
2 angles the same

In an isosceles triangle, you only need to know one angle to be able to find the other two, which is very useful if you remember it.

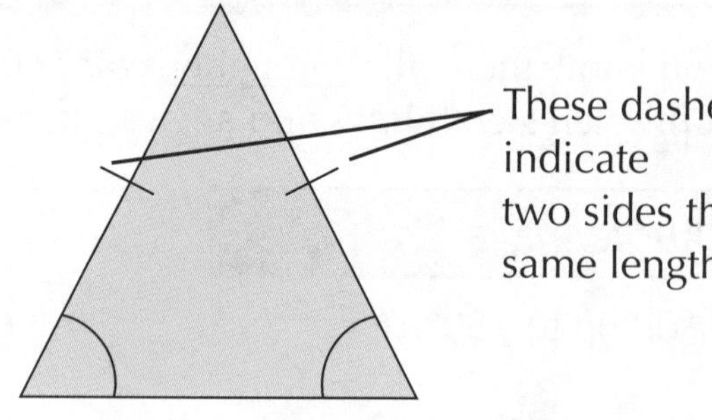

a)

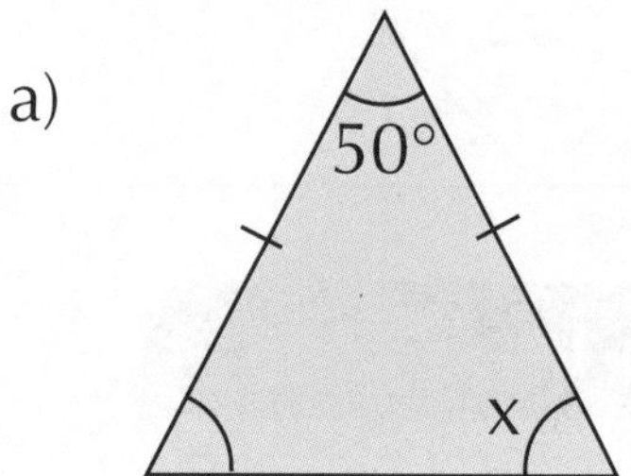

180° – 50° = 130°
The two bottom angles are both the same and they must add up to 130°, so each one must be half of 130° (= 65°).
So x = 65°.

b)

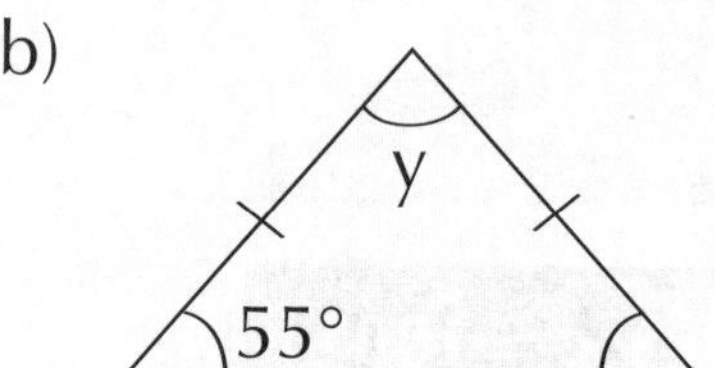

The two bottom angles must be the same, so 55° + 55° = 110°.
All the angles add up to 180° so y = 180° – 110° = 70°.

7 Irregular Polygons: Interior and Exterior Angles

An irregular polygon is basically any shape with lots of straight sides which aren't all the same. There are two formulae you need to know:

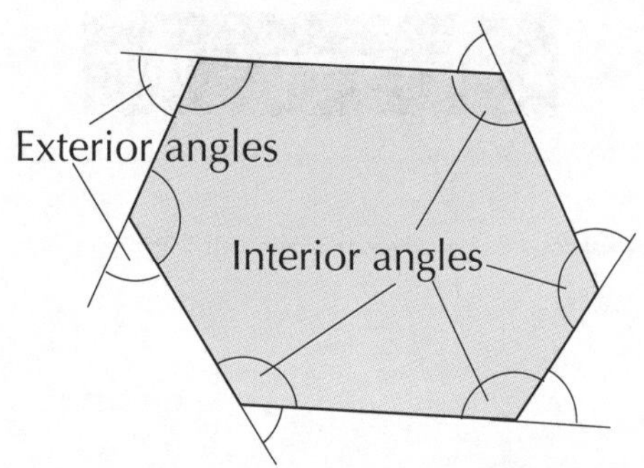

Sum of exterior angles = 360°

Sum of interior angles = (n – 2) × 180°
(where n is the number of sides)

The (n – 2) × 180° formula comes from splitting the inside of the polygon up into triangles using full diagonals. Each triangle has 180° in it so just count up the triangles and times by 180°. There's always 2 less triangles than there are sides, hence the (n – 2).

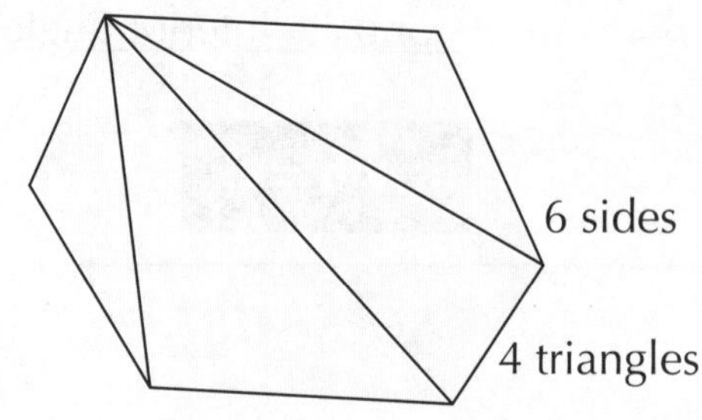

Geometry

8 Parallel Lines

Whenever a line goes across 2 parallel lines, then the two bunches of angles are the same. (The arrows mean those 2 lines are parallel.)

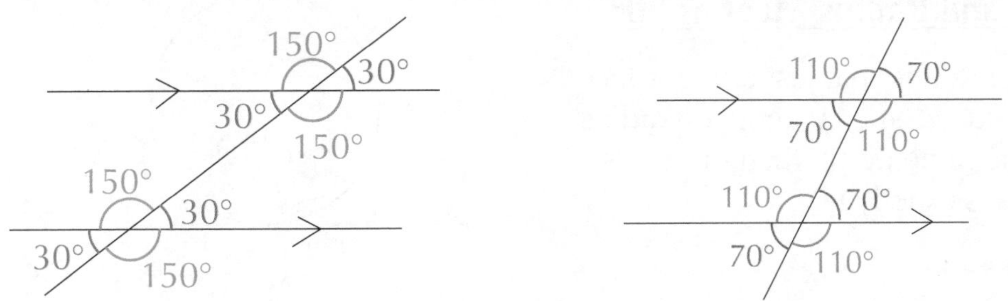

Whenever you have two parallel lines there are only two different angles: a small one and a big one and they always add up to 180°.
For example: 30° and 150° or 70° and 110°.

The trickiest bit about parallel lines is spotting them in the first place — watch out for these "Z", "C", "U" and "F" shapes popping up:

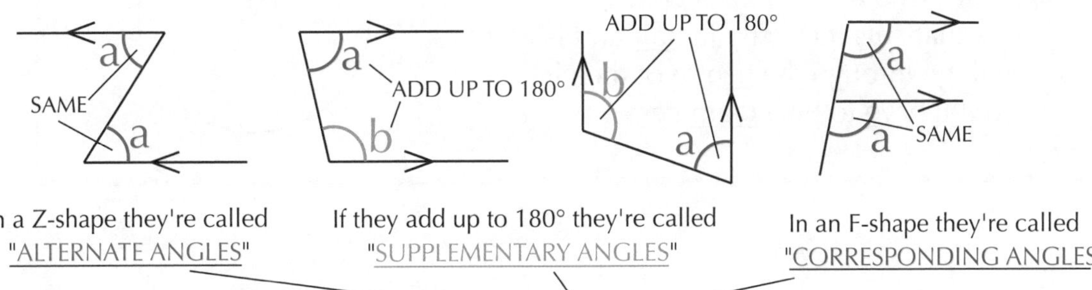

In a Z-shape they're called "ALTERNATE ANGLES"

If they add up to 180° they're called "SUPPLEMENTARY ANGLES"

In an F-shape they're called "CORRESPONDING ANGLES"

And it'd be a good idea to learn these three silly names, too!

If necessary, extend the lines to make the diagram easier to get to grips with:

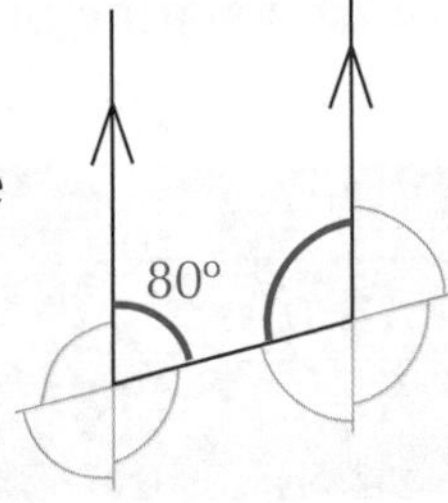

As promised, just eight simple rules to learn...

When you think you've got them all memorised, shut the book and try to write down all eight, each with a diagram. Don't forget to learn the three types of angles from the parallel lines bit.

Circle Geometry

Three Simple Rules — that's all

You'll have to learn these too if you want to be able to do circle problems.

1) Tangent and Radius Meet at 90°

A tangent is a line that just touches the edge of a curve. If a tangent and radius meet at the same point, then the angle they make is exactly 90°.

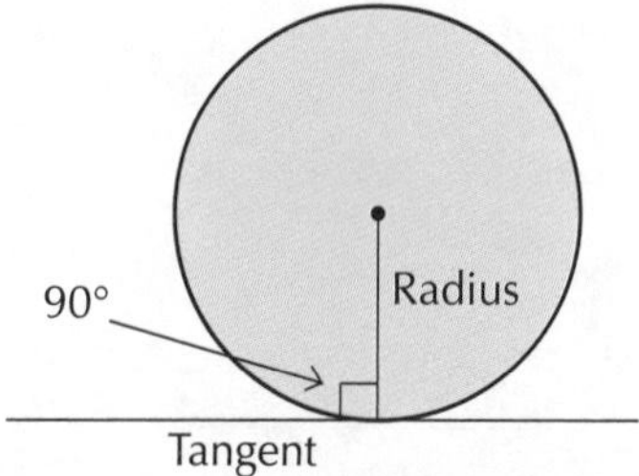

2) Sneaky Isosceles Triangles formed by Two Radii

Unlike other isosceles triangles they don't have the little tick marks on the sides to remind you that they're the same — the fact that two sides are radii is enough to make it an isosceles triangle.

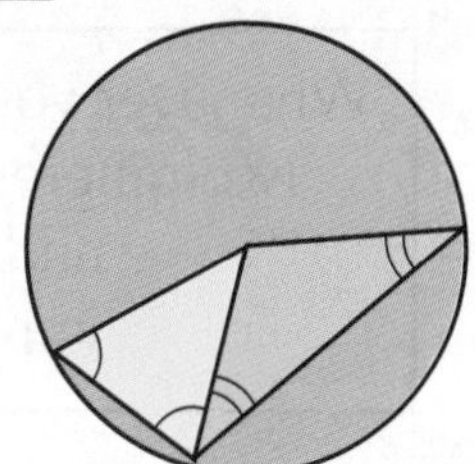

3) Chord Bisector is a Diameter

A chord is any line drawn across a circle. No matter where you draw a chord, the line that cuts it exactly in half and is at 90° to it will go through the centre of the circle and so it'll have to be a diameter.

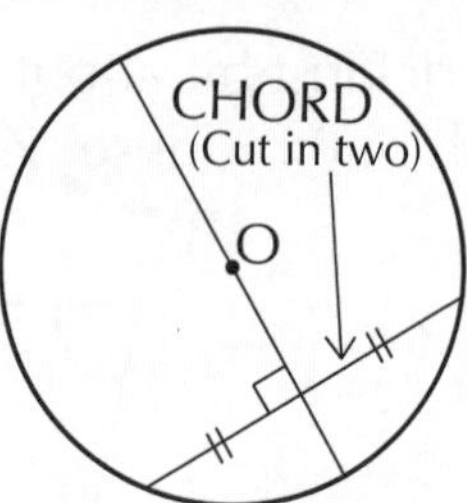

*And if you get **stuck...***

It's all too easy to find yourself staring at a geometry problem and getting nowhere — if so, this is what you do:

Go through the eleven rules one by one and apply each of them in turn in as many ways as possible — one of them is bound to work.

...Make that eleven simple rules to learn

Oops! Forgot about these three. Still, they won't take you long to learn, and then you can shut the book and see if you've remembered all eleven. Lucky old you.

Three-letter Angle Notation

*Using **Three Letters** to Specify **Angles***

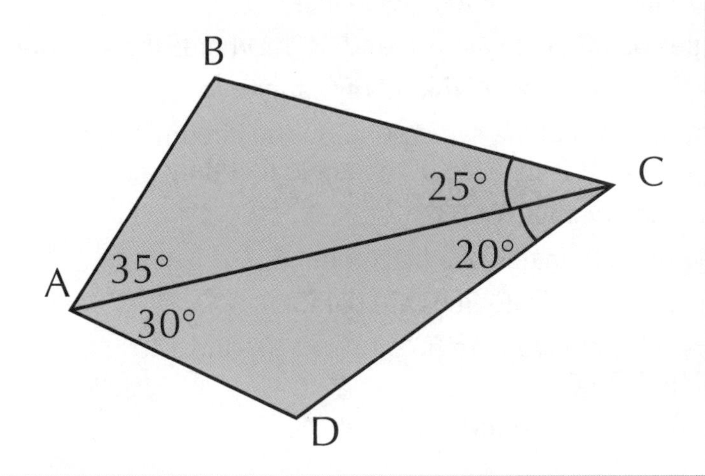

The best way to say which angle you're talking about in a diagram is by using three letters. For example in the diagram above, angle ACB = 25°. This is the way they'll do it in the exam, so like it or not you'll have to get the hang of it. Anyway, it's very simple:

1) The middle letter is where the angle is.
2) The other two letters tell you which two lines enclose the angle.

EXAMPLES FROM THE DIAGRAM ABOVE:

1) Angle BCD is at C and is enclosed by the lines BC and CD (you just split BCD into BC-CD). So angle BCD = 45°.
2) Angle ACD (AC-CD) is at C and is enclosed by the lines AC and CD. ACD = 20°.

Easy — the two points in the green box are all you need

It's vital you've got your head round it though. How annoying if you could remember how to work out all the angles in an exam question, but you weren't sure which they were asking for.

Warm-up and Worked Exam Questions

It's easy to think you've learnt a section until you get to the warm-up questions. But this geometry lark isn't easy, so don't panic if you've forgotten some of it — just go back over it now.

Warm-up Questions

1) What is the mathematical name for a 4-sided shape?
2) (a) Two of the angles of a triangle are 50° and 40°. What is the size of the third angle?
   (b) What name is given to this special kind of triangle?
3) A tangent and a radius meet at the same point on the circumference of a particular circle. What is the size of the angle that they make?
4) What is the supplementary angle of 63°?
5) Find the sum of the interior angles of a hexagon.
6) What symbols are used to indicate lines are parallel?
7) Four interior angles of a pentagon are 90°, 100°, 110° and 140°. Find the size of the fifth angle.
8) In a triangle ABC, use 3 letters to indicate angle C.

If you whizzed through that lot with no trouble then you're doing well.
Don't get cocky though — 'cos here comes the hard stuff...

Worked Exam Question

Calculator Not Allowed

1 PQRS is a quadrilateral.

Rule 3 on page 121 tells you what to do for quadrilaterals.

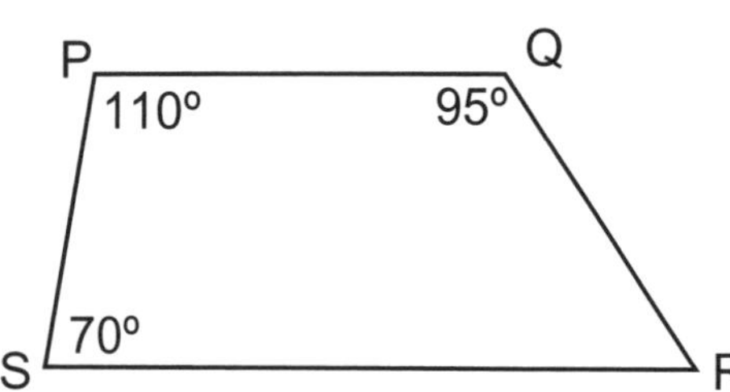

(a) Find the size of angle QRS.

All the angles in a quadrilateral add up to 360°.

So angle QRS = 360° – (110 + 95 + 70)° = 360° – 275° = 85°.

(1 mark)

(b) How do you know that PQ is parallel to SR?

Angle P + angle S = 110 + 70 = 180°,

and angle Q + angle R = 95 + 85 = 180°.

So P, S and Q, R are pairs of supplementary angles.

(2 marks)

(c) What type of quadrilateral is PQRS? Explain how you know.

It is a trapezium because it has one pair of parallel sides.

(1 mark)

This was covered quite a while back, on page 107. But it's a shape you need to know about for the exam. And if you can't remember it now, you definitely won't remember it then.

Exam Questions

Exam Questions

Calculator Allowed

2 Find angles a – m below.

Diagrams not to scale.

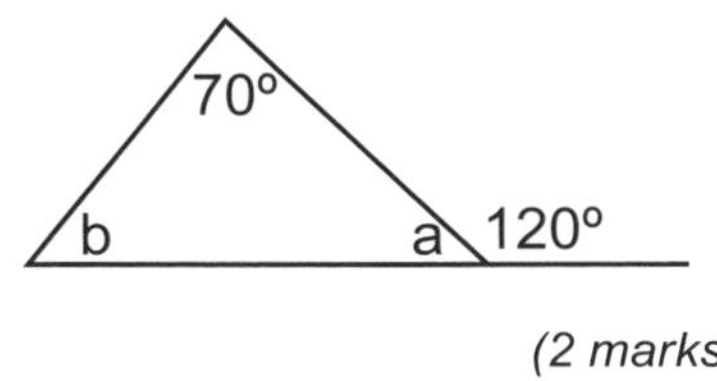

(2 marks)

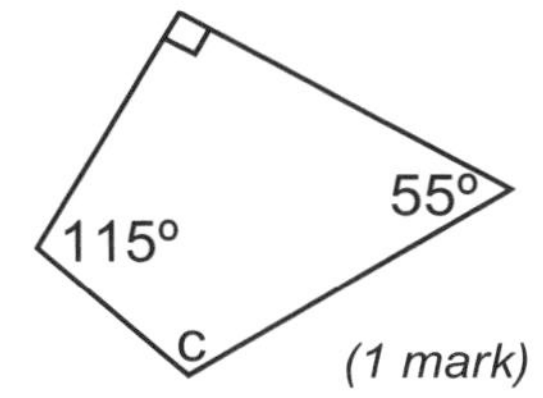

(1 mark)

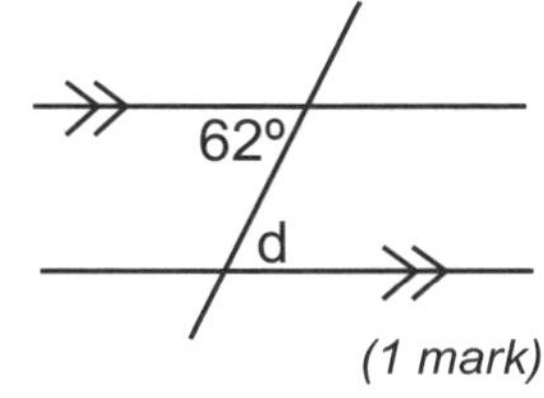

(1 mark)

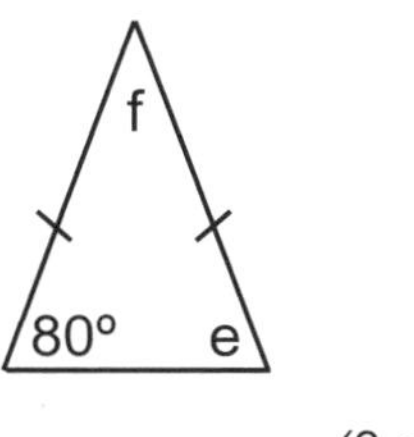

(2 marks)

68°
82°
76°
64°
g

(1 mark)

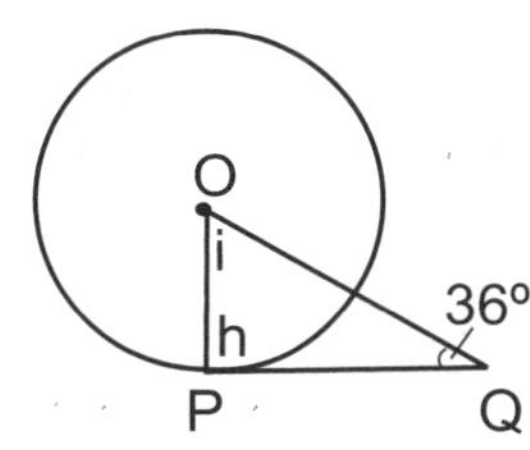

O is the centre of the circle.
PQ is a tangent to the circle.

(2 marks)

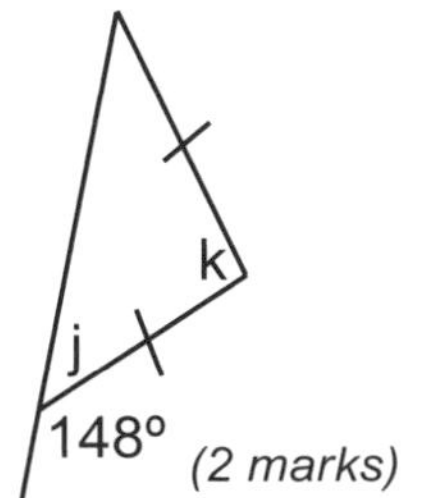

(2 marks)

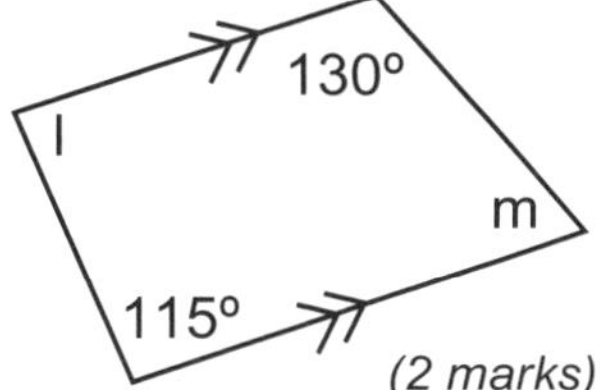

(2 marks)

3 Look at the diagram below. Give the letters of:

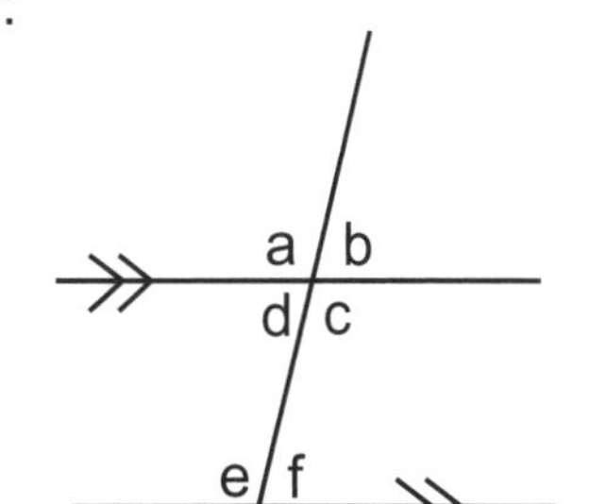

(a) Four pairs of corresponding angles. *(1 mark)*

(b) Two pairs of alternate angles. *(1 mark)*

(c) Two pairs of supplementary angles. *(1 mark)*

4 Seven of the interior angles of a nonagon (a nine-sided polygon) are:
105°, 115°, 125°, 135°, 140°, 145° and 155°. The remaining two angles are equal.
Find the size of each.

(3 marks)

Exam Questions

Exam Questions

Calculator Allowed

5 AB and CD are straight lines. Given that angle DXB = 55° and angle EXA = 48°, find the size of:

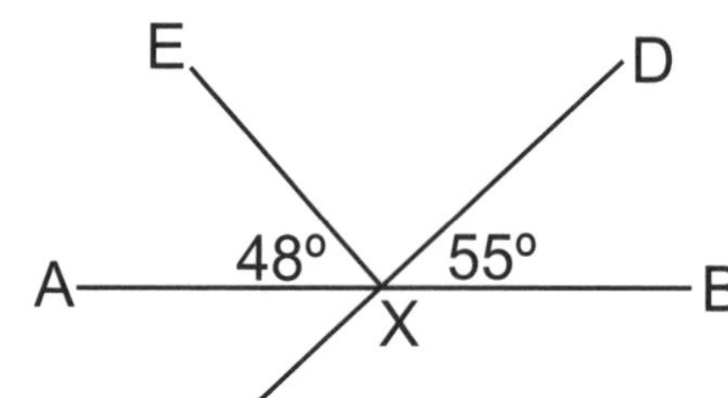

(a) angle EXD. *(1 mark)*

(b) angle BXC. *(1 mark)*

(c) angle CXE. *(1 mark)*

6 In quadrilateral EFGH, HX bisects angle EHG.

(a) Find angle XHG. *(2 marks)*

(b) Find angle HXF. *(1 mark)*

(c) What type of triangle is triangle EXH? Show your working. *(1 mark)*

7 O is the centre of the circle, and angle XOA = 52°. The line OX bisects the chord AB. Find:

(a) angle OXA. *(1 mark)*

(b) angle OAX. *(1 mark)*

(c) angle AOB. *(1 mark)*

8 ABCDEF is a **regular** hexagon, so all its sides and interior angles are the same. ABXY is a square.

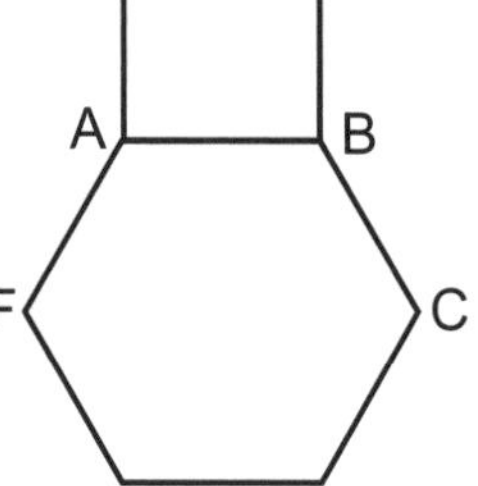

(a) If the sum of all the angles inside the hexagon is 720°, find the size of the obtuse angle YAF. *(3 marks)*

(b) Join F to Y. What is the size of angle AFY? *(2 marks)*

Length, Area and Volume

Identifying Formulae Just *by Looking* at Them

This isn't as bad as it sounds, since we're only talking about the formulae for 3 things:

LENGTH, AREA and VOLUME

The rules are as simple as this:

Length formulae (e.g. perimeter) always have lengths occurring singly.

Area formulae always have lengths multiplied in pairs.

Volume formulae always have lengths multiplied in groups of three.

In formulae of course, lengths are represented by letters, so when you look at a formula you're looking for groups of letters multiplied together in ones, twos or threes. But remember, π is NOT a length.

Examples

$6dw + \pi r^2 + 5d^2$ (area)

$2d^2w - 5t^3/4$ (volume)

$4\pi r + 12L$ (length)

$6\pi d - 8r/5$ (length)

$4\pi r^2 + 9d^2$ (area)

$Lwh + 8k^3$ (volume)

Remember, $r^2 = r \times r$. So in the first example, if we write it out in full, we have:

$(6 \times d \times w) + (\pi \times r \times r) + (5 \times d \times d)$.

At first that might look like groups of three multiplied together, but we're only interested in letters. That means the groups are multiplied together in twos, which means it's an area formula.

Watch out for these last two tricky ones:

$7c(3c + d)$ (area)

$3\pi h(F^2 + 4G^2)$ (volume)

Don't forget, the letters outside the brackets will be multiplied by the letters inside.

Identifying formulae can be tough at first

Once you get the hang of it though, it's easy. You're just interested in letters, not numbers or symbols. And it's the bits that are multiplied together that matter, not adding or subtracting bits.

Similarity and Enlargement

Congruence and Similarity

Congruence is another ridiculous maths word which sounds really complicated when it's not. If two shapes are congruent, they're simply the same — the same size and the same shape. That's all it is.

Congruent

— same size, same shape: A, B, and C are congruent (with each other).

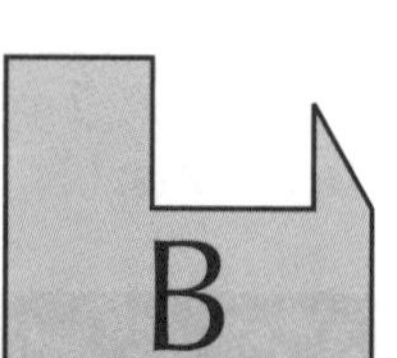

Similar

— same shape, different size: D and E are similar (but they're not congruent).

For shapes to be similar, the angles must be the same.

Areas and Volumes of Enlargements

This little joker catches everybody out.
The increase in area and volume is bigger than the scale factor. The rule is this simple:

For an enlargement of scale factor n:

The SIDES are	n times bigger
The AREAS are	n^2 times bigger
The VOLUMES are	n^3 times bigger

Simple... but very forgettable.

For example, if the scale factor is 2:

1) the lengths are twice as big, $(n = 2)$
2) each area is 4 times as big, $(n^2 = 4)$
3) the volume is 8 times as big, $(n^3 = 8)$
   as shown in the diagram:

All you have to do is remember it.

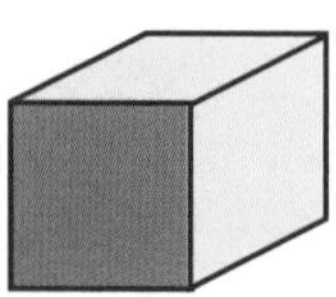
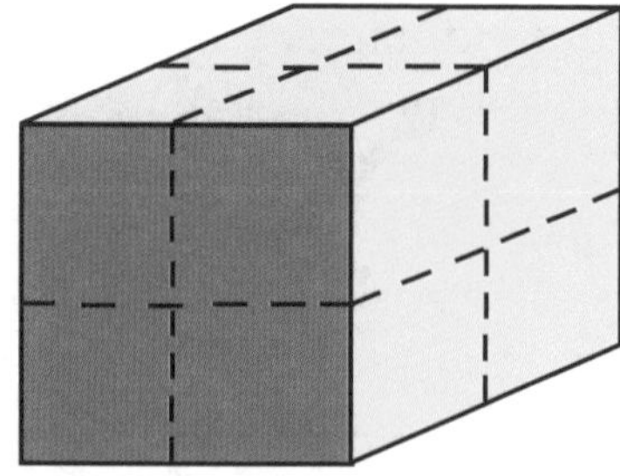

Learn the exact meanings of similar and congruent

Even the simplest words have new and very precise meanings in maths. Two similar shapes in maths means two shapes that have the same angles between their sides, but are different sizes.

Enlargements — The Four Key Features

There are four main things that you need to know about enlargements:

1) If the scale factor is bigger than 1 then the shape gets bigger.

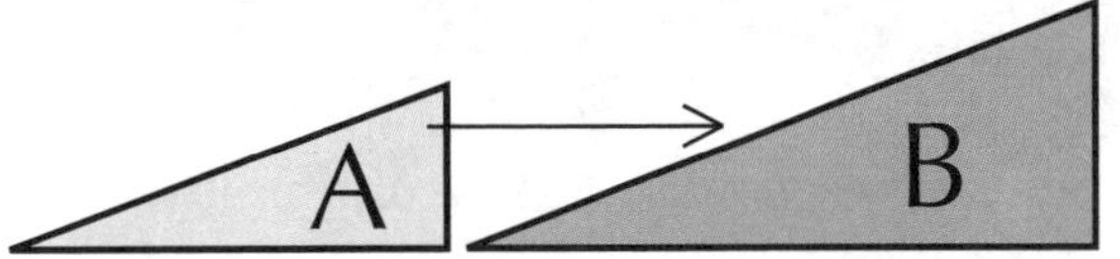

A to B is an Enlargement, Scale Factor 1½

2)

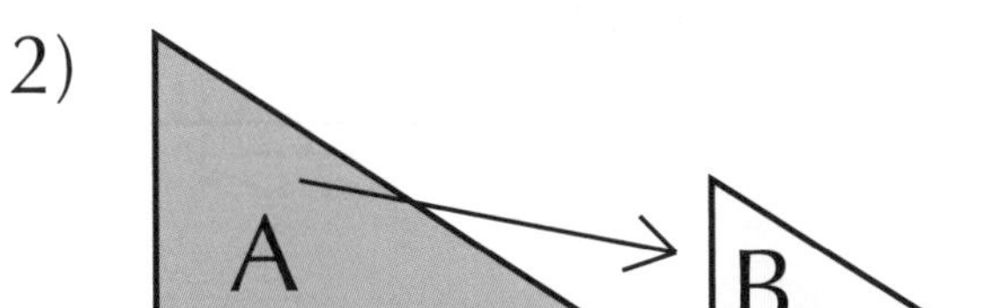

A to B is an Enlargement of Scale Factor ½

If the scale factor is smaller than 1 (i.e. a fraction like ½), then the shape gets smaller.

(Really this is a reduction, but you still call it an enlargement, Scale Factor ½)

3) Enlargement Scale Factor 3

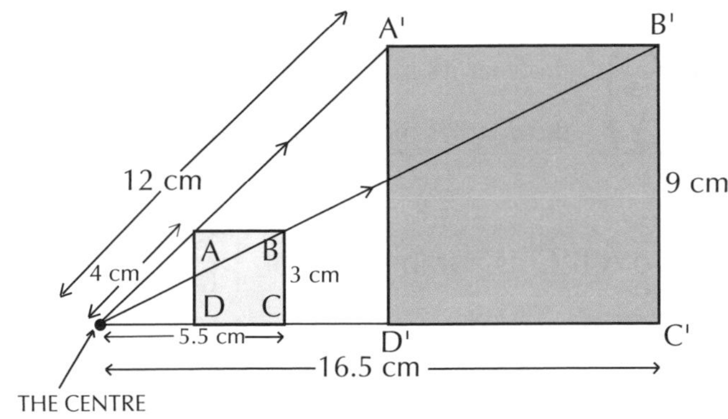

The scale factor also tells you the relative distance of old points and new points from the centre of enlargement.

This is very useful for drawing an enlargement, because you can use it to trace out the positions of the new points from the centre of enlargement, as shown in the diagram.

4) The lengths of the two shapes (big and small) are related to the scale factor by this very important formula triangle (see page 65) which you must learn:

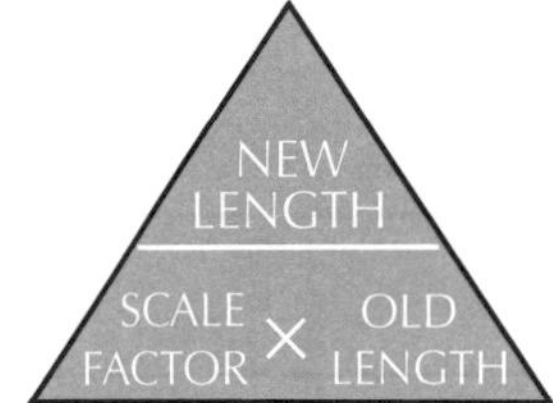

This now lets you tackle the classic "enlarged photo" exam question with no trouble:

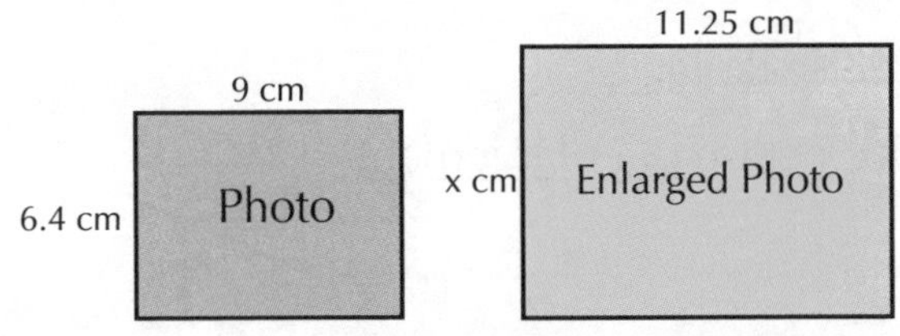

To find the width of the enlarged photo we use the formula triangle twice, firstly to find the scale factor, and then to find the missing side:

1) S.F. = new length ÷ old length = 11.25 ÷ 9 = 1.25

2) New width = scale factor × old width = 1.25 × 6.4 = 8 cm

Formula triangles are a great invention

You've got to really learn them though — this one for enlargement won't be any use at all if you can't remember whether the scale factor goes on the top or the bottom. You've been warned.

The Four Transformations

T ranslation — ONE Detail
E nlargement — TWO Details
R otation — THREE Details
R eflection — ONE Detail
Y

1) Use the word TERRY to remember the 4 types.
2) You must always specify all the details for each type.

1) TRANSLATION

You must specify this one detail:

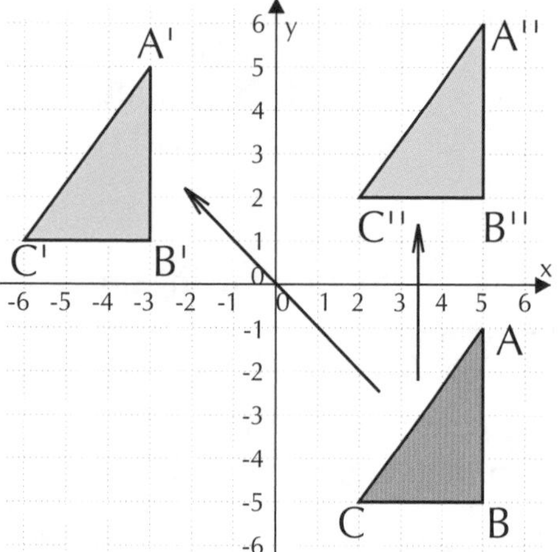

1) The translation vector:

$\begin{pmatrix} x \\ y \end{pmatrix}$ (how far it's moved along the x-axis)
(how far it's moved up or down the y-axis)

ABC to A'B'C' is a translation of $\begin{pmatrix} -8 \\ 6 \end{pmatrix}$.

ABC to A''B''C'' is a translation of $\begin{pmatrix} 0 \\ 7 \end{pmatrix}$.

2) ENLARGEMENT

You must specify these two details:

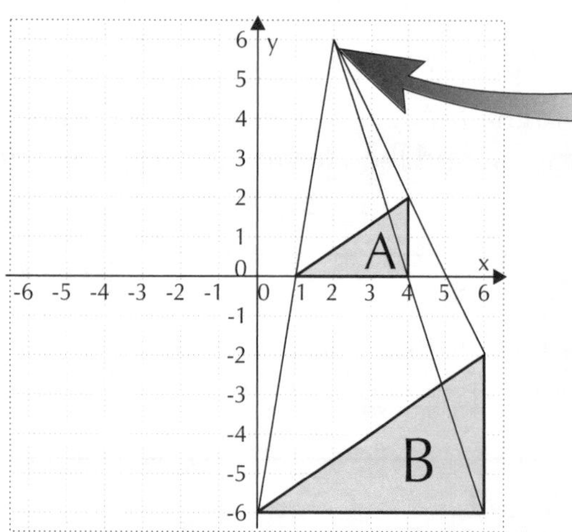

1) The scale factor
2) The centre of enlargement

A to B is an enlargement of scale factor 2 and centre (2,6).

B to A is an enlargement of scale factor 1/2 and centre (2,6).

The Four Transformations

3) ROTATION

You must specify these three details:

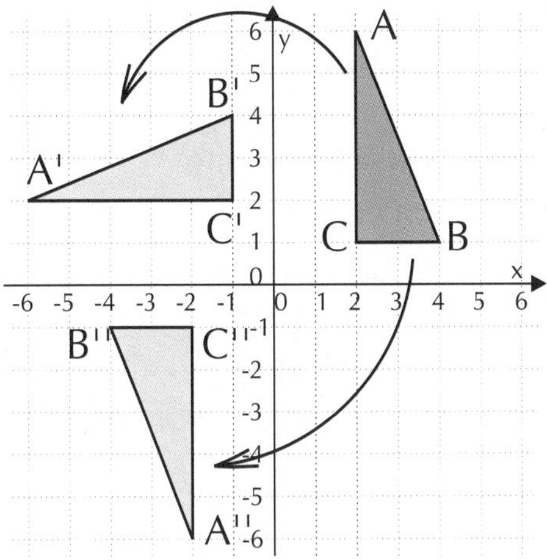

1) Angle turned
2) Direction (clockwise or anticlockwise)
3) Centre of rotation

ABC to A'B'C' is a rotation of 90°, anticlockwise, about the origin.

ABC to A''B''C'' is a rotation of half a turn (180°), clockwise, about the origin.

4) REFLECTION

You must specify this one detail:

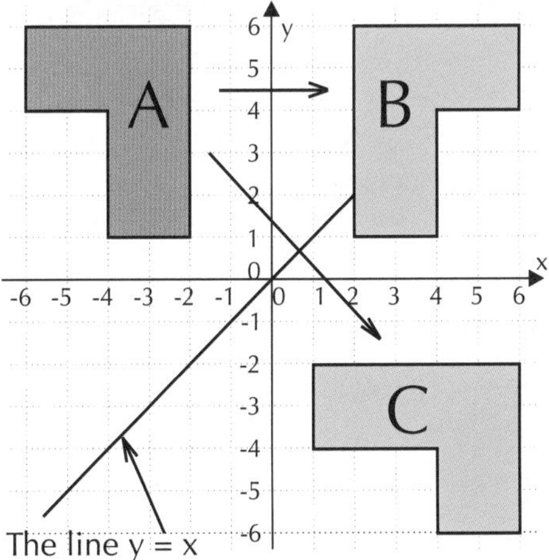

1) The mirror line

A to B is a reflection in the y-axis.

A to C is a reflection in the line y = x.
(That is, the y-value at each point along shape A is the same as the x-value at the same point on shape C. Just check for yourself.)

'Terry' can help you remember how many details you need

Then you need to remember what the details actually are, which might seem a bit harder. But when you start learning them, you'll realise it's actually pretty easy. For example, the detail that needs to be specified for reflection is the mirror line — you're not going to forget that.

Warm-up and Worked Exam Questions

With all these enlargements and rotations, it can be easy to think: "What on earth is the point?" Well, the point is that you have to know them or you'll lose marks in the exam. Simple really.

Warm-up Questions

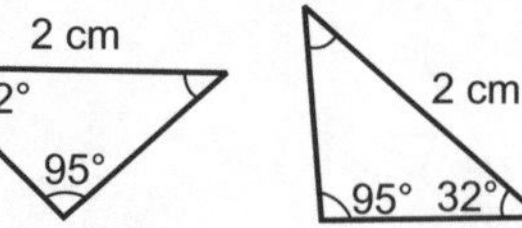

1) Look at these triangles.
   Are they similar, congruent or neither?
2) A triangle has a base of 4 cm and a height of 3 cm.
   It is enlarged using a scale factor of 3. What is the new base and height?
3) a and b are lengths. Is the formula ab a length, an area or a volume?
4) What word describes shapes that are the same size and the same shape?
5) The length of one side of a shape is 4 cm.
   When the shape is enlarged the side is 6 cm. What is the scale factor?
6) x, y and z are lengths. Is the expression $x + y + z$ a length, an area or a volume?
7) A triangle has coordinates (2,4), (3,4) and (3,6).
   What are the new coordinates after a translation of $\begin{pmatrix}3\\-1\end{pmatrix}$?
8) A shape with an area of 9 cm^2 is enlarged using a scale factor of 2.
   What is the new area?

Exam questions tend not to vary that much — once you've done these there's not really much they can ask you that'll be a shock in the exam.

Worked Exam Question

Calculator Allowed

1 For each of the pairs of rectangles below, the second rectangle is an enlargement of the first. For **each** pair, find:

(a) the scale factor of the enlargement. *(2 marks)*

(b) the missing length. *(2 marks)*

Questions like this are easy as long as you know the formula triangle for enlargements (page 131).

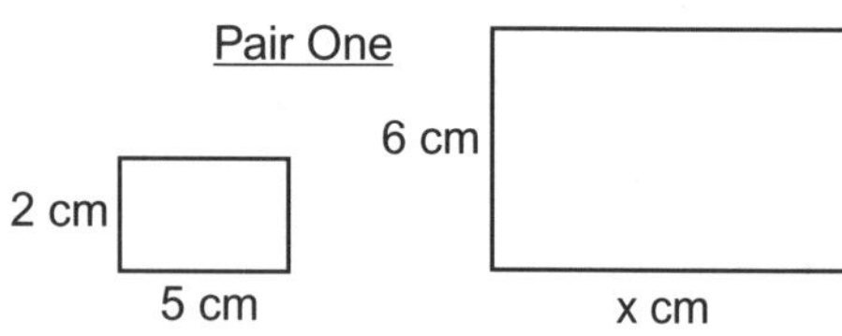

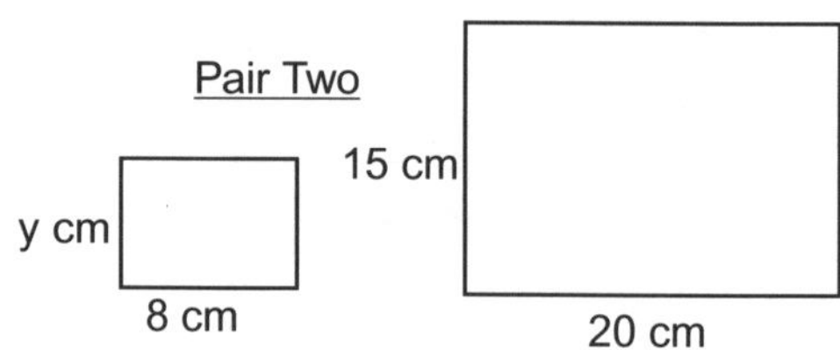

1 (a) For pair one, scale factor = 6 ÷ 2 = 3.

For pair two, scale factor = 20 ÷ 8 = 2.5.

(b) For pair one, side x = 5 x 3 = 15 cm.

For pair two, side y = 15 ÷ 2.5 = 6 cm.

Exam Questions

Exam Questions

Calculator Allowed

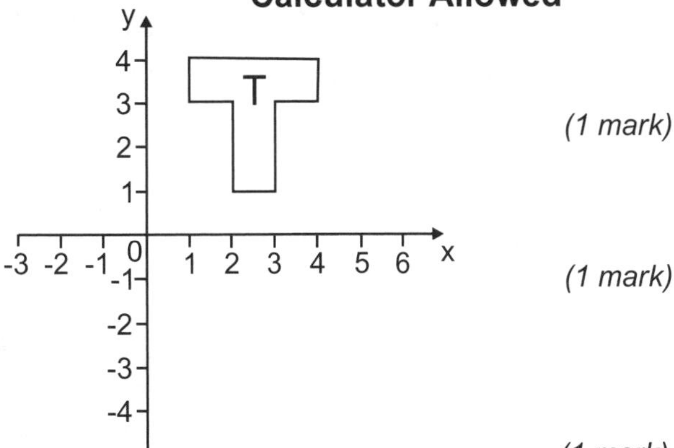

2 (a) Reflect the shape T in the line x = 1.
Label the new shape Q. *(1 mark)*

(b) Translate T using the vector $\binom{2}{-3}$.
Label the new shape R. *(1 mark)*

(c) Rotate T 180° about (1,0).
Label the new shape S. *(1 mark)*

(d) What single transformation would map S onto Q? *(2 marks)*

3 The two shapes in the diagram below are similar.

(a) What are the sizes of the following angles:

(i) WXY (ii) ABC (iii) BAF? *(4 marks)*

(b) What is the scale factor of the enlargement? *(1 mark)*

(c) Find the length of:

(i) UZ (ii) AB *(2 marks)*

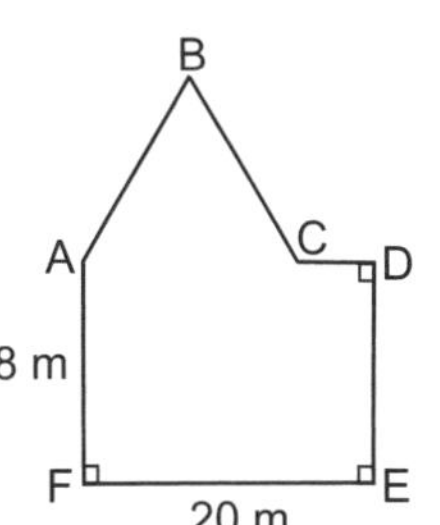

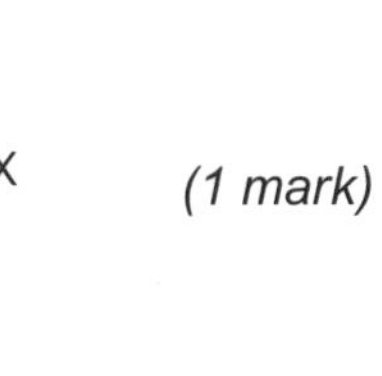

4 (a) These rectangles are similar.
Find the area of the larger one. *(2 marks)*

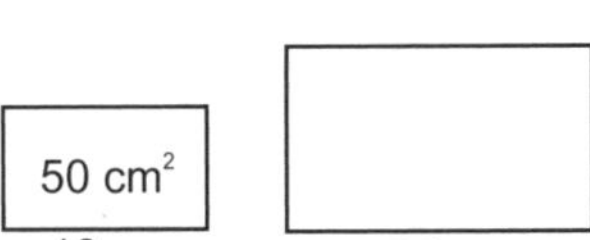

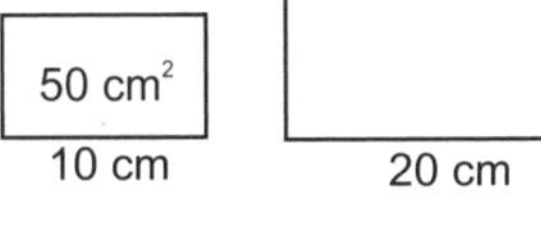

(b) These cuboids are similar.
Find the volume of the larger one. *(2 marks)*

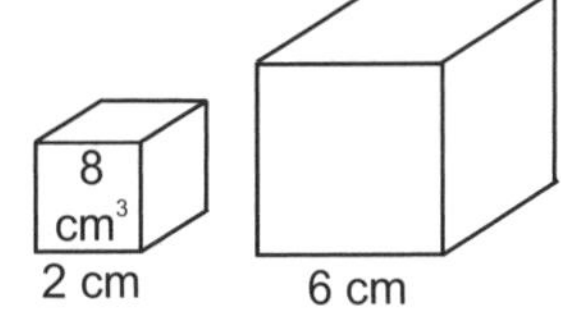

(c) These cylinders are similar. Find the volume of the smaller one, to the nearest whole number. *(2 marks)*

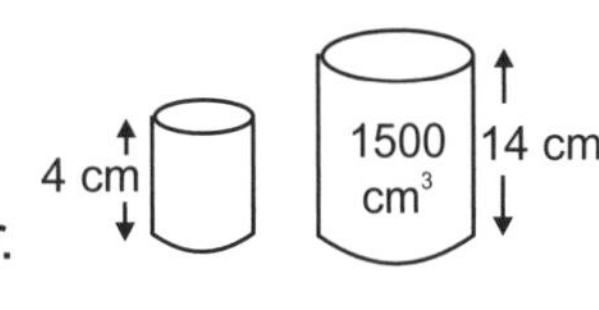

5 The letters e, f and g represent lengths. For each formula given below, say whether it represents a length, an area or a volume:

(a) efg (b) ef + fg (c) ef/g (d) $3e^2$ (e) πfg^2

(5 marks)

Pythagoras' Theorem

Pythagoras' Theorem and trigonometry (SIN, COS and TAN — see pages 138 and 139) both deal right-angled triangles.

The big difference between them is that Pythagoras' theorem just involves sides, while SIN, COS and TAN always involve angles as well as sides.

Method

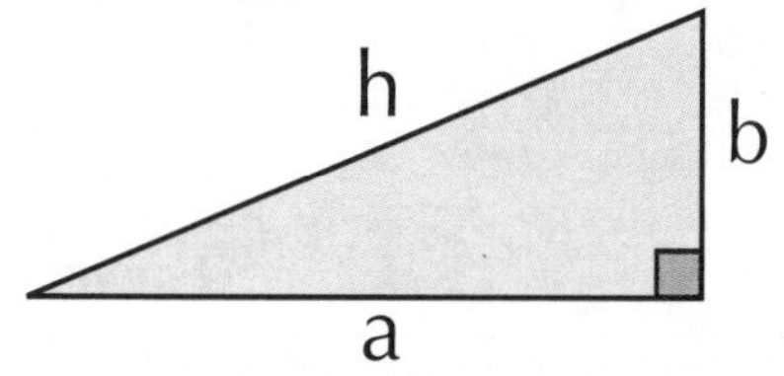

The basic formula for Pythagoras' theorem is:

$$a^2 + b^2 = h^2$$

where h stands for hypotenuse — which is the name for the side opposite the right angle in a right-angled triangle. It is always the longest side.

Remember — Pythagoras can only be used on right-angled triangles.

The trouble is, the formula can be quite difficult to use. Instead, it's better to just remember these three simple steps, which work every time:

1) SQUARE THEM: Square the two numbers (side lengths) that you are given.

2) ADD OR SUBTRACT: To find the longest side, add the two squared numbers. To find a shorter side, subtract the smaller squared number from the larger squared number.

3) SQUARE ROOT: After adding or subtracting, take the square root. Then check that your answer is sensible.

Example

"Find the missing side in the triangle shown."

ANSWER

Step 1) Square them: $12^2 = 144$, $13^2 = 169$

Step 2) We want to find a shorter side, so subtract: $169 - 144 = 25$

Step 3) Square root: $\sqrt{25} = 5$

So the missing side = 5 m.

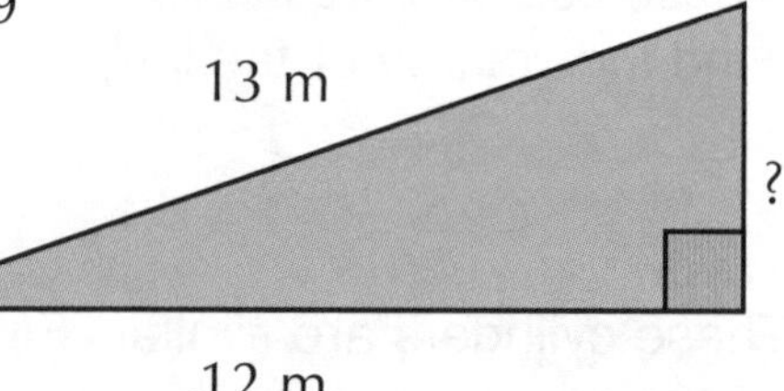

You should always ask yourself: "Is it a sensible answer?" — in this case you can say "yes," because it's a narrow triangle and the missing side is about half as long as the others.

Pythagoras — what a clever lad he was

All the brain power it took to come up with a formula which works every time like that one... It's a shame you can turn it into those three easy steps — now it doesn't seem that hard at all.

Bearings

Bearings — 3 Key Points

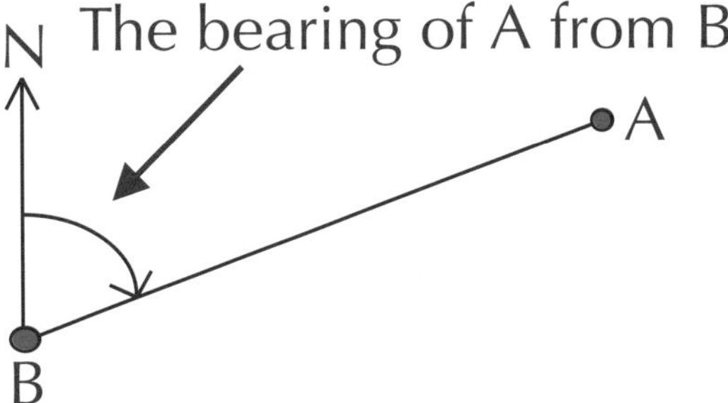

1) A bearing is the direction travelled between two points, given as an angle in degrees.
2) All bearings are measured clockwise from the northline. (Marked N in the diagram.)
3) All bearings should be given as 3 figures, e.g. 045° (not 45°), 316°, 009° (not 9°), etc.

The 3 Key Words

Only learn this if you want to get bearings right.

1) "FROM":	Find the word "from" in the question, and put your pencil on the diagram at the point you are going from.
2) "NORTHLINE":	At the point you are going from, draw in a northline.
3) "CLOCKWISE":	Now draw in the angle clockwise from the northline to the line joining the two points. This angle is the bearing.

Example

"Find the bearing of T from S."

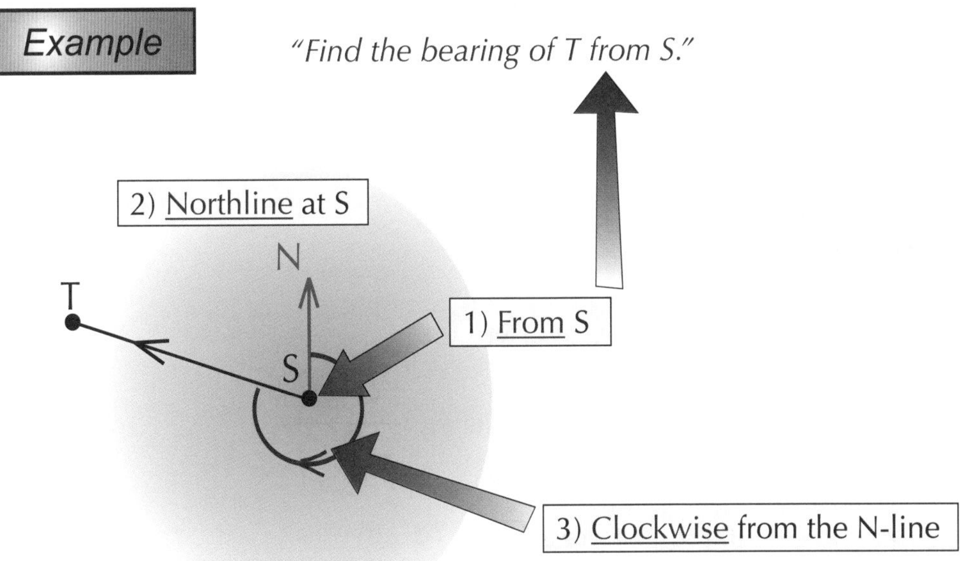

This angle is the bearing of T from S and is 290°.

Just three key words to learn and you can't go wrong

All you have to do is draw in your northline at whichever point you're going from. Then it's just a case of marking on the angle clockwise. Measure your angle, and there's your bearing.

Trigonometry — SIN, COS, TAN

Using formula triangles to do trigonometry makes the whole thing a lot easier, but always follow all these steps in this order. If you miss any out you're asking for trouble.

Method Using SIN, COS and TAN to solve right-angled triangles

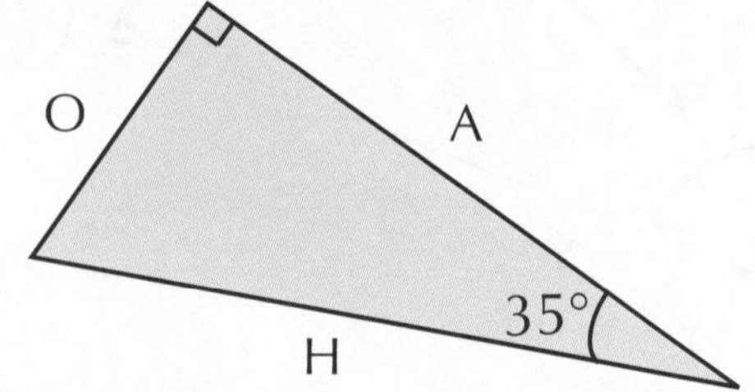

1) Label the three sides O, A and H
(opposite, adjacent and hypotenuse)

2) Write down from memory: "SOH CAH TOA"
(Sounds like a Chinese word, "Sokatoa!")

3) Decide which two sides are involved — O,H A,H or O,A
and select SOH, CAH or TOA accordingly

4) Turn the one you choose into a formula triangle, like this:

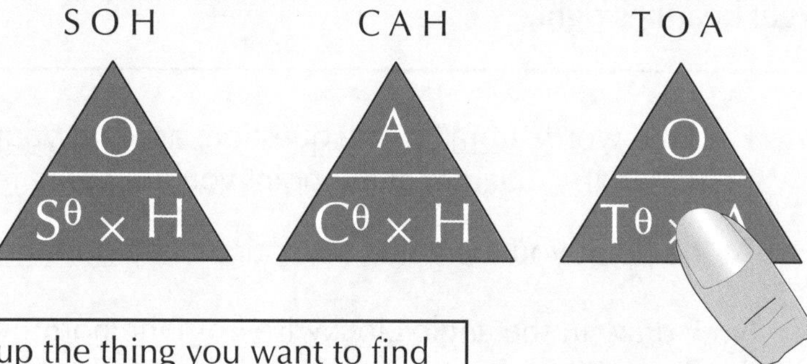

5) Cover up the thing you want to find
with your finger, and write down whatever is left showing

6) Translate into numbers and work it out

7) Finally, check that your answer is sensible

Seven Nitty Gritty Details

- The hypotenuse is the longest side.
  The opposite is the side opposite the angle being used (θ).
  The adjacent is the side next to the angle being used (θ).
- θ is a Greek letter called "theta", and is used to represent angles.
- In the formula triangles, S^{θ} represents SIN θ, C^{θ} is COS θ, and T^{θ} is TAN θ.
- To enter, say, SIN 30 into the calculator, just press SIN 30 = .
  (You should get 0.5 — if you don't, check you're in degrees mode — see page 39.)
- Remember, to find the angle — use inverse (see next page).
- Always use a diagram — draw your own if necessary.
- You can only use these formulae on right-angled triangles —
  you may have to add lines to the diagram to create one, especially on isosceles triangles.

Trigonometry — SIN, COS, TAN

Example 1

"Find x in the triangle shown."

Adj x, 60°, Hyp, 32 m, Opp

1) Label O, A, H
2) Write down "SOH CAH TOA"
3) The two sides <u>involved</u> are: O, A
4) So use

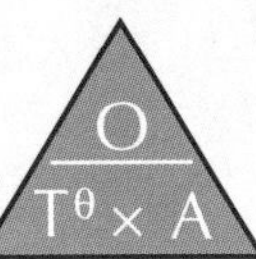

5) We want to find A so cover it up to leave: $A = {}^{O}\!/_{T^\theta}$

6) Translate: x = 32 / tan 60° Press:

18.475208

So <u>ANSWER</u> = <u>18.5 m</u>

7) Check it's sensible: <u>Yes</u>, it's about half as big as 32, as the diagram suggests.

Example 2

"Find the angle x in this triangle."

Note the usual way of dealing with an <u>isosceles triangle</u> — <u>split it</u> down the middle to get a <u>right angle</u>:

1) Split the triangle and thus angle x. θ = half of x.
2) Write down "SOH CAH TOA"
3) Two sides <u>involved</u>: O, H

x, 40 m, 40 m, 52 m

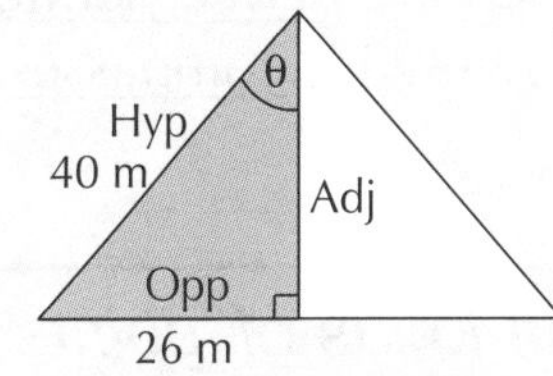

4) So use

5) We want to find θ so cover up S^θ to leave: $S^\theta = O/H$
6) Translate: $SIN\theta = {}^{26}\!/_{40} = 0.65$

<u>NOW USE INVERSE</u>: θ = INV SIN (0.65)

Press INV SIN 0.65 = 40.5416

So θ = <u>40.5°</u> Since θ = half of x, x = 40.5 × 2, i.e. <u>x = 81°</u>.

7) Is that sensible? — <u>Yes</u>, the angle looks like about 80°.

Angles of **Elevation** and **Depression**

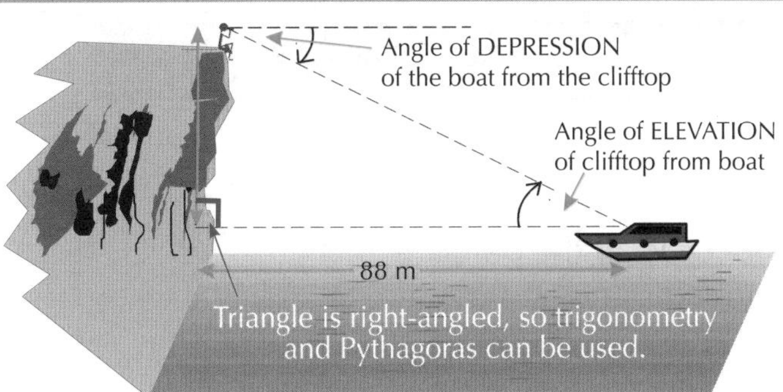

1) The angle of <u>depression</u> is the angle <u>downwards</u> from the horizontal.
2) The angle of <u>elevation</u> is the angle <u>upwards</u> from the horizontal.
3) The angle of elevation and angle of depression are <u>always equal</u>.

SOH CAH TOA — the most important word in trigonometry

<u>Don't</u> start getting stressed if they give you a random-looking triangle in an exam and ask you to find an angle. You'll usually be able to <u>divide it up</u> somehow to make sensible ones.

Loci and Constructions

A locus (plural loci — more ridiculous maths words) is just a line that shows all the points that fit in with a given rule. Make sure you learn how to do these properly using a ruler and compasses, as follows...

1 The locus of points which are "A Fixed Distance from a Given Point"

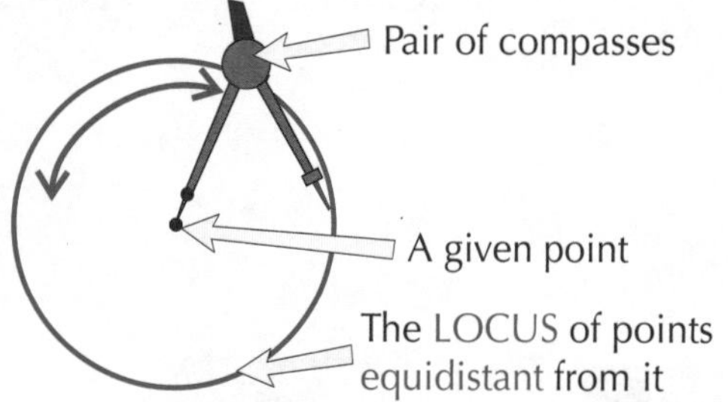

This locus is simply a circle.

2 The locus of points which are "A Fixed Distance from a Given Line"

This locus is an OVAL shape.

It has straight sides (drawn with a ruler) and ends which are perfect semicircles (drawn with compasses).

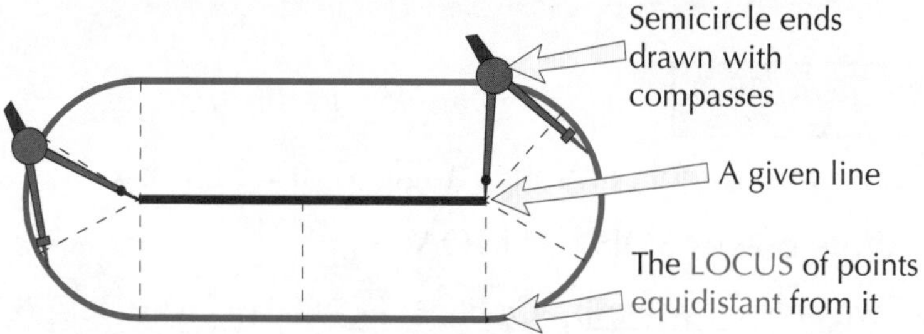

3 The locus of points which are "Equidistant from Two Given Lines"

1) Keep the compass setting the same while you make all four marks.
2) Make sure you leave your compass marks showing.
3) You get two equal angles — i.e. this locus is actually an angle bisector.

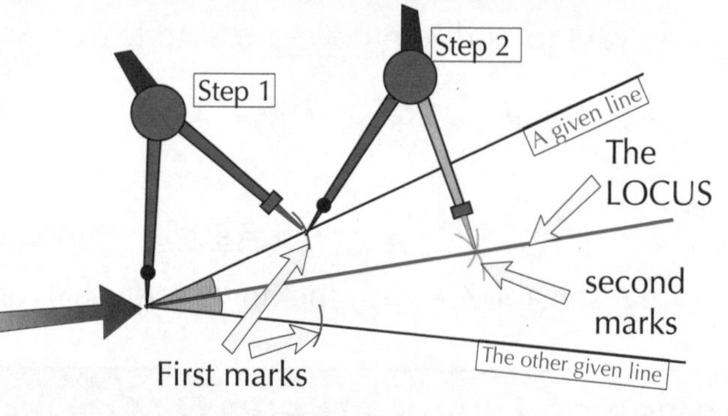

4 The locus of points which are "Equidistant from Two Given Points"

(In the diagram below, A and B are the two given points.)

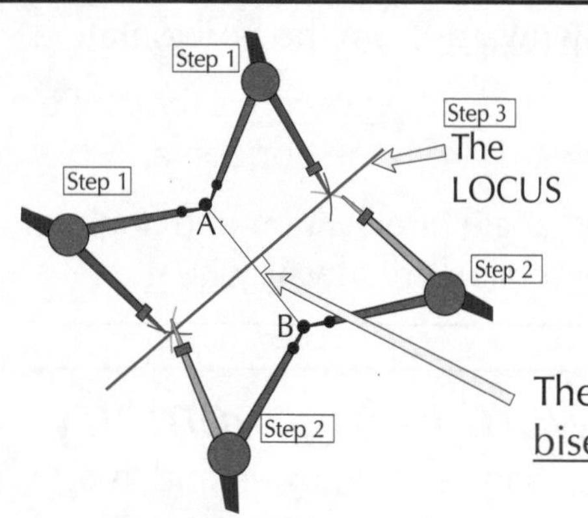

This locus is all the points which are the same distance from A and B.

The locus is actually the perpendicular bisector of the line joining the two points.

Loci and Constructions

5 Constructing accurate 60° angles

They may well ask you to draw an <u>accurate 60° angle</u>.

One place they're needed is for drawing an <u>equilateral triangle</u>.

Make sure you follow the method shown in this diagram, and that you can do it entirely from <u>memory</u>.

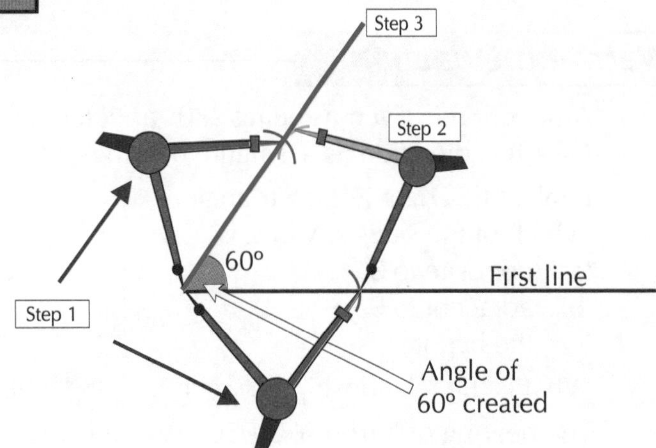

6 Constructing accurate 90° angles

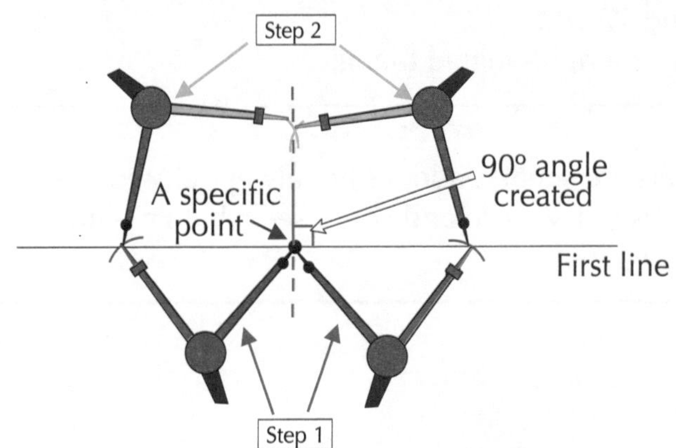

They might want you to draw an <u>accurate 90° angle</u>.

They won't accept it just done "<u>by eye</u>" or with a ruler — if you want to get the marks, you've got to do it the <u>proper</u> way with <u>compasses</u> like I've shown you here.

Make sure you can follow the method shown in this diagram.

7 Drawing the Perpendicular from a Point to a Line

This is similar to the one above but <u>not</u> quite the same — make sure you can do <u>both</u>.

Again, they won't accept it just done "<u>by eye</u>" or with a ruler — you've got to do it the <u>proper</u> way with <u>compasses</u>.

<u>Learn</u> the diagram.

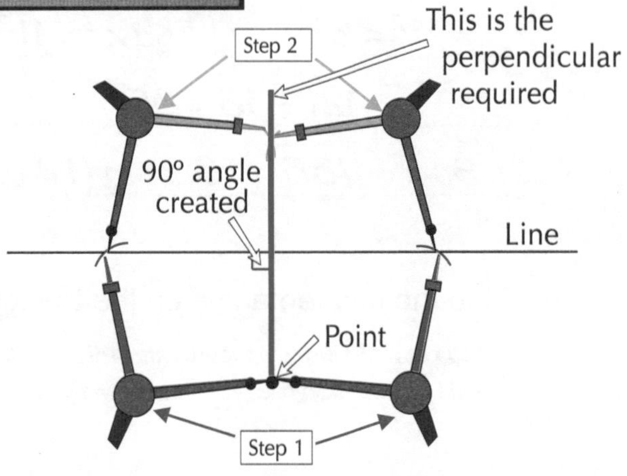

So don't forget your compasses for the exam

There are <u>seven</u> methods shown on the last two pages. Go through and make sure you can do <u>all</u> of them. Then close the book and try to do each just from <u>memory</u>. Then try again.

Warm-up and Worked Exam Questions

Now I know you can hardly wait to get on to those thrilling exam questions.
But you'll just have to be patient — these warm-up ones are just as important.

Warm-up Questions

1) A direction is given as being 280° anticlockwise from the northline. Give this direction as a 3-figure bearing.
2) Look at this right-angled triangle. Which of the sides x, y or z is
   (a) opposite to θ
   (b) adjacent to θ
   (c) the hypotenuse?

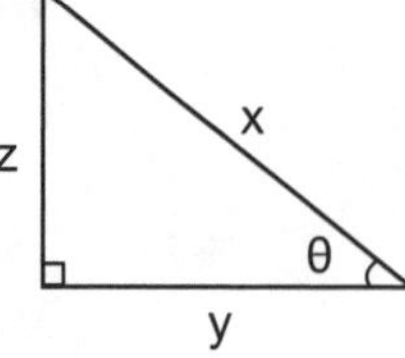

3) What is the relationship between x, y and z above, according to Pythagoras' Theorem?
4) The bearing of X from Y is 050°. What is the bearing of Y from X?
5) Define the term "angle of depression".
6) M is the point (0,0) on a graph and N is the point (3,4). Draw a triangle and use Pythagoras' Theorem to find the distance from M to N. (Units are not required.)
7) Describe the locus of points which are 4 cm from a point P.
8) A triangle has sides of length 8 cm, 15 cm and 17 cm. Use Pythagoras' Theorem to check whether it is a right-angled triangle.

Knowing the theory isn't enough here — examiners are sneaky, and it's not always clear straight away which bit of your knowledge you'll need to use. Try these and you'll see what I mean.

Worked Exam Question

Calculator Allowed

1 (a) Find the missing side on the triangle shown.

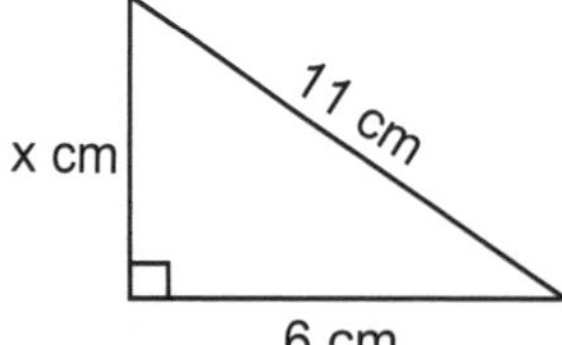

Easy – just use Pythagoras' theorem. $(a^2 + b^2 = h^2)$

$11^2 = 6^2 + x^2$, so $x^2 = 11^2 - 6^2$.

$= 121 - 36 = 85$.

So $x = \sqrt{85} = 9.2$ cm (1 d.p.)

(2 marks)

(b) Find the marked angle on the triangle shown.

You know the sides opposite and adjacent to the angle you want to find, so that means you use tan.

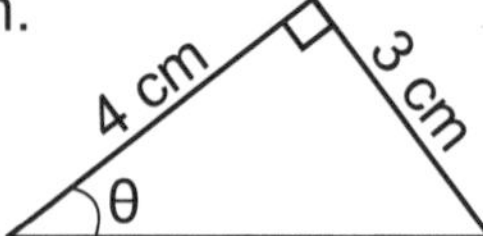

Don't be put off because the triangle has the right-angle at the top.

$\tan\theta$ = opposite ÷ adjacent = 3 ÷ 4 = 0.75, so

Press INV or SHIFT then tan 2.5 to give: $\theta = 36.9°$ (1 d.p.)

(3 marks)

Exam Questions

Exam Questions

Calculator Allowed

2 Find x, to 1 decimal place, in each of the following:

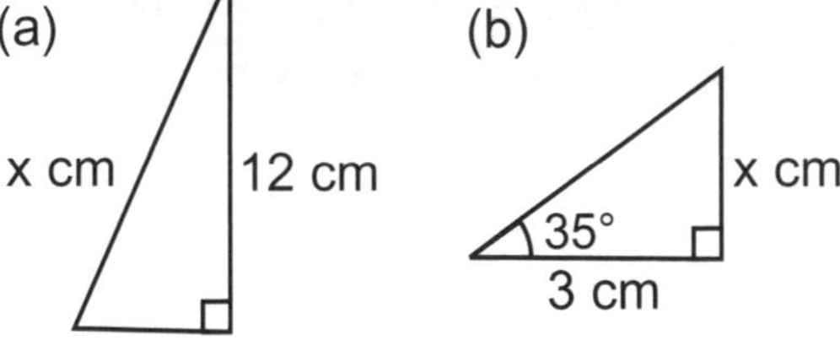

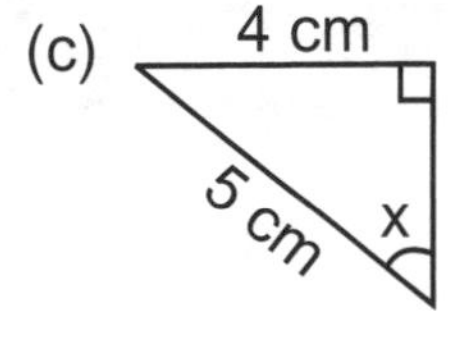

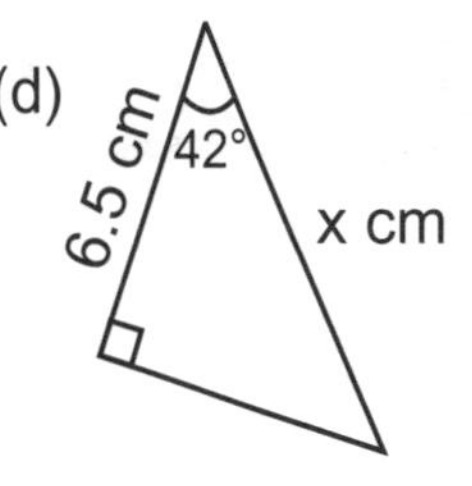

(8 marks)

3 (a) An equilateral triangle has sides of length 4 cm. Find its height.

(3 marks)

(b) An isosceles triangle has sides of length 7 cm, 7 cm and 10 cm. Find the angle between the two equal sides.

(3 marks)

4 The diagram shows the route of a bike race from Alton to Barton to Carlton and then back to Alton.

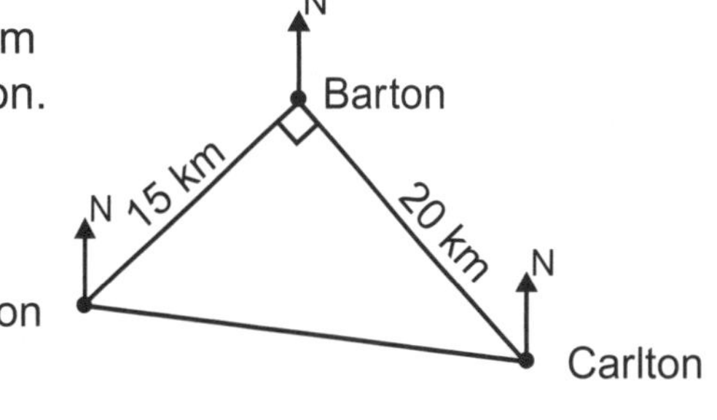

(a) Measure the bearing of:

(i) Barton from Alton
(ii) Carlton from Barton
(iii) Alton from Carlton

(3 marks)

(b) Find the total distance of the route from Alton to Barton to Carlton and then back to Alton.

(3 marks)

5 From a point on the ground 10 m from the base of a tower, I measure the angle of elevation of the top of the tower to be 64°. Find the height of the tower.

(2 marks)

6 A treasure chest is buried in a field. The chest is the same distance from AB as it is from BC, and equidistant from both B and C. Mark the point where it lies with a T.

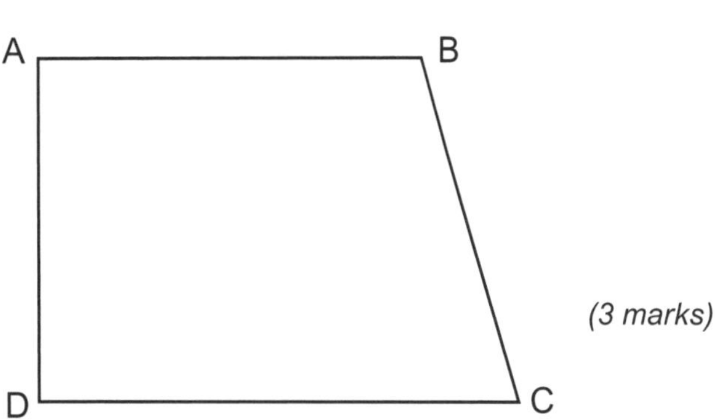

(3 marks)

Revision Summary for Section Three

This stuff about shapes isn't too hard, but there's no way you can get away with not revising. If you want to do well, you have to know all those geometry rules. So try these questions to see which bits you know and which need more work.

Keep learning these basic facts until you know them

1) What is a regular polygon? Draw the first 6, and describe their symmetry.
2) What are the 3 types of symmetry called? Draw an example of each.
3) Draw and name 6 different quadrilaterals and specify all their symmetry.
4) Name 3 different triangles. Draw them and describe their symmetry in full.
5) Write down the formulae for the area of 5 different types of shape.
6) What is π? What are the two circle formulae? When do you use them?
7) State 3 important steps for successfully finding the perimeter of a shape.
8) Give the formulae for the volumes of two types of solid.
9) What exactly is a prism? Draw one and show the two quantities needed to calculate its volume.
10) Explain what is meant by surface area and what a net is.
11) How are the two related? Is there a formula for working out surface area?
12) Draw the four important nets.
13) List the first 8 rules of geometry, and give extra details about the last 3.
14) Explain what acute and obtuse angles are and give 2 examples of each.
15) What is a quadrilateral?
16) Give details of the 3 simple rules for circle geometry.
17) What is the 3-letter notation for angles? Give an example.
18) What are the 3 rules for identifying formulae as being for length, area or volume?
19) Explain what is meant by: (a) congruence (b) similarity.
20) If an object is enlarged by a scale factor of 3, how much bigger will the area and volume be for the new shape?
21) What are the rules for this in terms of a scale factor n?
22) In enlargements, what is the effect of a scale factor <u>bigger</u> than 1?
23) What is the effect of a scale factor <u>smaller</u> than 1?
24) How do a scale factor and a centre of enlargement help you to draw an enlargement?
25) What is the formula triangle for enlargements?
26) Illustrate its use with the enlarged photo question.
27) What does TERRY stand for?
28) Give the details that go with each of the 4 types of transformation.
29) What is the formula for Pythagoras' theorem?
30) Name the three steps of the easy method for doing Pythagoras.
31) What are the three key points concerning bearings?
32) Give the three key words used to find or plot a bearing.
33) What is trigonometry about? What would a typical question be?
34) How do you decide which sides are the adjacent, opposite and hypotenuse?
35) What is the special word to help you to remember the trigonometry formulae?
36) How do you enter cos 60° into the calculator?
37) What is a locus? Describe in detail the four types you should know.
38) Write down how you would draw accurate 90° and 60° angles.

Probability

Probability can seem pretty mysterious if you don't understand it.
It's not as bad as you think, but you must learn the basic facts.

All Probabilities are Between 0 and 1

A probability of ZERO means it will never happen.
A probability of ONE means it will definitely happen.
You can't have a probability bigger than 1.

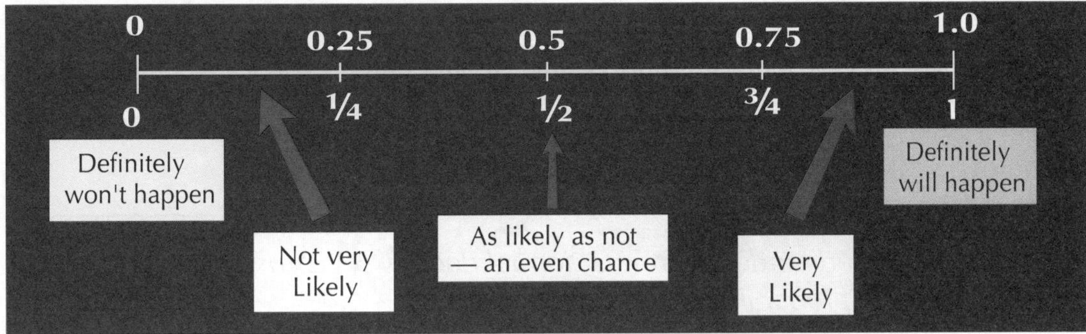

You should be able to put the probability of any event happening on this scale of 0 to 1.

Four Important Details

1) Probabilities can be given as a fraction, a decimal or a percentage.

E.g. The probability of event A is "¼" , "0.25" or "25%".

2) The notation : "P (x) = ½" should be read as: "The probability of event x happening is ½".

E.g. When you toss a coin, you'd write the probability of throwing a head as P (head).

3) Probabilities always add up to 1.

E.g. You pick a ball at random from a bag of red, blue and green balls.
P (red) = 0.2 and P (blue) = 0.3. What is P (green)?

The probabilities of the three possible outcomes add to 1.
So 0.2 + 0.3 + P (green) = 1, which gives P (green) = 1 – 0.2 – 0.4 = 0.5

(This gives us point 4...)

4) If the probability of an event occurring is p, then the probability of it not occurring is 1 – p.

E.g. If P (pass) = ¼, then P (fail) = 1 – ¼ = ¾

Theoretical Probability

There are basically two ways to find out the probability of something happening.

One way is to calculate it, like you would for coloured balls in a bag.
This is called theoretical probability.

Or you can do an experiment, and simply find out how many times the event happens compared to how many times you tried. This is called estimated probability (see the next page).

Theoretical Probability

Theoretical probability is the probability that is generally accepted to be a true mathematical chance of something happening.

The example below is all based on theoretical probability...

EXAMPLE: *A card is picked randomly from a normal deck of 52 cards (no jokers). Calculate the probability that the card will be:*

a) a black card
b) a Spade
c) a picture card
d) not a picture card
e) either a Club or Heart
f) an odd numbered black card

ANSWERS:

a) Half the cards in a normal pack are black.
So there's a 1 in 2 chance of picking a black, i.e. P (black) = $\frac{1}{2}$

b) There are 4 "suits" with an equal number of cards for each one.
So there's a 1 in 4 chance of picking a Spade, i.e. P (Spade) = $\frac{1}{4}$

c) There are 13 cards for each suit (you can count them to check).
Out of these, 3 are picture cards (Jack, Queen, King).
So there's a 3 in 13 chance of picking a picture card, i.e. P (picture card) = $\frac{3}{13}$

d) You can use the answer to c) for this.
P (picture card) = $\frac{3}{13}$, so P (not a picture card) = $1 - \frac{3}{13} = \frac{10}{13}$

e) Since there are 4 suits, the chance of picking a Club or Heart is 2 out of 4,
so P (Club or Heart) = $\frac{2}{4} = \frac{1}{2}$

f) This one's a bit trickier:
In each suit, there are 4 odd numbered cards (3, 5, 7, 9).
But there are only 2 black suits (Clubs and Spades).
So there must be 8 odd numbered black cards in the pack, which means there's an 8 in 52 chance of picking one out of the whole pack.
So P (odd-numbered black card) = $\frac{8}{52} = \frac{2}{13}$.

Estimated Probability

Estimated probability involves doing an experiment to find out how many times an event occurs from a certain number of tries.

Once you've done an experiment, you can use the results to estimate the probability of the same event happening in the future, using the formula below.

Estimated Probability

$$\text{P (event A)} = \frac{\text{number of times event occurred}}{\text{number of trials}}$$

EXAMPLE: *An unfair die is thrown 300 times. A "six" is the result 80 times. Estimate the probability of throwing a six with the die.*

ANSWER:

Based on the experiment: P (a "six" is thrown) $= \frac{80}{300} = \frac{8}{30} = \frac{4}{15}$

So $\frac{4}{15}$ is the estimated or experimental probability of getting a six with this unfair die.

You can now use this experimental probability to work out how many times you expect the same thing to happen for a certain number of tries. This is the simple formula:

expected number of occurrences = estimated probability × total number of tries

EXAMPLE: *If the unfair dice is thrown 750 times, how many sixes do you expect to get?*

ANSWER:

Expected number of sixes = estimated prob. × no. of tries $= \frac{4}{15} \times 750 = 200$

Not so mysterious after all

Another way of estimating probabilities is to use historical data, rather than doing experiments. E.g. you could estimate the probability of an earthquake occurring in a particular place based on how often they have occurred in the past. Yes, there's more to probability than balls and dice...

Combined Probability

Combined Probability — two or more events

Combined probability just means there's more than one event, e.g. throwing a die and a coin. The main thing you need to be able to do is find all the possible outcomes, either by listing them, or making a table. You can then use this to calculate probabilities.

Listing All Possible Outcomes — do it Carefully

In a typical exam question you might well be asked to list all the possible outcomes. To get them all you've got to do it in a logical order — so that you don't miss any.

Example 1 *"A coin and a die are tossed together. List all the possible outcomes."*

Start with one outcome for the coin and then pair that with each outcome for the die.

e.g. H1 H2 H3 H4 H5 H6

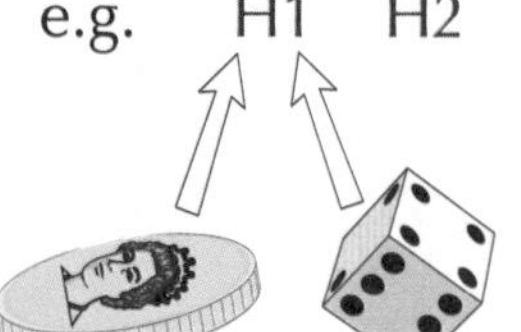

Then do the same with the other outcome for the coin (i.e. tails, T) ...

T1 T2 T3 T4 T5 T6

Sample Spaces are Tables for Showing All Outcomes

A much nicer way to represent all possible outcomes is to make a fancy table called a sample space.

Example 2 *"A green and a blue die are tossed together and the scores added. Draw a sample space to show the possible outcomes."*

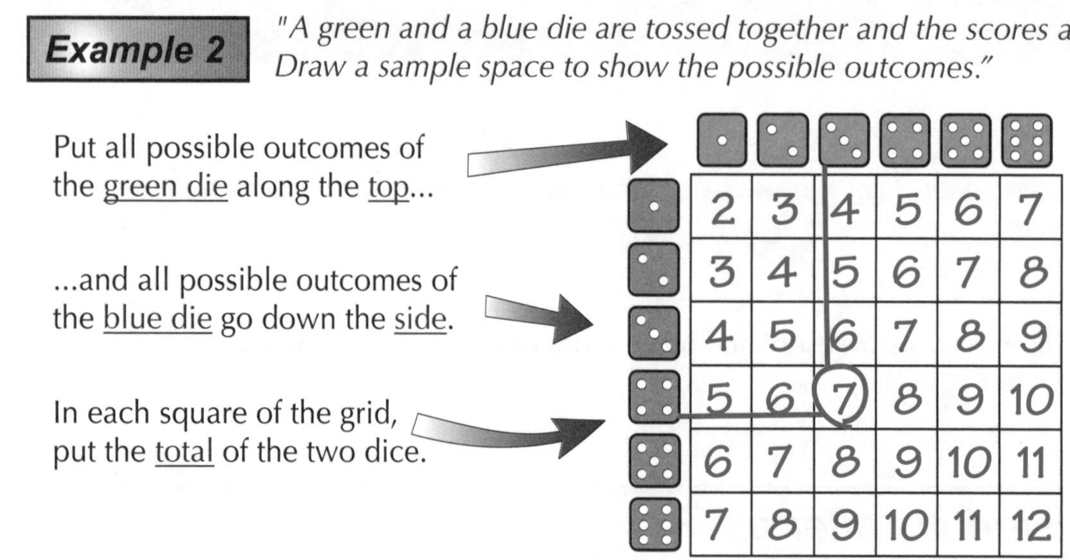

	1	2	3	4	5	6
1	2	3	4	5	6	7
2	3	4	5	6	7	8
3	4	5	6	7	8	9
4	5	6	7	8	9	10
5	6	7	8	9	10	11
6	7	8	9	10	11	12

Combined Probability

Calculating Combined Probabilities

Once you've found all the possible outcomes, it's easy to calculate probabilities based on it.

Example 1 continued...

"Calculate the probability of the coin being a head and the die showing less than 5"

From the previous page the possible outcomes are:

H1 H2 H3 H4 H5 H6
T1 T2 T3 T4 T5 T6 (note: there are 12)

The ones we want are H1, H2, H3 and H4 (i.e. 4 possible outcomes).
So there's a 4 in 12 chance of getting an outcome we want.

Which means P (head and die less than 5) $= \frac{4}{12} = \frac{1}{3}$

Example 2 continued...

"Calculate the probability of:
a) the total of the two dice being 9
b) the total being less than 7"

a) Looking at the sample space on the previous page:
- there are 4 nines in the table,
- there are 36 possible outcomes in total (6 × 6).

So there's a 4 in 36 chance of getting a 9.

i.e. P (total is 9) $= \frac{4}{36} = \frac{1}{9}$

b) Count the number of squares on the grid less than 7 — there's 15 of them.

So P (total is less than 7) $= \frac{7}{36}$

Admit it, that was a lot easier than you thought it would be.
With this method of calculating combined probabilities,
you basically just read off the answers, which is always nice.

With two events just list all the possible outcomes

Calculating probabilities nearly always boils down to working out...
(number of outcomes you want) ÷ (total possible outcomes) ... a handy fact to remember.

Warm-up and Worked Exam Questions

Probability is one of those ideas that suddenly clicks and is then simple forever. Check if you're at that stage yet by trying these warm-up questions — if not, keep trying and you soon will be.

Warm-up Questions

1) Today is November 24th. What is the probability of tomorrow being Christmas Day?
2) There are 10 coloured balls in a bag. You know that the probability of picking out a red one is P (red) = ½. How many red balls are in the bag?
3) If the probability of a bus arriving early or on time is 0.7, what is the probability of the bus arriving late?
4) A coin is tossed at the same time as a die is rolled. List all possible outcomes.
5) I roll a fair die. What is the probability of getting an odd number?

The probability of a probability question coming up in the exam is pretty close to one I'd say — and if you don't know what I mean by that then you're not ready to tackle these exam questions.

Worked Exam Question

Calculator Not Allowed

1 The two spinners below are spun and the results added to get a score. Both spinners have an equal chance of landing on each side.

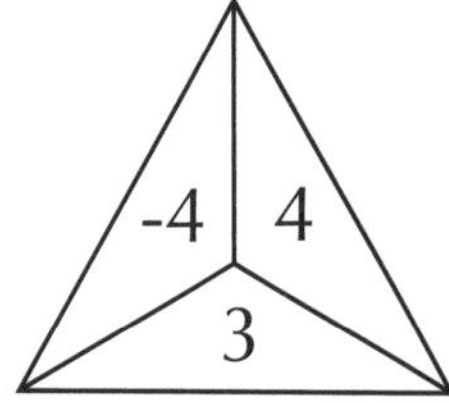

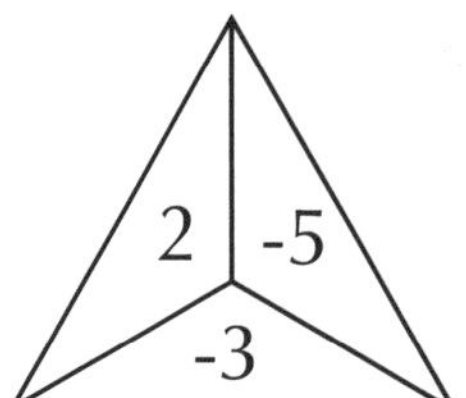

a) Draw a sample space to show all the possible outcomes.

The 3 possible outcomes for the first spinner

The 3 possible outcomes for the second spinner

	-4	4	3
2	-2	6	5
-5	-9	-1	-2
-3	-7	1	0

Put the totals in the middle. (Careful with all those minus signs...)

(2 marks)

b) Use your answer to a) to find the probability that the total score is negative.

From the table, there are 5 ways of getting a negative score,

from a total of 9 possible outcomes.

So P (negative score) = 5 / 9

(2 marks)

Exam Questions

Exam Questions

Calculator Allowed

2 The letters that spell the word PROBABILITY are placed in a bag. A letter is picked at random. Find:

(a) The probability of picking out an 'L'.
(1 mark)

(b) The probability of picking out an 'I' or a 'Y'.
(1 mark)

(c) The probability of picking out a vowel.
(1 mark)

(d) The probability of picking out an 'X'.
(1 mark)

3 A card is taken at random from a pack of 52 playing cards and then replaced. Find the probability of picking:

(a) a red card.
(b) a Queen.
(c) a Jack of Spades.
(d) a 5 or a 6.
(4 marks)

4 A bag holds red, blue and white counters. P (red) = 0.3, and P (red or blue) = 0.55.

(a) A counter is taken out and replaced. This is done 200 times. How many blue counters would you expect to get?
(2 marks)

(b) If there are 6 red counters, how many counters are there in the bag?
(2 marks)

(c) If there are 40 counters in the bag, how many are white?
(2 marks)

5 Chris spins the two spinners shown below and adds the numbers to get a score.

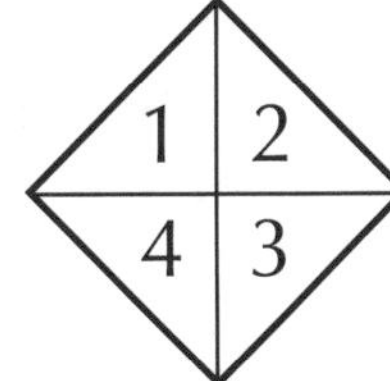

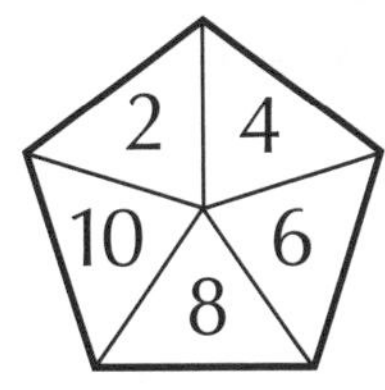

(a) Draw a diagram to show all the possible outcomes, including the total scores.
(3 marks)

(b) Find the probability of getting a score greater than 10.
(1 mark)

(c) Find the probability of getting the same number on both spinners.
(1 mark)

Graphs and Charts

Make sure you know all these easy details:

1 Line Graphs or "Frequency Polygons"

A line graph or "frequency polygon" is just a set of points joined up with straight lines.

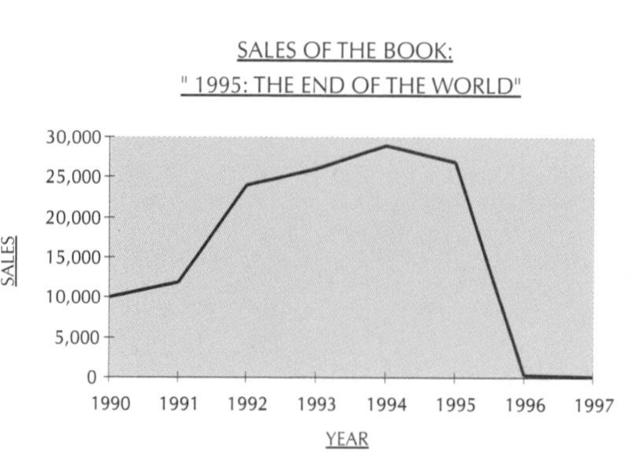

2 Bar Charts

Just watch out for when the bars should touch or not touch:

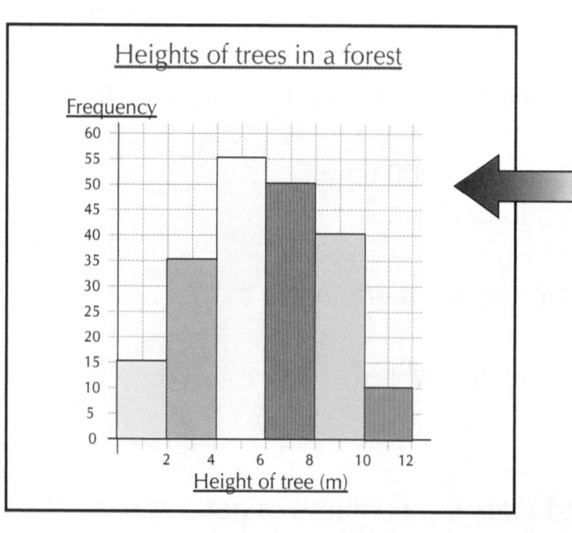

All the bars in this chart are for lengths. With anything like length or weight, where the measurements are different sizes but part of the same continuous scale, there mustn't be any spaces between bars.

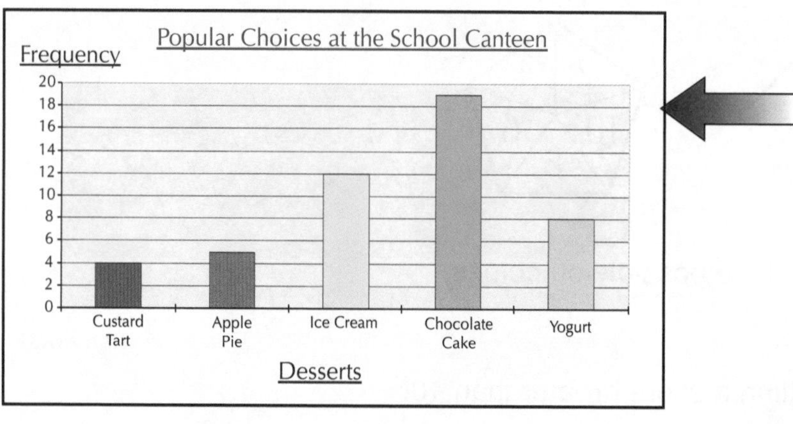

This bar chart compares totally separate items so the bars are separate.

A bar-line graph is just like a bar chart except you just draw thin lines instead of bars.

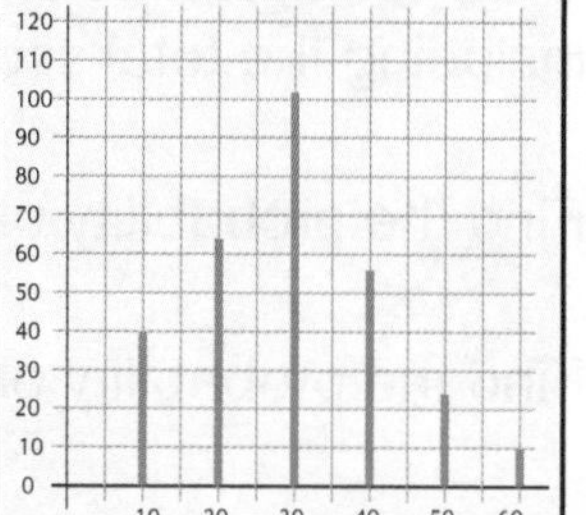

Graphs and Charts

3 Scatter Graphs

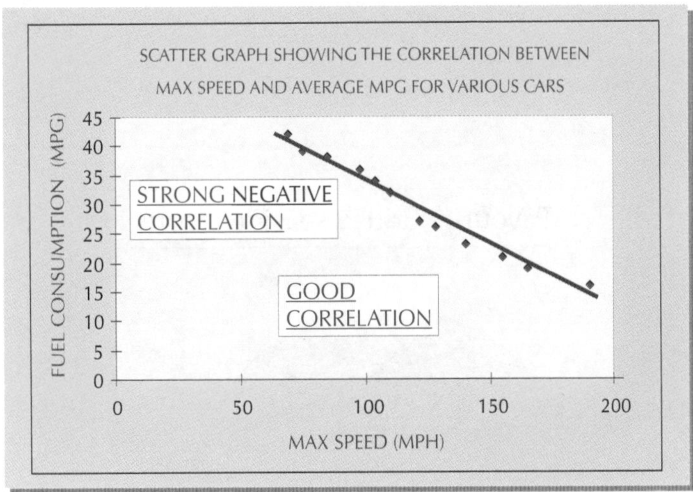

1) A scatter graph is just a load of points on a graph that end up in a bit of a mess rather than in a nice line or curve.
2) There's a fancy word to say how much of a mess they're in — it's correlation.
3) A good correlation (or strong correlation) means the points form quite a nice line, and it means the two things are closely related to each other.
4) A poor correlation (or weak correlation) means the points are all over the place and so there's very little relation between the two things.
5) If the points form a line sloping uphill from left to right, then there is positive correlation, which just means that both things increase or decrease together.
6) If the points form a line sloping downhill from left to right, then there is negative correlation. That just means that as one thing increases the other decreases.
7) So when you're describing a scatter graph you have to mention both things, i.e. whether it's a strong / weak / moderate correlation and whether it's positive / negative.

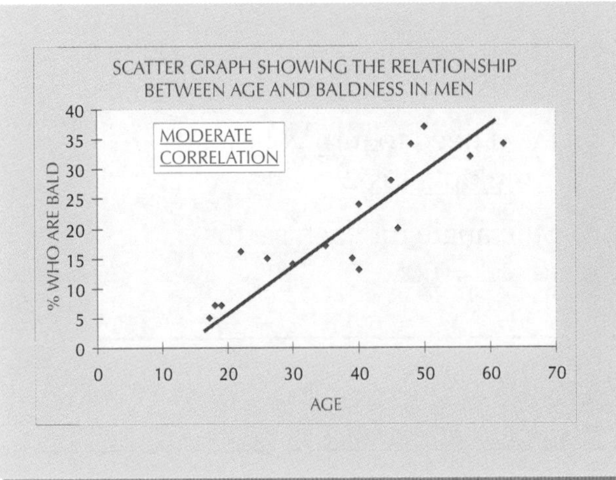

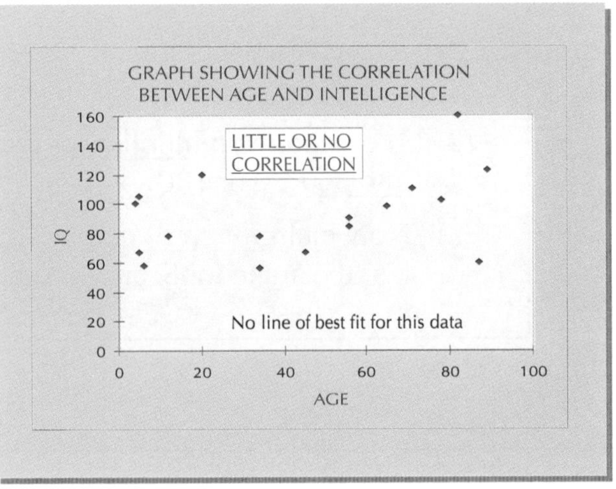

Graphs and Charts

4 Pie Charts

Learn this important rule for pie charts: **The TOTAL of everything = 360°**

EXAMPLE:

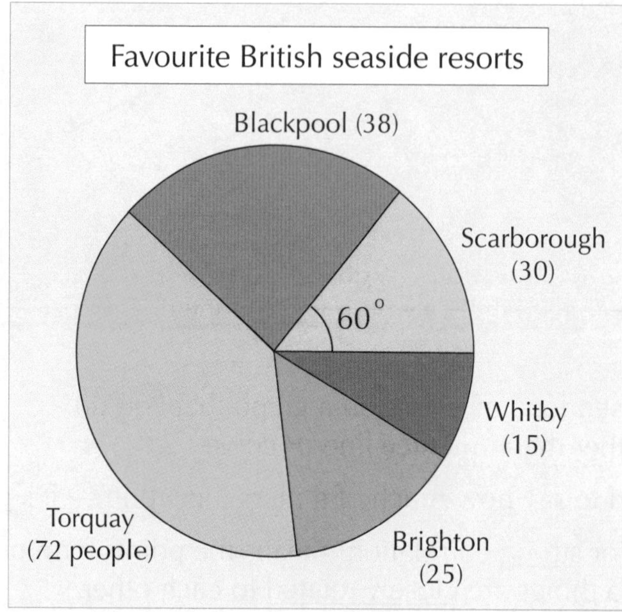

Resort	Blackpool	Scarborough	Whitby	Brighton	Torquay	Total
Number	38	30	15	25	72	180

↓ × 2

Angle		60°				360°

1) Add up all the numbers in each sector to get the total (it's 180 in the example above).
2) Then find the multiplier (or divider) that you need to turn your total into 360°. For 180 → 360 as above, the multiplier is 2.
3) Now multiply every number by 2 to get the angle for each sector. E.g. the angle for Scarborough will be 30 × 2 = 60°.

Graphs can tell you a lot just at a glance

You can probably look at a graph and see what it's telling you without much trouble. But that's not enough — you've got to be able to use the right words (like correlation) to talk about them.

Warm-up and Worked Exam Questions

For the exam you'll have to be able to draw all these different types of graphs.
You'll also need to be confident about explaining them using the right mathematical words.

Warm-up Questions

1) Two bar charts are drawn, one showing shoe sizes and the other showing lengths of feet. Which bar chart has spaces between the bars? Explain why.
2) A café sells more bowls of soup on cold days than on warm, sunny days. What type of correlation (positive or negative) is there between number of bowls sold and temperature?
3) A pie chart is drawn showing the favourite colours of 90 people. How many degrees represent one person on this chart?
4) Look at this graph. Is it showing a positive or a negative correlation?

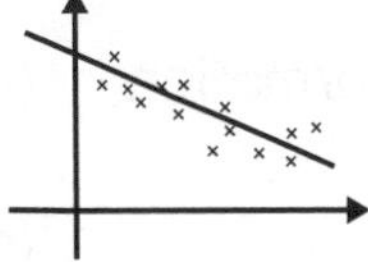

Practising lots of nice graph questions will help you make sure you can cope with them on exam day. If you managed the warm-up, you'll hopefully breeze through these.

Worked Exam Question

Calculator Allowed

1 A paint manufacturer wanted to name a new purple paint. The workers were asked to vote on possible names. The results are shown in the bar-line graph on the right.

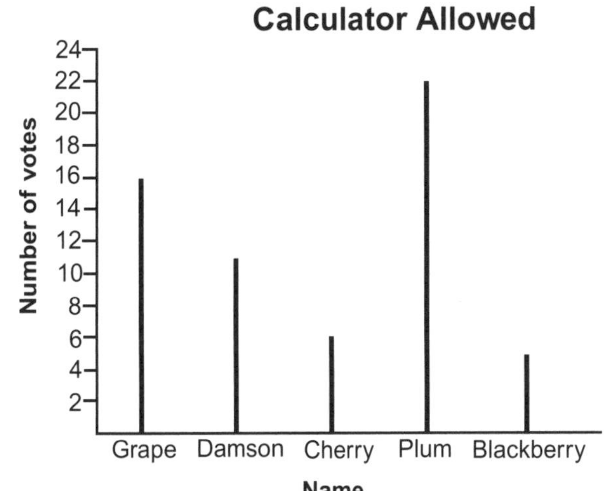

(a) Which colour got the most votes?

Plum

You can see straight away that this has the tallest line, so must have had the most votes. (1 mark)

(b) How many more people chose Plum than Blackberry?

Plum = 22. Blackberry = 5. 22 – 5 = 17 more people.

(1 mark)

(c) How many employees voted?

16 + 11 + 6 + 22 + 5 = 60.

It's really important with questions like these that you read off the numbers from the graph accurately. Use a ruler to follow a line across if you're not sure. (2 marks)

(d) What percentage chose Cherry?

6 chose cherry. (6 ÷ 60) × 100 = 10%.

(2 marks)

(e) What is the ratio of votes for Plum to votes for Damson, in its simplest form?

Ratio is 22 : 11 or 2 : 1.

Hopefully you'll notice at once that 11 and 22 can both be divided by 11 to give this ratio in its simplest form. (2 marks)

Exam Questions

Exam Questions

Calculator Allowed

2 A class of 30 children were asked to choose their favourite flavour of crisps. Their results are shown below.

Plain	**9**
Cheese and Onion	**8**
Salt 'n' Vinegar	**6**
Barbecue Beef	**5**
Prawn Cocktail	**2**

Display this information (a) in a bar chart.

(4 marks)

(b) in a pie chart.

(5 marks)

3 Write down which of the relationships (a) – (c) is shown by each graph below.

1 2

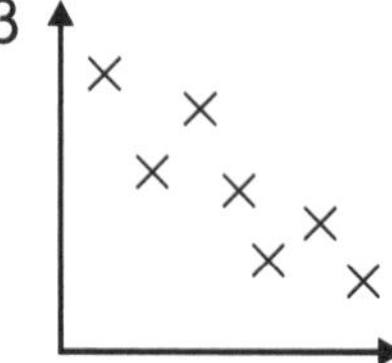

(a) Weight and hair length.

(1 mark)

(b) Cigarettes smoked per day and life expectancy.

(1 mark)

(c) Foot length and shoe size.

(1 mark)

4 This pie chart shows the favourite take-aways of a group of pupils:

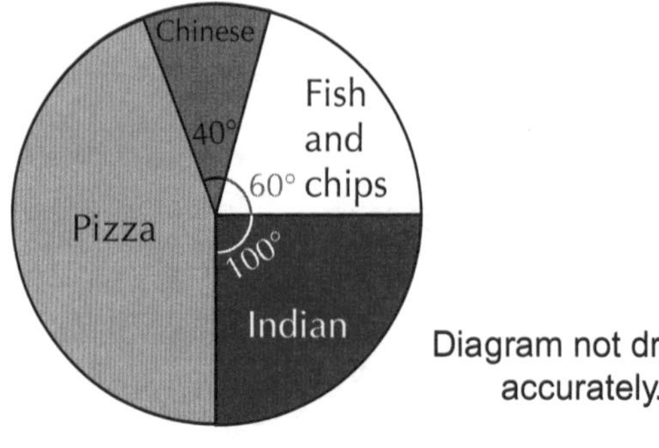

Diagram not drawn accurately.

(a) 10 pupils chose Indian. How many chose Chinese?

(2 marks)

(b) What fraction chose fish and chips?

(2 marks)

(c) How many pupils does this pie chart represent?

(2 marks)

(d) What percentage chose pizza? Give your answer to one decimal place.

(2 marks)

Mean, Median, Mode and Range

If you don't manage to learn these four basic definitions then you'll be passing up on some of the easiest marks in the whole exam.

1) *Mode* = *Most Common*

The mode = the most common value in a set of data.

Emphasise the 'o' in each when you say them, to help you remember.

2) *Median* = *Middle Value*

The median = the middle value in a set of data.

*Emphasise the 'm*d' in each when you say them.*

3) *Mean* = *Total of items ÷ Number of items*

The mean is what people usually think of as the average.

And it's a bit mean that you have to work it out.

4) *Range* = *How far from the smallest to the biggest*

The mean, median and mode are different kinds of average value. The range shows how much the values are spread out.

THE GOLDEN RULE:

Mean, median, mode and range should be easy marks, but even people who've bothered to learn them still manage to lose marks in the exam because they don't do this one vital step:

Always rearrange the data in ascending order.

(And then check you've got the same number of entries.)

Example *"Find the mean, median, mode and range of these numbers:*

6, -1, 5, -5, 0, 2, 8, 8, -7, 9, 6, 8." (12 numbers altogether)

1) First... put them in order: -7, -5, -1, 0, 2, 5, 6, 6, 8, 8, 8, 9 (✓12)

2) Mean $= \frac{\text{total}}{\text{number}} = \frac{-7 + -5 + -1 + 0 + 2 + 5 + 6 + 6 + 8 + 8 + 8 + 9}{12}$

$= 39 \div 12 = 3.25$

3) Median = the middle value (only when they're arranged in order of size, that is). When there are two middle numbers, as in this case, then the median is halfway between the two middle numbers.

-7, -5, -1, 0, 2, 5, 6, 6, 8, 8, 8, 9

← six numbers this side ↑ six numbers this side →

Median = 5.5

4) Mode = most common value, which is simply 8. (Or you can say "The modal value is 8".)

5) Range = distance from lowest to highest value, i.e. from -7 up to 9, = 16.

Frequency Tables

Frequency tables can either be done in rows or in columns of numbers. They can be quite confusing, but not if you learn these eight key points:

Nine Key Points

1) All frequency tables are the same.
2) The word frequency just means how many, so a frequency table is nothing more than a "How many in each group" table.
3) The first row (or column) just gives the group labels.
4) The second row (or column) gives the actual data.
5) You have to work out a third row (or column) yourself.
6) The mean is always found using: 3rd row total ÷ 2nd row total
7) The median is found from the middle value in the 2nd row.
8) The mode is easy — it's just the group with most entries.
9) The range is found from the extremes of the first row.

Example

Here is a typical frequency table shown in both row form and column form:

Number of letters received in a single day in thirty-two different households

No. of Letters	Frequency
0	5
1	9
2	8
3	6
4	3
5	0
6	1

column form

No. of Letters	0	1	2	3	4	5	6
Frequency	5	9	8	6	3	0	1

row form

There's no real difference between these two forms and you could get either one in an exam. Whichever you get, make sure you remember these three important facts:

1) The 1st row (or column) gives us the group labels for the different categories: i.e. "no letters", "one letter", "two letters", etc.
2) The 2nd row (or column) is the actual data and tells us how many (people) there are in each category i.e. 5 households had "no letters", 9 households had "one letter", etc.
3) But you should see the table as unfinished, because it still needs a third row (or column) and two totals for the 2nd and 3rd rows (or columns), as shown on the next page...

Frequency Tables

This is what the two types of table look like when they're completed:

No. of letters	0	1	2	3	4	5	6	totals	
Frequency	5	9	8	6	3	0	1	32	(Houses in street)
No. × Frequency	0	9	16	18	12	0	6	61	(Letters delivered)

No. of Letters	Frequency	No. × Frequency
0	5	0
1	9	9
2	8	16
3	6	18
4	3	12
5	0	0
6	1	6
TOTALS	32	61
	(Houses in street)	(Letters delivered)

So where does the third row come from?

The third row (or column) is always obtained by multiplying the numbers from the first 2 rows (or columns).

Third row = 1st row × 2nd row

Once the table is complete, you can easily find the mean, median, mode and range (see page 157) which is what they usually ask for in the exam.

Mean, Median, Mode and Range

This is easy enough if you learn it. If you don't, you'll drown in a sea of numbers.

1) Mean $= \dfrac{\text{3rd row total}}{\text{2nd row total}} = \dfrac{61}{32} = 1.91$ (Letters per household)

2) Median — imagine the original data set out in ascending order:

00000 111111111 22222222 333333 444 6
↑

The median is just the middle, which is here between the 16th and 17th digits. So for this data the median is 2. (Of course, when you get slick at this you can easily find the position of the middle value straight from the table.)

3) Mode — the group with the most entries, i.e. 1

4) The range is 6 – 0 = 6. The first row tells us there are houses with anything from "no letters" right up to "six letters" (but not 5 letters). (Always give it as a single number.)

Frequency tables just show how many there are in each group

Remember, when you get a frequency table with two rows (or columns), it's not finished. You've got to multiply the values in these two rows (or columns) together to get the third one.

Grouped Frequency Tables

These are a bit trickier than simple frequency tables, but they can look deceptively simple — like this one, which shows the distribution of the weights of 60 school kids.

Weight (kg)	31 — 40	41 — 50	51 — 60	61 — 70	71 — 80
Frequency	8	16	18	12	6

Class ***Boundaries*** *and Mid-Interval* ***Values***

These are the two little jokers that make grouped frequency tables so tricky.

1) The class boundaries are the precise values where you'd pass from one group into the next. For the above table the class boundaries would be at 40.5, 50.5, 60.5, etc. It's not difficult to work out what the class boundaries will be, just so long as you're clued up about it — they're nearly always "something.5" anyway, for obvious reasons.
2) The mid-interval values are pretty self-explanatory really — it's the middle value in each class. They usually end up being "something.5" as well. Mind you, a bit of care is still needed to make sure you get the exact middle.

You can calculate the mid-interval value by adding the numbers at each end of the class and dividing by 2. So for class 31-40, mid-interval value = (31 + 40) ÷ 2 = 35.5.

"Estimating" the ***Mean*** *using* ***Mid-Interval Values***

Just like with ordinary frequency tables you have to add extra rows and find totals to be able to work anything out. Also notice you can only "estimate" the mean from grouped data tables — you can't find it exactly unless you know all the original values.

1) Add a 3rd row and enter mid-interval values for each group.
2) Add a 4th row and multiply frequency by mid-interval value for each group.

Weight (kg)	31 — 40	41 — 50	51 — 60	61 — 70	71 — 80	TOTALS
Frequency	8	16	18	12	6	60
Mid-Interval Value	35.5	45.5	55.5	65.5	75.5	—
Frequency × Mid-Interval Value	284	728	999	786	453	3250

1) Estimating the mean is then the usual thing of dividing the totals:

$$\text{Mean} = \frac{\text{Overall Total (Final Row)}}{\text{Frequency Total (2nd Row)}} = \frac{3250}{60} = 54.2 \text{ (3 s.f.)}$$

2) The mode is still easy: the modal group is 51 — 60 kg (the one with the most entries).
3) The median can't be found exactly but you can at least say which group it's in. If all the data were put in order, the 30th / 31st entries would be in the 51 — 60 kg group.

Cumulative Frequency Tables

Usually you'll get a half-finished table and they'll ask you to complete it as a cumulative frequency table. This means adding a third row and filling it in (as shown in the example below).

*Four **Key** Points*

1) Cumulative frequency just means adding it up as you go along.
   So each entry in the table for cumulative frequency is just "the total so far".
2) You have to add a third row to the table — this is just the running total of the 2nd row.
3) If you're plotting a graph, always plot the cumulative frequency (from row 3) against the highest value in each group (from row 1), i.e. plot at the upper class boundaries.
   So for the example below, plot 13 at 160.5, 33 at 170.5, etc.
4) Cumulative frequency is always plotted up the side of a graph, not across.

Example

"Complete the table below for cumulative frequency:"

Height (cm)	141 – 150	151 – 160	161 – 170	171 – 180	181 – 190	191 – 200	201 – 210
Frequency	4	9	20	31	36	15	5

ANSWER: Add in the third row where each entry for row 3 (cumulative frequency) is just "the total so far" of the numbers for frequency (row 2).

Height (cm)	141 – 150	151 – 160	161 – 170	171 – 180	181 – 190	191 – 200	201 – 210
Frequency	4	9	20	31	36	15	5
Cumulative Frequency	4 (AT 150.5)	13 (AT 160.5)	33 (AT 170.5)	64 (AT 180.5)	100 (AT 190.5)	115 (AT 200.5)	120 (AT 210.5)

If you're asked to plot a graph, it'd be plotted from these pairs: (150.5, 4), (160.5, 13), (170.5, 33), (180.5, 64), etc. That's because the cumulative frequency has only reached those values (4, 13, 33, etc.) by the top end of each group, not at the middle of each group, and 150.5 is the actual class boundary between the first group and the next — a tricky detail.

Four key points to learn on this page

Completing cumulative frequency tables should be straightforward if you've learned and understood these four key points. You might then be asked to plot a graph using your table. Always use the upper class boundary, and plot the cumulative frequency up the side.

The Cumulative Frequency Curve

When you've plotted your cumulative frequency curve, it'll probably look something like this:

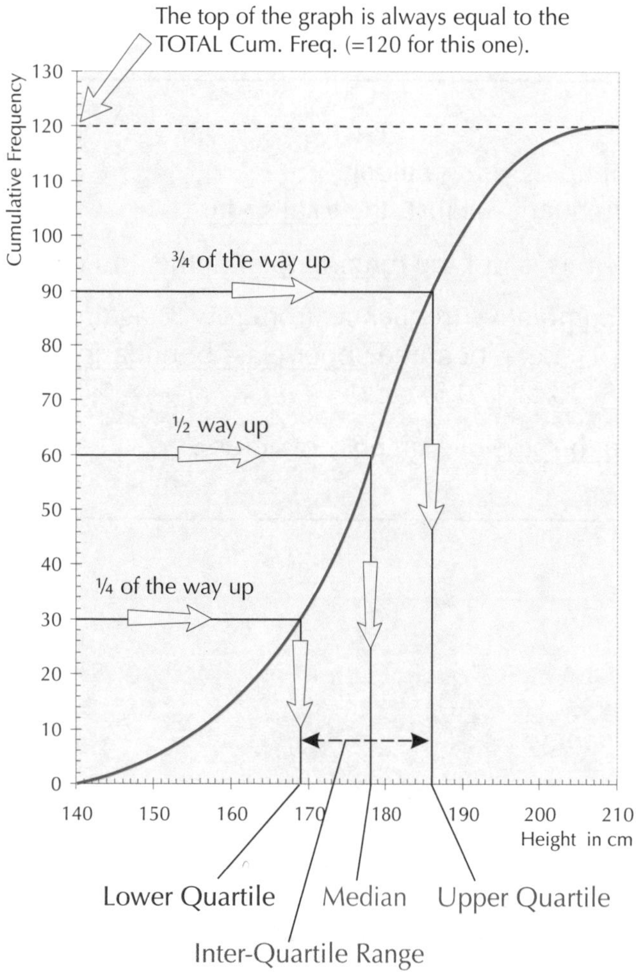

From the cumulative frequency curve you can get three vital statistics:

1) Median
Exactly halfway up, then across, then down and read off the bottom scale.

2) Lower and Upper Quartiles
Exactly ¼ and ¾ of the way up, then across, then down and read off the bottom scale.

3) The Inter-quartile Range
This is the distance on the bottom scale between the lower and upper quartiles.

So from the cumulative frequency curve on the left, we can easily get these results:

Median = 178 cm
Lower quartile = 169 cm
Upper quartile = 186 cm
Inter-quartile Range = 17 cm (186 – 169)

Interpreting the Shape

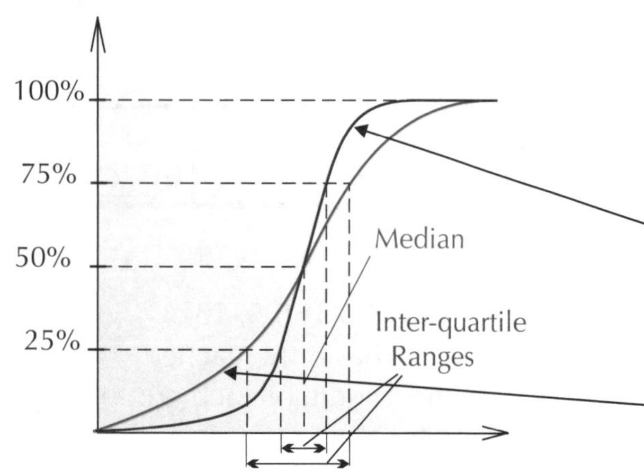

The shape of a cumulative frequency curve also tells us how spread out the data values are.

This 'tighter' distribution (with a small inter-quartile range) represents very consistent results, which is usually good. For example, if the curve shows the lifetimes of light bulbs, they're pretty similar and it's a good product compared to this curve, where the lifetimes show wide variation, meaning it's a poor quality product.

Learn how to get the three vital statistics from a curve

Make sure you know what these are and how to find them using a cumulative frequency curve. You could use the cumulative frequency table from the last page to draw your own curve.

Warm-up and Worked Exam Questions

Well, you've finally made it — this is the last set of questions in the book.
Just these to get through, and then you can have a long, well-deserved rest...

Warm-up Questions

1) Find the mean of 1, 2, 3, 4, 5, 6, 7, 8, 9 and 10.
2) What is the median of 10, 20, 12, 21, 19, 9, 5 and 18?
3) Find the range of the first 5 prime numbers.
4) Four numbers have a mean of 8. If 3 of the numbers are 5, 7 and 8, what is the 4th?
5) You are asked to complete this frequency table. How would you find the third row to complete it?

Number of pets	0	1	2	3	4
Frequency	11	9	12	5	3

6) Which type of frequency table can only be used to **estimate** the mean?
7) A grouped frequency table has as one of its groups 70-79 cm. What is the mid-interval value of this group?
8) How can you find the interquartile range from a cumulative frequency curve?
9) What does the shape of a cumulative frequency curve tell you?

Final set of exam questions — my last worked example — quite an emotional moment really.
(Except that there's still the practice exams to do. Sorry, forgot to mention that.)

Worked Exam Question

Calculator Allowed

1 Find the mean, median, mode and range of **1, 3, 0, 4, 2, 2, 1, 2, 4** and **1**.

Mean = (1 + 3 + 0 + 4 + 2 + 2 + 1 + 2 + 4 + 1) ÷ 10 = 20 ÷ 10 = 2.

Remember to include 0 as one of your values when you divide by the number of values.

Median: put the numbers in ascending order, i.e. 0, 1, 1, 1, 2, 2, 2, 3, 4, 4.

There are two middle numbers (underlined above), so find the average.

The average of 2 and 2 is obviously 2.

You need to find the number halfway between the 2 middle numbers – this is the same as finding the average of the 2 numbers.

Mode = 1 and 2.

The mode is the most common value, and 1 and 2 both appear 3 times in this set of data. It's OK to have more than one mode, if several values or groups are equally common.

Range = highest value – lowest value = 4 – 0 = 4.

(8 marks)

Exam Questions

Exam Questions

Calculator Allowed

2 Gina counts the number of letters in the names of everyone in her class. The frequency table on the right shows the results.

(a) Complete the table.

(b) Find the mean number of letters per name.

(c) Find the median number of letters per name.

Number of letters	Frequency	No. of letters × frequency
3	4	
4	3	
5	3	
6	3	
7	2	
8	4	
9	1	
Totals		

(5 marks)

3 In an attempt to improve their service, a bank decided to investigate the waiting times of their customers. The table below shows the results.

Waiting time (seconds)	1-30	31-60	61-90	91-120	121-150	151-180	181-210
Frequency	7	13	20	24	17	9	10

(a) What percentage of customers waited 3 minutes or less?

(2 marks)

(b) Estimate the mean waiting time, to the nearest whole second.

(4 marks)

(c) Find the modal waiting time.

(1 mark)

(d) Which group is the median waiting time found in?

(1 mark)

4 Here are the birth weights of babies born at a maternity unit in one week:

Weight (kg)	1.6-2.0	2.1-2.5	2.6-3.0	3.1-3.5	3.6-4.0	4.1-4.5	4.6-5.0
Frequency	1	2	4	6	9	5	1
Cumulative frequency							

(a) Complete the cumulative frequency row.

(2 marks)

(b) Draw the cumulative frequency curve. Use graph paper.

(3 marks)

(c) Use the curve to find the median weight.

(2 marks)

(d) Use the curve to find the interquartile range.

(3 marks)

Revision Summary for Section Four

Here's the really fun page. The inevitable list of questions to test how much you know. Remember, these questions will sort out exactly what you know and what you don't quicker than anything else can. And don't forget that's exactly what revision is all about — finding out what you don't know and then learning it until you do. Enjoy.

Keep learning these basic facts until you know them

1) How big or small can a probability be?
2) Draw a line to represent all probabilities with words to describe them.
3) Which three types of number can be used to represent probabilities?
4) How should P(x) = ½ be read?
5) What must the total probability always add up to?
6) What are the two formulae to do with estimated probability?
7) What is combined probability?
8) What is a sample space?
9) Give the names of the four different types of chart for displaying data.
10) Draw two examples of each type of chart.
11) When should the bars of a frequency chart touch and not touch?
12) What does correlation mean? Draw graphs of one positive and one negative correlation.
13) What are the three steps for finding the angles in a pie chart?
14) Give the definitions for mean, median, mode and range.
15) What is the Golden Rule in connection with mean, median etc.?
16) What are the nine key points for frequency tables?
17) How do you work out the mean and median from a frequency table?
18) How do you find the mode and range from a frequency table?
19) What is the difference between a frequency table and a grouped frequency table?
20) What are the two things that make grouped frequency tables so tricky?
21) How do you estimate the mean from a grouped frequency table?
22) What are the four key points to remember for cumulative frequency tables?
23) Do you need to think about class boundaries when plotting a cumulative frequency curve from a table of values? Why?
24) Sketch a typical cumulative frequency graph.
25) What are the three vital statistics you can obtain from a cumulative frequency graph?
26) Explain exactly how you obtain them, and illustrate on your graph.
27) What does the shape of a cumulative frequency curve tell you?

Once you've been through the topics in this book, you should feel pretty confident about knowing the maths — but you've still got to be able to answer questions on it in an exam. Doing the practice test that follows will help give you an idea what to expect in the real thing. There are three parts to it — non-calculator questions in Paper 1, calculator questions in Paper 2, and a mental mathematics test.
If you're doing tiers 3-5 or 4-6 you might not have learnt every bit, but it's still good practice.

Key Stage 3 — Mathematics Test

Paper 1 Tier 5 – 8
Calculator NOT allowed

Instructions

- The test is one hour long.
- Make sure you have these things with you before you start: pen, pencil, rubber, ruler, angle measurer or protractor, pair of compasses and tracing paper.
- The easier questions are at the start of the test.
- Try to answer all of the questions.
- Don't use any rough paper — write all your answers and working in this test paper (marks may be awarded for working).
- Check your work carefully before the end of the test.

This means write down your answer or show your working and your answer.

You must not use a calculator in this test.

Formulae

Trapezium

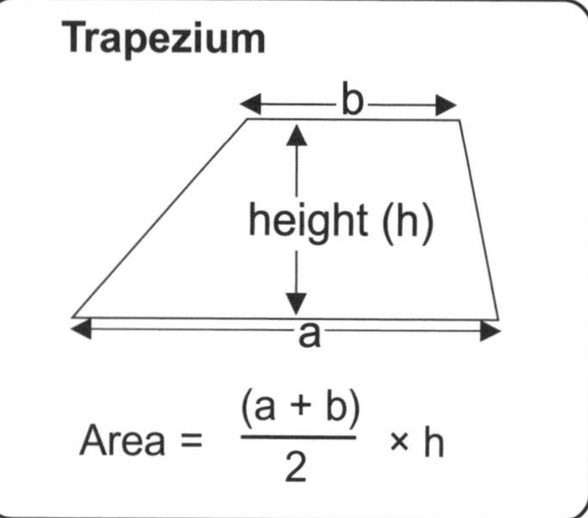

$$\text{Area} = \frac{(a + b)}{2} \times h$$

Prism

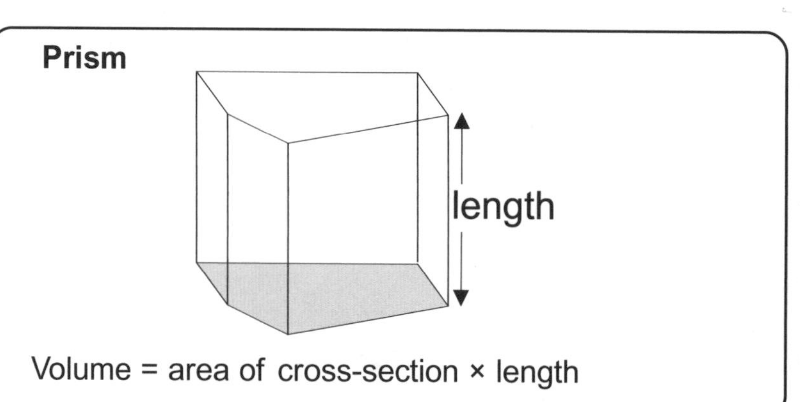

Volume = area of cross-section × length

1 Fill in the next two numbers in this sequence.

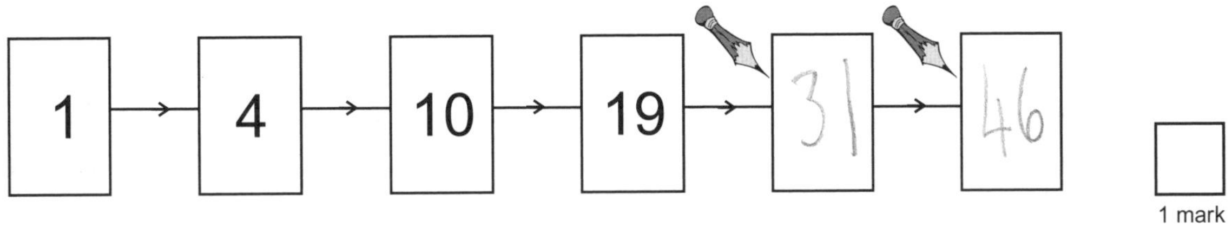

1 mark

2 In a Maths test Aaron scored 15 out of 20.

(a) Write down Aaron's mark as a percentage.

75 %

1 mark

In the same test Julie scored 12 out of 20.

(b) Write down Julie's mark as a percentage.

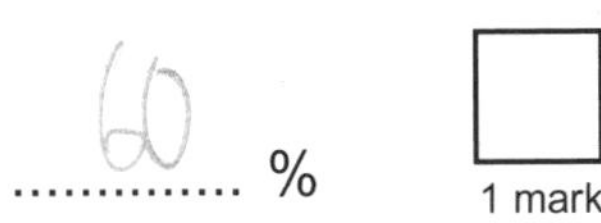

1 mark

3 Write these fractions in order of size, starting with the smallest.

0.3	**½**	**2/5**	**0.2**
0·2	0·3	2/5	½

3 marks

4 The diagram below shows a regular hexagon.
Find the size of the marked angles. Do **not** use a protractor.

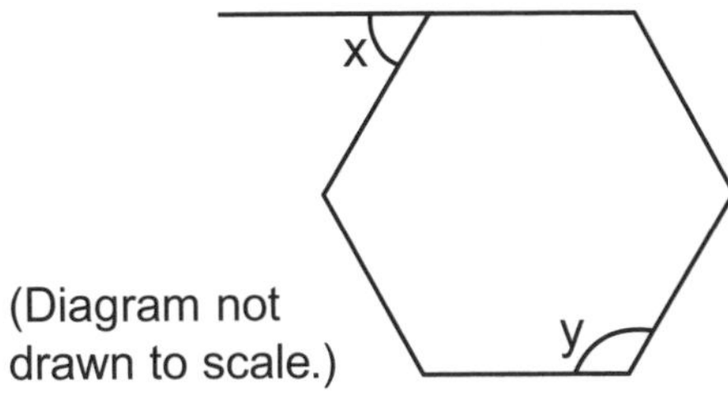

(Diagram not drawn to scale.)

x = 60 °

1 mark

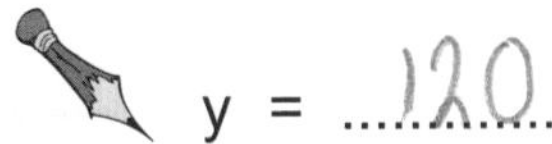

1 mark

5 Simplify these expressions.

(a) 4a + 3 + 2a = ...

1 mark

(b) a + 2 + a + 5 = ...

1 mark

6 (a) Using the line drawn for you on this grid, draw an isosceles triangle with an area of 12 cm^2.

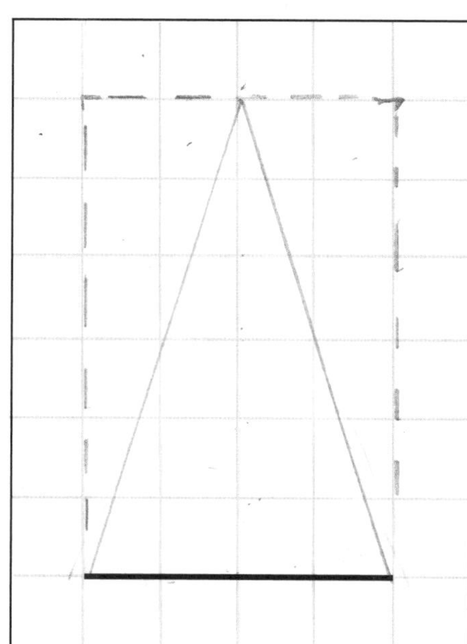

1 mark

(b) Using the line drawn for you on this grid, draw a right-angled isosceles triangle with an area of 8 cm^2.

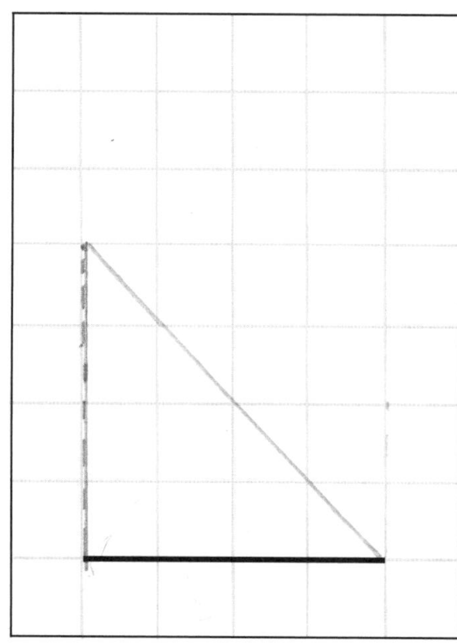

1 mark

7 Fill in the missing numbers.

(a) 1/4 of 100 = 1/3 of ....75....

1 mark

(b) 1/3 of 90 = 1/2 of ....60....

1 mark

(c) 1/2 of 24 = 3/4 of ....16....

1 mark

8 (a) Josh got the following marks out of 10 for his homework last month:
5, 7, 8, 10. What was his median mark?

 ....7.5....

1 mark

(b) The month before that he also handed in 4 pieces of homework.
They were all marked out of 10, and he got 10 once and 8 twice.
The range of his marks for that month was 5.
What was his other mark that month?

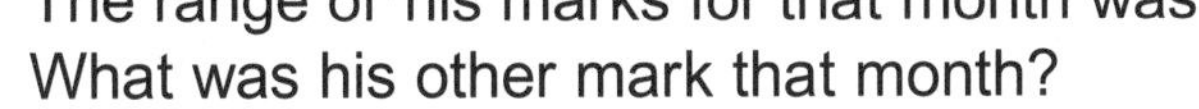

 ....5....

1 mark

9 This diagram (not drawn to scale) shows the route for a Fun Run.

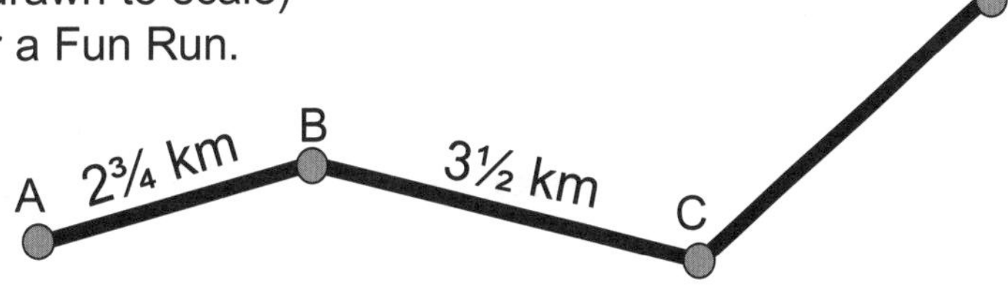

The run starts at A and finishes at D. B and C are checkpoints.

(a) How far is it from A to C?

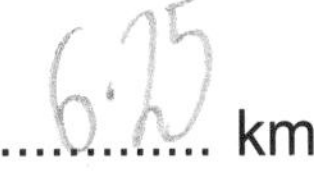 ....6.25.... km

1 mark

(b) The distance from B to D is 7¼ km.
How far is it from C to D?

 ....3.75.... km

1 mark

(c) What is the total distance from A to D?

 ....10.... km

1 mark

10 Emma is given a box of 20 chocolates. 12 of the chocolates have soft centres, 5 have whole nut centres and the rest have hard centres.

Emma is going to pick a chocolate at random from the box.

(a) Complete these sentences.

(i) The probability that the chocolate will have a

.... centre is ¼.

1 mark

(ii) The probability that the chocolate will have a

hard centre is ....

1 mark

(b) Before Emma picks her chocolate, her friend Chris eats two whole nut chocolates from the full box. If Emma now chooses the chocolate at random from the box, what is the probability that she will get a soft centre?

....

1 mark

(c) A different box of chocolates contains 24 chocolates. The table below shows the probability of getting each type of chocolate. Use the probabilities to work out how many chocolates of each type are in this box.

Write your answers in the table.

Type	Probability	Number of chocolates
Soft centre	2/3	
Whole nut centre	5/24	
Hard centre	1/8	

3 marks

11 There are 30 pupils in a class.
10 of these pupils have a pet dog at home.

(a) The pie chart is not drawn accurately.
What should the angles be?

..............° and ....°

2 marks

(b) 15 of the pupils in this class have a pet cat at home.
From this information, what percentage of the pupils who have a pet dog also have a pet cat?

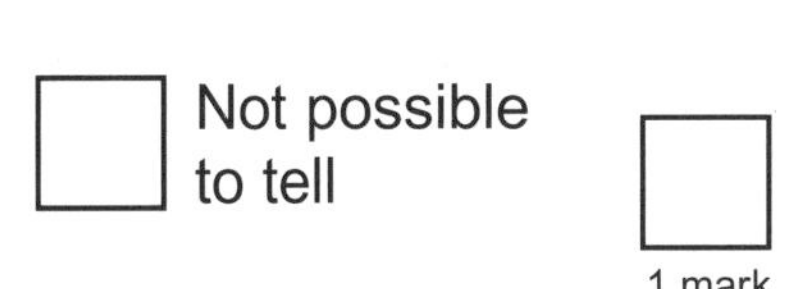

☐ 5% ☐ 10% ☐ 50% ☐ Not possible to tell

1 mark

12 Solve these equations. Show your working.

$4p - 3 = 5$

p = ...

1 mark

$2m + 7 = 15$

m = ...

1 mark

$4x + 3 = x + 24$

x = ...

1 mark

$2(5q + 8) = 6$

q = ...

1 mark

13 Here are six number cards.

1 2 3 4 5 6

(a) Arrange these six cards to make the calculations below.
The first one has been done for you.

867 = 5 4 1 + 3 2 6

1083 = ☐ ☐ ☐ + ☐ ☐ ☐

1 mark

381 = ☐ ☐ ☐ + ☐ ☐ ☐

1 mark

(b) Now arrange the six cards to make a difference of 135.

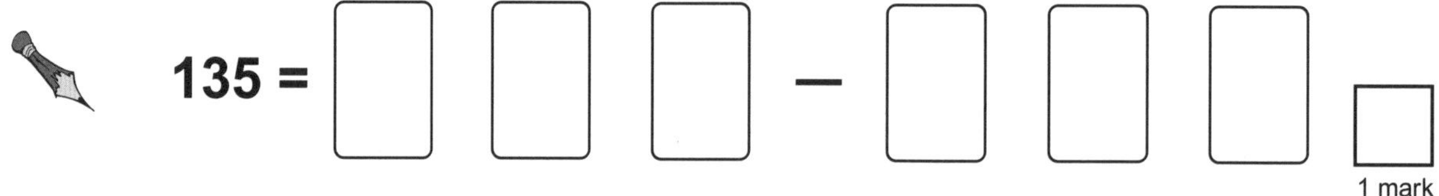

1 mark

14 The diagram shows two isosceles triangles.
The lines PQ and RS are parallel.

(The diagram is not drawn accurately.)

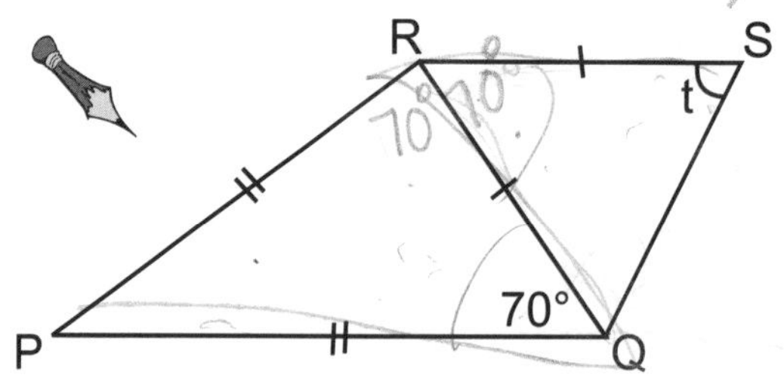

(a) There are two more angles on this diagram that are 70°.
Label them as **70°** on the diagram.

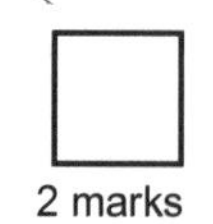

2 marks

(b) Calculate the size of the angle marked t.
Show your working.

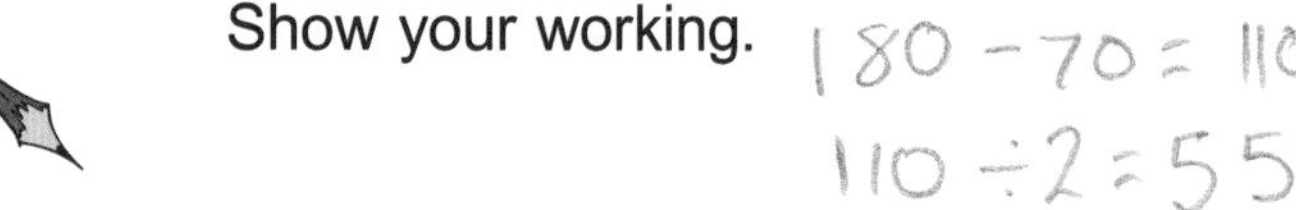

2 marks

15 (a) Solve these inequalities. Show your working.

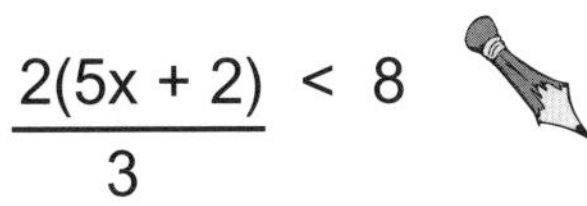

$$\frac{2(5x + 2)}{3} < 8$$

x .... 1 mark

$$\frac{2(9 - y)}{3} > 4$$

y .... 1 mark

(b) John had to solve the inequality $x^2 < 16$.
His answer was $x < 4$.
Write down a value of x, which is less than 4, which shows that his answer is incorrect.

x = ... 1 mark

16 O is the centre of this circle.
Angle OCB is 50°. Angle OAB is 25°.

(The diagram is not drawn accurately.)

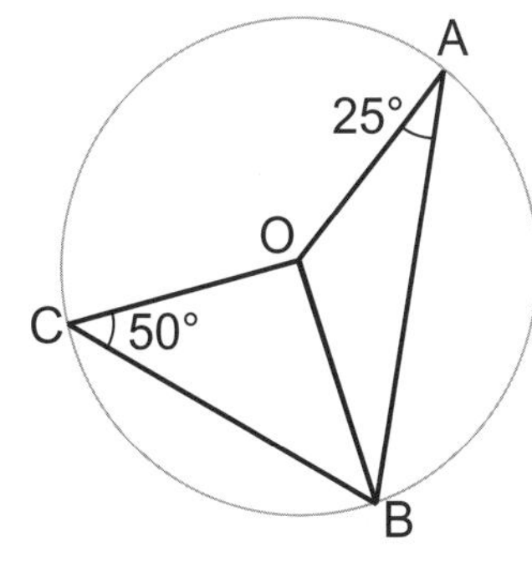

Write down the size of angle OBC.

.... ° 1 mark

Write down the size of angle OBA.

.... ° 1 mark

What is the size of the obtuse angle AOC?

.... ° 1 mark

17 Tick the statements that are true.

(a) ☐ When x is even, $x(x + 3)$ is odd. ☐ When x is even, $x(x + 3)$ is even.

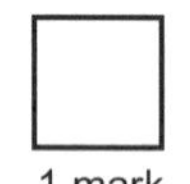

1 mark

(b) ☐ When x is odd, $x^2 + 1$ is even. ☐ When x is odd, $x^2 + 1$ is odd.

1 mark

(c) ☐ $x^2 + x$ is always odd.

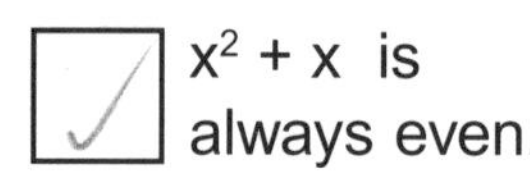

$x^2 + x$ is always even.

1 mark

18 The diagram shows a triangle drawn on a square grid.

The points A, B and C are the vertices of the triangle.

D is the mid-point of line AB and E is the mid-point of line BC.

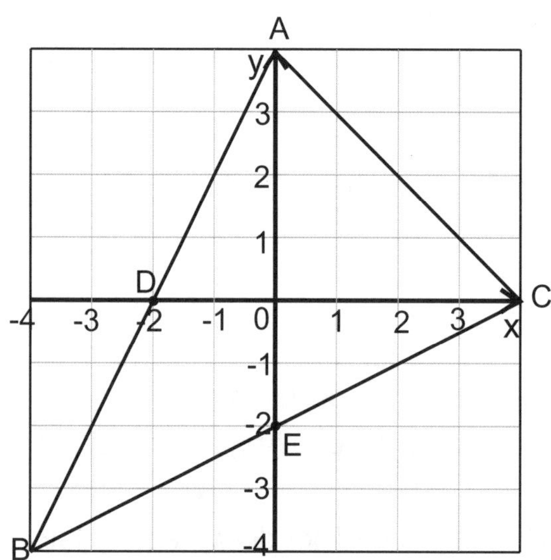

(a) Match the correct line to each equation below. One has been done for you.

x = 0	**line through A and C**
y = 0	**line through A and E**
x + y = 4	**line through A and B**
y = 2x + 4	**line through D and C**

3 marks

(b) Write down the equation of the line through B and C.

....

1 mark

19 Rebecca measured the heights of a group of 40 girls from her year group at school.
The graph shows her results.

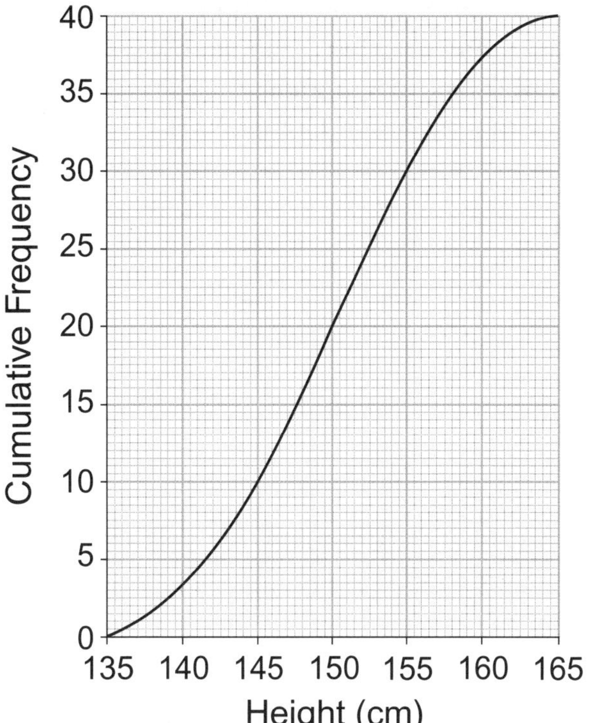

(a) Use the graph to estimate the median height of this group of girls.

median = ..150.. cm

1 mark

(b) Use the graph to estimate the inter-quartile range of the heights of this group of girls.

inter-quartile range = ..35.. cm

2 marks

(c) Rebecca then measured the heights of a second group of 40 girls from a different year group.

Results: The median height was 142 cm.
The inter-quartile range was 9.5 cm.

Compare the heights of the girls in the second group with the heights of the girls in the first group.
Which is likely to be older, the first group or the second group?

1 mark

20 The bar graph shows the percentage increase in sales of books by two publishing companies, Company A and Company B.

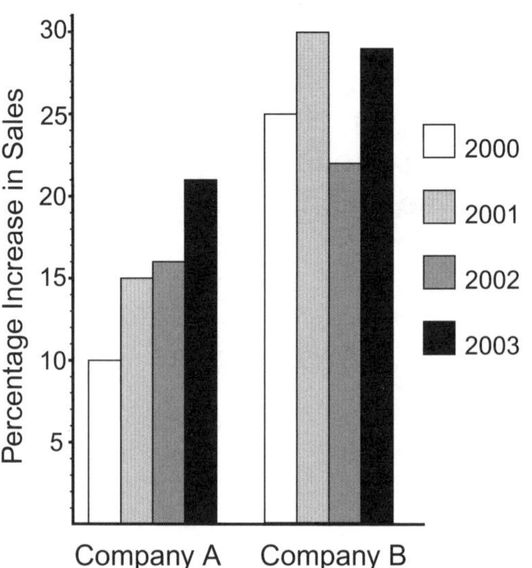

(a) In 2001 Company A's sales were 15% more than in the previous year.
By what percentage did Company B increase its sales in 2001?

Percentage increase in sales = ...30... %

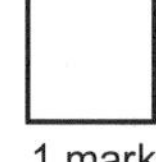

1 mark

(b) The bars for Company B are all taller than the bars for Company A.
Does this mean that Company B had higher sales than Company A?

☐ **Yes**  ☑ **No**

Explain your answer.

They might not have higher sales just higher increases

1 mark

(c) Did Company B's sales go down in 2002 compared with sales in 2001?

☑ **Yes** ☐ **No**

Explain your answer.

The bar is shorter

1 mark

Key Stage 3 — Mathematics Test

Paper 2 Tier 5 – 8

Calculator allowed

Instructions

- The test is one hour long.
- Make sure you have these things with you before you start: pen, pencil, rubber, ruler, angle measurer or protractor, pair of compasses and tracing paper.
- The easier questions are at the start of the test.
- Try to answer all of the questions.
- Don't use any rough paper — write all your answers and working in this test paper (marks may be awarded for working).
- Check your work carefully before the end of the test.

This means write down your answer or show your working and your answer.

You may use a calculator in this test.

Formulae

Trapezium

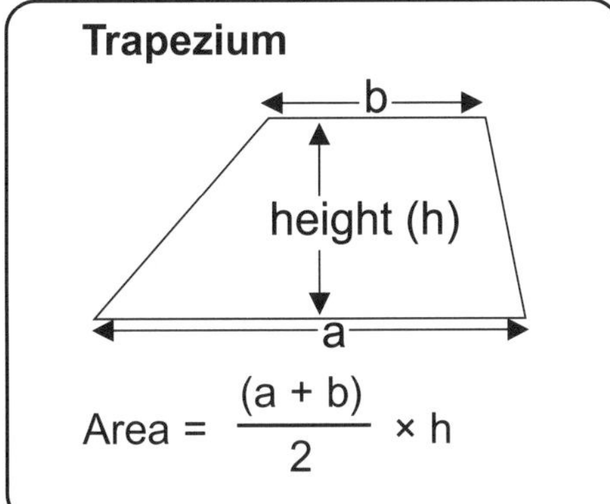

$$\text{Area} = \frac{(a + b)}{2} \times h$$

Prism

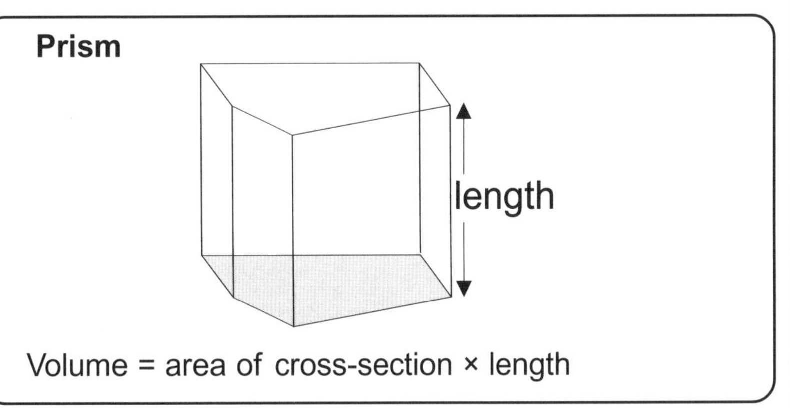

Volume = area of cross-section × length

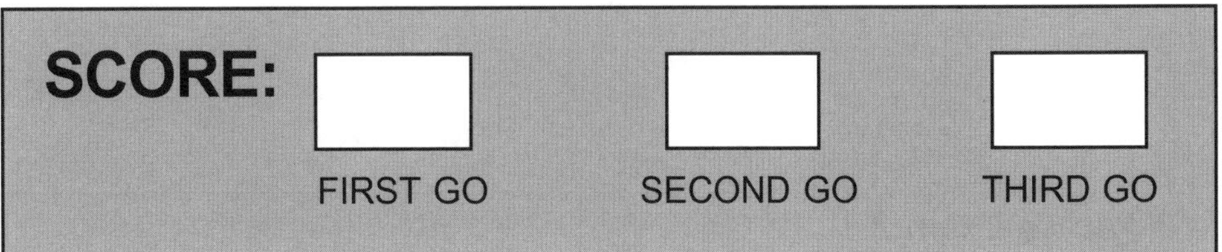

1 Fill in the missing numbers in these fractions.

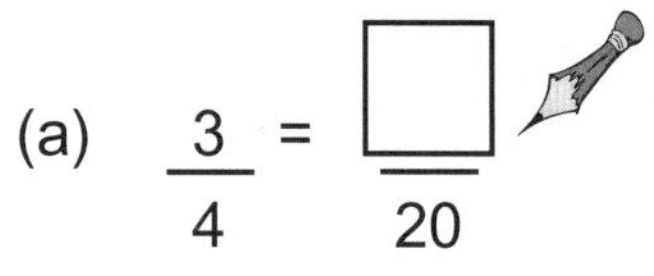

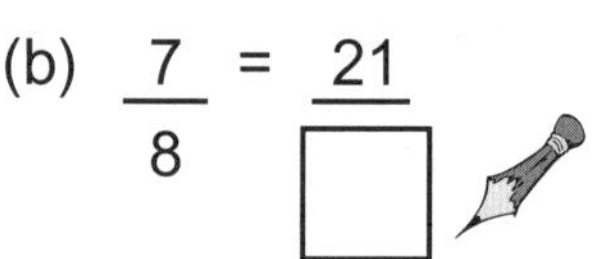

2 marks

2 Look at this number chain.

(a) Fill in the missing numbers in the number chains below.

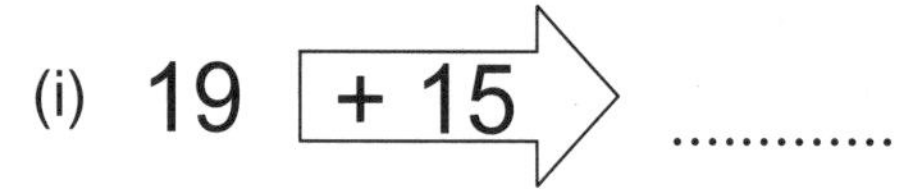

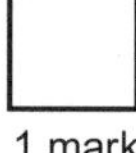

1 mark

(ii) .... ÷ 2.5 70

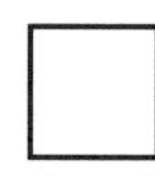

1 mark

(b) Fill in the missing numbers in the arrows.

(i) 38 + ... 950

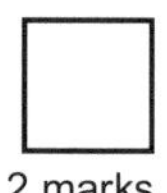

2 marks

3 One Saturday the attendance at a football match was 11 623.

(a) The local paper always gives the attendance to the nearest thousand.

Write down, in figures, the attendance to the nearest thousand.

1 mark

(b) The local radio station always gives the attendance to the nearest hundred.

Write down, in figures, the attendance to the nearest hundred.

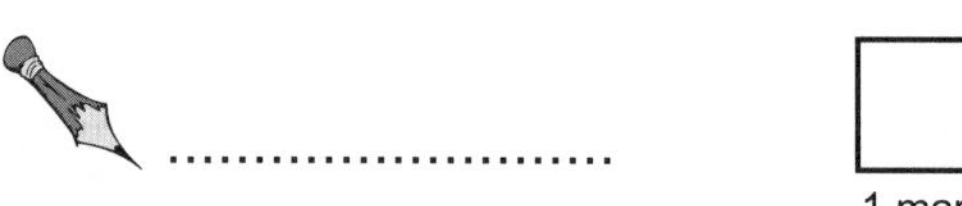

1 mark

4 This table shows the monthly payments and total amount repaid when a loan of £5000 is paid back over 3 years (36 monthly payments).

Provider	Monthly Payment (£)	Total Repaid (£)
Bank A	179.94	6477.84
Bank B	193.38	
Bank C	189.35	

(a) Find the total repaid if you borrow from Bank B.
Write your answer in the table.

1 mark

Find the total repaid if you borrow from Bank C.
Write your answer in the table.

1 mark

(b) How much less do you pay if you borrow from Bank A rather than from Bank C?

You pay £ .... less

1 mark

5 The diagram shows two cuboids. They both have the same volume.

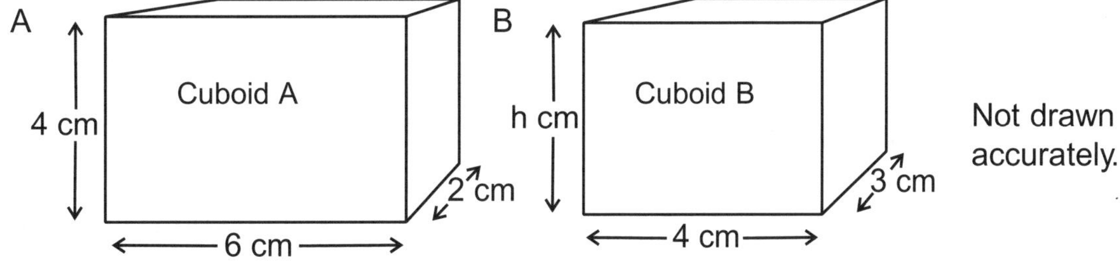

(a) What is the volume of cuboid A? Give the unit.

....

2 marks

(b) Work out the length marked h.

.... cm

1 mark

6 A short-stay car park costs 70p. One day the cash in the ticket machine was emptied after the first hour and the money was counted. The table shows the coins collected in the first hour.

Coin	Number of coins
£1	0
50p	36
20p	35
10p	12
5p	8

(a) Work out the total amount of money collected.

£ ....

1 mark

(b) How many motorists had paid 70p to park?

....

1 mark

7 (a) A cyclist travels for 3 hours at an average speed of 18 mph. How far does the cyclist travel?

.... miles

1 mark

(b) A car travels 147 miles in 3½ hours. What is the car's average speed?

.... mph

1 mark

(c) A train travels 153 miles at an average speed of 68 mph. How long does the train take?

.... hours

1 mark

8 (a) Write 800 000 000 in standard form. ....

1 mark

(b) Write 0.012 in standard form. ....

1 mark

(c) Work out 800 000 000 × 0.012, giving your answer in standard form. ....

1 mark

9 In a sale all prices are reduced by 15%.

(a) Toby wants to buy a jacket which cost £42 before the sale.
How much will Toby save if he buys the jacket in the sale?

He will save £ ....

1 mark

(b) Ricky buys a pair of jeans in the sale. They normally cost £54.
How much does Ricky pay for the jeans in the sale?

He will pay £ ....

1 mark

(c) Chris pays £15.30 for a pair of shoes in the sale.
How much did the shoes cost before the sale?

The shoes cost £ ....

1 mark

10 (a) The label on a tin of tuna shows this information.
How many grams of protein does 200 g of tuna provide?

TUNA STEAK	
150 g	
This tin provides:	
Energy	171 kcal
Protein	40.5 g
Fat	0.75 g
(of which saturates)	(0.3 g)

.... g

1 mark

(b)

PINK SALMON	
200 g	
Typical values per 100 g:	
Energy	155 kcal
Protein	23.0 g
Fat	7.0 g
(of which saturates)	(1.3 g)

The label on a tin of pink salmon shows this information.

Which contains more energy,
100 g of tuna or 100 g of pink salmon?
Show your working.

2 marks

11 A mobile phone tariff has a service charge of £5 per month, and a calling charge of 35 pence per minute.

(a) Complete the table below to show the cost of using this tariff for one month.

Calling time (minutes)	0	20	40	60
Cost of tariff (pence)	500		1900	

1 mark

(b) Plot a straight line graph on the grid below to show the cost of this tariff. Label your line **Tariff A**.

1 mark

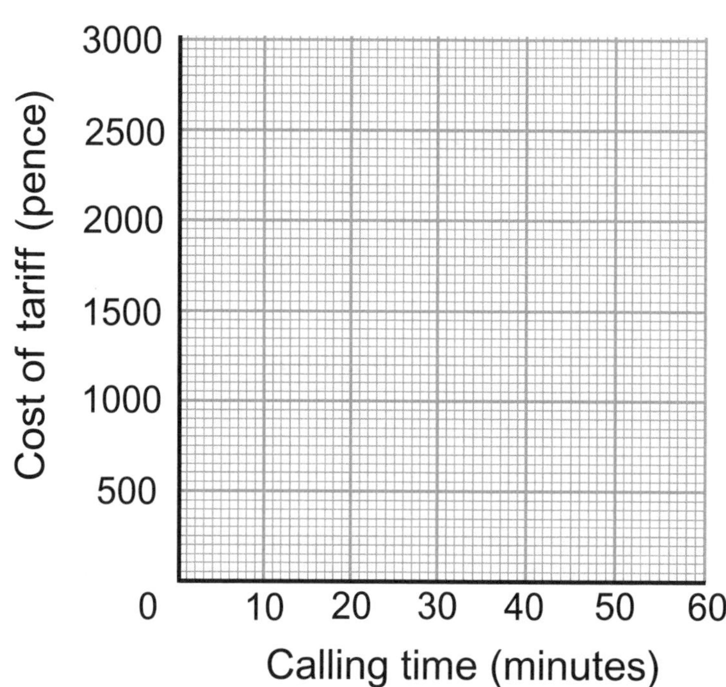

(c) A different tariff has **no** service charge, but calls cost 48p per minute. Complete the table below to show the cost of using this tariff for one month.

Calling time (minutes)	0	25	50
Cost of tariff (pence)		1200	

1 mark

(d) Plot a straight line on the grid above to show the cost of this tariff. Label your line **Tariff B**.

1 mark

(e) Look at your graphs. After how many minutes of calling time is the cost the same for both tariffs?

.... minutes

1 mark

12 A wheel on Stella's car has a diameter of 56 cm (including the tyre).

(a) Calculate the circumference of the wheel, giving your answer to the nearest centimetre.

Circumference = ... cm

1 mark

(b) When Stella drives between two sets of traffic lights, the wheel turns 142 times. What distance does the car travel between the two sets of traffic lights? Give your answer to the nearest metre.

The car travels .... m

2 marks

13 The cost of hiring a machine to strip wallpaper is calculated using the formula **C = 6n + 15**,
where **C** is the cost in pounds,
and **n** is the number of days the machine is hired for.

(a) Philip hires the machine for 7 days. How much will it cost him?

It will cost him £ ....

1 mark

(b) It cost Jane £33 to hire the machine.
How many days did she hire it for?

She hired the machine for .... days.

1 mark

14 Every Year 7 pupil in a school must choose to begin learning one of four languages. The probability of a pupil choosing each language was found, based on the choices made in the last two years. This information is shown in the table below.

French	German	Spanish	Russian
0.3		0.35	0.1

(a) What is the probability that a pupil will choose German?

P (German) = ...

1 mark

(b) There are 240 pupils due to join Year 7 this year.
Based on the choices made in the last 2 years, how many pupils would the school expect to choose French? Show your working.

.... pupils

1 mark

15 Most people take a short cut across the grass at the corner of this street.

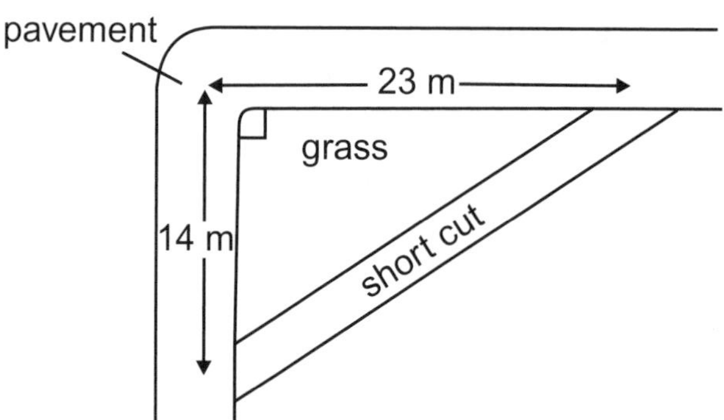

(a) Calculate the length of the short cut, correct to the nearest metre.

Length of short cut = ...m

2 marks

(b) How much further would you walk if you went around the corner by staying on the pavement, rather than using the short cut?

.... m further.

1 mark

16 The diagram shows a sketch of the curve $y = x(x - 4)$.

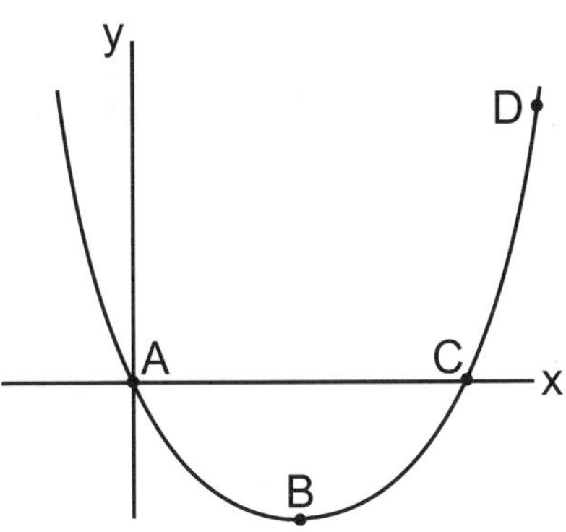

(a) What are the coordinates of points A, B, and C?

A (........ , ...) B (........ , ...) C (........ , ...)

3 marks

(b) The x-coordinate of D is 5. What is its y-coordinate?

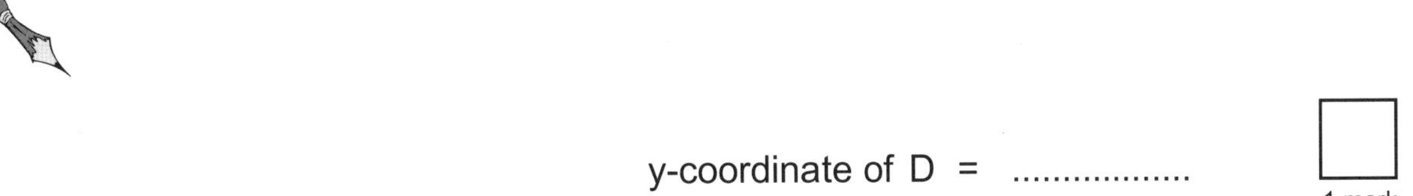

y-coordinate of D = ...

1 mark

17 In a park a tree grows on horizontal ground.
From a point on the ground 15 m from the base of the tree,
the angle of elevation of the top of the tree is 42°.

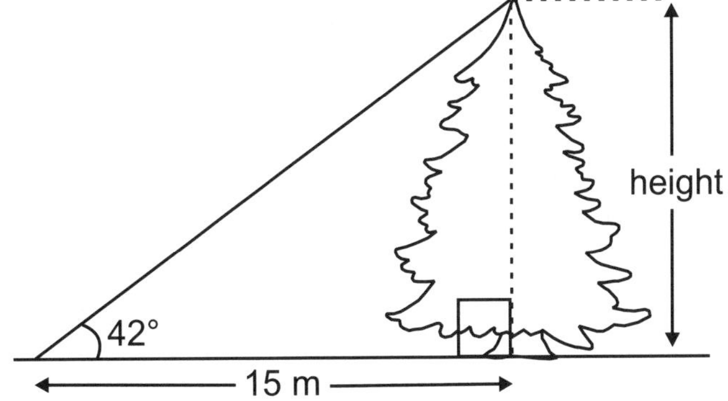

Calculate the height of the tree, correct to 3 significant figures.
Show your working.

Height of tree = ... m

2 marks

18 The diagram, which is drawn to scale, shows a small field.

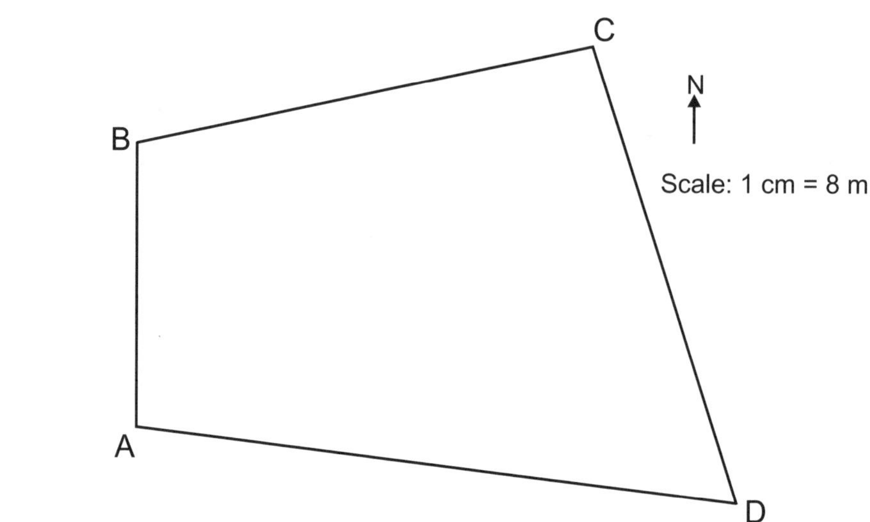

(a) On the diagram draw the locus of points **in the field** which are the same distance from B as they are from C.

1 mark

(b) On the diagram draw the locus of points **in the field** which are 40 m from D.

1 mark

Some treasure is buried in the field.
The treasure is equidistant from B and C, and 40 m from D.

(c) Mark the position of the treasure with a cross and label it **T**.

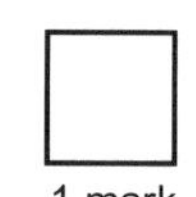
1 mark

(d) What is the bearing of C from A?
(Note that the line AB runs north-south.)

Bearing = ...°

1 mark

19 Triangles ABC and PQR are similar. Angles A and P are equal, angles B and Q are equal and angles C and R are equal.

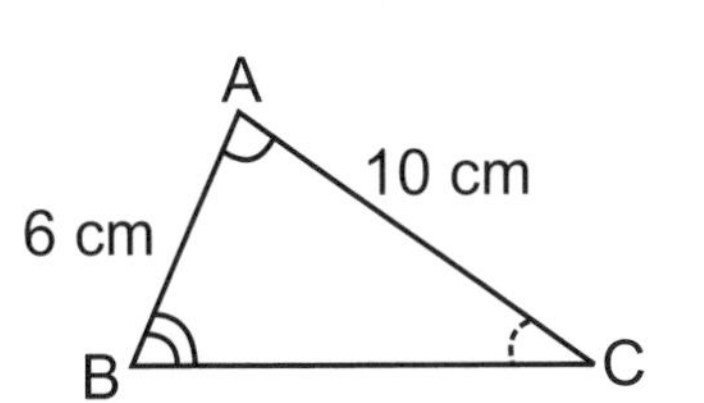

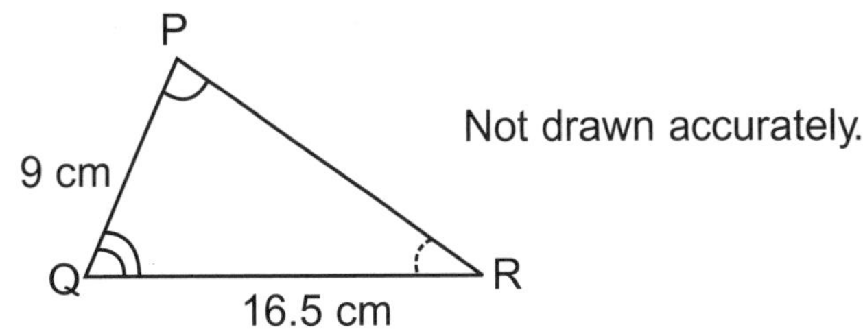

(a) Work out the length of PR.

PR = ... cm

1 mark

(b) Work out the length of BC.

BC = ... cm

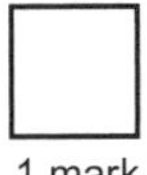

1 mark

(c) Express the ratio length AB : length PQ in its simplest terms.

length AB : length PQ = ... : ....

1 mark

20 Phil buys 4 chocolate bars and 1 packet of mints. It costs him £1.34.
Chris buys 3 chocolate bars and 3 packets of mints. It costs her £1.50.

Use simultaneous equations to find how much one chocolate bar costs and how much one packet of mints costs.
Call the price of one chocolate bar **x** pence.
Call the cost of one packet of mints **y** pence.

Price of one chocolate bar = ... p

Price of one packet of mints = ... p

4 marks

Key Stage 3
Mental Mathematics Test

In your mental maths test you get thirty questions read out to you, and you write your answers on a sheet like the one on the right. Each question is read out twice, and you have 5, 10 or 15 seconds to answer.

There are a few things you can do to make sure you get all the marks you can:

1) Listen really well, and follow all the instructions. You don't get a chance to ask questions once the test starts.
2) Write your answers clearly and in the right place. You can write down your working, but it won't get any marks.
3) Don't get put off if you miss a question or can't work it out in time — stay calm and focus on the next one.
4) Nothing beats getting practice, so have a go at the test below and any others you can get your hands on.

If you can, get someone else to read the questions out loud and time you.

"Now we are ready to start the test. For the first group of questions, you will have 5 seconds to work out each answer and write it down."

1 Write in figures the number that is ten more than one thousand.

2 What number should you multiply eight by to get seventy-two?

3 What is twenty-five percent of forty-eight?

4 Look at the equation. When **x** equals three, what is the value of **y**?

5 Add seven to minus sixteen.

6 A block of wood has a density of twelve grams per cubic centimetre. If it has a volume of one hundred cubic centimetres, what is its mass?

"For the next group of questions, you will have 10 seconds to work out each answer and write it down."

7 A bag of sugar weighs six and three-quarter pounds. About how many kilograms is that? Ring the best answer on your answer sheet.

8 Thirty-six children were asked what their favourite colour was. The pie chart shows the results. How many children chose blue?

9 Look at the graphs of $\mathbf{x + y = 3}$ and $\mathbf{y = 0.5x + 1.5}$. What is the solution of these two equations?

10 What is the area of this parallelogram?

11 What is five eighths of sixty-four?

12 Write down the next two terms in this sequence.

13 Look at the equation. Solve it to find the value of **x**.

14 Light travels at a speed of about three hundred thousand kilometres in one second. Write down in standard form approximately how far it will travel in twenty seconds.

15 A recipe asks for two parts sugar to three parts butter. If Emma uses one hundred and eighty grams of sugar, how much butter should she use?

16 Look at the expression. When **r** is seven, work out the value of this expression.

17 Tony is one point five metres tall. His sister Deborah is twenty percent taller. What height is Deborah?

18 Look at the calculation. Use it to work out fourteen multiplied by eight.

19 Look at the inequality. How many integer solutions are there?

20 What is twenty-five percent of one third of one hundred and fifty?

21 I roll an unfair die ninety-six times. Twelve of these times, I roll a one. Estimate the probability of rolling a one with this die.

"For the next group of questions, you will have 15 seconds to work out each answer and write it down."

22 Look at the expression. If **y** equals thirty-five point eight, what is the value of **x**?

23 What would be the last digit of seventy-four to the power four?

24 What is the median of the numbers on your answer sheet?

25 Your answer sheet shows the answer to sixty-seven multiplied by twenty-five. Use this to help you work out sixty-seven multiplied by twenty-three.

26 Write an approximate answer to the calculation on your answer sheet.

27 What is the cube root of twenty-seven one hundred and twenty-fifths?

28 On the grid, sketch the straight line with the equation **y** equals minus **x** minus two.

29 The diagram shows a triangle. What is the size of the angle marked **x**?

30 Fill in the missing number in the number sentence.

"Put your pens down. The test is finished."

Mental Mathematics Answer Sheet

Time: 5 seconds

1			
2			
3		48	
4		y = 2x + 3	
5		-16	
6	g	12 g/cm³	

Time: 10 seconds

7 | 1 | 1.5 | 2 | 2.5 | 3

8

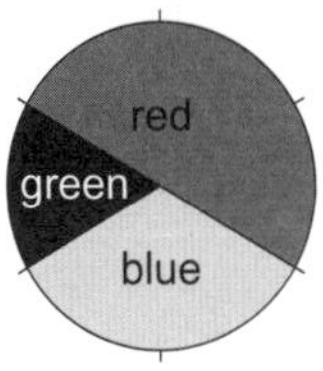

children

9

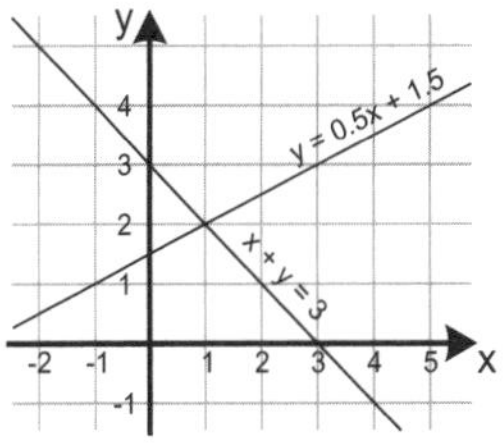

x = y =

10

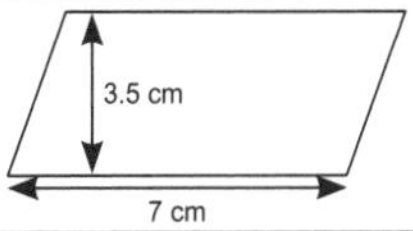

cm²

11		64	

12 | 2 | 3 | 5 | 8 | 13

13	x =	6x – 3 = 21	
14	km	300 000 km	
15	g	180 g	
16		$r^2 - 3.2$	
17	m	1.5 m	
18		14 × 18 = 252	
19		-3 < t < 7	
20		150	
21			

Time: 15 seconds

22		$y = 2x^2 + 3.8$	
23		74^4	

24 | 32 | 25 | 47 | 23 | 36 | 30 | 29

25		67 × 25 = 1675 67 × 23	
26		(82 × 4.9) ÷ 22	
27		$\frac{27}{125}$	

28

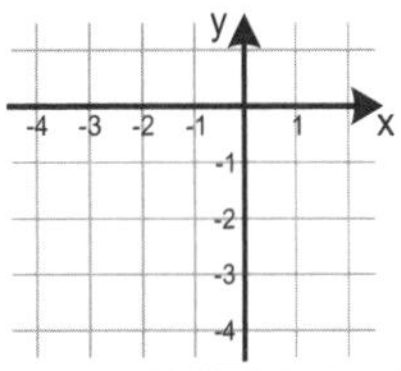

29

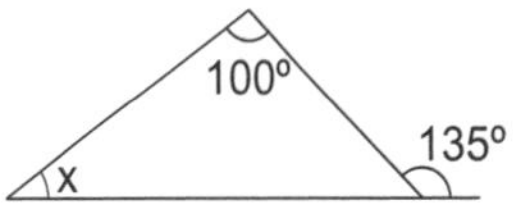

°

30 | 2.5 × 6 = ... × 2.4

Section One — Numbers

Page 6 (Warm-up Questions)

1) (a) **12, 15, 18** (b) **10, 15, 20** (c) **11, 13, 17, 19**
2) (a) **15, 17** (odd numbers) (b) **15, 21** (triangle numbers)
   (c) **49, 64** (square numbers)
3) **31, 37, 41, 43, 47**
4) (a) **44** (even) (b) **125** (cube) (c) **28** (decreasing in sevens)
5) (a) **1, 2, 4, 7, 8, 14, 28, 56** (b) **1, 2, 3, 4, 6, 9, 12, 18, 36**
   If you don't understand where these numbers came from, you need to have a look at the method on page 1.
6) (a) **16, 25, 36** (b) **8, 27** (c) **3, 21, 36**
   (d) **8, 12, 16, 30, 36** (e) **3, 21, 25, 27, 43**
7) (a)

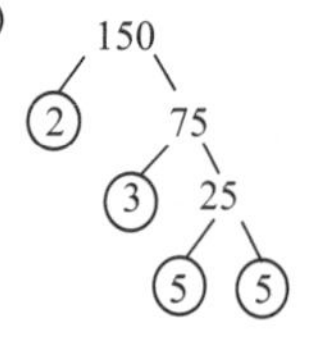

(b)

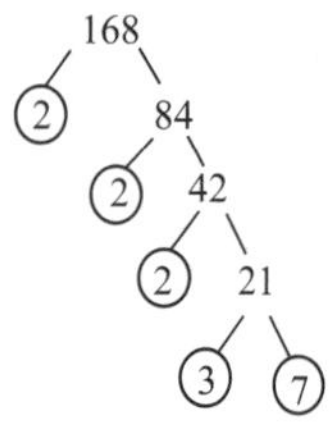

168
2 84
2 42
2 21
3 7

So **150 = 2 × 3 × 5 × 5** So **168 = 2 × 2 × 2 × 3 × 7**

8) 273 ÷ 3 = 91, 273 ÷ 7 = 39.
   So 273 has more factors than just 273 and 1.
9) (Also accept same triangle in different positions)

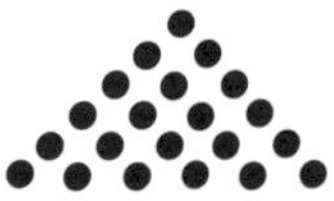

Page 7 (Exam Questions)

2) (a) **29, 35** (in that order — 1 mark each)
   (b) **80, 78** (in that order — 1 mark each)
3) **11, 13, 15, 17, 19** (in any order — 2 marks)
4) **1, 2, 4, 8, 16** (2 marks for all correct or 1 mark if only 1 mistake, i.e. 1 missing or 1 incorrect number.)
5) **36**

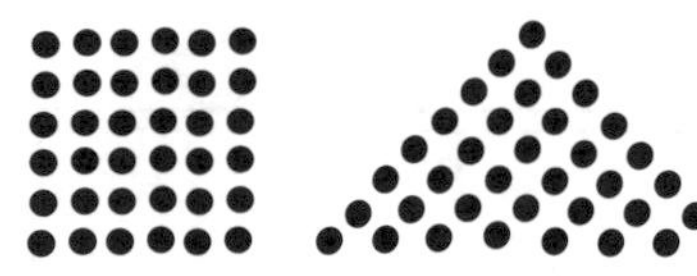

(Also accept same triangle in different positions)
(1 mark for answer and 1 mark each for diagrams)

6) (a)

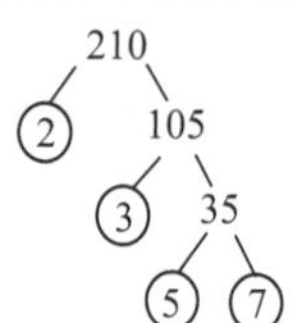

(b)

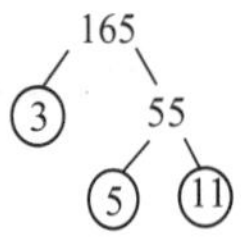

165
3 55
5 11

So **210 = 2 × 3 × 5 × 7** (2 marks) So **165 = 3 × 5 × 11** (2 marks)

   (c) The number is 15 because 3 and 5 are the common factors of 210 and 165, and 3 × 5 = **15**. (1 mark)

Page 14 (Warm-up Questions)

1) (a) Divide top and bottom by 9 to give **1/3**.
   (b) Divide top and bottom by 15 to give **1/4**.
   (c) Divide top and bottom by 13 to give **1/8**.
2) (a) 7 ÷ 10 = 0.7 0.7 × 100 = **70%**
   (b) 2 ÷ 5 = 0.4 0.4 × 100 = **40%**
   (c) 3 ÷ 20 = 0.15 0.15 × 100 = **15%**
3) (a) 84% = 84/100. Cancel down (divide top and bottom by 4) to give **21/25**.
   (b) 60% = 60/100. Cancel down (divide both by 10 then 2) to give **3/5**.
   (c) 30% = 30/100. Cancel down (divide both numbers by 10) to give **3/10**.
4) (a) **7.9** (b) **7.90** (c) **7.895**
   These can be tricky, so if you make a mistake just have another look at page 10.
5) (a) **70** (b) **73** (c) **72.6**
6) (a) **12 800** (b) **3.79** (c) **0.000 560**
   If the decider is a 5, you must round up.

Page 15 (Exam Questions)

3) (a) This is approximately 48 ÷ 6 = **8**. (1 mark)
   (b) This is about half of 125, but that gives 62.5, which is halfway between 60 and 65. 123.6 is less than 125 though, so the answer will be closest to **60**. (1 mark)
   (c) This is approximately $\frac{40 \times 30}{7 \times 4} = \frac{1200}{28}$ which is about $\frac{1200}{30} = 40$
   (1 mark for a first equation similar to that above, and 1 mark for the final answer. Accept answers in the range 38 to 44 inclusive.)
4) % won by Bingham Bears $= \frac{17}{20} \times 100 = \frac{1700}{20} =$ **85%** (1 mark)
   % won by Hockley Hares $= \frac{21}{25} \times 100 = \frac{2100}{25} =$ **84%** (1 mark)
   So the Bingham Bears have performed better. (1 mark)
5) (a) **22.5 m** (1 mark) (b) **9.5 m** (1 mark)
   (c) The least the distance around the outside of the court could be is (22.5 × 2) + (9.5 × 2) = 64 m (1 mark)
   1 km = 1000 m 1000 ÷ 64 = 15.625 (1 mark) = **16** times (2 s.f.) (1 mark)

Page 21 (Warm-up Questions)

1) (a) C.f. = 100, so divide by 100 to give **100 m**
   (b) C.f. = 100 000, so divide by 100 000 to give **0.78956 km**
   (c) C.f. = 100 000, so multiply by 100 000 to give **56 cm**
2) (a) C.f. = 1000, so divide by 1000 to give **600 litres**
   (b) C.f. = 1, so the answer is just **1067 ml**
   (c) C.f. = 1000, so multiply by 1000 to give **6.5 cm³**
3) (a) C.f. = 1000, so multiply by 1000 to give **0.08 g**
   (b) C.f. = 1000, so divide by 1000 to give **0.072 tonnes**
   (c) C.f. = 1 000 000, so divide by 1 000 000 to give **2.1 tonnes**
4) (a) 2 ÷ 5 = **0.4** (b) 1 ÷ 8 = **0.125** (c) 3 ÷ 7 = **0.429** (3 s.f.)
5) (a) 26/100 = **13/50** (b) 8/100 = **2/25** (c) 625/1000 = **5/8**
6) (a) $\frac{8}{5} + \frac{4}{5} = \frac{12}{5} = \mathbf{2\frac{2}{5}}$ (b) $\mathbf{-\frac{9}{16}}$
   (c) $\frac{2 \times 6}{3 \times 7} = \frac{12}{21} = \mathbf{\frac{4}{7}}$ (d) $\frac{3}{5} \times \frac{5}{2} = \frac{15}{10} = \frac{3}{2} = \mathbf{1\frac{1}{2}}$

Page 22 (Exam Questions)

3) (a) Turn all the fractions into decimals:
   3/5 = 0.6 1/3 = 0.33 (2 d.p.) 4/10 = 0.4
   So the order is: **0.2**, **0.3**, **1/3** (or 0.33), **4/10** (or 0.4), **0.45**, **3/5** (or 0.6)
   (2 marks — award 1 mark if one of the numbers is out of place)
   You can't rank fractions in order of size of their top numbers if their bottom numbers are different — 3/5 is larger than 4/10, for example. If you can't tell what order they go in, turn them all into decimals or percentages.
   (b) 1 litre = 1¾ pints, so 2 pints is just over 1 litre 500 cm³ = 0.5 litres
   0.5 gallons = ½ × 4.5 litres = 2.25 litres
   So the order is **500 cm³, 1 litre, 2 pints, 0.5 gallons**
   (2 marks — or 1 mark if at least two of the numbers are in the right place)
   You're pretty unlikely to get this right unless you've learnt the conversions on page 17. It's a bit boring, but you can do it.
4) Number of blue marbles = 2/7 of 21 = 2/7 × 21 = 6. (1 mark)
   Number of red marbles = 1/3 of 21 = 1/3 × 21 = 7. (1 mark)

So number of green marbles = 21 – (6 + 7) = **8.** (1 mark)

5) (a) 1 mile = 1.6 km (1 mark) So 24 ÷ 1.6 = **15 miles** (1 mark)

Remember to check whether your answer is sensible — this one is, because you know that a mile is a bit longer than a kilometre.

(b) (i) £1 = 1.445 Euros So 100 ÷ 1.445 (1 mark) = **£69.20** (1 mark)
(ii) 1 litre = 4.5 gallons 135 litres ÷ 4.5 = 30 gallons (1 mark)
30 gallons costs 20.25 Euros 20.25 ÷ 1.445 = £14.01 (1 mark)
It costs £14.01 per 30 gallons, so 14.01 ÷ 30 = £0.467 per gallon
= 47 pence per gallon to the nearest penny. (1 mark)

(c) 5.5 × 50 000 = 275 000 cm (1 mark) = **2.75 km** (1 mark)

Page 28 (Warm-up Questions)

1) (a) 20/100 × 200 = **£40** (b) 45/100 × 560 = **£252**
(c) 30/100 × 12.5 = **£3.75**

2) (a) 26 ÷ 40 = 0.65 0.65 × 100 = **65%**
(b) 18 ÷ 30 = 0.6 0.6 × 100 = **60%**
(c) 64 ÷ 80 = 0.8 0.8 × 100 = **80%**

3) £64 = 70% £64 ÷ 70 = 0.91 (2 d.p.) 0.91 × 100 = **£91**

4) % change = (5 000 ÷ 25 000) × 100 = **20%**

5) In the ratio 2 : 3 : 5 there are 2 + 3 + 5 = 10 parts altogether.
So divide the total sum to be shared by 10: £6200 ÷ 10 = £620
Dan: £620 × 2 = **£1240** Chris: £620 × 3 = **£1860**
Angela: £620 × 5 = **£3100**

6) £850 = 117.5 % 850 ÷ 117.5 = 7.234 7.234 × 100 = **£723.40**

Page 29 (Exam Questions)

2) (a) 15% = 10% + 5%. So 15% of £60 = £6 + £3 = **£9** (1 mark)

(b) 15% = 10% + 5%. £8.50 + £4.25 = £12.75.
So £12.75 is 15% of **£85** (1 mark)
You could probably tell at a glance that this will be the only possibility from the table — the values for £15 and £60 will be too small.

(c) 2 × £85 = £170. £4.25 is 5% of £85, so 5% of £170 must be 2 × £4.25 = **£8.50** (1 mark)

(d) £3 is 5% of £60, so £1.50 must be 5% of (£60 ÷ 2) = **£30** (1 mark)

3) (a) (38 ÷ 85) × 100 = **44.7%** (3 s.f.) (1 mark)
(b) (133 ÷ 292) × 100 = **45.5%** (3 s.f.) (1 mark)
(c) £69.99 = (100 – 28)% = 72% (1 mark)
(£69.99 ÷ 72) × 100 = **£97.21** (2 d.p.) (1 mark)
(d) (i) 5 : 20 = **1 : 4** (1 mark)
(ii) If the ratio remains the same, then the number of Buffy rentals remains ¼ of the number of X-men rentals. (1 mark)
36 ÷ 4 = **9.** (1 mark)
Check whether 9 : 36 is in the ratio 1 : 4 — yes, 36 = 4 x 9.

Page 34 (Warm-up Questions)

1) (a) $\mathbf{5.6 \times 10^6}$ (b) $\mathbf{7.29 \times 10^7}$ (c) $\mathbf{1.01 \times 10^4}$
If you've put 7.2853462×10^7, you probably wouldn't get the marks in an exam. The whole point of standard form is to write long numbers in a convenient way, so you need to give your answer to a sensible number of decimal places.

2) (a) $\mathbf{7.6 \times 10^{-5}}$ (b) $\mathbf{3.79 \times 10^{-3}}$ (c) $\mathbf{5.07 \times 10^{-4}}$

3) (a) Add the powers: $\mathbf{6^5}$ (b) Subtract the powers: $\mathbf{7^6}$
(c) Anything to the power 0 = 1, so 1 × 5 = **5**
(d) The power ½ means square root, so $\sqrt{49}$ = **7**
(e) The cube root of 64 = **4**

4) (a) **10.4** (b) **4.16** (c) **1680000** (d) **3.63** (e) **9.59**
(All answers are correct to 3 s.f.)

Page 35 (Exam Questions)

3) $(8.9 \times 10^6 \div 2.7 \times 10^7) \times 100$ (1 mark) = **33%** to 2 s.f. (1 mark)

4) (a) $\mathbf{6.28 \times 10^6}$ (2 d.p.) (1 mark — also accept 6.278×10^6)
(b) 6 278 000 ÷ 82.2 = **76 375** (nearest whole number) (2 marks — award 1 mark if the value of 6.28×10^6 was used in the calculation instead, or if the answer was given to something other than the nearest whole number.)

5) (a) When multiplying, add the powers = 12×10^{11} (1 mark) which is $\mathbf{1.2 \times 10^{12}}$ in standard form. (1 mark)
(b) Because you can't use your calculator, it's easiest to express these numbers in standard form and then add the powers = $3 \times 10^{-3} \times 2 \times 10^{-3}$ (1 mark) = $\mathbf{6 \times 10^{-6}}$ (1 mark)

6) (a) $64 \times 4096 = 8^2 \times 8^4$ (1 mark) = 8^6 = **262 144** (1 mark)
(b) $16\ 777\ 216 \div 32\ 768 = 8^8 \div 8^5$ (1 mark) = 8^3 = **512** (1 mark)
(c) $(8^2)^3 = 8^6$ (1 mark) = **262 144** (1 mark)

Section Two — Algebra

Page 46 (Warm-up Questions)

1) (a) $\mathbf{2x + 5}$ **is correct.**

2) Charlotte has $\mathbf{3x}$ apples.

3) (a) $\mathbf{5x + 4}$ (b) $\mathbf{y + x - 1}$ (c) $\mathbf{2x^2 + 2x - 3}$

4) (a) $\mathbf{2a + 6}$ (b) $\mathbf{6u - 15}$ (c) $\mathbf{3x^2 + 2x}$ (d) $\mathbf{4b^2 - 6b}$

5) (a) $y^2 + y + 2y + 2 = \mathbf{y^2 + 3y + 2}$
(b) $(w - 3) \times (w - 3) = w^2 - 3w - 3w + 9 = \mathbf{w^2 - 6w + 9}$
(c) $6p^2 - 2p + 3p - 1 = \mathbf{6p^2 + p - 1}$
(d) $q^2 - q + q - 1 = \mathbf{q^2 - 1}$

6) (a) $\mathbf{2(y + 2)}$ (b) $\mathbf{2x(2y - 3)}$ (c) $\mathbf{3x(x + 3)}$ (d) $\mathbf{4a(a - 2)}$
(e) $\mathbf{u(3u - 7)}$
Check you've done it right by multiplying out — it's amazing how often you'll have done something silly, even if you're pretty confident about your answer.

Page 47 (Exam Questions)

3) There are 6 lots of N, plus an extra 5, so the correct two are:
6N + 5 and **5 + 6N** (2 marks for both correct. 1 mark for one error.)

4) Bill has $\mathbf{5y}$. (1 mark) Clive has $\mathbf{y + 4}$. (1 mark)

5) (a) $\mathbf{6x + 2y + 7}$ (1 mark) (b) $\mathbf{2x + 4}$ (1 mark)

6) (a) $(u - v)(u + v) = u^2 + uv - vu - v^2 = \mathbf{u^2 - v^2}$
(2 marks — 1 mark for a similar method but an incorrect answer.)
uv and vu are the same thing, of course - it just means v x u.
(b) $-2x(-3x + y - 2) - x^2 = 6x^2 - 2xy + 4x - x^2 = \mathbf{5x^2 - 2xy + 4x}$
(2 marks — 1 mark for a similar method but an incorrect answer.)
Careful with the signs — check your answer carefully.

7) $(a + 2)^2 = (a + 2)(a + 2) = \mathbf{a^2 + 4a + 4}$.
(2 marks — 1 mark if there is evidence of multiplying the brackets.)

8) (a) **36(b + 1)** is incorrect — it would give 36b + 36. (1 mark)
(b) **12(3b + 1)** (1 mark)

Page 53 (Warm-up Questions)

1) (a) **11, 14. There is a difference of +3.**
(b) **26, 35. The difference increases by 2.**
(c) **108, 324. Times the previous term by 3.**
(d) **2, ½. Divide the previous term by 4.**
(e) **16, 26. Add the two previous terms together.**

2) (a) n^{th} term = dn + (a – d), so n^{th} term = -2n + (8 – -2) = **10 – 2n.**
(b) n^{th} term = a + (n – 1)d + ½(n – 1) (n – 2)C,
so n^{th} term = 3 + (n – 1) × 3 + ½ × (n – 1) × (n – 2) × 2
= 3 + (n – 1) × 3 + (n – 1) (n – 2)
= 3 + 3n – 3 + n^2 – 3n + 2
= $\mathbf{n^2 + 2}$

3) (a) **-6** (b) **6** (c) **-1** (d) **7** (e) **9** (f) **-9**
(g) 2 × -3 = -6 and 4 × -2 = -8. -6 + -8 = **-14**
(h) 2 × -3 = -6 and 4 × -2 = -8. -6 – -8 = -6 + 8 = **2**

4) $\mathbf{(2p)^2 = 4p^2}$ $\mathbf{(2p)^2 = 2^2 \times p^2}$ $\mathbf{(2p)^2 = 2p \times 2p}$

5) (a) $\mathbf{x^2y^2}$ or $\mathbf{xy \times xy}$ or similar. (b) $\mathbf{8x^3}$ or $\mathbf{2x \times 2x \times 2x}$ or similar.

Page 54 (Exam Questions)

3) (a) $5 \times -4 = -20$ and $5 + -4 = 1$, so the numbers are **5 and -4**. (1 mark for any 2 numbers that times to give -20 and 2 marks for the correct answer.)

(b) $12 \times -1 = -12$ and $12 + -1 = 11$, which is the largest sum. (2 marks, or 1 mark for any other two numbers that times to give -12.)

4) (a) $2 \times 3 = 6$; $6 \times 3 = 18$, so next term is $18 \times 3 =$ **54** (1 mark)

(b) 5th term is $54 \times 3 =$ **162** (1 mark)

5) (a) The sequence drops by 3 each time so missing terms, shown in bold, are: 6, **3**, 0, **-3**, -6, **-9** (1 mark for any two correct. 2 marks for all 3.)

(b) Divide previous number by 3 each time so missing terms, shown in bold, are: 27, **9**, **3**, 1, 1/3, **1/9** (1 mark for any two correct. 2 marks for all 3.)

(c) The previous 2 terms are added together so missing terms, shown in bold, are: 5, 10, 15, 25, **40**, 65, **105** (2 marks)

6) For the 2nd term, n = 2, so 2nd term $= 2^2 + 1 = 4 + 1 =$ **5**. (1 mark)

For the 3rd term, n = 3, so 3rd term $= 3^2 + 1 = 9 + 1 =$ **10**. (1 mark)

7) Correct answer is **a × a × (b – c) × (b – c) × (b – c)** (1 mark)

Page 63 (Warm-up Questions)

1) (a) $3x = 13 - 4 = 9$. So $x = 9 \div 3$, i.e. $\boldsymbol{x = 3}$.

(b) $17 = 5 + 2x$. So $2x = 17 - 5 = 12$. So $x = 12 \div 2$, i.e. $\boldsymbol{x = 6}$.

(c) $2x + 6 = 8$. $2x = 8 - 6 = 2$. So $\boldsymbol{x = 1}$.

(d) $4x = 10 + 5 = 15$. So $x =$ **15/4**.

(e) $5x = 8 - 13 = -5$. So $x = -5 \div 5$ i.e. $\boldsymbol{x = -1}$.

2) (a) Take 3w away from both sides to give **q = p – 3w**

(b) Take q away from both sides to give 3w = p – q

Then divide both sides by 3 to give $\mathbf{w} = \frac{p-q}{3}$

3) When $x = 0.3$, $x^2 + 3x - 1 = -0.01$
When $x = 0.4$, $x^2 + 3x - 1 = 0.36$, so the solution lies **between 0.3 and 0.4**.
You can tell by looking at this equation that x must be less than 1, because $x^2 + 3x$ must be equal to 1. So just start sticking a few "nought-point-somethings" into the equation and see what gets you closest.

4) (a) $3 \times -2 =$ **-6** (b) $-2 \times -2 =$ **4**

(c) $d^2 = (-2^2) = -2 \times -2 = 4$. But the formula was $-(d^2)$, so the answer is **-4**.

(d) $3 + 2 + 5 + -2 =$ **8** (e) $3 - 2 + 5 - -2 =$ **8**

(f) $(3 \times 2) + (2 \times 5) + (5 \times -2) = 6 + 10 + -10 =$ **6**.

(g) $(3 + 2) \div -2 = 5 \div -2 =$ **-2.5** (h) $3 + 2 \div -2 = 3 + -1 =$ **2**

Page 64 (Exam questions)

4)
vw ÷ u = 2.5 — **v ÷ w** = 2.5
u + v + w = 11 — **2u + v – w** = 11
uv ÷ w = 10 — **2v** = 10
(1 mark for each correct pairing.)

5) (a) Add 3 to both sides to give 7k = 14. Divide both sides by 7 to give **k = 2**. (1 mark)

(b) Subtract t from both sides to give 2t + 5 = 12. (1 mark)
Next subtract 5 from both sides to give 2t = 7.
Dividing both sides by 2 gives **t = 3½** (1 mark)

6) Divide both sides by 3 to give s ÷ 3 = t – v.
Add v to both sides to give **t = s ÷ 3 + v** (1 mark)

7) (a) (ii) a + 2b = 1/2 × (2a + 4b) = 1/2 × 16 = **8**. (1 mark)

(iii) 2d – 6b = -2 × (3b – d) = -2 × 7 = **-14** (1 mark)

(iv) 2a + 7b – d = 2a + 4b + 3b – d = 16 + 7 = **23** (1 mark)

(b) Any accurate combination, but easiest is **2a + 10b – 2d**
2a + 4b + 2(3b – d) = 2a + 10b – 2d = 30
(2 marks, or 1 mark for incorrect answer but similar method.)

8) (a) $V = \frac{1}{3} \times 3^2 \times 7 =$ **21 cm³**
(1 mark for correct answer, and 1 mark for correct unit.)

(b) $48 = \frac{1}{3} \times l^2 \times 9 = 3l^2$, so $l^2 = 48 \div 3 = 16$, so **l = 4 cm**
(1 mark for correct answer, and 1 mark for correct unit.)

Page 69 (Warm-up Questions)

1) a) F / m × a

b) 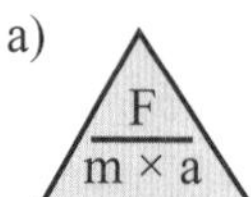

c) 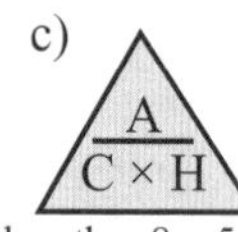

d) O / T × A

2) Scale factor = new length ÷ old length = 8 ÷ 5 = **1.6**
New length (w) = 1.6 × 3 = **4.8 cm**
You can turn the formula given in the question into a formula triangle first, to help you use different bits of it without making any mistakes.

3)

Mass	Volume	Density
10 kg	100 cm³	10 ÷ 100 = **0.1 kg/cm³**
0.02 × 1 = 0.02 kg = **20g**	1 cm³	0.02 kg/cm³
500 g	500 ÷ 125 = **4 cm³**	125 g/cm³
1.2 × 15 = **18 kg**	15 cm³	1.2 kg/cm³

4) (a) 1 hour 15 minutes = 60 + 15 = **75 minutes**

(b) 1.15 hours = 1.15 × 60 = **69 minutes**

Page 70 (Exam questions)

2) (a) Time = distance ÷ speed = 45 ÷ 60 = **0.75 hours** (or ¾ of an hour, or 45 minutes) (1 mark)

(b) 2 hours 30 minutes = 2.5 hours (1 mark)
speed = distance ÷ time = 1800 ÷ 2.5 = **720 km/h** (1 mark)

(c) 285 minutes = 285 ÷ 60 = 4.75 hours (1 mark)
distance = speed × time= 45 × 4.75 = **213.75 km** (1 mark)

3) 750 m = 0.75 km. Time = 0.75 ÷ 1.2 = 0.625 hours
0.625 hours = 0.625 × 60 = 37.5 minutes = **0 hours 37 minutes 30 seconds** (1 mark for 37.5 minutes or 2 marks for the correct answer.)

4) (a) 10 minutes = 1/6 of an hour. (1 mark)
0.8 ÷ 1/6 = **4.8 km/h**. (1 mark)

(b) 150 m = 0.15 km (1 mark)
15 seconds = 15/(60 × 60) = 15/3600 hours (1 mark)
0.15 ÷ 15/3600 = **36 km/h** (1 mark — accept answers in the range 35.7-36 km/h)
Try not to round during calculations — if you leave the value for time as a fraction instead of using a rounded decimal, this works out exactly. Nice.

5) (a) Volume of butter = 5 × 4 × 4 = 80 cm³ (1 mark)
Density = mass ÷ volume = 300 ÷ 80 = **3.75 g/cm³** (1 mark)

(b) Volume = 3 × 4 × 4 = 48 cm³ (1 mark)
Density is 3.75 g/cm³. Mass = 48 × 3.75 = **180 g**. (1 mark)

6) (a) Force = mass × acceleration = 7 × 3 = **21 kg m/s²** (1 mark)

(b) Mass = force ÷ acceleration (1 mark) = 21 ÷ 5 = **4.2 kg** (1 mark)

Page 77 (Warm-up Questions)

1) Fourth corner is **(5, 10)**
Gradient from (0, 10) to (5, 0) is -10 ÷ 5 = **-2**
Gradient from (0, 0) to (5, 10) is 10 ÷ 5 = **2**
If you find this tough, try drawing a quick sketch graph. You can sketch on the diagonals as well — it makes it much easier.

2) (a) AB: from (0, -3) to (3, 0) has gradient -3 ÷ -3 = **1**.
AD: from (0, 3) to (3, 0) has gradient 3 ÷ -3 = **-1**.

(b) (i) BD is **x = 0** (ii) AC is **y = 0**

3) (a) gradient 5 ÷ 5 = **1** (b) gradient (5 – 2) ÷ (4 – 1) = **1**

(c) gradient (15 – 5) ÷ (10 – 5) = **2**

(d) gradient (2 – 4) ÷ (6 – 2) = **-0.5**

4) (a) **Speed in kilometres per hour**

(b) **Density in kilograms per centimetre cubed**

(c) **Rate of water flow in litres per second**

Page 78 (Exam Questions)

2) (a) **He is not correct.**
Gradient is (3 – 0) ÷ (3 – 1) = 3/2 = 1.5 not 2/3 (1 mark)

(b) Lorna's line has the same gradient and goes through (0, 0) so has equation **y = 1.5x**. (1 mark)

3) (a) AB is $\mathbf{y = 2}$ (1 mark) (b) BC is $\mathbf{x = 4}$ (1 mark)

(c) AC has gradient $(-2 - 2) \div (4 - -4) = -4 \div 8 = -0.5$ (1 mark) and goes through the origin (0, 0) so has equation $\mathbf{y = -0.5x}$ (1 mark)

(d) BD has gradient 0.5 (1 mark) and goes through the origin so has equation $\mathbf{y = 0.5x}$ (1 mark)

4) (a) A is **(0, 0, 3)** (1 mark) (b) E is **(5, 4, 3)** (1 mark)

5) (a)

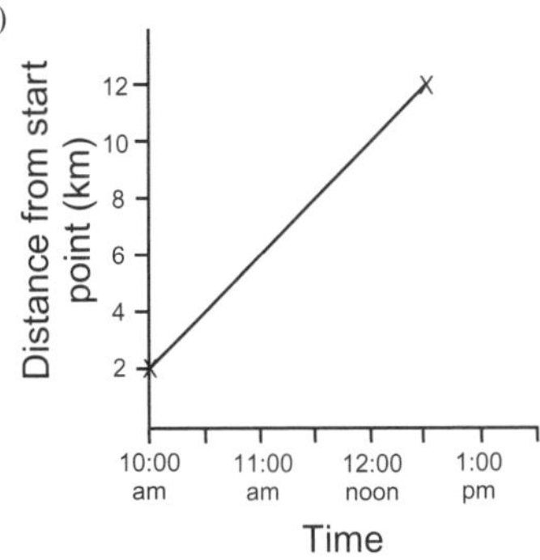

(1 mark for plotting the points in the correct places, 1 mark for joining them with a straight line.)

(b) From 10:00 to 12:30 is the change along the x-axis = 2.5 hours. The change in the distance (y-axis) = 10 km. So gradient is $10 \div 2.5 = \mathbf{4}$ (2 marks for correct answer, or 1 mark for correct method)

(c) Speed is **4 km/h** (1 mark)

Page 83 (Warm-up questions)

1) **B** and **D**, because they are of the form $y = mx + c$. A has x^2 in it so would be a bucket shape, and C has $3/x$ in it so would be symmetrical about the line $y = x$.

2) (a) **(iii)**, because it has the x^2 bucket shape, which rules out (ii), the shape is not upside down which rules out (iv), and the graph does not pass through (0, 0), which rules out (i).

(b) **(ii)**, because the graph goes up from bottom left, ruling out (i) and (iii) and it passes through (0, 0), which rules out (iv).

(c) **(iv)**, because the graph goes down from top left, ruling out (i) and (ii), and it passes through (0, 0), ruling out (iii).

For a lot of people, this isn't the type of thing that becomes obvious once you understand it. It's the type of thing that needs careful learning, so go back over pages 79 - 82 until you've got all the little rules about graph shapes memorised.

Page 84 (Exam Questions)

2) $\mathbf{y = 2x + 5}$. (1 mark) Graph A slopes upwards and crosses the y-axis at +5, so the x-term must be positive and the equation must contain +5.
$\mathbf{x + 2y = 6}$. (1 mark) Graph B slopes downwards, so must have a negative gradient (i.e. $-x$). It also crosses the y-axis at +3, so it can't be $y = 5 - x$ or $y = -3x + 5$. If you rearrange this equation to make y the subject you can see how this is the correct equation: take away x from both sides to give $2y = 6 - x$. Then divide both sides by 2 to give $y = 3 - \frac{1}{2}x$.

3) (a) **B**. (1 mark) Straight line graphs have equations of the type $y = mx + c$, where m is the gradient. So the equation $y = 2x + 3$ corresponds to a graph with a gradient of 2.

(b) **C**. (1 mark) y is the same (i.e. -3) at all points along this line, so the graph must be a horizontal line at -3 below the x-axis.

(c) **D** (1 mark) and **F**. (1 mark) With D, x and y add up to 8, so where x is 5 y must be 3. F is a vertical line where x is always 5, and at some point it must pass through $y = 3$.

(d) **A**. (1 mark) $y = x^2$, so if one value is zero then the other must be too.
If you find this hard it's a good idea to do a little sketch of what the graph would look like — you might get confused if you just try to picture them.

4) (a) A: $y = 0$, so $0 = x^2 - 9$. Therefore $x^2 = 9$, so $x = 3$ or -3. Point A is to the left of the origin, so A **(-3, 0)**. (1 mark)
B: $x = 0$, so $y = 0 - 9$, i.e. $y = -9$. So B **(0, -9)**. (1 mark)
C: This is the same as point A but to the right of the origin, so x is positive, i.e. C **(3, 0)**. (1 mark)

(b) D is a reflection of B, so it must be the same distance above the line $y = 2$ as B is below it. From 2 down to -9 is a distance of 11 units, so D must be 11 above 2 = 13. So D **(0, 13)**. (1 mark)

Page 92 Warm-up Questions

1)

x	-2	0	2	4
y	-8	**-2**	**4**	**10**

2)

x	-4	-3	-2	-1	0	1	2	3
y	19	**8**	1	**-2**	**-1**	**4**	**13**	26

3) $\mathbf{y = mx + c}$.

4) The gradient is the number in front of x, so it's **-5**.

5) Equation should be of the form $y = mx + c$. m is the gradient, 3, and c is the y-intercept, -4, so the equation is $\mathbf{y = 3x - 4}$.

6) The gradient tells you the **speed**.

7) **Distance** is always plotted up the vertical axis of a travel graph.

Page 93 (Exam questions)

2) (a)

x	-3	-2	-1	0	1	2	3
y	19	**9**	3	**1**	**3**	9	**19**

(1 mark for every 2 correct answers.)

(b)

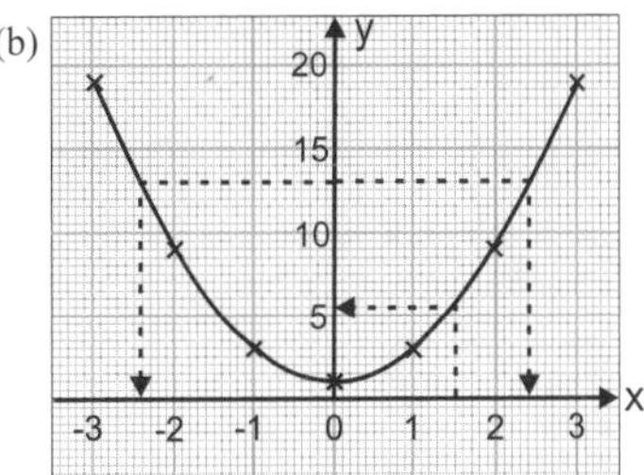

(1 mark for axes with sensible scale. 1 mark for plotting points correctly and for joining points with a smooth curve.)

(c) Read up from x-axis at $x = 1.5$. Read across from curve to y-axis to get **5.5** (1 mark — accept answers in the range 5-6)

(d) Find $y = 13$ on the y-axis. Read across in both directions to the curve, and then down to the x-axis. Answers should be about **-2.4** and **2.4** (2 marks for answers in the range -2.3 to -2.5 and 2.3 to 2.5, 1 mark for answers in the range -2.2 to -2.6 and 2.2 to 2.6).

3) (a)

x	0	2	4
y	**3**	**5**	**7**

(1 mark)

(b)

x	0	2	4
y	**12**	**8**	**4**

(1 mark)

(c)

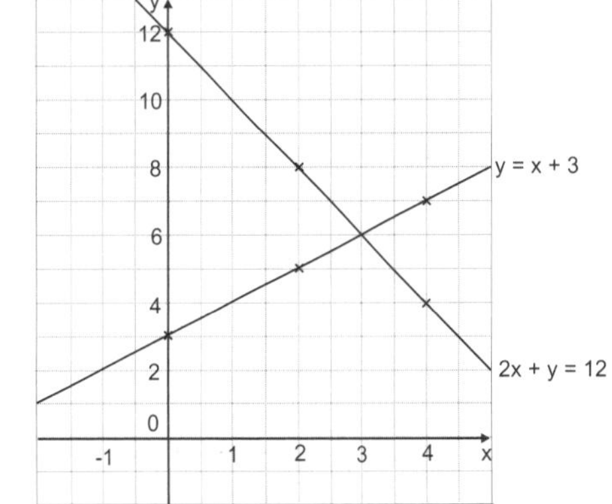

(1 mark for each set of correctly plotted points, joined by a straight line.)

(d) Where the lines cross $x = 3$ and $y = 6$, so the coordinates of that point are **(3, 6)**. (1 mark)

4) (a) Each big square on the bottom scale is worth half an hour or 30 minutes, so one half-square must be worth 15 minutes. Read up from this point until you meet the curve, then across to give **3 km**. (1 mark)
A quick way to tell where you should read across from is to look at where the slope of the graph first changes. You know the girls slowed down from a jog to a walk, and the point where this happens is the point where the gradient of the graph changes (because the gradient = speed).

(b) The flat part of the graph is where they are stopped. This part covers 10 small squares, or **30 minutes**. (1 mark)

(c) Speed = gradient = distance up ÷ distance along
= 8 ÷ 1.25 = **6.4 km/h.** (1 mark)
You could also use the graph to find distance and time, and work it out using speed = distance ÷ time.

(d) The last section of this graph, where the gradient is the steepest, corresponds to the time they were in the car. This section begins at **14:45**. (1 mark)

(e) Speed = distance up ÷ distance along = 6 ÷ 0.25 = **24 km/h.** (1 mark)

(f) Before their rest they jogged and walked 8 km. After they walked 8 – 6 = 2 km. So altogether they walked and jogged 8 + 2 = **10 km.** (1 mark)

Page 98 (Warm-up Questions)

1) (a) Label the equations 1 and 2.
Multiply equation 1 by 2, and then subtract one equation from the other to eliminate the y's. Solve this equation to find x. Then substitute the value for x into one of the original equations and solve it to find y.
(Or you could eliminate the x's by the same method.)

(b) Accurately draw the graphs of the 2 equations on graph paper.
Find the coordinates of the point where the two graphs cross.
These values for x and y are the solution of the equations.

2) (a)

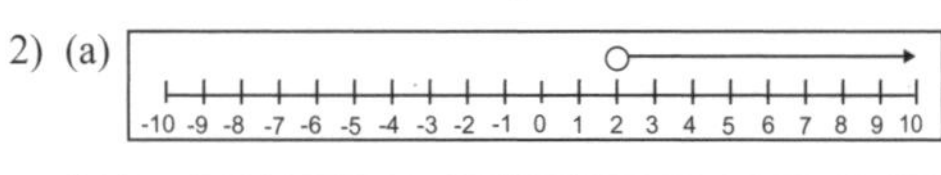

(b)

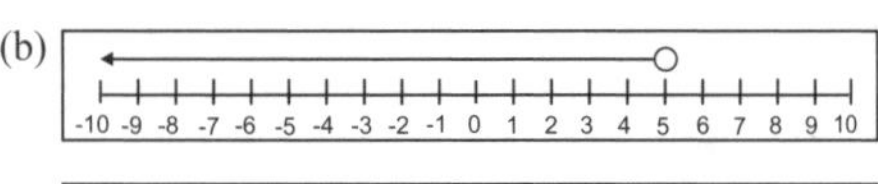

(c)

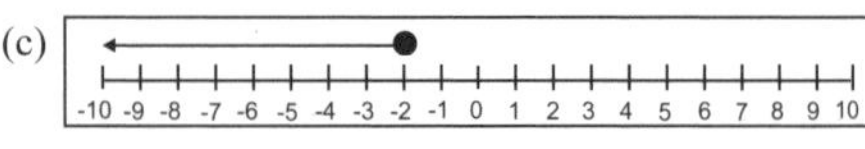

(d)

-10 -9 -8 -7 -6 -5 -4 -3 -2 -1 0 1 2 3 4 5 6 7 8 9 10

Page 99 (Exam Questions)

3) $5x - 2 < 2x + 13$.
Take $2x$ from both sides: $3x - 2 < 13$. (1 mark)
Add 2 to both sides : $3x < 15$. (1 mark)
Divide both sides by 3: $\boldsymbol{x < 5}$. (1 mark)

4) (a)

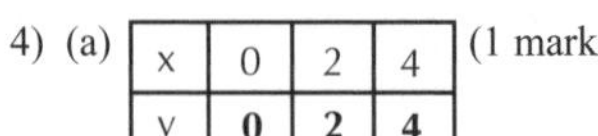

x	0	2	4
y	**0**	**2**	**4**

(1 mark)

(c)

x	0	2	4
y	**6**	**4**	**2**

(1 mark)

(b)
(d)
(e)
(f)

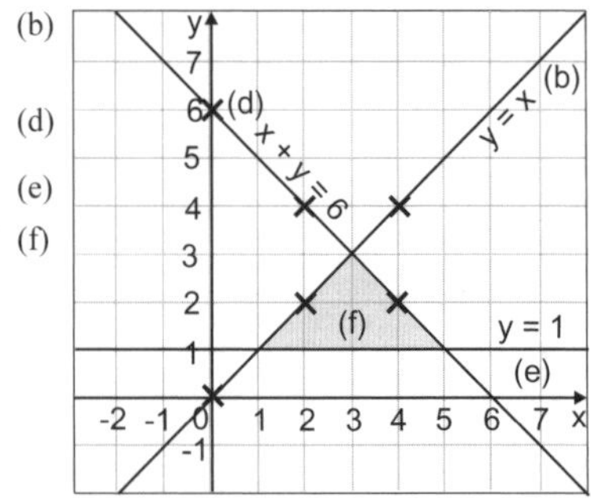

(1 mark each for correctly plotting the graphs for parts (b) and (d) and for joining them with straight lines. 1 mark for correctly drawing the line y = 1. 1 mark for shading in the area enclosed by these lines, as shown above.)

Page 100 (Exam Questions)

5) $5x + 2y = 33$ (1)
$2x + y = 14$ (2) (1 mark for both equations correct)
First match up the numbers in front of either the xs or the ys in both equations. In this case it's probably easiest to multiply equation 2 by 2:
$5x + 2y = 33$ — (1)
(2) × 2: $4x + 2y = 28$ — (3) (1 mark)
Then subtract equation (3) from equation (1) to give $x = 5$. (1 mark)
Substitute this value for x into one of the original equations, e.g. (2):
$2x + y = 14$ gives $10 + y = 14$.
So $y = 14 - 10 = 4$. (1 mark)
It takes him 5 minutes to iron a shirt.
It takes him 4 minutes to iron a pair of jeans. (1 mark)

6) (a) (b) Either use tables of values or the gradient and y-intercept to plot each line. (1 mark for each correctly drawn and labelled line.)

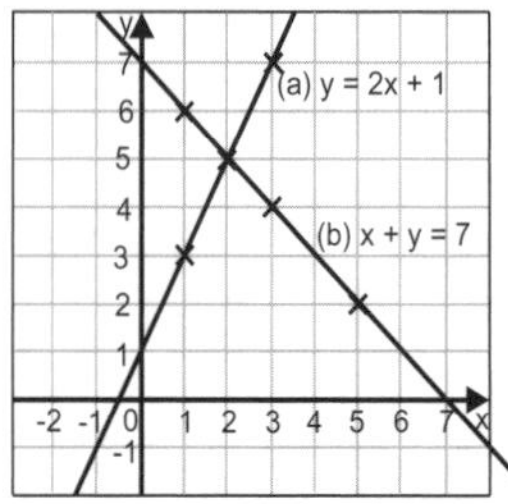

(c) The answer is just the coordinates of the point where the two graphs cross, i.e. $\boldsymbol{x = 2, y = 5}$. (1 mark)

7) $7 + 3x < 2 + 5x$.
First take away $5x$ from both sides to give $7 - 2x < 2$.
Then take away 7 from both sides to give $-2x < -5$.
Then divide both sides by -2 to give $\boldsymbol{x > 2.5}$.
(2 marks for correct answer. If incorrect, 1 mark for a similar method.)

-10 -9 -8 -7 -6 -5 -4 -3 -2 -1 0 1 2 3 4 5 6 7 8 9 10 (1 mark)

Watch out for that "big exception" from page 96 — when you divide by a negative number, the inequality sign flips round. If you're not sure, you can avoid this altogether by collecting x terms on the side where they'll be positive.

Section Three — Shapes

Page 108 (Warm-up Questions)

1) **2**

2) **5**

3) Interior angle = 180° – exterior angle.
So exterior angle = 180° – 140° = **40°**.

4) **Parallelogram**

5) (a) Exterior angle = 360° ÷ no. of sides, so no. of sides = 360° ÷ exterior angle = 360° ÷ 45° = **8 sides.**
(b) Interior angles = 180° – 45° = **135°**.

6) (a) **Kite.** (b) It has **1 line of symmetry**.

7) **Regular tetrahedron, tetrahedron** or **triangular-based pyramid**.

Page 109 (Exam Questions)

2)

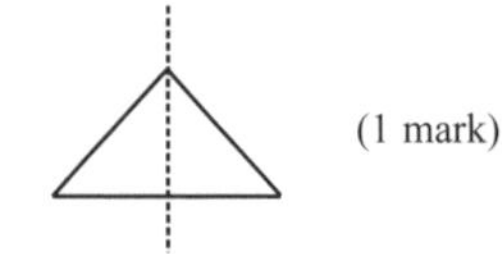

(1 mark)

3) (a)

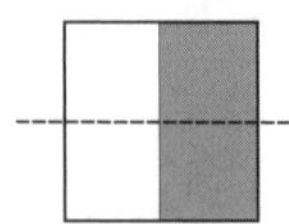

(1 mark for correct line as shown. No mark if incorrect line included.)

(b)

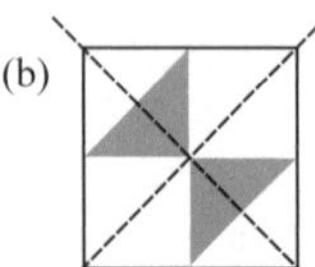

(2 marks for 2 correct lines as shown. 1 mark for 1 correct line as shown. No mark if incorrect line included.)

4) (a)

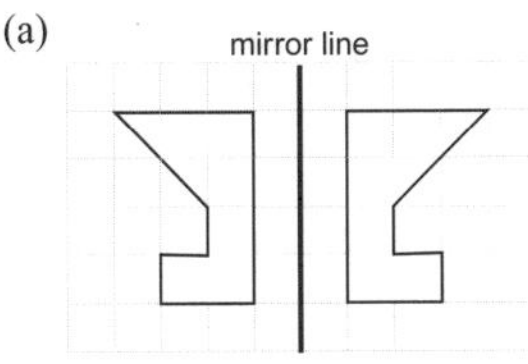

(1 mark for correct distance from the mirror line; 1 mark for correct shape.)

(b)

(2 marks for the correct triangle. If triangle is incorrect, then 1 mark for at least 1 correct side.)

5) (a) **6** (1 mark) (b) **2** (1 mark)

(c) $\mathbf{p} = 360° \div 6 = \mathbf{60°}$. (1 mark)

$\mathbf{q} = 180° - p = 180° - 60° = \mathbf{120°}$. (1 mark)

In a regular hexagon, each sector triangle is equilateral, so $\mathbf{r} = \mathbf{s} = (180° \div 3) = \mathbf{60°}$. (1 mark for each angle) **OR**

r is the same as the exterior angles = **60°**. (1 mark)

$\mathbf{s} = (180° - \text{angle r}) \div 2 = \mathbf{60°}$. (1 mark)

Page 118 (Warm-Up Questions)

1) Area = ½ × base × vertical height = ½ × 12 × 5 = **30 cm²**.
2) **12**
3) Area = length × width, i.e. 20 = 5 × width, so width = 20/5 = **4 cm**.
4) **3 cm**. The radius is half the diameter.
5) **Cylinder** or **circular prism**.
6) **8** *Vertices is the plural of vertex — the fancy maths word for corner.*
7) Length of 1 side = 24 ÷ 4 = 6 cm. So area = 6 × 6 = **36 cm²**
8) Area = $\pi \times r^2$, so area = π × 10 × 10 = **314 cm²**
9) **Tangent**
10) Area of 1 face = 5 × 5 = 25 cm². Area of 6 faces = 6 × 25 cm = **150 cm²**

Page 119 (Exam Questions)

2) Area of a parallelogram = base × vertical height.
Area of one parallelogram = 20 × 9 = 180 (1 mark)
Double 180 to get **360 cm²** (1 mark) (1 mark for correct units.)

3) (a) Volume of a cuboid = length × width × height.
So volume of loaf = 20 × 10 × 10 (1 mark) = **2000 cm³** (1 mark)

(b) Thickness = 20 ÷ 25 (1 mark) = **0.8 cm** or **8 mm** (1 mark)

4) (a) Area of rectangle = 12 = p × 8, so p = 12 ÷ 8 (1 mark) = **1.5 cm** (1 mark);

(b) Area of triangle = 12 = ½ × 4 × q, so q = 2 × (12 ÷ 4) (1 mark) = **6 cm** (1 mark)

(c) Area of trapezium = 12 = ½ × (6 + r) × 3 (1 mark)
So 6 + r = 12 ÷ 1.5 So r = 12 ÷ 1.5 – 6 = **2 cm.** (1 mark)

5) (a) Circumference = π × diameter, so circumference = π × 60 (1 mark)
= **188.5 cm (1 d.p.)** (1 mark)

(b) 1 km = 1000 m. Number of revs = 1000 m ÷ 188.5 cm (1 mark)
Must work in the same units, so 1000 m ÷ 1.885 m (1 mark)
= 530.5 (to 1 d.p.) Complete revs = **530** (1 mark)

6) (a) Perimeter = (2 × 3b) + (2 × 2b) = 6b + 4b = 10b. (1 mark)
b = 24 ÷ 10 = **2.4 cm** (1 mark)

(b) Length = 3b. So if b = 2.4, length = (2.4 × 3) = 7.2 cm (1 mark)
Width = 2b. So if b = 2.4, width = (2.4 × 2) = 4.8 cm (1 mark),
so area = 7.2 × 4.8 = **34.6 cm² (3 s.f.)** (1 mark)

Page 120 (Exam Questions)

7) Area of square = 8 × 8 = 64 cm² (1 mark)
Diameter of circle is 8cm, so radius = 4 cm (1 mark)
Area of circle = π × r² = π × (4 × 4) = 50.27 cm² (2 d.p.) (1 mark)
Shaded area = 64 – 50.27 = **13.73 cm² (2 d.p.)** (1 mark)

8) Volume of triangular prism = area of cross section × length (1 mark)
Area of cross section = ½ × base × height = ½ × 20 × 30 = 300 cm²
(1 mark) Volume = 300 × 40 = **12 000 cm³** (1 mark)

9) (a) Area of circle = π × 4.5 × 4.5 = 63.62 cm² (2 d.p.) (1 mark).
Quarter-circle = 63.62 ÷ 4 (1 mark) = **15.9 cm²** (1 d.p.) (1 mark).

(b) For circle: C = π × diameter = π × 2 × 4.5 = 28.3 cm (1 d.p.) (1 mark)
For quarter-circle: arc = 28.3 ÷ 4 = 7.1 cm (1 d.p.) (1 mark)
Perimeter = 7.1 + 4.5 + 4.5 = **16.1 cm** (1 d.p.) (1 mark)

10) (a)

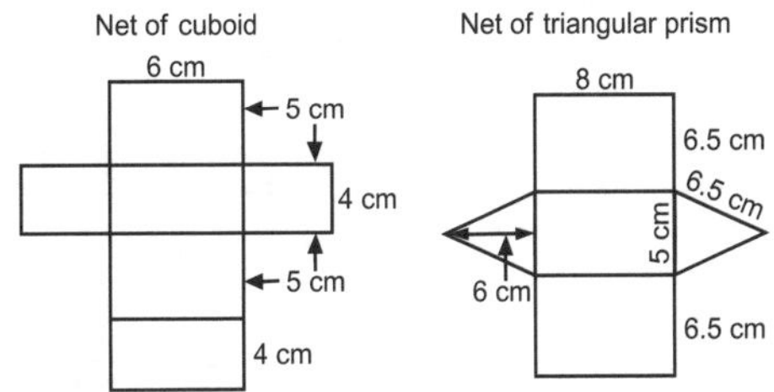

(Or similar — other nets possible. 3 marks for each net — 1 mark for correct shape, 1 mark for correctly labelling the three lengths of side, 3 marks if all correct. Marks will not be lost if more dimensions are given than is strictly necessary, as long as this labelling is accurate.)

(b) To compare, work out the surface area of each.
Cuboid: top and bottom = 2 × (6 × 5) = 2 × 30 = 60 cm²,
Front and back = 2 × (6 × 4) = 2 × 24 = 48 cm²,
2 ends = 2 × (4 × 5) = 2 × 20 = 40 cm².
Total S.A. = 60 + 48 + 40 = **148 cm²**
(2 marks — 1 mark for incorrect answer but correct method.)
Triangular prism: triangular ends = 2 × (½ × 5 × 6) = 2 × 15 = 30 cm²,
Base = 8 × 5 = 40 cm²
2 sloping sides = 2 × (6.5 × 8) = 2 × 52 = 104 cm².
Total S.A. = 30 + 40 + 104 = **174 cm²**
(2 marks — 1 mark for incorrect answer but correct method.)
They do not have the same surface area. (1 mark)
(The triangular prism has the larger surface area.)

Page 126 (Warm-up Questions)

1) **Quadrilateral**

2) (a) Angles in a triangle add up to 180°, so 3rd angle = 180° – (50° + 40°) = **90°**

(b) **Right-angled** triangle

3) **90°** or **right-angle**
If you haven't learnt the 12 geometry rules properly, questions like this one will be impossible. If you have learnt them, they'll be simple. It's worth the effort.

4) Supplementary angles add up to 180°, so 180° – 63° = **117°**
5) Sum of interior angles = (n – 2) × 180° = (6 – 2) × 180° = **720°**
6) **Arrows**
7) Sum of interior angles = (5 – 2) × 180° = 540°.
5th angle = 540° – (90° + 100° + 110° + 140°) = 540° – 440° = **100°**.
8) **BCA** or **ACB**

Page 127 (Exam Questions)

2) (1 mark for each correct angle.)

a: Angles on a straight line add up to 180°. 180 – 120 = **60°**.
b: Angles in a triangle add up to 180°. 180 – (70 + 60) = 180 – 130 = **50°**. c: Angles in a quadrilateral add up to 360°.
360 – (90 + 115 + 55) = 360 – 260 = **100°**.
d: Alternate angles where a line crosses 2 parallel lines are equal. = **62°**.
This is like the z-shape of parallel lines from page 123. But it doesn't look exactly like the diagram on that page, so watch out in the exam.

e: This is an isosceles triangle because 2 sides are equal, so the bottom 2 angles are equal too = **80°**.
f: Angles in a triangle add up to 180°. 180 – (80 + 80) = 180 – 160 = **20°**.
g: Sum of exterior angles in a polygon = 360°.
360 – (76 + 68 + 82 + 64) = 360 – 290 = **70°**.
h: Angle between a radius and a tangent to a circle = **90°**
i: Angles in a triangle add up to 180°. 180 – (36 + 90) = 180 – 126 = **54°**.
j Angles on a straight line add up to 180°. 180 – 148 = **32°**.
k: This is an isosceles triangle because two sides are equal, so two of the angles are equal, too.
180 – (32 + 32) = 180 – 64 = **116°**.

l: Supplementary angles add up to 180°. 180 – 115 = **65°**.
m: Supplementary angles add up to 180°. 180 – 130 = **50°**,
or Angles in a quadrilateral add up to 360°.
360 – (115 + 65 + 130) = 360 – 310 = **50°**.

3) (a) Corresponding angles are in the same position at each parallel line, so **a = e, b = f, d = h, c = g**. (All are needed for 1 mark.)
(b) Alternate angles form a Z shape, so **d = f and e = c**. (Both are needed for 1 mark.)
(c) Supplementary angles are found in the corners of the typical C-shape made by a line crossing 2 parallel lines, so **d with e** and **c with f**. (Both are needed for 1 mark.)

4) A nonagon has 9 sides. Sum of interior angles = (n – 2) × 180 = (9 – 2) × 180 = 1260°. (1 mark)
Total of given angles is 105 + 115 + 125 + 135 + 140 + 145 + 155 = 920.
Sum of 2 remaining angles = 1260 – 920 = 340. (1 mark)
Angles are equal so each angle = 340 ÷ 2 = **170°**. (1 mark)

Page 128 (Exam Questions)

5) (a) Angle EXD = 180 – (48 + 55) = **77°**. (1 mark) (Because angles on a straight line add up to 180°.)
(b) Angle BXC = 180 – 55 = **125°**. (1 mark) (DC is also a straight line.)
(c) Angle CXE = 180 – angle EXD = 180° – 77° = **103°** (1 mark)

6) (a) In EFGH, angle EHG = 360 – (100 + 94 + 86) = **80°**. (1 mark)
HX bisects angle EHG (cuts it in half), so angle XHG = 80 ÷ 2 = **40°**. (1 mark)
(b) HXFG is a quadrilateral too. So angle HXF = 360 – (94 + 86 + 40) = 360 – 220 = **140°**. (1 mark)
(c) In triangle EHX, angle H = 40, angle X = 180 – 140 = 40.
2 angles are the same, therefore it is **isosceles**. (1 mark)

7) (a) OX is part of the diameter that bisects AB, so using rule 3 from page 124 angle OXA must be **90°** (1 mark)
(b) Angle OAX = 180 – (52 + 90) = **38°** (1 mark)
(c) Triangle AOB is isosceles because it's formed by two radii. Therefore angle AOX = angle BOX, so angle AOB = 2 × 52 = **104°** (1 mark)

8) (a) Angle YAB = 90°, because it's an angle in a square. (1 mark)
Angle BAF = 720° ÷ 6 = 120°, because ABCDEF is a regular hexagon. (1 mark) So obtuse angle YAF = 360 – (90 + 120) = 360 – 210 = **150°**, because angles YAB, BAF and YAF are angles round a point. (1 mark)
(b) Line AB is common to hexagon ABCDEF and square ABXY, so they have sides of equal length. AF = AY, so triangle YAF is isosceles. (1 mark)
Angle AFY = (180° – angle YAF) ÷ 2 = (180° – 150°) ÷ 2 = 30° ÷ 2 = **15°** (1 mark)

Page 134 (Warm-up Questions)

1) **Similar**
2) Base = 3 × 4 cm = **12 cm**. Height = 3 × 3 cm = **9 cm**.
3) This is 2 lengths multiplied together, so it's an **area**.
4) **Congruent**
5) New length ÷ old length = 6 ÷ 4 = **1.5**
6) This formula is for a **length** — 3 lengths added together gives a length.
7) Each coordinate moves 3 units to the right and one down, so add 3 to each of the first numbers and take away one from each of the second numbers to give **(5,3)**, **(6,3)**, **(6,5)**.
8) If the scale factor is 2, the area is 2^2 = 4 times the size.
New area = 9 × 4 = **36 cm²**.

Page 135 (Exam Questions)

2) (a)
(b)
(c)

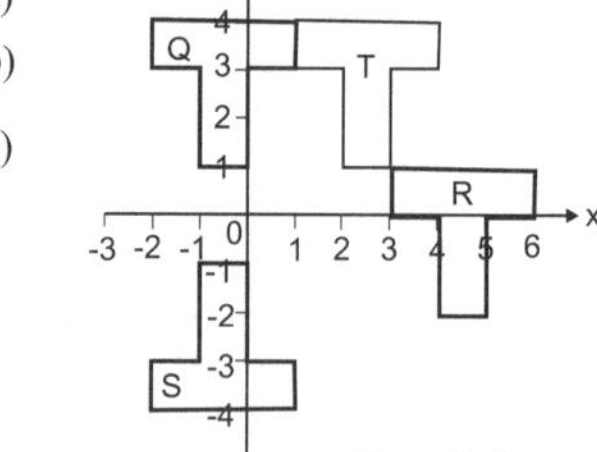

(1 mark for each correctly positioned shape.)

(d) **Reflection** (1 mark) **in the x axis** or **the line y = 0** (1 mark)

3) (a) (i) Angle WXY is a right-angle = **90°** (1 mark);
(ii) The shapes are similar, so angles in the same places are the same. Therefore angle ABC is the same as angle UVW = **60°** (1 mark);
(iii) The shapes are hexagons, so the sum of the interior angles = (6 – 2) × 180° = 720°. (1 mark)
Angle BAF = 720° – (90 + 90 + 90 + 240 + 60) = 720 – 570 = **150°** (1 mark)
A common mistake with questions like this is forgetting about one of the angles. Reflex angles like angle BCD can be easy to miss. Remember, you know this angle even though it isn't marked on because the shapes are similar, so it's the same as angle VWX on the other shape.
(b) Scale factor = new length ÷ old length = 35 ÷ 20 = **1.75** (1 mark)
(c) (i) UZ = 8 × 1.75 = **14 m** (1 mark)
(ii) AB = 21 ÷ 1.75 = **12 m** (1 mark)

4) (a) Scale factor = 20 ÷ 10 = 2, so scale factor for area is 2 × 2 = 4. (1 mark)
4 × 50 cm² = **200 cm²** (1 mark)
(b) Scale factor = 6 ÷ 2 = 3, so scale factor for volume is 3 × 3 × 3 = 27. (1 mark) 27 × 8 cm³ = **216 cm³** (1 mark)
(c) Scale factor = 14 ÷ 4 = 3.5, so scale factor for volume is 3.5 × 3.5 × 3.5 = 42.875 (3 d.p.) (1 mark) 1500 ÷ 42.875 = **35 cm³** (nearest whole number) (1 mark)

5) (a) 3 lengths multiplied together means this is a **volume** (1 mark)
(b) 2 lengths multiplied means this is an **area** (and 2 areas added together is still an area) (1 mark)
(c) 2 lengths divided by one length is a **length** (1 mark)
(d) Ignore the 3 because it's a number not a length. A length squared is the same as 2 lengths multiplied together, so this is an **area** (1 mark)
(e) Ignore π because it's a number not a length.
3 lengths multiplied together gives a **volume** (1 mark)

Page 142 (Warm-up Questions)

1) Must be clockwise, so 360 – 280 = **080°**.
2) (a) **z** (b) **y** (c) **x**
3) $\mathbf{y^2 + z^2 = x^2}$
4) Northlines are parallel, so using supplementary angles, 180 – 050 = 130°.

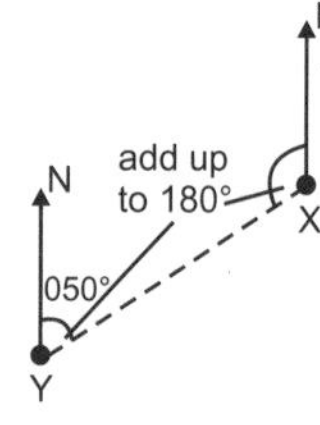

This gives the anticlockwise angle at X from the Northline. To get the clockwise angle (the bearing), subtract 130 from 360 = **230°**.
Questions like this are confusing when you try to understand what's going on just by reading them. Draw yourself a little sketch, and you'll probably find you recognise that parallel lines U-shape straight away (see page 123).

5) **The angle of depression is the angle downwards from the horizontal.**
6) Plot the points on a sketch graph to form a right-angled triangle with MN as the hypotenuse. Then use Pythagoras' Theorem:
$MN^2 = 3^2 + 4^2 = 25$, so MN = **5**.
7) **A circle with centre P and radius 4 cm.**
8) **Yes**. If it is right-angled then Pythagoras' Theorem must work for it. Check if it does: 17^2 (the longest side) = $8^2 + 15^2 = 64 + 225 = 289$.
So 289 should be 17^2. Find the square root of 289, and yes it is 17.

Page 143 (Exam Questions)

2) (a) $x^2 = 5^2 + 12^2$ (1 mark) $= 25 + 144 = 169$, $x = \sqrt{169}$ = **13 cm** (1 mark)

(b) Tan 35° = opp/adj = $x/3$ (1 mark), so $x = 3 \times \tan 35°$ = **2.1 cm** (1 d.p.) (1 mark)

(c) Sin x = opp/hyp = $4 \div 5$ (1 mark) = 0.8. So x = inv. sin 0.8 = **53.1°** (1 d.p.) (1 mark)

(d) Cos 42° = adj/hyp = $6.5/x$ (1 mark), so $x = 6.5 \div \cos 42°$ = **8.7 cm** (1 d.p.) (1 mark)

3) (a) First draw the triangle and put in the height, as in diagram below.

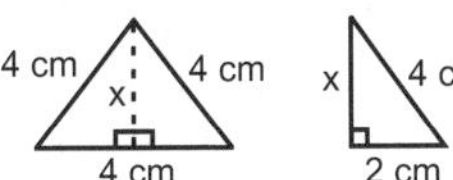

Split the triangle in half as shown to give a right-angled triangle. (1 mark) Pythagoras' theorem can now be used to find the missing side, which is the height. $4^2 = 2^2 + x^2$ (1 mark), i.e. $16 = 4 + x^2$, so $x^2 = 16 - 4 = 12$.

So $x = \sqrt{12}$ = **3.5 cm** (1 d.p.) (1 mark)

(b) Draw the triangle and put in the height to give 2 right-angled triangles, as in the diagram on the right. (1 mark)

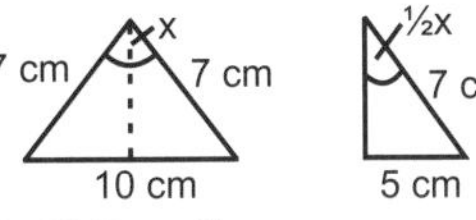

Sin $\frac{1}{2}x$ = opp/hyp = $5 \div 7$ (1 mark)
so $\frac{1}{2}x$ = 45.6°. (1 d.p.) so $x = 45.6° \times 2$ = **91.2°** (1 mark)

4) (a) (i) **047°** (1 mark), protractor at A, clockwise to B. (Accept answers in the range 046° to 048°.)

(ii) **137°** (1 mark), protractor at B, clockwise to C. (Accept answers in the range 136° to 138°.)

(iii) **277°** (1 mark). It is easier to measure anticlockwise from C, 83°, then subtract from 360°. (Accept answers in the range 276° to 278°.)

(b) $AC^2 = 15^2 + 20^2$ (1 mark) $= 225 + 400 = 625$. $AC = \sqrt{625} = 25$ km

(1 mark) Total distance of route = 25 + 20 + 15 = **60 km**. (1 mark)

5) Draw a diagram similar to that on the right.
Tan 64° = h ÷ 10 (1 mark), so h = 10 × tan 64° = **20.5 m** (1 d.p.) (1 mark)

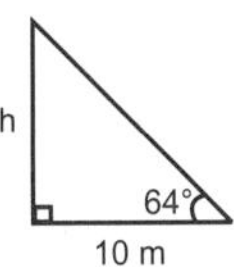

6) Firstly, draw the locus of points equidistant from the 2 given lines, AB and BC, by bisecting the angle (ABC) between them. (1 mark). Secondly, draw the locus of points which are equidistant from the 2 given points, B and C, by constructing the perpendicular bisector of the line BC. (1 mark) At the point where these loci meet is the treasure, T (1 mark). Your answer should look similar to that below.

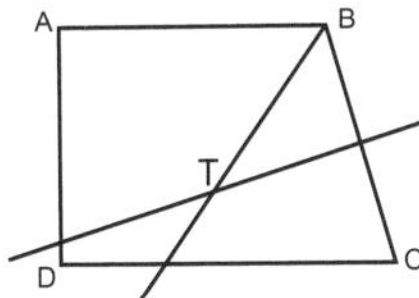

If you didn't get this one, have another look at page 140.

Section Four — Statistics and Probability

Page 150 (Warm-up Questions)

1) **0**

2) $10 \times \frac{1}{2}$ = **5**

3) $1 - 0.7$ = **0.3**

4) **Heads and 1, H & 2, H & 3, H & 4, H & 5, H & 6, Tails and 1, T & 2, T & 3, T & 4, T & 5, T & 6.**

5) There are 3 possible odd numbers, 1, 3 and 5. So the probability is $3/6 = \frac{1}{2}$.

Page 151 (Exam Questions)

2) (a) There are 11 letters altogether and only 1 is an 'L', so probability = **1/11**. (1 mark)

(b) There are 2 'I's and 1 'Y', so probability = **3/11**. (1 mark)

(c) There are 4 vowels altogether (1 × O, 1 × A, 2 × I), so probability = **4/11**. (1 mark)

(d) There are no 'X's, so it's impossible to pick out that letter. Therefore probability = 0/11 = **0**. (1 mark)

3) (a) Half of the cards are red, so probability = ½ (1 mark)

(b) There are 4 queens, so probability = 4/52 = **1/13** (1 mark)

(c) There is only one jack of spades, so probability = **1/52** (1 mark)

(d) There are four 5s and four 6s, so probability = 8/52 = **2/13** (1 mark)

4) (a) P (blue) = 0.55 – 0.3 = 0.25. (1 mark) If done 200 times you'd expect to get 200 × 0.25 = **50**. (1 mark)

(b) P (red) = 0.3 so total counters = 6 ÷ 0.3 = **20**. (2 marks for correct answer, 1 mark for correct working if answer is incorrect.)

(c) P (white) = 1 – 0.55 = 0.45 (1 mark), so number of white counters is 0.45 of 40 = 0.45 × 40 = **18** (1 mark).

5) a) Draw a sample space like this:

	2	4	6	8	10
1	3	5	7	9	11
2	4	6	8	10	12
3	5	7	9	11	13
4	6	8	10	12	14

(3 marks for a correct diagram, lose a mark for each mistake.)

b) Count all the numbers greater than 10 — there are six of these. There are 20 possible outcomes, so P (score greater than 10) = 6/20 = **3/10**. (1 mark)

c) There are two ways of getting the same number on both spinners, either (2, 2) or (4, 4). So P (same number on spinners) = 2 / 20 = **1/10**. (1 mark)

Page 155 (Warm-up Questions)

1) **The bar chart showing shoe sizes, because these are separate items.** *For measurements like lengths, all possible measurements must be included and so the bars are joined.*

2) **Negative**, because the amount of soup sold increases as the temperature decreases.

3) 360° ÷ 90 = **4°**

4) **Negative**

Page 156 (Exam Questions)

2) (a)

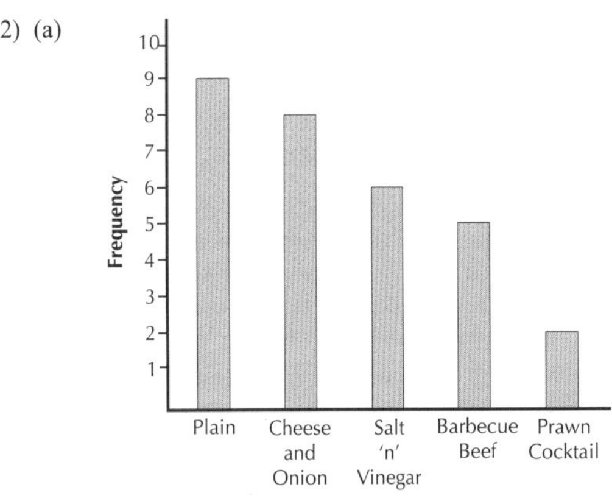

(1 mark for numbering vertical axis and naming bars correctly.
1 mark for labelling axes with titles similar to those above.
1 mark for bars of equal width with spaces between them.
1 mark for correct heights of bars.)

(b)

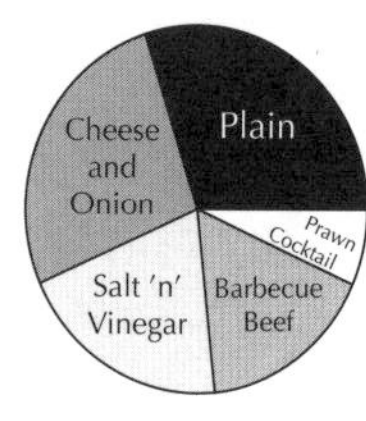

(5 marks if the sectors are all correctly drawn and labelled, with angles as in the method below. 4 marks if the correct method has been used and at least three of the sectors are correctly drawn and labelled. If the diagram is incorrect, marks can be awarded for the method, as shown below.)
Each person is represented by 360° ÷ 30 = 12°. (1 mark). Angle sizes:
Plain = 9 × 12° = 108° Cheese and Onion = 8 × 12° = 96°
Salt 'n' Vinegar = 6 × 12° = 72° Barbecue Beef = 5 × 12° = 60°
Prawn Cocktail = 2 × 12° = 24°
(2 marks if all correct, 1 mark if a minimum of 2 correct.)
Remember to check that your angles add up to 360 degrees: 108 + 96 + 72 + 60 + 24 = 360. If they don't, then you've made a mistake.

3) (a) **2** (1 mark) because there's no connection between these 2 things, and this graph shows no correlation.
(b) **3** (1 mark) because this graph shows negative correlation, and the more someone smokes, the shorter their life expectancy.
(c) **1** (1 mark), because this graph shows positive correlation, and as a foot gets longer the shoe size goes up.

4) (a) Indian: 10 people = 100°, so each person = 100° ÷ 10 = 10° (1 mark)
Chinese = 40°, so 40° ÷ 10° = **4 pupils** (1 mark)
(b) Angle for fish and chips is 60°. Total angle in a circle is 360°. So fraction of pupils choosing fish and chips = 60/360 (1 mark) = **1/6**. (1 mark)
(c) Every 10° is one person, so 360° ÷ 10° (1 mark) = **36 pupils**. (1 mark)
(d) Angle for pizza = 360° – (40° + 60° + 100°) = 160°, (1 mark) so percentage is (160 ÷ 360) × 100 = **44.4%**. (1 d.p.) (1 mark)

Page 163 (Warm-up Questions)

1) Sum of numbers = 1 + 2 + 3 + 4 + 5 + 6 + 7 + 8 + 9 + 10 = 55; So mean is 55 ÷ 10 = **5.5**.
2) The numbers in ascending order are 5, 9, 10, 12, 18, 19, 20 and 21. There is no middle number, so the answer is halfway between the middle two (12 and 18). The average of 12 and 18 is (12 + 18) ÷ 2 = **15**.
3) The first 5 prime numbers are 2, 3, 5, 7 and 11, so the range is 11 – 2 = **9**.
4) If the mean is 8, the sum of the 4 numbers is 8 × 4 = 32.
The sum of the 3 given numbers is 5 + 7 + 8 = 20.
So the 4th number is 32 – 20 = **12**.
If the first bit of this working out sounds strange, just think about how you'd work out the mean. You'd add up all the numbers and then divide by however many numbers there were. So if you've got the mean and you know how many numbers there were, you can go backwards by multiplying the mean by how many numbers there were.
5) You would multiply together the numbers from the first two rows, i.e. **3rd row = 1st row (number of pets) × 2nd row (frequency)**.
6) A **grouped frequency table**.
7) (70 + 79) ÷ 2 = **74.5 cm**.
8) **Find the upper quartile by looking across to the curve from the point ¾ of the way up the vertical axis, then reading down to the horizontal axis. Find the lower quartile by repeating this for a point ¼ of the way up the vertical axis. Then take the lower quartile away from the upper quartile to get the interquartile range.**
9) **The shape of a cumulative frequency curve tells you how spread out the data values are.**

Page 164 (Exam Questions)

2) (a) The table should be as shown below (1 mark)

Number of letters	Frequency	No. × freq.
3	4	**12**
4	3	**12**
5	3	**15**
6	3	**18**
7	2	**14**
8	4	**32**
9	1	**9**
Totals	**20**	**112**

(b) mean = 3rd row total ÷ 2nd row total (1 mark) = 112 ÷ 20 = **5.6** (1 mark)

(c) Imagine the original data set out in ascending order:
3333 444 555 666 77 8888 9 The middle number is between the 10th and the 11th, so it's halfway between the 10th number = 5, and 11th = 6. So median = **5.5**. (2 marks — 1 mark for 5 or 6)

3) (a) 3 minutes = 3 × 60 = 180 seconds. Customers served in 3 minutes or less = 7 + 13 + 20 + 24 + 17 + 9 = 90. (1 mark)
Percentage = 90 ÷ 100 (total no. of customers) × 100 = **90%**. (1 mark)

(b)

Waiting time (seconds)	1-30	31-60	61-90	91-120	121-150	151-180	181-210	Totals
Frequency	7	13	20	24	17	9	10	**100**
Mid-interval value	**15.5**	**45.5**	**75.5**	**105.5**	**135.5**	**165.5**	**195.5**	—
Freq. × mid-interval value	**108.5**	**591.5**	**1510**	**2532**	**2303.5**	**1489.5**	**1955**	**10 490**

(1 mark for correctly calculated mid-interval values, 1 mark for correctly calculated frequency × mid-interval values, 1 mark for totals. This information need not be arranged in a table as above to gain the marks.)
Mean = overall total (final row) ÷ frequency total (2nd row)
= 10 490 ÷ 100 = **105 secs** (nearest whole second) (1 mark)
To make sure you haven't accidentally left out any values, complete the 3rd and 4th rows of the grouped frequency table, including the 'totals' column.
(c) **91-120 seconds**, (1 mark) because this group has the highest frequency.
(d) There are 100 customers, so the middle one must be between the 50th and 51st customers. Up to 90 seconds there are 7 + 13 + 20 = 40 customers. The next 24 waited between 91 and 120 seconds, so the 50th and 51st fall in this interval. **91-120 seconds**. (1 mark)

4) (a)

Weight (kg)	1.6-2.0	2.1-2.5	2.6-3.0	3.1-3.5	3.6-4.0	4.1-4.5	4.6-5.0
Frequency	1	2	4	6	9	5	1
Cumulative frequency	1	1 + 2 **= 3**	3 + 4 **= 7**	7 + 6 **= 13**	13 + 9 **= 22**	22 + 5 **= 27**	27 + 1 **= 28**

(2 marks if all correct, 1 mark if at least four correct.)

(b) (c) (d)

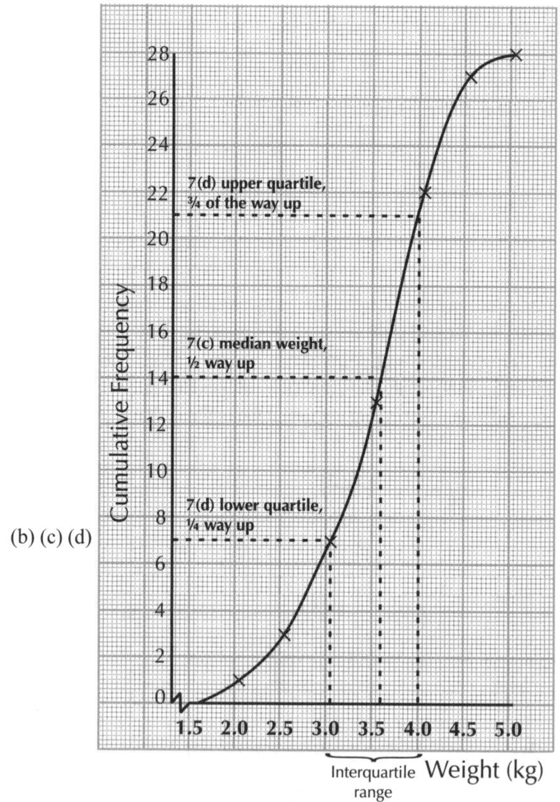

(b) Curve must be plotted at upper limits (2.05, 2.55, 3.05, 3.55, 4.05, 4.55, 5.05) with all points correct and a smooth curve drawn in for the full 3 marks. Axes must have a similar scale to that in the example shown, and must be labelled correctly. Award 2 marks only if curve is not smooth or if axes are incorrect or not properly labelled or if up to 2 of the 7 points are plotted incorrectly, and 1 mark if more than one of the above mistakes are made, or if 3 to 5 points are plotted incorrectly. No marks if more than 5 points are plotted incorrectly.
(c) Median: Line drawn at 14 on vertical axis (half the total cumulative frequency). Reading from horizontal axis should be about **3.6 kg** (2 marks for an answer in the range 3.5-3.7 kg. 1 mark for an answer in the range 3.4-3.8 kg.)

(d) Lower quartile is ¼ of the way up the vertical axis = 7.
Read off bottom axis to give about 3.05 kg.
Upper quartile is ¾ of the way up the vertical axis = 21.
Read off bottom axis to give about 4.0 kg.
Interquartile range = 4.0 – 3.05 = **0.95 kg**
(1 mark for correct working and 2 marks for an answer in the range 0.8-1.1 kg, or 1 mark for an answer in the range 0.7-1.2 kg.)

EXAM PAPER ANSWERS

Paper 1 — Calculator Not Allowed

1 The difference is increasing by 3 each time. To continue this pattern you first add 12 and then 15 onto the previous numbers to give **31, 46** (1 mark)

2 (a) 15/20 = 75/100 = **75%** (1 mark)

(b) 12/20 = 60/100 = **60%** (1 mark)

3 Turn the fractions into decimals: 1 ÷ 2 = 0.5. 2 ÷ 5 = 0.4.
So the order is **0.2, 0.3, 2/5, ½**.(1 mark for 0.2 first, 1 mark for ½ last, 1 mark for middle terms in correct order.)

4 This is a regular polygon, so work out x using the formula exterior angle = 360° ÷ no. of sides. So x = 360 ÷ 6 = **60°**. (1 mark)
Work out the size of y (the interior angle) using the formula interior angle = 180° – exterior angle. So y = 180 – 60 = **120°**. (1 mark)

5 (a) **6a + 3** (1 mark) (b) **2a + 7** (1 mark)

6 (a)

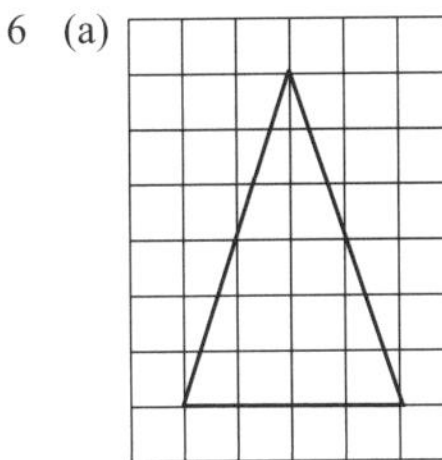

(1 mark)

(b)

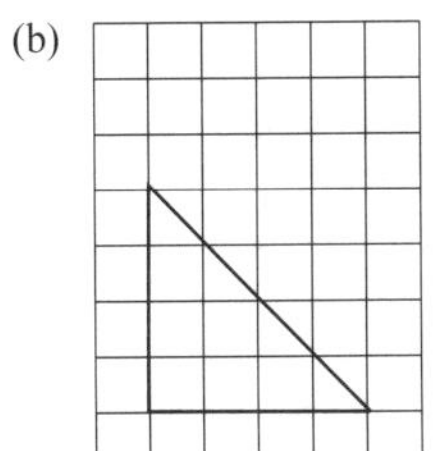

Or

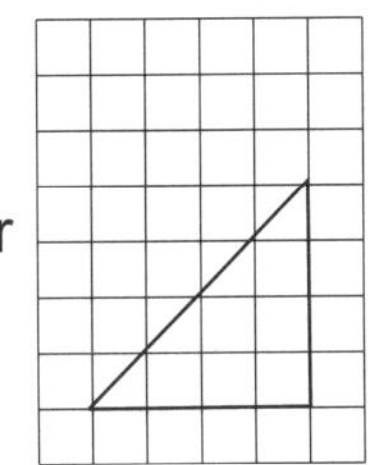

(1 mark)

7 (a) 1/4 of 100 = 100 ÷ 4 = 25. 25 × 3 = **75**. (1 mark)

(b) 1/3 of 90 = 90 ÷ 3 = 30. 30 × 2 = **60**. (1 mark)

(c) 1/2 of 24 = 24 ÷ 2 = 12. If 12 is 3/4, then 1/4 is 12 ÷ 3 = 4, so 4/4 = 4 × 4 = **16**. (1 mark)

8 (a) The marks are in ascending order, so the median should be the one in the middle. But there are 2 in the middle, so the median is halfway between these = **7.5** (1 mark)

(b) **5** (1 mark)

9 (a) 2¾ + 3½ = **6¼ km** (1 mark) (b) 7¼ – 3½ = **3¾ km** (1 mark)

(c) 2¾ + 7¼ = **10 km** (1 mark)

10 (a) (i) 5/20 = 1/4, so it's **whole nut**. (1 mark)

(ii) No. of hard centres = 20 – (12 + 5) = 3, so probability = **3/20**. (1 mark)

(b) Chris has taken 2 chocolates, so there are 20 – 2 = 18 left.
So the probability of getting a soft centre now is 12/18 or **2/3**. (1 mark)

(c) Soft centre = (24 ÷ 3) × 2 = **16**. (1 mark) Whole nut centre = **5**. (1 mark)
Hard centre = (24 ÷ 8) = **3**. (1 mark)

11 (a) Total = 30. To turn 30 into 360°, × by 12 (as 30 goes into 360 12 times).
10 × 12 = **120°**. (1 mark)
20 × 12 (because 30 – 10 = 20) = **240°** (1 mark)

(b) **Not possible to tell.** (1 mark)
This might seem like a trick question, but think about it and you'll see that there's no way you can tell what % have both pets. It could be that all 10 children with dogs also have a cat, or it could be that 15 of the 20 children without a dog have a cat instead. Or it could be something in between. They just haven't told you enough. Be very careful when they give you this "not possible to tell" option though — you've got to be absolutely sure there's no way you can work it out.

12 4p – 3 = 5. Add 3 to both sides to give 4p = 8.
Divide both sides by 4 to give **p = 2**. (1 mark)
2m + 7 = 15. Take 7 away from both sides to give 2m = 8.
Divide both sides by 2 to give **m = 4**. (1 mark)
4x + 3 = x + 24. Take x away from both sides to give 3x + 3 = 24.
Take 3 away from both sides to give 3x = 21.
Divide both sides by 3 to give **x = 7**. (1 mark)
2(5q + 8) = 6. Divide both sides by 2 to give 5q + 8 = 3.
Take 8 away from both sides to give 5q = -5.
Divide both sides by 5 to give **q = -1**. (1 mark)

On the last one, if you want, you can multiply out the brackets first and then solve it — it's the same equation either way. Just remember to do the same thing to both sides when you're solving it.

13 (a) 1083 = **652 + 431** or **651 + 432** or **632 + 451** or **631 + 452**
OR any of these pairs in reverse order. (1 mark)
381 = **246 + 135** or **245 + 136** or **236 + 145** or **235 + 146**
OR any of these pairs in reverse order. (1 mark)

(b) 135 = **456 – 321** (1 mark)

14

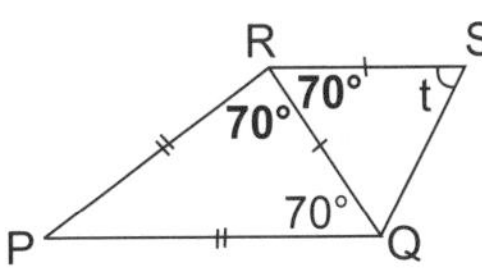

(a) Triangle PQR is isosceles, so angle **PRQ** should be labelled 70°. (1 mark)
PQ and RS are parallel, so angle **QRS** should be labelled 70°. (1 mark)
Look back to pages 122 and 123 if you didn't get this second one.

(b) Triangle QRS is isosceles, so angles t and RQS must be the same
So t = (180 – 70) ÷ 2 (1 mark) = **55°**. (1 mark)

15 (a) $\frac{2(5x+2)}{3} < 8$ Multiply both sides by 3 to give $2(5x + 2) < 24$.
Divide both sides by 2 to give $5x + 2 < 12$.
Take 2 away from both sides to give $5x < 10$.
Divide both sides by 5 to give $\mathbf{x < 2}$. (1 mark)

$\frac{2(9-y)}{3} > 4$ Multiply both sides by 3 to give $2(9 – y) > 12$.
Divide both sides by 2 to give $9 – y > 6$.
Add y to both sides to give $9 > 6 + y$.
Take 6 from both sides to give $3 > y$, or $\mathbf{y < 3}$. (1 mark)

(b) John's answer is wrong, because numbers from -4 downwards are less than +4, but can be squared to give 16 or more.
Accept **x = -4**, or **any answer less than -4**. (1 mark)

16 Both the triangles must be isosceles, because both have two sides that are radii of the circle. So angle OBC must be equal to OCB = **50°** (1 mark)
For the same reason, angle OBA must be equal to OAB = **25°** (1 mark)
AOC = 360 – (angle COB + angle BOA), since angles around a point add up to 360°. Angle COB = 180 – (50 + 50) = 80°.
Angle BOA = 180 – (25 + 25) = 130°.
So AOC = 360 – (80 + 130) = **150°**. (1 mark)

17 (a) **When x is even, $x(x + 3)$ is even** should be ticked. (1 mark)

(b) **When x is odd, $x^2 + 1$ is even** should be ticked. (1 mark)

(c) **$x^2 + x$ is always even** should be ticked. (1 mark)
The simplest way to tackle questions like these is to pick an even or an odd number, and substitute it into the equation.

18 (a) **y = 0 — line through D and C**. (1 mark)
x + y = 4 — line through A and C. (1 mark)
y = 2x + 4 — line through A and B. (1 mark)

(b) Gradient = 4 ÷ 8 = 0.5. Line crosses y-axis at -2.
So the equation of the line through B and C is $\mathbf{y = \frac{1}{2}x - 2}$ (1 mark)

19 (a) Look halfway up the y-axis to the cumulative frequency of 20.
Draw a line across until it meets the curve, and read off the value on the x-axis at this point. So the median is about **150 cm** (1 mark)

(b) As above, but at ¼ and ¾ of the way up. So inter-quartile range is approx. 155 cm – 145 cm (1 mark) = **10 cm**
(1 mark – accept answers in the range 9-11 cm).

(c) The second group has a lower average (but similar spread of values), so are generally less tall, and **the girls in the first group are likely to be older**. (1 mark)

20 (a) **30%** (1 mark)

(b) **No. The graph just shows the percentage increase in sales, not the sales themselves. So Company B could have large increases, but a much smaller number of sales.** (1 mark)

(c) **No. The percentage increase in sales was less, but it was still an increase in sales.** (1 mark)
A sneaky little question that one — for some reason you just assume that the graph will show the amount sold, rather than the percentage increase in the amount sold. That's why you have to really keep your wits about you in an exam and make sure you read every question properly.

[There are 60 marks available in total for Paper 1]

Paper 2 — Calculator Allowed

1 (a) $20 \div 4 = 5$. $3 \times 5 = 15$, so fraction is **15/20**. (1 mark)
(b) $21 \div 7 = 3$. $8 \times 3 = 24$, so fraction is 21/**24**. (1 mark)

2 (a) (i) $19 + 15 =$ **34**, $34 \times 2.5 =$ **85**. (Both must be correct for 1 mark.)
(ii) $70 \times 2.5 =$ **175** (1 mark)
(b) (i) $950 - 38 =$ **912** (1 mark) (ii) $950 \div 38 =$ **25** (1 mark)

3 (a) **12 000** (1 mark) (b) **11 600** (1 mark)

4 (a) Bank B: £193.38 × 36 = **£6961.68** (1 mark)
Bank C: £189.35 × 36 = **£6816.60** (1 mark)
This should be 2 easy marks — all you need to do is multiply each of the numbers they give you in the table by 36. It's all there in the question, so don't let any extra bits like the size of the loan confuse you.
(b) £6816.60 – 6477.84 = **£338.76** (1 mark)

5 (a) 6 cm × 2 cm × 4 cm = **48** (1 mark) **cm³** (1 mark)
(b) $4 \times 3 \times h = 48$ cm³, so $h = 48 \div 12 =$ **4 cm**. (1 mark)

6 (a) $(36 \times 50) + (35 \times 20) + (12 \times 10) + (8 \times 5) = 2660$p
= £(2660 ÷ 100) = **£26.60** (1 mark)
(b) $2660 \div 70 =$ **38** (1 mark)

7 (a) Distance = speed × time = 18 × 3 = **54 miles** (1 mark)
(b) Speed = distance ÷ time = 147 ÷ 3.5 = **42 mph** (1 mark)
(c) Time = distance ÷ speed = 153 ÷ 68 = **2.25 hours** or **2¼ hours** (1 mark)
It might seem like a waste of time learning formula triangles, but if you know them they make questions like this so much easier.

8 (a) $\mathbf{8 \times 10^8}$ (1 mark) (b) $\mathbf{1.2 \times 10^{-2}}$ (1 mark) (c) $\mathbf{9.6 \times 10^6}$ (1 mark)

9 (a) $15 \div 100 = 0.15$. $0.15 \times 42 =$ **£6.30** (1 mark)
(b) $15 \div 100 = 0.15$. $0.15 \times 54 =$ £8.10. £54 – £8.10 = **£45.90** (1 mark)
(c) £15.30 = 85%. 15.30 ÷ 85 = £0.18. £0.18 × 100 = **£18** (1 mark)

10 (a) 1 g provides $40.5 \div 150 = 0.27$.
So 200 g provides $0.27 \times 200 =$ **54 g** (1 mark)
(b) 100 g of pink salmon provides 155 kcal.
100 g of tuna provides (171 kcal ÷ 150) × 100 = 114 kcal. (1 mark)
So **100 g of pink salmon** contains more energy. (1 mark)

11 (a) For 20 minutes it costs $500 + (20 \times 35) =$ **1200**.
For 60 minutes it costs $500 + (60 \times 35) =$ **2600**.
(Both answers required for 1 mark.)
(b) (d) (e) (1 mark for line correctly drawn.)

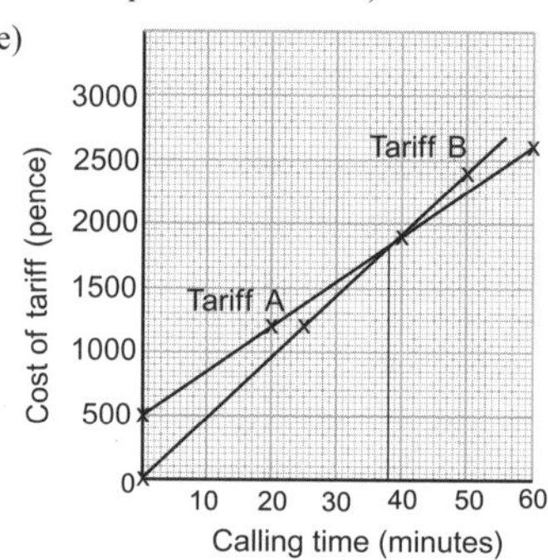

(c) **0** for 0 min, $50 \times 48 =$ **2400** for 50 min.
(Both answers required for 1 mark)
(d) See graph above. (1 mark for line correctly drawn.)
(e) Where graphs are correct, **38 minutes**. (1 mark — accept answers in the range **37 to 39**. Where graphs are incorrect, 1 mark for reading off **correct value where the two lines cross ± 1 minute.**)

12 (a) Circumference = π × diameter = $\pi \times 56$
= **176 cm (nearest centimetre)** (1 mark)
(b) 176 cm = (176 ÷ 100) m = 1.76 m. Distance = 1.76 × 142 = 249.92 m
= **250 m (nearest metre)** (2 marks for correct answer, or 1 mark for correct method if answer incorrect.)

13 (a) $C = (6 \times 7) + 15 = 42 + 15 =$ **£57** (1 mark)
(b) $6n + 15 = 33$, so $6n = 33 - 15 = 18$, so $n = 18 \div 6 =$ **3 days** (1 mark)

14 (a) $1 - (0.3 + 0.35 + 0.1) = 1 - 0.75 =$ **0.25** (1 mark)
(b) $240 \times 0.3 =$ **72 pupils** (1 mark — must show working to get the mark.)

15 (a) Short cut length² = $14^2 + 23^2 = 196 + 529 = 725$.
So short cut length = $\sqrt{725}$ = **27 m** (to nearest metre)
(2 marks for correct answer, or 1 mark for correct method if answer incorrect.)
(b) Distance on pavement = 23 + 14 = 37 m.
Distance of short cut = 27 m, so it is 37 – 27 = **10 m** further. (1 mark)

16 (a) A: **(0,0)**. (1 mark)
C: You know that $y = 0$. Substituting in the equation $y = x(x - 4)$, $0 = x(x - 4)$, so <u>either</u> $x = 0$ <u>or</u> $x - 4 = 0 \Rightarrow x = 4$. You can see from the graph that $x = 0$ at point A, and x is positive at point C. So $x = 4$ must be correct for point C, and the coordinates are **(4,0)**. (1 mark)
B: You know that $x = 2$, because B is halfway between points A and C. So put that value into the equation $y = x(x - 4)$ to find y:
$y = 2(2 - 4) = 2 \times -2 = -4$.
So the coordinates of point B are **(2,-4)**. (1 mark)
(b) $y = x(x - 4) = 5 \times (5 - 4) =$ **5** (1 mark)

17 Height (opposite) = 15 (adjacent) × tan 42° (1 mark) = **13.5 m** (1 mark)
Formula triangles are really useful for trigonometry questions like this, so if you don't know them you need to go over page 138 again.

18 (a) (b) (c)

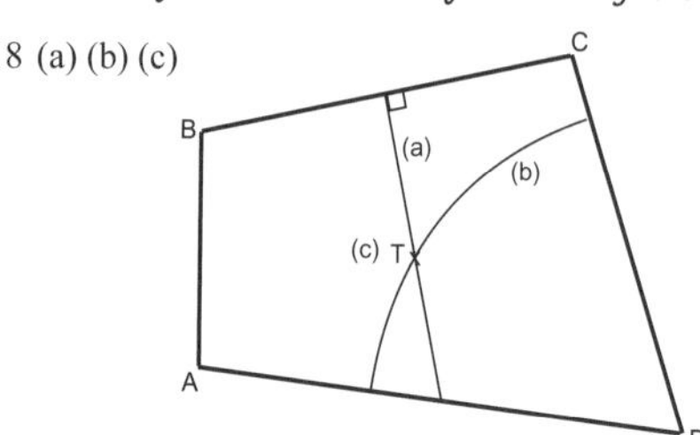

(a) (1 mark for a line drawn with a ruler exactly halfway along the line BC, at 90° to the line BC.)
(b) (1 mark for a line drawn with compasses which is the arc of a circle with centre D and radius 40 ÷ 8 = 5 cm.)
(c) (1 mark for correctly marking and labelling the point where the two lines cross.)
(d) **051°**. (1 mark)
Use a protractor and measure clockwise from the northline.

19 (a) Scale factor = 9 ÷ 6 = 1.5. PR = 10 cm × 1.5 = **15 cm**. (1 mark)
(b) BC = 16.5 ÷ 1.5 = **11 cm** (1 mark) (c) 6 : 9 = **2 : 3** (1 mark)

20 $4x + y = 134$ (equation 1)
$3x + 3y = 150$ (equation 2) (1 mark for giving correct starting equations.)
It's now easiest to match up the numbers in front of the ys by multiplying equation 1 by 3 to give $12x + 3y = 402$ (equation 3).
$3x + 3y = 150$ (equation 2).
Take away equation 2 from equation 3 to give $9x = 252$.
(1 mark for correct method similar to this.)
Divide both sides by 9 to give $x = 28$.
Substitute this value into equation 1 to find y: $4x + y = 134$
$= (4 \times 28) + y = 134$, so $y = 134 - 112 = 22$ or $y = 22$.
i.e. A chocolate bar costs **28p** (1 mark) and a packet of mints costs **22p** (1 mark).

[There are 60 marks available in total for Paper 2]

Mental Mathematics Test

1) **1010**
2) **9**
3) **12**
   Look at your answer sheet as you listen to the questions — there are often important bits written down for you, that make it much easier.
4) **9**
5) **-9**
6) **1200**
   This is a bit of a challenge for 5 seconds — the questions get harder as you go. You can note down the 100 cm³ and come back to this, but don't miss other questions by worrying about this one.
7) **3**
8) **12**
9) x = **1** y = **2**
10) **24.5**
11) **40**
12) **21   34**
13) **4**
14) **6 × 10⁶**
   You can scribble the 6 000 000 on the answer sheet and use it for working out, but remember to write the answer too, otherwise you won't get any marks.
15) **270**
16) **45.8**
17) **1.8**
18) **112**
19) **9** Accept a list of all integer solutions, i.e. -2, -1, 0, 1, 2, 3, 4, 5, 6.
20) **12.5**
21) **1/8** Accept equivalent probabilities, e.g. 12/96.
22) **4** or **-4** Accept either.
23) **6** Do not accept 256.
24) **30** *To be sure, write the numbers out in order.*
25) **1541**
26) **18 ≤ answer ≤ 21**
27) **3/5** Accept equivalent fractions or decimals.
28)

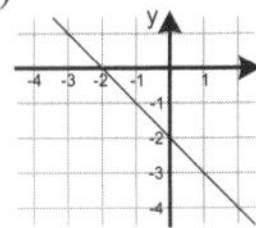

Accept line at least two diagonals in length.
Accept line not drawn accurately, provided intention is clear.

29) **35**
30) **6.25**

[There are 30 marks available in total for the Mental Maths paper]

Working out your grade

- *Add up all your marks for the three papers.*
- *Look up your total in this table to see what level you got.*

Total marks	0 – 26	27 – 32	33 – 38	39 – 59	60 – 96	97 – 150
Level	N	4	5	6	7	8

Important

- *The practice exams cover tiers 5-7 and 6-8. If you're doing tiers 3-5 or 4-6, you could get a level 2 or 3 instead of an N.*
- *The grades are only a guide — these papers are meant to be a real test of how well you've revised, so if they show up gaps in your knowledge don't panic, just go back to the topics and go over them again. The more practice you do the better ...*

Index

A

accuracy 12
adjacent, trigonometry 138
algebra 41 - 101
alternate angles 123
angle notation 125
angle of depression 139
angle of elevation 139
angles
103, 121, 122, 123, 124, 137
arc 112
areas 17, 110, 111, 115, 129
area method for expanding out brackets 45
area of cross-section 116
average 157
axes 89

B

balance method for equations 60
bar charts 152
bar-line graph 152
bearings 137
BODMAS 56
brackets 43-45, 55, 61, 62, 71
brackets buttons 38
bucket shaped graphs 80

C

calculators 20, 36-39, 68
centre of enlargement 131, 132
centre of rotation 133
charts 152-154
chords 112, 124
chord bisector 124
circles 112, 113, 124, 140
circle geometry 124
circular prism 116
circumference 111
class boundary 161
clockwise 137
coefficients 94
combined probability 148-149
common denominator 19
common difference 48
common factor 44
compasses 140
complicated shapes 114-115
congruence 130
constructions 140-141
conversion factors 16
conversions 16, 17
converting decimals to fractions 9
coordinates 71-72, 85
correlation 153
corresponding angles 123
COS 138, 139
cross-multiplying 61, 62
cross-sectional area 116
cube 107, 117
cube numbers 5
cube root 32, 33, 37
cubics 59
cuboid 13, 107, 117
cumulative frequency 161-162

D

data 157-159
decimals 9, 10, 18, 23
decimal point 10, 11, 30
denominator 19
density 66
depression, angle of 139
diameter 111, 112, 124
distance 66-67, 91
drawing a perpendicular line 141
drawing a reflection 104
drawing angles 141
drawing curves 89

E

edge 117
elevation, angle of 139
enlargements 130, 131-132
equals sign 60
equation of a straight line graph 76, 86, 87
equations 41, 57-58, 60-61, 86, 94-95
equilateral triangles 102, 107, 141
estimated probability 146, 147
estimating 13
estimating the mean 160
even numbers 4
expanding out brackets 43-45
experimental probability 146, 147
exterior angles 103, 121, 122

F

face 117
factor tree 2
factorising 44
factors 1, 44
feet 17
FOIL method for expanding out brackets 45
formula triangles 65, 66
formulae
41, 49-50, 55-56,
61-62, 66-68, 129
fractions 8, 9, 18-20, 23
fraction button 20, 145
frequency 158-161
frequency polygons 152
frequency tables 158-161

G

gallons 17
geometry 121-124
gradient 75-76, 86-87, 91
graph method for simultaneous equations 95
graphical inequalities 97
graphs 73-76, 79-82, 85-91,
95, 97, 152-154
"greater than or equal to" 96
"greater than" 96
grouped frequency tables 160

H

height, of shapes 110
heptagon 102
hexagon 102
horizontal line graphs 73
hypotenuse 136, 138

I

identifying formulae 129
imperial units 17
inches 17
indices 32
inequalities 96, 97
intercept 86
interior angles 103, 122
inter-quartile range 162
inverse proportion 82
irregular polygons 122
isosceles triangles 107, 122, 124

K

kilograms 17
kite 107
kilometres 17

L

length 129
"less than or equal to" 96
"less than" 96
letters 52
line graphs 152
line symmetry 102, 104
listing all possible outcomes 148
litre 17
loci/locus 140, 141
lower quartile 162

M

mass 65, 66
mean 157, 158, 159-160
median 157, 158, 159, 160, 162
metric-imperial conversions 17
mid-interval values 160
miles 17
millimetres, mm 17
minus signs 51
mirror line 104, 133
modal group 160
mode 157, 158, 159, 160
modes on the calculator 39
multiples 1
multiplying out brackets 43-45

N

negative correlation 153
negative numbers 51
nets 117
non-subject terms 61, 62

Index

northline, bearings 137
n^{th} term 49-50
number line 42, 51
number patterns 48
number sequences 4, 5
number of sides, shapes 102

O

octagon 102
odd numbers 4
opposite, trigonometry 138
order of rotational symmetry 106
origin 74
original value, percentages 24
ounces 17

P

parallel lines 123
parallelograms 107, 121
pentagon 102
percentages 9, 23-24
perimeters 114
perpendicular 141
pi, π 112, 129
pie charts 154
pints 17
plane symmetry 104
plotting points 89
plotting straight line graphs 85-87
polygon 102
positive correlation 153
pounds 17
power $^{1/2}$, roots 33
powers 32, 38, 44
prime numbers 2-3
prime factors 2
prisms 116-117
probability 145-149
pyramid 117
Pythagoras' Theorem 136

Q

quadrants 71
quadrilaterals 121
quartiles 162

R

radii/radius 111-112, 124
range 157-159
ratios 25-27
rearranging formulas 61-62
rectangles 107, 121
reduction 131
reflections 104, 106, 133
regular polygons 102-3
relationships between variables 153
rhombus 107
right-angled triangle 107, 136, 138
roots 32, 33
rotations 133
rotational symmetry 102, 107
rounding off 10, 11, 13

S

sample space 148
scale factor 130, 131, 132
scatter graphs 153
sequences 4
shading a region on a graph 97
shapes 102, 107
significant figures 11
similarity 130
simplifying equations 42
simultaneous equations 94-95
SIN 136, 138-139
six steps for rearranging formulas 62
six steps for solving equations 61
smooth curve 89
SOH CAH TOA 138-139
solids 107, 117
solving equations 57-61, 94-95
speed 17, 66-68, 76, 91
sphere 107
spread of data 162
square root 32, 33
square-based pyramid 107
squared brackets 44
squares 102, 107, 121
squaring both sides of equations 61
squaring both sides of formulas 62
standard form/standard index form 30, 31, 39
stones 17
straight line equations 79, 85
straight line graphs 73-76, 79, 85-87
subject terms 61, 62
substituting values into formulae 55-56
supplementary angles 123
surface area 117
symmetry 102, 104, 105-107

T

tables of values 85, 95
TAN 138-139
tangent 112, 124
terms in algebra 42
theoretical probability 146
theta 138
three-letter angle notation 125
time 66-68, 91
tonnes, tons 17
tracing paper 106
transformations 132-133
translation 132
trapezium 107, 111
travel graphs 91
trial and error method for equations 58
trial and improvement for equations 59
triangles 107, 122, 136, 139
triangle numbers 5
triangular prism 107, 116, 117
trigonometry 138-139

U

units 17, 67
upper quartile 162

V

variation 162
vectors 132
vertex 117
vertical heights of shapes 110
vertical line graphs 73
volumes 17, 66, 116, 129

W

weight 17

X

x = a graphs and y = a graphs 73
x and y coordinates 71-72
x-axis and y-axis 75
x^2 graphs 80
x^3 graphs 81

Y

y = -ax graphs 74
y = -x graphs 74
y = a graphs 73
y = ax graphs 74
y = mx + c 79, 86-87
y = x graph 74
y intercept 79
yards 17

Z

z coordinates 72